D1608734

AGING AND COGNITION

AGING AND COGNITION

Research Methodologies and Empirical Advances

Edited by

Hayden B. Bosworth and Christopher Hertzog

American Psychological Association
Washington, DC

Published by
American Psychological Association
750 First Street, NE
Washington, DC 20002
www.apa.org

To order
APA Order Department
P.O. Box 92984
Washington, DC 20090-2984
Tel: (800) 374-2721;
Direct: (202) 336-5510
Fax: (202) 336-5502;
TDD/TTY: (202) 336-6123
Online: www.apa.org/books/
E-mail: order@apa.org

In the U.K., Europe, Africa, and the Middle East, copies may be ordered from
American Psychological Association
3 Henrietta Street
Covent Garden, London
WC2E 8LU England

Typeset in New Century Schoolbook by Circle Graphics, Columbia, MD

Printer: Edwards Brothers, Ann Arbor, MI
Cover Designer: Minker Design, Sarasota FL
Technical/Production Editor: Devon Bourexis

The opinions and statements published are the responsibility of the authors, and such opinions and statements do not necessarily represent the policies of the American Psychological Association.

Library of Congress Cataloging-in-Publication Data

Aging and cognition : research methodologies and empirical advances / edited by Hayden B. Bosworth and Christopher Hertzog. — 1st ed.
    p. cm.
  Includes bibliographical references and index.
  ISBN-13: 978-1-4338-0454-0
  ISBN-10: 1-4338-0454-9
  1. Cognition in old age. 2. Cognition—Age factors. I. Bosworth, Hayden B. II. Hertzog, C. K. (Christopher K.), 1952-

  BF724.55.C63A47 2009
  155.67'13—dc22

                                                                    2008046651

British Library Cataloguing-in-Publication Data
A CIP record is available from the British Library.

Printed in the United States of America
First Edition

APA Science Volumes

Attribution and Social Interaction: The Legacy of Edward E. Jones

Best Methods for the Analysis of Change: Recent Advances, Unanswered Questions, Future Directions

Cardiovascular Reactivity to Psychological Stress and Disease

The Challenge in Mathematics and Science Education: Psychology's Response

Changing Employment Relations: Behavioral and Social Perspectives

Children Exposed to Marital Violence: Theory, Research, and Applied Issues

Cognition: Conceptual and Methodological Issues

Cognitive Bases of Musical Communication

Cognitive Dissonance: Progress on a Pivotal Theory in Social Psychology

Conceptualization and Measurement of Organism–Environment Interaction

Converging Operations in the Study of Visual Selective Attention

Creative Thought: An Investigation of Conceptual Structures and Processes

Developmental Psychoacoustics

Diversity in Work Teams: Research Paradigms for a Changing Workplace

Emotion and Culture: Empirical Studies of Mutual Influence

Emotion, Disclosure, and Health

Evolving Explanations of Development: Ecological Approaches to Organism–Environment Systems

Examining Lives in Context: Perspectives on the Ecology of Human Development

Global Prospects for Education: Development, Culture, and Schooling

Hostility, Coping, and Health

Measuring Patient Changes in Mood, Anxiety, and Personality Disorders: Toward a Core Battery

Occasion Setting: Associative Learning and Cognition in Animals

Organ Donation and Transplantation: Psychological and Behavioral Factors

Origins and Development of Schizophrenia: Advances in Experimental Psychopathology

The Perception of Structure

Perspectives on Socially Shared Cognition

APA Decade of Behavior Volumes

Computational Modeling of Behavior in Organizations: The Third Scientific Discipline

Couples Coping With Stress: Emerging Perspectives on Dyadic Coping

Developing Individuality in the Human Brain: A Tribute to Michael I. Posner

Emerging Adults in America: Coming of Age in the 21st Century

Experimental Cognitive Psychology and Its Applications

Family Psychology: Science-Based Interventions

Inhibition and Cognition

Medical Illness and Positive Life Change: Can Crisis Lead to Personal Transformation?

Memory Consolidation: Essays in Honor of James L. McGaugh

Models of Intelligence: International Perspectives

The Nature of Remembering: Essays in Honor of Robert G. Crowder

New Methods for the Analysis of Change

On the Consequences of Meaning Selection: Perspectives on Resolving Lexical Ambiguity

Participatory Community Research: Theories and Methods in Action

Personality Psychology in the Workplace

Perspectivism in Social Psychology: The Yin and Yang of Scientific Progress

Primate Perspectives on Behavior and Cognition

Principles of Experimental Psychopathology: Essays in Honor of Brendan A. Maher

Psychosocial Interventions for Cancer

Racial Identity in Context: The Legacy of Kenneth B. Clark

The Social Psychology of Group Identity and Social Conflict: Theory, Application, and Practice

Strengthening Research Methodology: Psychological Measurement and Evaluation

Transcending Self-Interest: Psychological Explorations of the Quiet Ego

Unraveling the Complexities of Social Life: A Festschrift in Honor of Robert B. Zajonc

Visual Perception: The Influence of H. W. Leibowitz

Contents

Contributors

Rolf Adolfsson, MD, Umeå University, Umeå, Sweden
Duane F. Alwin, PhD, Pennsylvania State University, University Park
Brian J. Ayotte, PhD, Durham VA Medical Center, Durham, NC
Lars Bäckman, PhD, Karolinska Institute, Stockholm, Sweden
Allison A. M. Bielak, PhD, University of Victoria, Victoria, British Columbia, Canada
Hayden B. Bosworth, PhD, Duke University Medical Center, Durham, NC
Leslie J. Caplan, PhD, National Institutes of Health, Bethesda, MD
Carolyn B. Crow, MA, Victoria, British Columbia, Canada
Roger A. Dixon, PhD, University of Alberta, Edmonton, Alberta, Canada
Ryne Estabrook, MA, University of Virginia, Charlottesville
Daniel Grühn, PhD, North Carolina State University, Raleigh
Christopher Hertzog, PhD, Georgia Institute of Technology, Atlanta
David F. Hultsch, PhD, University of Victoria, Victoria, British Columbia, Canada
Robert F. Kennison, PhD, California State University, Los Angeles
Gisela Labouvie-Vief, PhD, University of Geneva, Geneva, Switzerland
Margie E. Lachman, PhD, Brandeis University, Waltham, MA
Kayan L. Lewis, PhD, Texas Department of State Health Services, Austin
Scott B. Maitland, PhD, University of Guelph, Guelph, Ontario, Canada
Mike Martin, PhD, University of Zurich, Zurich, Switzerland
Harold Mouras, PhD, National Center for Scientific Research, Amiens, France
John R. Nesselroade, PhD, University of Virginia, Charlottesville
Lars-Göran Nilsson, PhD, Stockholm University, Stockholm, Sweden
Lars Nyberg, PhD, Umeå University, Umeå, Sweden
Christina Röcke, PhD, University of Zurich, Zurich, Switzerland
Christopher B. Rosnick, PhD, MPH, Southern Illinois University, Edwardsville
Carmi Schooler, PhD, National Institutes of Health, Bethesda, MD
Amber Watts, MA, University of Southern California, Los Angeles
Elizabeth M. Zelinski, PhD, University of Southern California, Los Angeles
Daniel Zimprich, PhD, University of Zurich, Zurich, Switzerland

Foreword

In early 1988, the American Psychological Association (APA) Science Directorate began its sponsorship of what would become an exceptionally successful activity in support of psychological science—the APA Scientific Conferences program. This program has showcased some of the most important topics in psychological science and has provided a forum for collaboration among many leading figures in the field.

The program has inspired a series of books that have presented cutting-edge work in all areas of psychology. At the turn of the millennium, the series was renamed the Decade of Behavior Series to help advance the goals of this important initiative. The Decade of Behavior is a major interdisciplinary campaign designed to promote the contributions of the behavioral and social sciences to our most important societal challenges in the decade leading up to 2010. Although a key goal has been to inform the public about these scientific contributions, other activities have been designed to encourage and further collaboration among scientists. Hence, the series that was the "APA Science Series" has continued as the "Decade of Behavior Series." This represents one element in APA's efforts to promote the Decade of Behavior initiative as one of its endorsing organizations. For additional information about the Decade of Behavior, please visit http://www.decadeofbehavior.org.

Over the course of the past years, the Science Conference and Decade of Behavior Series has allowed psychological scientists to share and explore cutting-edge findings in psychology. The APA Science Directorate looks forward to continuing this successful program and to sponsoring other conferences and books in the years ahead. This series has been so successful that we have chosen to extend it to include books that, although they do not arise from conferences, report with the same high quality of scholarship on the latest research.

We are pleased that this important contribution to the literature was supported in part by the Decade of Behavior program. Congratulations to the editors and contributors of this volume on their sterling effort.

Steven J. Breckler, PhD
Executive Director for Science

Virginia E. Holt
*Assistant Executive Director
for Science*

Preface

This book originated in a conference held June 2007 at Pennsylvania State University to honor the distinguished career and scientific contributions of Dr. K. Warner Schaie. As a pioneer in the field of cognition in aging, Dr. Schaie has contributed substantially to our understanding of adult cognitive development, and his colleagues and friends were proud to honor him at this conference.

From 1981 through his recent retirement in 2007, Dr. Schaie was the Evan Pugh Professor of Human Development and Psychology at the Pennsylvania State University. Prior to that, Dr. Schaie held faculty positions at West Virginia University and the University of Southern California, where he was also the director for research at the Andrus Gerontology Center. He now resides in Seattle, Washington, where he is a part-time faculty member at the Department of Psychiatry and Behavioral Sciences at the University of Washington.

In a very real sense, the move of Dr. Schaie and his wife and colleague, Sherry L. Willis, to Seattle completes a major circle in his life. Dr. Schaie graduated with a PhD from the University of Washington in 1956 after conducting a dissertation on aging and psychometric intelligence. This cross-sectional study eventually evolved into Dr. Schaie's major life work. He converted it into the Seattle Longitudinal Study (SLS)—the huge, ongoing longitudinal research project that he is best known for—by conducting a 7-year longitudinal follow-up of the dissertation sample in 1963 and by adding a new, concurrent independent cross-sectional sample. This sequential sampling scheme—longitudinal follow-ups on all previous participants, combined with a new cross-sectional sample every 7 years—has continued to this day, assembling the largest multiple-cohort study of psychological development in history.

The SLS has yielded not only significant findings about change in intelligence across the adult life span but also methodological advances in studying the interaction of individual development, secular trends (cohort), and time. Dr. Schaie has clarified the differential life course of intellectual abilities, improved our understanding of when a reliable decline in intellectual abilities can be observed, and determined how large a decline can be expected. His work has provided insight into possible demographic shifts in intellectual performance where he examined patterns of generational (cohort) differences in intellectual abilities as well as their magnitude. He was also concerned with examining the stability of the factor structure of the psychometric abilities across the adult life course. His work has also helped to explain the causes of individual differences in age-related ability change in adulthood, including life events, disease status, genetic variability, patterns of activity, and environmental and family contexts.

Using SLS data, Dr. Schaie has consistently challenged the stereotype of universal cognitive decline in old age, arguing that cognitive and intellectual ability in adulthood is malleable. He has argued strongly the position that intellectually engaging activities promote enhancement and maintenance of cognitive functioning. This argument evolved into the training component of the SLS

in which he and Sherry Willis demonstrated training improvements in persons
with a prior history of cognitive decline.

Dr. Schaie is the author of more than 275 journal articles and chapters on
the psychology of aging. He is author or editor of 51 books, including the text-
book *Adult Development and Aging* (5th ed., with S. L. Willis)[1] and all six edi-
tions of the *Handbook of the Psychology of Aging* (coedited with James E. Birren).[2]
He has remained remarkably productive as a scientist through his 70s. A recent
check of the Web of Knowledge (http://www.isiknowledge.com) showed over
3,000 citations to his work (which underestimates the impact because it ignores
citations of books). In the last 10 years he has produced journal publications
with colleagues and students, and a major book reviewing and summarizing
findings from the SLS, published in 2005.

Dr. Schaie is a fellow in Divisions 1, 3, 5, 7, and 20 of the American Psychological Association (APA). He is the past president of APA Division 20
(Adult Development and Aging; 1973–1974). He is a consulting editor for *Psychology and Aging*. He continues to serve as a reviewer for numerous APA journals. He was a member of the APA Council of Representatives (1976–1979;
1983–1986), and a member of the APA Board of Social and Ethical Responsibilities (1990–1991). He received the APA Division 20 Distinguished Contribution
Award (1982) and the APA Division 20 Distinguished Mentor Award (1996). In
1992, he received the Distinguished Scientific Contributions Award from APA.

Dr. Schaie has received several additional awards and honorary degrees
recognizing his contributions to the field of adult development and aging. In
1997, he received an honorary doctorate (Dr. phil. h.c.) from the Friedrich-
Schiller University of Jena, Germany, and an honorary ScD degree from West
Virginia University (2002). In 1997, he was elected to the Akademie für Gemein-
nützige Wissenschaften zu Erfurt (Academy of Sciences in the Public Interest,
Erfurt, Germany). He received the Kleemeier Award (1987) for Distinguished
Research Contributions from the Gerontological Society of America, and the
MENSA lifetime career award (2000).

As further testimony of Dr. Schaie's influence on the field of cognitive
aging, the authors of this edited volume indicate how Dr. Schaie's work has
informed or inspired their current work. Examples of how Dr. Schaie's work
influenced a whole cadre of investigators include Hultsch's examination of the
accuracy of adults' retrospections about their intellectual functioning using data
from the SLS (chap. 9); Zelinski's discussion of cohort effects using the Long
Beach Longitudinal Study (LBLS), which was started by Dr. Schaie in 1978, and
how the design and measurement approach of the LBLS was very much inspired
by Dr. Schaie's SLS (chap. 6); and Bosworth's inclusion of Willis and Schaie's
work of everyday cognition to inform interventions to improve adherence to
health behaviors, including medication adherence (chap. 11).

In addition to contributing substantively to the fields of cognitive aging,
specifically, and gerontology, in general, Dr. Schaie has trained successive gen-

---

[1] Shaie, K. W., & Willis, S. L. (2001). *Adult development and aging* (5th ed.). Upper Saddle River,
NJ: Prentice Hall.

[2] Birren, J. E., & Willis, S. L. (2006). *Handbook of the psychology of aging* (6th ed.). Burlington, MA:
Elsevier.

erations of gerontologists and researchers. He has directly and indirectly trained hundreds of scientists in the study of adult development and aging, through his work with students on the SLS and through courses he has taught over the years, including one on research methods in aging that was part of the annual USC gerontology summer institutes. As attested by the various contributing authors, he has encouraged and inspired new generations of gerontologists to think more critically about a wide range of issues and problems and continue advancing the field of gerontology, to which Dr. Schaie has contributed so much. To this end, many of the authors who are direct academic descendants or colleagues collaborated on this volume in his honor.

Aging and Cognition

Introduction

Hayden B. Bosworth and Christopher Hertzog

There have been significant substantive and methodological developments in the field of aging and psychological functioning in older adulthood. The proportion of older adults in the populations of Western countries continues to increase as birth rates decline and health care improves. It is of critical importance to our society to understand not only the functional capacity of older adults but also the extent to which the age changes we observe today accurately predict the status of future generations of older adults.

This book considers aging in its cognitive, social, and psychological contexts. It summarizes new research findings and significant challenges to the field of adult development. In addition, it explains and evaluates new methodologies for measuring developmental change, and it considers possible applications of the findings for interventions to improve older adults' cognitive functioning. The authors are scientists who have made recent and significant contributions to the cognitive, social, and psychological development of aging and the identification of critical needs for future research.

We have divided this book into three major parts. Part I: Methodological Issues in the Study of Developmental Change explores new methods for evaluating developmental change. This part comprises chapters 1 through 5. In chapter 1, Alwin discusses the present state of knowledge of cognitive aging, especially cohort differences in patterns of cognitive performance in populations of general interest.

The scientific study of developmental changes relies heavily on the ability to measure behavioral and psychological attributes. With a few exceptions, the quality of measurement in behavioral science has generally been suspect. Since the 1960s, within the life span tradition, concepts of factorial invariance have been instrumental in helping to allay concerns regarding measurement quality. In chapter 2, Nesselroade and Estabrook examine factorial invariance to assess its applicability in light of contemporary measurement concerns. Some extensions and elaborations of the concepts are presented and discussed.

In chapter 3, Zimprich and Martin discuss the use of multilevel factor analysis to understand further intellectual development in old age. The authors report that cross-sectional and longitudinal correlations among cognitive abilities appear to converge. An analytic framework and a detailed example are presented in the chapter; this method provides a way to separate three different sources of variance existent in a variable that has been measured longitudinally.

An important issue for developmental researchers in examining measures is underlying structure and measurement equivalence/invariance. In chapter 4, Maitland and colleagues use the Temperament and Character Inventory (TCI), a common personality measure, as an example for discussing measurement equivalence/invariance.

In chapter 5, Zelinski and colleagues discuss that whereas the methodological limitations of relying on cross-sectional methods are well known, increasing attention to methodological considerations such as selection, attrition, and retest, related to longitudinal studies needs to be considered. Specifically, the authors examine issues related to the requirements of convergence assumption, which posits that results of cross-sectional and longitudinal analyses are similar and can be combined. Thus, the authors argue that it is critical to assess cohort effects and that it is important that models of aging be developed within the larger context of these changes.

Part II: Cognitive, Social, and Psychological Development in Adulthood discusses various factors associated with aging. This part comprises chapters 6 through 10. In chapter 6, Schooler and Caplan examine the role that social issues such as socioeconomic status may have on bestowing increased advantages with age. Socially and structurally determined environmental conditions and psychological functioning are shown to have a reciprocally causal relationship, leading to "spirals" of continually increasing advantages for those who are already psychologically or socially advantaged. The authors suggest that these spirals affect the cognitive functions, psychological and physical health, and social status of individuals over the life course so that differences between the initially psychologically and socially advantaged and disadvantaged are magnified by age.

Beliefs about control in key life domains have implications for affect and action. Those who have a greater sense of control are more optimistic about the future and are more likely to use adaptive strategies for prevention, compensation, or remediation of aging-related declines. In chapter 7, using the Midlife in the United States (MIDUS) longitudinal sample, Lachman, Rosnick, and Röcke, and examine patterns of change in control beliefs and life satisfaction over a 10-year period. The authors present evidence for interindividual differences in intraindividual change in control beliefs and life satisfaction using person- and variable-centered methodological approaches, and they examine, psychosocial and health-related antecedents of stability and change trajectories. Possible mechanisms linking control beliefs and differential patterns of subjective well-being are considered as well.

In chapter 8, Hertzog examines the intriguing question of whether people's behaviors influence the course of their own cognitive development. *Cognitive enrichment* is a generic term that captures the concept that individuals' actions can influence their cognitive status. Hertzog summarizes three different mechanisms through which behaviors may influence cognitive aging. The chapter ends with a review of the current controversy of cognitive enrichment effects.

In chapter 9, Labouvie-Vief, Grühn, and Mouras discuss the relationship between cognition and emotion within the context of dynamic integration theory. This theory proposes an inverted U-shaped function—that describes the degrading effects of highly arousing situations, levels of activation or demand can be mediated through cognitive and emotional resources. The theory predicts that older adults in particular may have difficulty dealing with highly arousing situations and may develop self-protective coping strategies. The authors illustrate the resulting framework with behavioral and neurobiological findings.

In chapter 10, Hultsch and colleagues examine issues related to older adults' perceptions of change in their memory performance. They use longitudinal data from the Victoria Longitudinal Study to examine changes in adults' perceptions of their memory ability relative to actual changes in performance. The results suggest that perceptions of change in personal characteristics are driven to a significant degree by expectations of what will happen rather than by what actually happens.

In Part III: Applying Research Findings, the final chapter of the book considers the challenge of using aging and cognition research findings to improve the lives of older adults. Within the past couple of decades, there has been increased interest in everyday cognition, or how older adults address complex cognitive tasks in their everyday lives. This interest has been driven by both methodological and theoretical concerns. Despite this increased focus on everyday cognition, applying basic research to "real-world" settings remains a significant challenge. In chapter 11, Bosworth and Ayotte outline how basic cognitive functioning underlies performance in applied everyday tasks and illustrate these relationships in the context of medication adherence.

With research methods, findings, and applications, this book has something to offer all professionals who deal with cognitive and psychological development among older adults. In particular, researchers in the fields of cognitive aging; gerontology; health psychology; developmental psychology; personality and social psychology; experimental psychology; evaluation, measurement, and statistics; and clinical psychology will find much to appreciate here.

Part I

Methodological Issues in the Study of Developmental Change

1

History, Cohorts, and Patterns of Cognitive Aging

Duane F. Alwin

The idea that historical events and processes influence the nature and composition of society, via the uniqueness in the experiences of different birth cohorts, has been prominent in the disciplines of economics, sociology, demography, political science, and psychology over the past century and before. In the 1950s, for example, sociologist Samuel Stouffer (1955) found that popular support for the toleration of communists, atheists, and socialists followed lines of demarcation associated with historical location, with the more recent birth cohorts being significantly more tolerant than their elders. He argued that this was, in part, attributable to the higher levels of education of the more recently born, whose higher levels of schooling fostered greater openness toward freedom of speech and the exchange of ideas. In the 1970s, political scientist Ronald Inglehart (1977) found post–World War II birth cohorts in Western Europe sought freedom and self-expression, in contrast to the pre-war cohorts, who were more interested in economic security and political order. He argued from a Maslowian "hierarchy of needs" perspective that more recent cohorts had the luxury of economic prosperity that could not be taken for granted by their elders, who, during their youth, had to focus more on basic needs (see also Inglehart, 1986, 1990). Economist Richard Easterlin (1987), in a pathbreaking series of studies, hypothesized that the numerically large sets of birth cohorts making up the so-called Baby Boom were at a significant socioeconomic disadvantage relative to that of their predecessors, simply because of their size. He argued that the number of persons born in a particular year has far-reaching consequences, given its effects on competition for jobs and the strain it produces on the opportunity structure. Individuals in large cohorts, according to Easterlin, will be less likely to marry and more likely to put off having children; mothers will be more likely to work outside the home; and, as young adults, these individuals will more likely experience psychological stress and feelings of alienation. Many of these ideas have proven to be

Duane F. Alwin is the inaugural holder of the Tracy Winfree and Ted H. McCourtney Professorship in Sociology and Demography, The Pennsylvania State University. The research reported here was supported by a grant to the author titled "Latent Curve Models of Cognitive Aging" (R01-AG021203-06). The author acknowledges the collaboration of colleagues Scott Hofer and Linda Wray in the development of the ideas presented here, but he is solely responsible for the presentation made in this chapter. Chris Hertzog gave the chapter a close reading, helping remove several weaknesses, and Paula Tufiş and Alyson Otto provided valuable assistance.

true (see Pampel, 1993). And recently, political scientist Robert Putnam (2000) suggested in his popular book *Bowling Alone* that civic engagement has declined, not because individual Americans have become less civic-minded but mostly because earlier-born, engaged Americans have died off and been replaced by younger more alienated ones, who are less tied to traditional institutions, such as the church, the lodge, the bridge club, and the bowling league.

These ideas about cohort differences and their persistence across a variety of content domains are a few examples that show the value of the kind of "cohort theorizing" that has taken place and the kinds of "cohort effects" in existence, according to social and behavioral science researchers, in the recent past. In sociology, the existence of cohort effects was recognized by Karl Mannheim (1952/1927) and Norman Ryder (1965), and since then ideas about their role in contributing to social change have flourished.[1] In psychology, these ideas about the unique historical experiences of birth cohorts were introduced largely through the work of K. Warner Schaie and many of his colleagues—Paul Baltes, John Nesselroade, Hayne Reese, and others—especially with respect to the interpretation of age-related patterns of cognitive performance but also with respect to personality and related constructs (Baltes, 1968; Baltes & Mayer, 1999; Baltes, Cornelius, & Nesselroade, 1979; McKlosky & Reese, 1984; Schaie, 1965, 1984, 2008; Schaie, Willis, & Pennack, 2005; Willis & Schaie, 2006). Not only has Schaie made contributions to understanding cohort effects, he has also made singular contributions to the understanding of the nature of adult development of cognitive abilities, across the entire adult life span, and the many influences that contribute to individual differences in life-span trajectories. Schaie's research is exemplary as a life-span developmental perspective on cognitive change and aging, and his contributions involving the Seattle Longitudinal Study (SLS) reflect a multicausal, multidimensional, and multicohort approach to the study of cognitive aging. His research involving the SLS offers an unparalleled and comprehensive account of the development of cognitive capacities across the adult life span, and few studies offer the longitudinal perspective on adult maturation and change that is characteristic of Schaie's work (e.g., Schaie, 1996, 2005).

Within the framework of Schaie's legacy regarding the comprehensive study of intellectual and cognitive capacities, this chapter discusses the present state of our knowledge of cognitive aging, and especially of cohort differences in patterns of cognitive performance in populations of general interest.[2]

---

[1]For a recent summary of the literature on cohort effects with respect to attitudes, beliefs, and self-identifications, see Alwin and McCammon (2003, pp. 40–41).

[2]Consistent with most contemporary uses, I use the term *cohort effects* to refer to the stable residues of historical experiences common among persons born at the same time. Schaie's and others' work (e.g., Flynn, 1999) on this topic uses the term *generation* instead of cohort. This is more typical in psychology than in the social sciences. I prefer the term *cohort*, given the many uses of the term *generation* and the confusion engendered by multiple meanings of the term (see Alwin & McCammon, 2003, 2007; Alwin, McCammon, & Hofer, 2006; Roscow, 1978). As used here, a cohort is a group of persons born in the same calendar year, and for some purposes groups of persons born in adjacent years—nothing is assumed other than their common historical location. Members of a given cohort experience various phases of the life cycle at the same time; the common unfolding of their lives is embedded in historical time, and consequently biography and history are uniquely intertwined. By contrast, the concept of generation has other meanings (see Alwin & McCammon, 2007).

I organize the discussion around seven empirical principles that can be derived from Schaie's half-century of research. In achieving these objectives, I draw on examples from the contemporary literature that illustrate the issues raised and some of the current debates about the influences of cohort experiences on cognitive aging. I should point out that it is not my intention to canvass the entire research record of Schaie on intellectual and cognitive capacities but to focus on a limited set of issues. For purposes of illustration, I rely mainly on results obtained in my earlier research (Alwin, 1991; Alwin & McCammon, 1999, 2001) using the publicly available repeated cross-sectional data sets from the General Social Survey (GSS), a nationally representative sample of the adult household population of the United States (Alwin, 1991; Alwin & McCammon, 1999, 2001). I also briefly discuss the results of our recent investigation of cohort effects on cognitive processes in the Health and Retirement Study (HRS) (Alwin, 2009a; Alwin, McCammon, Wray, & Rodgers, 2008). For the most part, our findings support the hypotheses developed by Schaie on the basis of the SLS about patterns of cognitive aging, especially with regard to the patterns in test scores associated with aging, although our research registers some interesting disagreement about the nature of cohort differences and their sources.[3]

K. Warner Schaie's Legacy

Several important general conclusions can be derived from Schaie's research on cognitive development in adulthood, which are relevant to the theme of historical factors and cohort effects (Schaie, 2005). Seven discussed here are (a) the idea that age-related differences in cognitive scores do not necessarily imply aging—they may reflect the influences of historical or cohort factors as well; (b) the statistical identification of aging and cohort effects is generally not possible unless one is willing to make the assumption of minimal period influences; (c) evidence for "typical" or "normal" cognitive aging suggests that significant cognitive decline does not occur for most performance measures until well after age 60 and for some not until after age 70; (d) evidence for the stability of individual differences in cognitive functioning through old age suggests a high degree of stability, despite average mean shifts; (e) the interpretation of historical effects on cohorts suggests that more recent cohorts have higher levels of average cognitive performance, which can be attributed to 20th century events and experiences, for example, the expansion of education, thought to be relevant to the promotion of cognitive reserve; (f) the empirical identification of cognitive decline as a risk factor for mortality; and (g) the development of the hypothesis that cohort differences in cognitive function are in part because of population processes and mortality selection. I take up each of these in the following discussion, noting along the way their relevance to contemporary understanding of the nature of cohort effects on processes of cognitive aging.

---

[3]It is hoped that in future years, when the SLS data become publicly available, some of these differences can be reconciled through the application of common set of techniques of data analysis.

Age-Related Differences

Age-related differences in cognitive scores do not necessarily imply aging. For some time, the idea that age-related differences may be caused in part by differences in socialization experiences has been a prominent way to understand social contrasts between people born at different times. The German sociologist, Karl Mannheim (1927, p. 298) argued that the earliest impressions, marked by the historical location of one's birth year, were some of the most powerful influences on the individual over the entire life span and therefore that birth cohort was an important ingredient in understanding human orientations. It was a natural extension of this foundational theorizing, and in part because of it, that Ryder (1965) popularized the term *cohort* (by which he meant "birth cohort") among sociologists and demographers to account for social change (see also Riley, 1973). Put simply, society changes as the cohort composition of society changes, and given the natural social metabolism of cohort replacement, if (a) cohorts are distinct in terms of their experiences and their consequences and (b) people are stable over most of their lives following an early period of socialization, then one can observe the remnants of these cohort differences in society, as time passes.

It is clear that Schaie was influenced by this kind of cohort theorizing. In some of his earliest work on age differences in psychological functioning (e.g., Schaie, 1959), he suggested that cross-sectional differences in age could be due to historical location, or cohort, as well as to aging.[4] For example, cohorts could differ in their cognitive performance because of their historically linked differences in exposure to educational opportunities, later born cohorts having the advantage. Schaie's work on cohort effects has generally suggested that more recent birth cohorts have higher levels of cognitive performance when observed at the same age (see Schaie, 1996, 2005). However, in contrast to Schaie's work, the bulk of the literature on age differences in cognitive scores has largely ignored this premise (to its detriment), almost universally interpreting age differences in levels of cognitive performance solely in terms of processes of aging.

In the social sciences it is generally well understood that in cross-sectional data the influences of aging and cohort are confounded in the comparisons of age groups, so despite the importance of considering both the influences of cohort and age on cognitive scores, it is not a simple matter to disentangle their unique contributions in cross-sectional comparisons. Also, it can be further shown that in over-time comparisons within cohorts, what Schaie refers to as *time sequential designs,* the influences of aging and period effects are naturally inseparable (Alwin, McCammon, & Hofer, 2006; e.g., also see Riley, 1973). Much has been written about the confounding of age, period, and cohort effects, and the difficulties of mathematically identifying their independent effects (e.g., see Mason & Fienberg, 1985; Mason, Mason, Winsborough, & Poole, 1973; Yang, Fu, & Land, 2004).

---

[4]According to Schaie (see Schaie, Willis, & Pennak, 2005, p. 44), his work on cohort differences in cognitive abilities was influenced by the writings of Kuhlen (1940) and Matilda White Riley (Riley, Johnson, & Foner, 1972).

Schaie (1965, 1970) wrote about the identification problem and proposed a strategy toward solving the problem that contains several internal inconsistencies (see later in this chapter). I do not review these issues in depth here because they are discussed adequately elsewhere, except to note that although there is an agreed-on need to reckon with potential cohort differences, the critical problem is that they are naturally confounded with age differences and therefore often ignored. In the next section I discuss how it is possible to identify both aging and cohort effects using longitudinal data (either repeated cross-sectional designs or panel designs involving the same persons observed over time) if one is willing to assume minimal period effects. In the following, I mention Schaie's early (1965, 1970) discussion of these issues.

Identification Issues

The point of the discussion in the preceding section is that if one were to look at a cross-section of adults in American society with respect to a set of cognitive performance measures, it would be easy to confuse effects of aging with the possibility that they might instead reflect differences resulting from unique cohort experiences. Earlier-born cohorts not only are older and more experienced at a given time point, they also grew up in different time periods and were exposed to a different range of educational opportunities. By contrast, people born more recently are not only younger but they also experienced their period of youthful socialization at different historical times, that is, they have different historical locations. So, if one is looking at a phenomenon that is influenced both by aging, that is, the amount of experience or maturity as well as the particular slice of history in which one is located when growing up, the results of empirical analyses can be quite puzzling. Similarly, if one is studying the changes in a single cohort (or set of cohorts) over time, effects that might otherwise be attributable to age-related change are confounded with period effects, and disentangling the two sets of influences can be difficult (Mason & Fienberg, 1985).

Using the earlier discussion as preliminary, let me briefly summarize what is typically meant by the terms *aging, period,* and *cohort* effects (Alwin et al., 2006; Alwin, Hofer, & McCammon, 2006). *Aging effects* refers to patterns of within-person change associated with the passage of biographic time, linked to species-specific biological (life cycle) and/or psychological processes of maturation and development and/or to culturally constructed age-graded experiences, that is, life stages or phases. By contrast, *cohort effects* refers to enduring attributes of persons associated with unique placement of birth cohorts in historical time, resulting from the unique intersection of biographical and historical time. Cohort effects may also reflect culturally constructed "generational" experiences, but this is not a necessary element in the definition of cohort effects. Finally, *period effects* refers to changes in persons associated with the occasion of measurement, that is, changes in persons because of historical events and processes. Period effects may be a generalized phenomenon in the sense that the effects occur regardless of age or social circumstances—the idea is that for the most part, by definition, a period effect influences just about every member of a given society.

I assume from the earlier discussion that variables representing these three main sets of factors can be thought of as affecting the mean levels of cognitive functioning: aging (A), chronological time or period (P), and birth cohort (C). These are conceptual categories of variables representing rich and complex sets of influences that operate primarily through (a) processes of aging and life cycle changes, (b) those effects due to the distinctiveness of the time of measurement or historical period, and (c) processes influencing specific cohorts. The problem is, however, that within a given occasion of observation, A (age) and C (cohort) are perfectly correlated. And in a series of sequential replications within cohorts, A (age) and P (chronological time) are perfectly correlated (Mason & Fienberg, 1985). Because Age = Time – Birth Date (A = P – C), it is rarely possible to separate the influences of aging, cohorts, and time periods in any purely exploratory fashion using cross-sectional data. One needs to be able to impose a strong set of assumptions about the nature of one or more of these three sources of variation to identify these separate influences unequivocally. Moreover, contrary to what was suggested by Schaie (1965) and Baltes (1968) early in these discussions, adding sequential observations on the same cohorts does not make the problem go away, it only adds complexity. Finally, as Schaie and others (e.g., Duncan, 1985) have pointed out, I should emphasize that the problem could be solved if direct measures of aging, cohort experiences, and relevant period factors were available. Although this is generally problematic for "aging," especially given our inability to directly measure the degree of biological or psychological aging (Austad, 1997; Kirkwood, 1999), this approach has been tried for cohort and period effects (e.g., Farkas, 1977; O'Brien, 2000).

Consider the hypothesized relative contributions of age (A), period (P), and cohort (C) factors to cognitive test scores using the following linear equations:

$$E(Y) = \beta_0 + \beta_A \text{ Age} + \beta_C \text{ Cohort} + \beta_P \text{ Period} \qquad (1)$$

$$E(Y) = \beta_0 + \beta_A \text{ Age} + \beta_C \text{ Cohort} + \beta_P (\text{Cohort} + \text{Age}) \qquad (2)$$

$$E(Y) = \beta_0 + (\beta_A + \beta_P) \text{ Age} + (\beta_C + \beta_P) \text{ Cohort} \qquad (3)$$

$$E(Y) = \beta_0 + \beta_1 \text{ Age} + \beta_2 \text{ Cohort} \qquad (4)$$

where the coefficients in Equation 1 refer to the potential effects of age, period, and cohort (the notation is for the unstandardized coefficients at the population level) on some cognitive test performance score of interest. These equations reflect a set of linear and additive assumptions about the effects of these three factors, which is done for convenience, and these may not reflect an actual situation. It is the logic of the problem I wish to emphasize here. There are several things to note in the above development. First, it can be shown that the model in Equation 1 is underidentified, because as I mentioned previously, Period = Cohort + Age. Thus, Equation 2 can be rewritten in terms of two unknown parameters rather than three. Moving from Equations 2 through 4, one sees the consequences of analyzing age and cohort ignoring period—that is, by rewriting the variable period in Equation 1 as equal to Cohort + Age, one sees that the effects of Age and Cohort (in Equation 4) each contain a piece that is attributable to period effects. Note that $\beta_1 = \beta_A + \beta_P$ and $\beta_2 = \beta_C + \beta_P$, and that, given the present set of working hypotheses, in equation (1) $\beta_A < 0$, $\beta_C > 0$, and $\beta_P > 0$. This means that $\beta_1 < 0$, unless period effects are stronger than aging effects, and $\beta_2 > 0$, regardless of the relative magnitudes of β_C and β_P (see Firebaugh, 1989, 1992).

As I noted earlier, here I put aside the issue of functional form and focus on the logic of the problem, that is, the linear form of the model is simply a convenient specification for now. It is clear that all three of these processes—aging, cohort, and period effects—could be operating and that both cohort and aging explanations of intercohort differences may be true to some extent. It is the nature of the data, not the nature of the phenomena, that prevents a clear interpretation of age, period, and cohort effects. However, note that in the above, if one is willing to assume there are no period effects, that is, $\beta_P = 0$, then the patterns in the data reduce to interpretations of aging and cohort effects, that is, $\beta_1 = \beta_A$ and $\beta_2 = \beta_C$. Schaie's (1965, 1970) early work in this area demonstrated, as I have shown above, that if one is willing to make a strong set of assumptions that period effects are nonexistent, then it is possible to simplify the problem and identify the effects of aging and cohort factors on patterns of cognitive test score performance, assuming one has sequential replications across several cohorts. However, most people agree that the arbitrary Schaie ANOVA designs (time sequential, cohort sequential) are not a solution to the problem (Schaie, 1965, 1970).

It has been known for some time that having what is often called "side information," or assumptions about the nature of certain historical, aging, or cohort processes, it may be possible to simplify the problem. If one can make strong theoretical assumptions about the nature of certain influences, for example, setting either cohort, aging, or period effects to some known value, for example, $\beta_P = 0$, it is possible to creatively interpret survey data in service of the goal of identifying cohort phenomena when they exist. Short of such strong assumptions, it is usually not possible to cleanly disentangle these processes empirically *from such data alone*. There is a recent literature that suggests other possibilities regarding the identification of age, period, and cohort effects (Yang, Fu, & Land, 2004).

Schaie's (1965, 1970) work demonstrated the need to assume there are no period effects, if one wants to decipher aging and cohort effects from repeated cross-sectional data. However, the assumption that there are no period effects is not an arbitrary assumption and can only be imposed if it makes sense to do so. In this context, it appears to be a plausible assumption, although Flynn's (1984, 1999) work suggests there may also be period effects. Making this assumption can assist in creatively interpreting the age and cohort patterns. I can think of few reasons to expect there to be period effects on most measures of cognitive performance in studies conducted over the latter half of the past century.[5] For verbal school-based learning, there may be an issue of "word obsolescence,"

---

[5]C. Hertzog (personal communication, April 29, 2008) suggested that the testing policies of No Child Left Behind may have a period effect on standardized tests within the full range of K through 12, which is something that may be detected in future research.

which reflects changing fashions in the use of words (Alwin, 1991, p. 48), but these are not very useful interpretations in the general case. Most of the available evidence suggests that, although people may be reading less now, the standard vocabulary of modern American English has not changed over much of this time (Alwin, 1991; Alwin & McCammon, 1999, 2001; Glenn, 1994; Hauser & Huang, 1997; Huang & Hauser, 1998; Weakliem, McQuillan, & Schauer, 1995), and there is little support for an effect tied to the occasion of measurement, that is, period effects are zero, or $\beta_P = 0$.

Let us assume for present purposes that there are no period effects on cognitive test scores, at least for representative samples. Moving forward, if there are no period effects on cognitive performance measures (Alwin & McCammon, 1999, 2001), then it is possible to use repeated cross-sectional data to study the effects of aging and cohorts on cognitive performance measures (in Schaie's terminology, *time sequential studies*). However, it is important to stress that these are representative of the population at each occasion of measurement and do not represent panels of respondents followed through time. In this case, one can simply regress the outcome variable of interest on two factors (net of any controls, written in a more complex functional form, if necessary): aging and cohort, that is, $E(Y) = \beta_0 + \beta_1 \, Age + \beta_2 \, Year \, of \, Birth$.

I introduce an example here for purposes of demonstrating the nature of aging and cohort effects on processes of cognitive aging, based on my previous research on cohort effects in the case of vocabulary knowledge, using longitudinal data sets from nationally representative samples in the GSS for which measures of cognitive performance are available. The GSS is a repeated cross-sectional representation of the adult household population of the United States (Davis & Smith, 2001). The sample and data I present are described elsewhere (Alwin, 1991; Alwin & McCammon, 1999, 2001), and I note only for present purposes that the analyses concern a 10-item vocabulary knowledge test, and, from the point of view of the population of interest, the results here can be generalized to the noninstitutionalized adult community-dwelling population in the United States in the years from 1974 to 1998.[6]

In Figure 1.1, I have plotted some theoretical expectations for intercohort differences in vocabulary knowledge. In terms of the equational representation of these expectations, they pertain to a model in which β_1 is negative and β_2 is positive, that is, as age increases vocabulary knowledge declines and as birth year increases, vocabulary knowledge increases. Except perhaps for functional form, this is consistent with the theoretical expectations prevalent in the research literature regarding the effects of aging and cohort; and whatever the form of the relationship, a more or less monotonic decline from recent cohorts to earlier ones is expected. In the analyses on which the results presented later are based, I used a curvilinear functional form, with the rate of change due to age to be increasing with age (for a more nuanced discussion of these issues, see Alwin & McCammon, 1999, 2001). The purpose here is simply to sensitize the reader to the typical set of expectations associated with postulated aging and cohort effects. I come back to these theoretical expectations for intercohort differ-

---

[6]There are more recent GSS surveys that also contain this 10-item vocabulary score, at least through 2006.

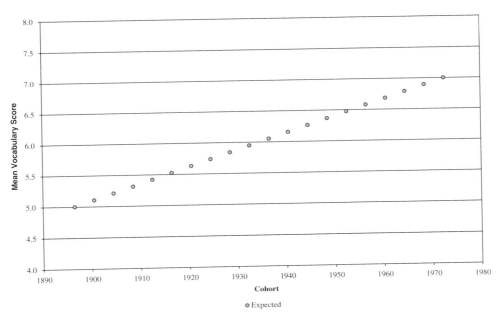

Figure 1.1. Theoretical expectations for cohort differences in vocabulary knowledge: U.S. adult population.

ences in vocabulary knowledge subsequently, when I return to a consideration of Schaie's contributions to the understanding of cohort effects on cognitive performance.

Cognitive Decline

When does cognitive decline begin? The early work of Cattell (1941, 1971; see also Horn & Cattell, 1966) suggested that the decline in some aspects of ability, particularly *fluid abilities* (abilities considered to involve basic problem solving skills, regardless of the social and cultural context), begins relatively early in adulthood, and it is only *crystallized abilities* (abilities involving the investment of fluid abilities in the social and cultural context) that tend to remain stable into old age and decline much later. Schaie led the way in challenging these arguments, making the case that significant cognitive decline does not occur for most dimensions of cognitive function until well after age 60 and for some not until after age 70 (Schaie, 1996, 2005). Of course, there is no such thing as a pure measure of either fluid or crystallized abilities, and to some extent all verbal tests are heavily loaded with the ingredients involved in crystallized abilities (Hertzog, 2008).

Admittedly, there is disagreement with respect to the inevitability of cognitive decline, and there is certainly heterogeneity in the experience of cognitive aging. Despite this, the overall aggregate trend for many, if not most, dimensions of human abilities is one of decline. Individual differences aside, there is general agreement that there are systematic age-related declines in cognitive functioning in many performance domains from midlife (in some cases) into older age. One of the early debates in the field of cognitive aging—between Baltes and Schaie on one hand and John Horn and Gary Donaldson on the other—involved the question of the typical levels of decline in cognitive function and the timing of that decline (see, e.g., Baltes & Schaie, 1976; Horn & Donaldson, 1977, 1980). Baltes and Schaie (1976) argued that much of early theorizing about systematic declines in cognitive abilities from midlife onward were in error and that many cognitive functions remained intact into very old age, challenging what they called the myth of intellectual decline. Horn and Donaldson (1977, 1980) argued that this was in part an issue of what is being measured. Recalling the Cattellian duality—the distinction between fluid and crystallized abilities (Cattell, 1971)—and the differing relationship of these two concepts to age, they argued that many fluid intelligence abilities experience declines from early adulthood through old age. Horn and Donaldson (1980, p. 479) drew the conclusion from their data that with age there is a loss of neurological base for intellectual functions (although they had no measures of these), and that loss is probably reflected most notably in performance measures reflecting fluid intellectual abilities.[7]

Some of the best evidence for the life-span development of various cognitive abilities is Schaie's (1996) SLS (see also Salthouse, 1991), which began tracking a cross-section of the adult population in 1956 at 7-year reinterview intervals. Schaie's early work (1983) concluded, on the basis of 21 years of the SLS, that "reliably replicable age changes in psychometric abilities of more than a trivial magnitude cannot be demonstrated prior to age 60" (p. 127). His more recent work has tended to bear out these conclusions (Schaie, 1989, 1990, 1994, 1996, 2005; see also Hertzog & Schaie, 1986, 1988; Schaie & Hertzog, 1983), and he has made a strong case for stability in many measured abilities over most of the adult life span. Schaie and his colleagues have argued that there is relative stability of mean performance levels throughout most of the life span, with some decline in old age, because of the onset of the dementias and other disease-related impediments to complete cognitive functioning.

This seemingly straightforward problem of identifying the age at which change begins and the pattern of change in the population is actually quite complex and has not been fully resolved. Many of these methodological and sampling issues were well described in the early debate over this question of when change begins (Baltes & Schaie, 1976; Horn & Donaldson, 1977, 1980) and are further developed in recent work (Alwin & Hofer, 2008). Longitudinal studies, while providing the essential measurement of within-person change, require repeated exposures to cognitive tests, and this usually results in practice-related gains in performance in the opposite direction of age-related declines. It has been argued that practice-related gains cannot be statistically controlled for in most longitudinal studies (Thorvaldsson, Hofer, Hassing, & Johansson, 2008). Numerous other effects confound simple description of aggregate aging-

---

[7]C. Hertzog (personal communication, April 29, 2008) reminded me how remarkable it is that psychometricians can infer a neurological substrate without even measuring it. Perhaps future studies involving neural imaging can test the Horn and Donaldson hypothesis (see, e.g., Hayes & Cabeza, 2008).

related change with cohort differences, differential mortality selection, initial sample selection, and health-related change.

Stability of Individual Differences

As noted earlier, in his 1964 presidential address to the American Sociological Association, Norman Ryder (1965) argued that the concept of cohort is a powerful concept in the explanation of social change not only because of the potential for unique experiences occurring during the impressionable years of socialization but also because of the strong tendencies for human stability. There is a great deal of evidence that individual differences in cognitive test scores, among other dimensions of individual differences, are quite stable over rather lengthy periods of the life span. As is the case with many human traits that reflect both ontogenic and sociogenic influences, individual differences in test scores are relatively less stable in childhood and early adolescence, but with age the differences among persons tend to stabilize, at least through midlife (Alwin, 1994, 2008, 2009b). There is no question that environment plays an important role in cognitive development, and it also has a role in the maintenance of individual differences over the life span. No one would likely dispute the possibility that major environmental inputs can contribute to the flexibility and change in older age in a range of abilities, but available evidence suggests a picture of high degrees of stability of individual differences in cognitive functioning into old age (Alwin, 2008, 2009a).

Patterns of individual stability and patterns of stability of individual differences are two different things—one does not necessarily imply or ensure the other (Alwin, 1994). Where the stability of individual differences in human abilities has been taken as problematic, measures of cognitive and intellective variables are highly stable over most of the adult life span, and results from recent research suggest that levels of molar stability are relatively low in the childhood years and increase with age (Alwin, 1994, 2008). Stability results for the adult years show there is very little change in the distributional placement of individuals relative to others after the age of 20. For example, Schaie's results from the SLS reflect the typical pattern—Hertzog and Schaie's (1986) estimate of the stability of the common factor underlying individual differences in a version of Thurstone's Primary Mental Abilities is .92 over a 14-year period (see also Schaie, 1983, 1990, 1996, 2005). They also showed that levels of stability increase with age. Similarly, Kohn and Schooler (1978) found a normative stability value of .93 for their concept of ideational flexibility assessed over a 10-year period. The entire range of studies indicates that stability grows in magnitude from adolescence onward and from the age of 40, the typical "molar stability" of intellectual ability is roughly .9 (Alwin, 2008). I conclude from this discussion that individual differences in cognitive abilities is one of the most stable components of human behavior that has been studied, although results differ at various points in the life cycle.

It needs to be emphasized at this point that the stability of individual differences in cognitive abilities has little, if anything, to do with the pattern of stability in average or typical trajectories over the life span. However, these results may seem to pose a serious threat to some interpretations arguing that socialization or learning affecting basic individual differences in intellectual abilities continues well into adulthood (e.g., Kohn & Schooler, 1978, 1983). Obviously, some openness to change is possible during adulthood, but if stability is viewed as a function of constancies of person–situation or person–structural linkages, then continuities over time may be viewed as reflections of the stability of socially structured experience. Only if changes in the social environment in later life were to contribute to levels of functioning would the environmental interpretation be relevant. The proper adjudication of the issue of whether a socioenvironmental interpretation exists for the instability of cognitive abilities would have to focus on the segment of the population that experiences change in social locations at different points in the life cycle, so that life-course linkages to changes in socially structured experiences could be determined. Schooler's (1987) analysis of the development of intellectual flexibility over the life span through exposure to changes in the complexity of the environment represents one attempt to apply theories of social structure and personality to human development (see, e.g., Kohn & Schooler, 1983; Kohn & Slomczynski, 1990; Schooler, 1987), but data from this research program have not been adequately organized to reflect life-span variations in stability (Alwin, 1995, pp. 163–164). Generalizing from findings in other domains, it may be that the greatest change occurs in persons whose environments are changing most rapidly, but those who remain in stable environments are least likely to change (Alwin, 1994; Alwin, Cohen, & Newcomb, 1991; Baltes, 1997; Musgrove, 1977).

Historical Influences

Interpretation of historical effects on cohorts through chronicles of 20th century events and experiences are thought to be relevant to the process. Several decades ago, psychologist Kenneth Gergen (1973) made an important set of observations that are relevant in the present context. He argued that "contemporary" theories of social behavior are "primarily reflections of contemporary history" (p. 309; for a more detailed discussion of Gergen's ideas, see Alwin et al., 1991). He suggested we think in terms of a "*continuum of historical durability,* with phenomena highly susceptible to historical influence at one extreme and the more stable processes at the other" (p. 318). Some phenomena may be closely tied to innate and irreversible physiological givens, and many would argue that patterns of cognitive aging are an example of such phenomena. On the other hand, "learned dispositions," Gergen suggested, may in some cases "overcome the strength of some physiological tendencies" (p. 318). In a more recent essay, elaborating on the same point, Gergen (1980) suggested that evidence of cohort differences in developmental trajectories of a wide range of human characteristics is invariably found among cohorts born in different historical eras within the same culture. He suggested that "depending upon the socio-historical circumstances, differing age-related trajectories are found in value commitments, personality characteristics, *mental capabilities,* political ideology, communication patterns and so on" (p. 37).

I believe Gergen (1980) may have overstated the case somewhat, but it is now well-accepted that age-related trajectories of cognitive performance observed in samples of individuals from age-heterogeneous populations may be due in part to the spurious effects of historically linked cohort experiences. Historical processes are implicated by the fact that cohort groups differ markedly in their levels of schooling, which are predictive of levels of cognitive performance. In our recent research we argued that generalizations about processes of cognitive aging can be improved by examining such issues in broad representative samples of populations of interest and by considering the relevance of demographic processes in estimating aging functions in samples of such populations. We argued that it is important to consider the historical processes of educational expansion and cohort differences in schooling outcomes as they relate to assessments of cognitive functioning in aging populations (Alwin, 2009a).

The demographic literature concerned with cohort effects on cognitive functioning has focused primarily on differences between cohorts in levels (or intercepts) of performance (e.g., Alwin, 1991; Alwin & McCammon, 1999, 2001). By contrast, the developmental literature has phrased the issue of cohort variation in terms of the existence (or lack thereof) of "simple age-graded nomothetic and universal patterns of behavioral development" (Baltes et al., 1979, p. 86). Both of these issues may be investigated within the framework of growth models by explicitly examining the differences between two sets of models—one that posits intraindividual change across all cohorts to follow the same overall age-based trajectory (Bell, 1953, 1954; McArdle & Bell, 2000) and one that allows for potential differences in intercepts and slopes across cohorts (Miyazaki & Raudenbush, 2000). A question for future research on cognitive aging is whether the patterns of cognitive decline witnessed in contemporary data are likely to be observed in similar studies conducted 50 years from now on the cohorts of today's children (Alwin et al., 2008). For purposes of the present discussion, I set aside the issue raised by Baltes et al. (1979), focusing instead on cohort differences in levels of cognitive performance.

Cohort experiences can affect cognitive scores, for example, verbal and quantitative abilities, through several mechanisms. Childhood and youth are periods for learning vast amounts of new information, and this information becomes a resource for further development. Such knowledge may be affected by the distinctiveness of cohort experiences. One of the major mechanisms for the transmission of knowledge is formal schooling; it is often assumed that greater amounts of time spent in school, as assessed by years of schooling completed, should be related to greater amounts of knowledge across a wide range of domains. More recently born cohorts' greater access to schooling should better prepare them for adult life compared with earlier born cohorts. Indeed, psychometricians have known for a long time that standardized test scores tend to rise from one generation to another. The tendency for test scores on standardized intelligence tests to increase over time has been called the *Flynn effect*, named after James Flynn, a political scientist at the University of Otago in New Zealand, who quantified the pervasiveness of the pattern (Flynn, 1984, 1987, 1998, 1999; Neisser, 1997, 1998). Flynn found that increasing raw scores appear on every major test, in every age range and in every modern industrialized country, although the tests most closely linked to school content show the smallest increases (see the review by Neisser, 1997, pp. 441–442; see also Flynn, 1998, p. 61). Flynn (1984, p. 48) argued that increased educational levels accounted for much, but far from all, of these IQ gains. The test scores continue to increase despite the fact that cohort-specific levels of schooling reached an asymptote with those born in 1945 and after (Alwin, 2009a).

One of the interesting things about the Flynn argument (e.g., Flynn, 1998, 1999) is that it is most apparent among measures that are highly loaded in fluid abilities and least apparent in measures of crystallized abilities, which is not what one would expect. Indeed, less or no gains were found for acculturated skills acquired through schooling, that is, crystallized learning. If cohort factors were operating to produce Flynn's effect, one would expect this to make his patterns even more apparent in the case of crystallized abilities. About the role of cohort and period effects in intelligence test scores, Flynn (1998, p. 61) had this to say:

> Gains may be age specific, but this has not yet been established and they certainly persist into adulthood. The fact that gains are fully present in young children means that causal factors are present in early childhood but not necessarily that they are more potent in young children than among older children or adults.

Thus, it is not clear from Flynn's writing whether he considers the effect exclusively a cohort phenomenon or also due to period factors (see also Flynn, 1999). By contrast, Schaie, Willis, and Pennak (2005) made the argument that what Flynn has found are cohort effects, that is, that the changes Flynn observes at the macrolevel are primarily reflections of differences in cohort experiences and that the largest gains, as suggested by the SLS data, are for cohorts born in the early part of the last century. This argument is consistent with the theoretical expectations illustrated in Figure 1.1 and consistent with a "progressive" view of the consequences of the expansion of education cognitive and intellectual improvement (see also Schaie, 2005, 2008).

Schaie's work on cohort effects has generally suggested that more recent birth cohorts have higher levels of cognitive performance when observed at the same age (Schaie, 2005, 2008; see also Schaie, Willis, & Pennak, 2005). Several observations can be drawn from these researchers' results. First, when intracohort trajectories are shown for measures of both fluid and crystallized abilities, virtually all intercohort comparisons undertaken holding age constant (i.e., within age groups) reveal patterns favoring later-born cohorts. Second, although the available trends show a great deal of uniformity across measures, supporting a conclusion that there are systematic and substantial positive advances as seen in the intercohort trends, there are some inconsistencies. There are some trends that are negative, and some trends change their direction at some points on the birth cohort continuum. Indeed, the cohort differences from 1889 to 1952 for verbal ability show positive intercohort gains, but following the 1952 birth cohort, there is a decline in scores (Schaie et al., 2005, p. 50). There are other examples as well such as a decline in number fluency from the 1910 cohort. Third, although most of the attention given to the consideration of "massive IQ gains" has focused on the post–World War II cohorts, Schaie et al.'s data presented an intercohort pattern that extends back to those born in the early 1900s, and they argued that there are generally positive trends over the past century (Schaie et al., 2005). They argued that one of the major reasons for this trend is that sociocultural factors were working to ensure that advances in educational attainment and shifts in the occupational structure would result in protective factors, or what is often called *cognitive reserve* would compensate for the risks to cognitive health linked to neurobiological diseases that come with longevity (Stern, 2007).

Consistent with some of Schaie's findings, I would point out that the tendency for test scores to rise has not always been the case, nor is it the case for all domains. During the 1960s and 1970s, serious concern was expressed about the declining performance by the young on measures of verbal ability. Average verbal scores on standardized tests such as the Scholastic Aptitude Test (SAT) and the American College Testing Service (ACT) tests (Wirtz & Howe, 1977) declined systematically from the mid-1960s through the mid-1980s. There are, of course, serious problems with interpreting changes in college-admissions test scores as if they reflect true aggregate levels of verbal and quantitative skills of high school students, given the changing composition of the test-taking population, but most observers of the test-score declines conceded that, net of these compositional shifts, the test-score decline was real (e.g., Blake, 1989). Responding to the need for better information based on national probability samples, Alwin (1991) used data from nine representative samples of the U.S. population in the GSS between 1974 and 1990, showing that there were systematic education-adjusted differences among cohorts in the GSS vocabulary test score, especially beginning with those born subsequent to 1946. He concluded that these differences were a reflection of the same social processes that produced the test score decline of the 1960s and 1970s.

These conclusions are apparent from the data presented in Figure 1.2, where we have added the observed mean vocabulary scores from the GSS data, super-

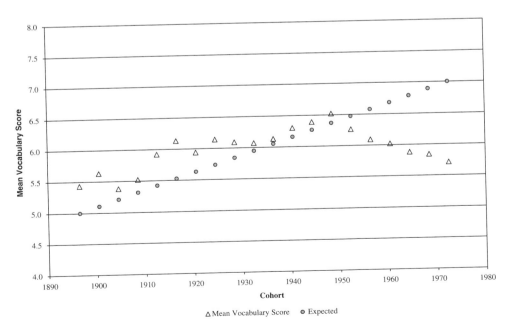

Figure 1.2. Vocabulary test scores: General Social Surveys, 1974–1998. Data from Alwin and McCammon (2001).

imposed on the theoretical model discussed previously in the text surrounding Figure 1.1. These results show the raw GSS vocabulary test score data across cohort groupings beginning before the 1900s through cohort groups born in the late 1960s and early 1970s. These results depart in one critical way from the theoretical mode, particularly the decline in vocabulary test scores from the 1950 cohort onward. As shown in Figure 1.2, there are cohort patterns that differ systematically from those expectations but that are completely consistent with the cohort interpretation given by Schaie (2005) for the "verbal meaning" score in his analyses.

Glenn (1994) confirmed the existence of this intercohort trend in vocabulary knowledge and argued that the trend could be interpreted by reference to inter-cohort differences in media exposure, that is, television watching and newspaper reading. Since the publication of Alwin's (1991) and Glenn's (1994) studies, other work has reinforced the cohort interpretation of the test-score decline. Much concern has focused on literacy and what schools are teaching, and recent historical analyses of reading difficulty in student texts are quite revealing. For example, Hayes, Wolfer, and Wolfe (1996) argued that schools have contributed to lower verbal scores because of a progressive simplification of the language used in schoolbooks. Reviewing 800 textbooks used in elementary, middle, and high schools between 1919 and 1991, they found that the vocabulary of the school-books became progressively easier after World War II. They concluded that daily use of simplified textbooks across 11 years of schooling produces "a cumulating deficit in students' knowledge base and advanced verbal skill" (Hayes et al., 1996, p. 493). The systematic "dumbing down" of American reading textbooks provides a strong basis for a sociohistorical interpretation of the decline in verbal test scores in the 1960s and 1970s, a decline not experienced to the same extent by the quantitative scores (Chall & Conard 1991, pp. 1–4). Thus, despite the fact that more recent cohorts (post-1946 cohorts) have much higher levels of school-ing, according to this argument they are learning less. (For alternative views, see Wilson & Gove, 1999; Schaie et al., 2005; for debate surrounding their argu-ments, see Alwin & McCammon, 1999, 2001; Schaie, 2008.)

In Figure 1.3, I have superimposed a third pattern on the previous two figures. These are the cohort-specific vocabulary test scores in the 1974–1998 GSS data, adjusted for age and schooling. These results show some rather sur-prising patterns in that once they adjusted to the age and schooling levels of the population as a whole, the earlier-born cohorts have systematically higher scores. Overall, the results point to a conclusion that, despite their higher levels of school-ing, post–World War II birth cohorts have scored systematically lower on cogni-tive tests compared with those born earlier in the century. This is a pattern that is identified in our recent research using the HRS data (see Alwin, 2009a; Alwin et al., 2008). This set of results is puzzling, and even potentially alarming, and it will, I hope, challenge researchers to further explore the patterns observed here.

Something important to note in this case is that the pattern of numbers in Figure 1.3 is exactly the opposite of what is predicted in Figure 1.1. Possible expla-nations that may account for the cohort-specific differences in intercepts observed in these results include (a) historical effects on socialization, learning cognitive development; and/or (b) mortality selection favoring the earlier born cohorts, such that differential survival of most cognitively fit in the earlier-born cohorts are at

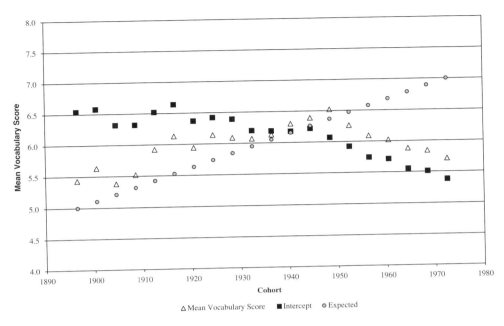

Figure 1.3. Vocabulary test scores: General Social Surveys, 1974–1998, adjusted for age and schooling. Data from Alwin and McCammon (2001).

a comparative advantage relative to the later-born cohorts. There is clearly more than a single explanation of the trends observed in Figure 1.3 and quite possibly a different explanation for cohort disparities at different points across the cohort axis. The experiences of the 1960s cohorts, both in school and in the extracurricular world, may have systematically lowered vocabulary knowledge, but this does not account for the relatively higher scores of persons in the earliest-born cohorts. For the latter there are other possibilities, namely compositional phenomena linked to mortality selection—I return to this in the next section.

Although an argument can be made for differences in the experiences among cohorts in levels of schooling that might account for cohort differences in cognitive test performance, this explanation is counterintuitive in the present case, as our results from the HRS cognitive performance data show the opposite pattern, that is, one in which the intercepts of earlier-born cohorts are higher than those of later-born cohorts. And, when intercohort differences in the level of schooling are controlled, the differences in intercepts are accentuated rather than reduced or removed (Alwin, 2009a; Alwin et al., 2008, p. 81).

Cognitive Decline and Mortality

Cognitive decline is a risk factor for mortality. One of the important ingredients in the interpretation I provide here for the results in the earlier-born region of Figure 1.3, is the idea that processes involved with respect to mortality selection, especially the selectivity on the basis of health-related factors associated with cognitive function. Lower cognitive performance in adults has been reported to be associated with earlier mortality in several studies. Research by Schaie and his colleagues (Bosworth & Schaie, 1999; Bosworth, Schaie, & Willis, 1999) using the SLS investigated the question of the cognitive, social, and demographic risk factors for mortality. They found that a decrease in cognitive performance tended to be a better predictor of subsequent mortality than was the level of cognitive performance.

We have investigated the relationship between mortality patterns and age-related trajectories of performance using the HRS cognitive performance measures (verbal score, two recall measures, and a serial subtraction assessment of working memory; see Alwin, 2009a; Alwin et al., 2008). We examined patterns of mortality in the 1996–2002 HRS for several birth cohort groups from the AHEAD subsample—those born 1890–1908, 1909–1913, 1914–1918, and 1919–1923—and found that within wave, there is a significant effect for mortality pattern and age group (and education, when it is included), but there is no evidence of an interaction effect between mortality pattern and age group (results not presented here). There is a clear difference in cognitive performance between members of a given cohort (in this case a group of cohorts) who are nearer to death in any wave of the study relative to those who prove themselves to have greater longevity. Whatever factors are selective with respect to mortality in these data, they appear to be associated with level of cognitive performance. These results illustrate the phenomena of *mortality selection* with respect to cognitive performance, and they strongly suggest that this process reflects one possible explanation of the pattern of intercohort differences in intercepts reported in the preceding analysis.

Given this pattern of cognitive scores among groups defined by patterns of mortality, and given that heterogeneity in longevity decreases with age, the later-born cohorts, as a whole, have lower mean levels of cognitive performance, than does the subset of these cohorts that will survive to the ages represented by the earlier-born cohorts. These results suggest that comparisons of age differences in cognitive performance, particularly when undertaken cross-sectionally, should take age-specific mortality rates into account. We note, however, that if the phenomenon of interest declines with age but is positively related to longevity, then the bias introduced by ignoring mortality selection is conservative. That is, under such circumstances, ignoring mortality selection results in an underestimate of age-related decline (Alwin, 2009a).

One solution to this is to account for cohort differences in longevity by controlling statistically for intercohort differences in expected age at death. We have used this approach to account for heterogeneity in cohort experiences in variables linked to survivorship, at least at the cohort level (Alwin et al., 2008, pp. 82–85). We know of no research that has attempted to control for individual differences on expected longevity, although the examination of the history of panel respondents who have experienced mortality—which eventually will include all respondents in the HRS—represents an appropriate strategy for analyzing cognitive change in what may be a more informative time metric. These results are quite general, extending to several measures of cognitive functioning in the HRS data, and they confirm the expectation that mortality selection is a plausible explanation for the intercohort differences in the HRS immediate work recall measure reported before in this chapter. These results reinforce the conclusions that models of the aging process should allow for free-intercepts models with respect to cohort differences. Such models appear to reflect a better assessment of the aging function than the more conventional "age-based" or "convergence" models that are common in the growth modeling literature, which assume there are no cohort differences in processes of cognitive aging (see the review of these issues by Alwin et al., 2008; see also Thorvaldsson et al., 2008).

Cohort Differences and Mortality Selection

As I noted earlier, the pattern of numbers represented in Figure 1.3 presents a picture of intercohort differences in vocabulary scores that is counterintuitive, given Schaie's "progress model." As noted, perhaps the most plausible explanation of the pattern of intercohort differences in intercepts reported here for the earlier born cohorts involves the phenomenon of mortality selection (e.g., Baltes, 1968; Schaie, Labouvie, & Barrett, 1973). A given birth cohort can be thought of as a collection of subpopulations defined by longevity, and cohorts differ substantially in their representation of these subpopulations (Alwin et al., 2008, p. 82). Mortality is obviously selective, and to the extent that selectivity is linked to factors associated with levels of cognitive performance, then mortality selection is a potential explanation for the findings just noted. Because the variable of interest, in this case cognitive functioning, is positively related to longevity, then the younger group will necessarily have a lower age-standardized mean than that of the older group, net of any "real" cohort differences (Vaupel & Yashin, 1985). Indeed, it might be the case that such performance-linked selectivity in survivorship might be masking a "true" cohort effect that favors more recent-born cohorts. Therefore, a strong argument can be made that differential age-specific mortality rates should be taken into account when examining age differences in cognitive performance, or when comparing cohorts in patterns of age-related within-cohort change (Alwin, 2009a).

Analyzing Aging Trajectories in a Demographic Context

This chapter has dealt with many important issues organized around seven principles from Schaie's research. Some of these observations are well known; others are less well understood. It is widely known, for example, that age-related differences in cognitive scores do not necessarily imply aging because of the potential influence of cohort and period effects (Alwin, McCammon, & Hofer, 2006). I have referred repeatedly to the terms *cohort* and *period* in this chapter, and I have raised many issues with respect to the analysis of cognitive aging data. What is less well-understood concerning the issues raised in the foregoing discussion are the modern statistical methods that can be used for separating aging and cohort effects. In this final section I provide a brief discussion of solutions to this problem involving *latent curve* or *latent growth curve* models, which allow for cohort effects. I assume some background on the part of the reader in the methods of studying the effects of time and within-person change (see, e.g., Singer & Willett, 2003; Willett, 1989; Willett & Sayer, 1994).

Latent Curve Models in a Demographic Context

Models of individual growth and development can be conceptualized within the general framework offered by structural equation models (SEM) or covariance structure analysis (e.g., Bollen & Curran, 2006; McArdle, 1986, 1988, 1991; McArdle & Anderson, 1990; McArdle & Bell, 2000; McArdle & Epstein, 1987; McArdle & Hamagami, 2001; Meredith & Tisek, 1990; Willett & Sayer, 1994). This approach is referred to as *latent growth curve* or *latent curve* (LC) analysis because the variables representing individual-level intercepts and slopes are incorporated in the model as *latent common factors*. LC models are well suited to the study of aging because they focus on continuous processes of change and can allow for measurement errors in the variables assessed over time. Given this formulation, LC models have a natural kinship to confirmatory factor models and models for factorial invariance (Alwin, 1988; McArdle & Bell, 2000; Meredith, 1993; Meredith & Horn, 2001).

All latent change models begin with the specification of a within-person (i.e., intraindividual) model for individual change over the period of measurement—these are often referred to as *time-based* or *occasion-based* models, though for a given individual measured longitudinally, there is a perfect correlation between time of measurement and age. When these models are aggregated across individuals, the latent factor means represent the average trajectory, whereas the factor variances reflect the person-to-person variability of the individual-level curves.

There are other ways to analyze these LC (or growth) models. For example, such models can also be viewed as a special application of multilevel models in which occasions of measurement are nested within persons, where the Level 1 model is used to specify the population function of change, that is, time in study, chronological age, time to event (Bryk & Raudenbush, 1992; Goldstein, 1995; Hox, 2000, 2002). The LC model is statistically equivalent to a random coefficients model for change over time when time values are discrete across occasions for all or most individuals. The multilevel approach permits more flexible specification of time in that values can be different for each individual at each occasion. In this approach, time, as modeled by the basis parameters for the slope factor in the SEM approach, is instead included as a variable in the multilevel regression model (Hox, 2002).

Latent Curve Models Within Cohorts

Capitalizing on the heterogeneity of birth cohorts that may exist in a data set, separate occasion-based models can be specified for each cohort, and with the appropriate between-person model constraints, the cohort-specific models can then be combined to relatively quickly construct age trajectories that represent the processes of aging across an age range equal to the span of measurement (in years) plus the number of the birth cohorts in the sample (Alwin, Hofer, & McCammon, 2006). Models such as these in which within- and between-person models are combined are referred to as *age-based* models. In these models, the distinction between occasion-based and age-based models is reduced to insignificance. Given the possibility to aggregate these models of intraindividual change across individuals from different birth cohorts, combining observed within-person change and between-person differences, one can construct trajectories for a broad range of ages that follow the same overall age function. Such approaches are referred to by a variety of names, including *convergence models* (McArdle, Anderson, & Aber, 1987; McArdle & Bell, 2000; McArdle & Hamigami, 2001), *accelerated longitudinal designs* (Bell, 1953, 1954; Miyazaki & Raudenbush, 2000; Raudenbush & Chan, 1992), *cohort sequential designs* (Baltes & Nesselroade, 1979; Muthén & Muthén, 2000, 2004), *age-vector models* (Mirowsky & Kim, 2007; Mirowsky & Ross, 2008) or simply *age-based modeling*. In any event, it can be seen that using data collected over a relatively short period of time, one can construct a longitudinal age curve spanning much larger number of years than is represented in the design.

The causal diagrams in Figure 1.4 present an illustration of a generic occasion-based growth curve model for four waves of data, embedded within each of two hypothetical birth cohorts—one born in 1940 and the other in 1941. This example can be generalized to the case of multiple cohorts (C > 2). Although I do not present the mathematical formula here, this is a model for latent intraindividual change in a given variable that is derived from the specification of two models: (a) a measurement model and (b) a model for intraindividual change, where the measurement model for the *pth* person for a given observed variable *y* measured at time *t* is assumed to follow the assumptions of classical measurement theory, and the intraindividual change model is stated for a single true score measured over time (Willett & Sayer, 1994). As noted earlier, consistent with the multilevel approach, the intraindividual growth model is sometimes called a *Level 1* model. Once this model is formulated and estimated, one can examine a *Level 2* model for explaining interindividual differences in levels (intercepts) and rates of change (slopes) in the Level 1 model (Willett & Sayer, 1994, pp. 363–364).

This model for within-person change in the generic case (see Figure 1.4) expresses change as a function of time, where an individual's score at a given point in time is a function of an intercept (or level) parameter, a linear slope parameter, a quadratic slope parameter reflecting some form of curvature, and a disturbance term. The arrows connecting the latent variables and the observed variables are called *latent basis parameters* or *factor loadings,* which are fixed to reflect the nature of the growth function with respect to time/age. The particular form of the model is then fit to the data, and the fit of the model is assessed using standard strategies for evaluating the model's goodness of fit. For example, if change is theorized to be a simple linear function of time, the quadratic latent variable would be omitted, and the latent basis parameters for the slope factor would be fixed, for example, at "years since initial testing" (where $t = 0, 1, 2, 3$ in waves separated by 1-year intervals, or some linear transformation of these values). Or, the time-basis parameters might be fixed to represent some form of curvature, for example, in a quadratic form. One does not in general assume that individual growth (decline) is a linear function of time, and therefore one should reserve the option to specify these coefficients as a way of formulating various hypotheses to be tested against the data, or as group-level parameters to be estimated (McArdle & Bell, 2000, pp. 81–82). This model may be modified where times of measurement vary across individuals (see Muthén & Muthén, 2004, p. 344).

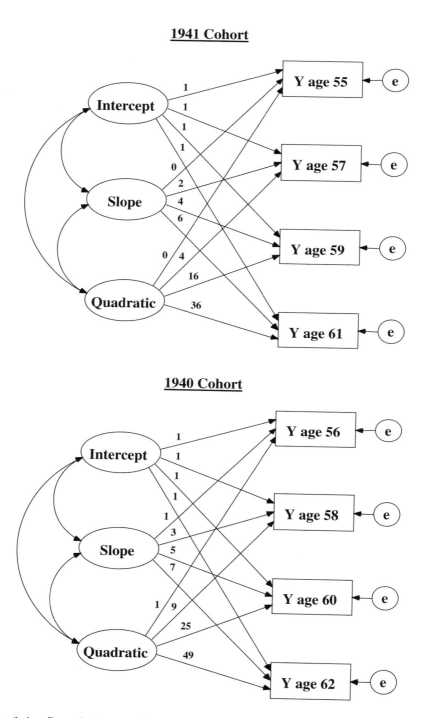

Figure 1.4. Causal diagram for age-based latent growth models using structural equation methods.

Tests of Cohort Effects

The demographic literature concerned with cohort effects has focused primarily on differences between cohorts in levels (or intercepts) of variables (see, e.g., Alwin, 1991; Alwin & McCammon, 1999, 2001). By contrast, in the developmental literature concerned with the role of cohort variation, the issue has been additionally phrased in terms of the existence (or lack thereof) of "simple age-graded nomothetic and universal patterns of behavioral development" (Baltes et al., 1979, p. 86). Both of these issues may be investigated within the framework of growth models by explicitly examining the differences between two sets of models—one that posits intraindividual change across all cohorts to follow the same overall age-based trajectory, that is, the convergence model (Bell, 1953, 1954; McArdle & Bell, 2000) and one that posits potential differences in intercepts and slopes across cohorts. Building on modeling strategies used by Miyazaki and Raudenbush (2000), McArdle, Anderson, and Aber (1987), and Muthén and Muthén (2000), a comparison between age-based and occasion-based LC models can be constructed in a way that provides a test for cohort differences in slopes and intercepts (Alwin, 2009a; Alwin, Hofer, & McCammon, 2006). This comparison can be implemented using the multiple-group model described previously in which the groups are defined by birth year. The age-based version of this model—in which the slopes and intercepts are constrained to be equal over groups—is a restricted version of the multiple-cohort occasion-based LC model. Because the latter model is nested within the less restrictive time-based, multiple cohort model in which intercepts and slopes are unconstrained across cohorts, the test for cohort effects comes down to a comparison of the likelihood-ratio fit statistics for various models that specify cohort-specific parameters that differ from those in the age-based model (Alwin, 2009a; Alwin, Hofer, & McCammon, 2006).

Results from our project involving cognitive measures from the HRS strongly suggest that failing to take cohort differences into account in the investigation of patterns of cognitive aging can bias the assessment of rates of cognitive decline in older age (Alwin, 2009a; Alwin, McCammon, Rodgers, & Wray, 2008). These types of results are expected to encourage other researchers to reject the more conventional age-based or convergence models that are common in the psychological literature, models which assume there are no cohort differences in processes of cognitive aging (McArdle, Fisher, & Kadlee, 2007). I believe that models allowing for cohort differences have great promise, and I encourage other students of cognitive aging to reconsider the conventional view in favor of a set of multi-group models that are sensitive to cohort differences, especially in the presence of mortality selection (Alwin, 2009a; Alwin et al., 2008).

Conclusions

Schaie's work on intellectual and cognitive change throughout adulthood addresses three major theses in research on the role of historical and social factors in processes of cognitive aging: (a) the theoretical justification for hypothesizing cohort differences in developmental patterns and processes that will result in observations of cohort differences in levels and overtime trajectories of cognitive function; (b) the methodological problems inherent in drawing inferences about cohort effects and dealing with competing hypotheses; and (c) the need to understand the population processes, especially those involving mortality selection, resulting in compositional differences among cohorts observed at a given time.

This chapter has covered seven principle empirical findings from Schaie's work that bear on the nature of cohort differences in cognitive functioning. First, building on the ideas of others, Schaie embraced the idea rather early on that age-related differences in cognitive scores do not necessarily imply aging—they may reflect the influences of historical or cohort factors as well. Second, Schaie played a role in the statistical identification of aging and cohort effects, arguing that this is generally not possible unless one is willing to make the assumption of minimal period influences. Schaie (1965, 1970) confronted these difficult issues early on and helped clarify the identification issues; there were no satisfactory solutions, except those that can be settled on the basis of theoretical knowledge and a priori assumptions. Third, on the basis of his results from the SLS, the best evidence for typical or normal cognitive aging suggests that significant cognitive decline does not occur for most performance measures until well after age 60 and for some not until after age 70. Fourth, Schaie's research provides strong evidence for the stability of individual differences in cognitive functioning through old age, which suggests a high degree of stability, despite average mean shifts. This is one of the important elements in positing cohort effects, namely, stability of individual differences. Fifth, Schaie's scholarly contributions, especially his most recent work, has supplied an interpretation of historical effects on cohorts. His work suggests that more recent cohorts have higher levels of average cognitive performance, which can be attributed to 20th century events and experiences, for example, the expansion of education, thought to be relevant to the promotion of intellectual abilities. Sixth, Schaie's research has been helpful in providing the empirical identification of cognitive decline as a risk factor for mortality. And seven, Schaie's research, taken together, helps provide the development of the hypothesis that cohort differences in cognitive function are in part attributable to population processes and mortality selection.

For the most part, our findings support the hypotheses developed by Schaie on the basis of the SLS about patterns of cognitive aging, although our research registers some interesting disagreement about the nature of cohort differences and their sources. I should note, however, that the results for the GSS vocabulary measure are quite consistent with Schaie's (2005) results pertaining to verbal ability. The ultimate question I have about the SLS results is whether population processes, specifically mortality selection, play a role in Schaie's findings, and if so, what is the nature of that role? It is hoped that in future years, when the SLS data become publicly available, that some of these differences in findings can be reconciled through the application of a common set of techniques of data analysis, such as those proposed above for separating the effects of aging and cohort (see also Alwin, 2009a; Alwin, Hofer, & McCammon, 2006).

References

Adams, J. (1978). Sequential strategies and the separation of age, cohort, and time-of-measurement contributions to developmental data. *Psychological Bulletin, 85,* 1309–1316.

Alwin, D. F. (1988). Structural equation models in research on human development and aging. In K. W. Schaie, R. T. Campbell, W. Meredith, & S. C. Rawlings (Eds.), *Methodological issues in aging research* (pp. 71–170). New York: Springer.

Alwin, D. F. (1991). Family of origin and cohort differences in verbal ability. *American Sociological Review, 56,* 625–638.

Alwin, D. F. (1994). Aging, personality and social change: The stability of individual differences over the adult life span. In D. L. Featherman, R. M. Lerner, & M. Perlmutter (Eds.), *Life-span development and behavior* (Vol. 12, pp. 135–185). Hillsdale, NJ: Erlbaum.

Alwin, D. F. (1995). Taking time seriously: Studying social change, social structure and human lives. In P. Moen, G. H. Elder Jr., & K. Lüscher (Eds.), *Examining lives in context: Perspectives on the ecology of human development* (pp. 211–262). Washington, DC: American Psychological Association.

Alwin, D. F. (2008). Social structure and cognitive aging. In S. M. Hofer & D. F. Alwin (Eds.), *Handbook of cognitive aging: Interdisciplinary perspectives* (pp. 418–444). Thousand Oaks, CA: Sage.

Alwin, D. F. (2009a). *The dynamic processes of aging: The aging mind in social and historical context.* Unpublished manuscript, Pennsylvania State University, University Park.

Alwin, D. F. (2009b). Social structure, cognition, and aging. In C. Phillipson & D. Dannefer (Eds.), *International handbook of social gerontology.* London: Sage.

Alwin, D. F., Cohen, R. L., & Newcomb, T. M. (1991). *Political attitudes over the life span: The Bennington women after fifty years.* Madison: University of Wisconsin Press.

Alwin, D. F., & Hofer, S. M. (2008). Opportunities and challenges for interdisciplinary research. In S. M. Hofer & D. F. Alwin (Eds.), *Handbook of cognitive aging: Interdisciplinary perspectives* (pp. 2–31). Thousand Oaks, CA: Sage.

Alwin, D. F., Hofer, S. M., & McCammon, R. J. (2006). Modeling the effects of time: Integrating demographic and developmental perspectives. In R. H. Binstock & L. K. George (Eds.), *Handbook of aging and the social sciences* (pp. 20–38). New York: Academic Press.

Alwin, D. F., & McCammon, R. J. (1999). Aging vs. cohort interpretations of intercohort differences in GSS verbal scores. *American Sociological Review 64,* 272–286.

Alwin, D. F., & McCammon, R. J. (2001). Aging, cohorts, and verbal ability. *The Journals of Gerontology: Series B. Psychological Sciences and Social Sciences 56,* S1–S11.

Alwin, D. F., & McCammon, R. J. (2003). Generations, cohorts, and social change. In J. T. Mortimer & M. J. Shanahan (Eds.), *Handbook of the life course* (pp. 23–49). New York: Kluwer Academic/Plenum Publishers.

Alwin, D. F., & McCammon, R. J. (2007). Rethinking generations. *Research in Human Development, 4,* 145–272.

Alwin, D. F., McCammon, R. J., & Hofer, S. M. (2006). Studying Baby Boom cohorts within a demographic context: Conceptual and methodological issues. In S. K. Whitbourne & S. L. Willis (Eds.), *The baby boomers at midlife: Contemporary perspectives on middle age.* Mahwah, NJ: Erlbaum.

Alwin, D. F., McCammon, R. J., Wray, L. A., & Rodgers, W. L. (2008). Population processes and cognitive aging. In S. M. Hofer and D. F. Alwin (Eds.), *Handbook of cognitive aging: Interdisciplinary perspectives* (pp. 69–89). Thousand Oaks, CA: Sage.

Austad, S. N. (1997). *Why we age—What science is discovering about the body's journey through life.* New York: Wiley.

Baltes, P. B. (1968). Longitudinal and cross-sectional sequences in the study of age and generation effects. *Human Development, 11,* 145–171.

Baltes, P. B. (1997). On the incomplete architecture of human ontogeny. *American Psychologist, 52,* 366–380.

Baltes, P. B., Cornelius, S. W., & Nesselroade, J. R. (1979). Cohort effects in developmental psychology. In J. Nesselroade & P. Baltes (Eds.), *Longitudinal research in the study of behavior and development* (pp. 61–87). New York: Academic Press.

Baltes, P. B., & Mayer, K. U. (1999). *The Berlin Aging Study: Aging from 70 to 100.* New York: Cambridge University Press.

Baltes, P. B., & Nesselroade, J. R. (1979). History and rationale of longitudinal research. In J. R. Nesselroade & P. B. Baltes (Eds.), *Longitudinal research in the study of behavior and development* (pp. 1–39). New York: Academic Press.

Baltes, P. B., & Schaie, K. W. (1976). On the plasticity of intelligence in adulthood and old age: Where Horn and Donaldson fail. *American Psychologist, 31,* 720–725.

Bell, R. Q. (1953). Convergence: An accelerated longitudinal approach, *Child Development, 27,* 45–74.

Bell, R. Q. (1954). An experimental test of the accelerated longitudinal approach. *Child Development, 25,* 281–86.

Blake, J. (1989). *Family Size and Achievement.* Berkeley: University of California Press.

Bollen, K. A., & Curran, P. J. (2006). *Latent curve models.* Hoboken, NJ: Wiley.

Bosworth, H. B., & Schaie, K. W. (1999). Survival effects in cognitive function, cognitive style, and sociodemographic variables in the Seattle Longitudinal Study. *Experimental Aging Research, 25,* 121–139.

Bosworth, H. B., Schaie, K. W., & Willis, S. L. (1999). Cognitive and sociodemographic risk factors for mortality in the Seattle Longitudinal Study. *The Journals of Gerontology: Series B. Psychological Sciences and Social Sciences, 54,* P273–P282.

Bryk, A. S., & Raudenbush, S. W. (1992). *Hierarchical linear models: Applications and data analysis methods.* Newbury Park, CA: Sage.

Cattell, R. B. (1941). Some theoretical issues in adult intelligence testing. *Psychological Bulletin, 38,* 592.

Cattell, R. B. (1971). *Abilities: Their structure, growth and action.* Boston: Houghton Mifflin.

Chall, J. S., & Conard, S. S. (1991). *Should textbooks challenge students? The case for easier or harder books.* New York: Teachers College Press.

Davis, J. A., & Smith, T. W. (2001). *General social surveys, 1972–2000: Cumulative codebook* [Machine-readable data file]. Chicago: National Opinion Research Center (producer); Storrs, CT: The Roper Center for Public Opinion Research, University of Connecticut (distributor).

Duncan, O. D. (1985). Generations, cohorts, and conformity. In W. M. Mason & S. E. Fienberg (Eds.). *Cohort analysis in social research: Beyond the identification problem.* (pp. 289–321). New York: Springer-Verlag.

Easterlin, R. A. (1987). *Birth and fortune: The impact of numbers on personal welfare.* Chicago: University of Chicago Press.

Farkas, G. (1977). Cohort, age, and period effects upon the employment of white females: Evidence for 1957–1968. *Demography, 13,* 33–42.

Firebaugh, G. (1989). Methods for estimating cohort replacement effects. In C. C. Clogg (Ed.), *Sociological methodology 1989* (pp. 243–262). Oxford, England: Blackwell.

Firebaugh, G. (1992). Where does social change come from? Estimating the relative contributions of individual change and population turnover. *Population Research and Policy Review, 11,* 1–20.

Flynn, J. R. (1984). The mean IQ of Americans: Massive gains. *Psychological Bulletin, 95,* 29–51.

Flynn, J. R. (1987). Massive IQ gains in 14 nations: What IQ tests really measure. *Psychological Bulletin, 101,* 171–191.

Flynn, J. R. (1998). IQ gains over time: Toward finding the causes. In U. Neisser (Ed.), *The rising curve: Long-term gains in IQ and related measures* (pp. 25–66). Washington, DC: American Psychological Association.

Flynn, J. R. (1999) Searching for justice: The discovery of IQ gains over time. *American Psychologist, 54,* 5–20.

Gergen, K. J. (1973). Social psychology as history. *Journal of Personality and Social Psychology, 26,* 309–320.

Gergen, K. J. (1980). The emerging crisis in life-span developmental theory. In P. B. Baltes & O. G. Brim Jr. (Eds.), *Life-span development and behavior* (Vol. 3, pp. 32–65). New York: Academic Press.

Glenn, N. D. (1994). Television watching, newspaper reading, and cohort differences in verbal ability. *Sociology of Education, 67,* 216–230.

Goldstein, H. (1995). *Multilevel statistical models* (2nd ed.). New York: Halsted.

Hauser, R. M., & Huang, M.-H. (1997). Verbal ability and socioeconomic success: A trend analysis. *Social Science Research, 26,* 331–376.

Hayes, D., Wolfer, L., & Wolfe, M. (1996). Schoolbook simplification and its relation to the decline in SAT-Verbal scores. *American Educational Research Journal, 33,* 489–508.

Hayes, S. M., & Cabeza, R. (2008). Imaging aging: Present and future. In S. M. Hofer & D. F. Alwin (Eds.), *Handbook of cognitive aging: Interdisciplinary perspectives* (pp. 308–326). Thousand Oaks, CA: Sage.

Huang, M.-H., & Hauser, R. M. (1998). Trends in black-white test-score differentials II. The WORDSUM vocabulary test. In U. Neisser (Ed.), *The rising curve: Long-term gains in IQ and related measures* (pp. 303–332). Washington, DC: American Psychological Association.

Hertzog, C. (2008). Theoretical approaches to the study of cognitive aging. In S. M. Hofer & D. F. Alwin (Eds.), *Handbook of cognitive aging: Interdisciplinary perspectives* (pp. 34–49). Thousand Oaks, CA: Sage.

Hertzog, C., & Schaie, K. W. (1986). Stability and change in adult intelligence: I. Analysis of longitudinal covariance structures. *Psychology and Aging, 1,* 159–171.

Hertzog, C., & Schaie, K. W. (1988). Stability and Change in Adult Intelligence: 2. Simultaneous analysis of longitudinal means and covariance structures. *Psychology and Aging, 3,* 122–130.

Hofer, S. M., & Alwin, D. F. (Eds.). (2008). *Handbook of cognitive aging: Interdisciplinary perspectives.* Thousand Oaks, CA: Sage.

Horn, J. L., & Cattell, R. B. (1966). Refinement and test of the theory of fluid and crystallized general intelligences. *Journal of Educational Psychology, 57,* 253–270.

Horn, J. L., & Donaldson, G. (1977). Faith is not enough: A response to the Baltes-Schaie claim that intelligence does not wane. *American Psychologist, 32,* 369–373.

Horn, J. L., & Donaldson, G. (1980). Cognitive development in adulthood. In O. G. Brim Jr. & J. Kagan (Eds.), *Constancy and change in human development* (pp. 445–529). Cambridge MA: Harvard University Press.

Hox, J. J. (2000). Multilevel analyses of grouped and longitudinal data. In T. D. Little, K. U. Schnabel, & J. Baumert (Eds.), *Modeling longitudinal and multilevel data: Practical issues, applied approaches and specific examples* (pp. 15–32). Mahwah, NJ: Erlbaum.

Hox, J. J. (2002). *Multilevel analysis: Techniques and applications.* Mahwah, NJ: Erlbaum.

Inglehart, R. (1977). *The silent revolution: Changing values and political styles among western publics.* Princeton, NJ: Princeton University Press.

Inglehart, R. (1986). *Intergenerational changes in politics and culture: The shift from materialist to postmaterialist value priorities.* In R. G. Braungart & M. M. Braungart (Eds.), *Research in political sociology* (pp. 81–105). Greenwich, CT: JAI Press.

Inglehart, R. (1990.) *Culture shift in advanced industrial society.* Princeton, NJ: Princeton University Press.

Kirkwood, T. (1999). *Time of our lives—the science of human aging.* Oxford, England: Oxford University Press.

Kohn, M. L., & Schooler, C. (1978). The reciprocal effects of the substantive complexity of work and intellectual flexibility: A longitudinal assessment. *American Journal of Sociology, 84,* 24–52.

Kohn, M. L., & Schooler, C. (1983). *Work and personality: An inquiry into the impact of social stratification.* Norwood, NJ: Ablex.

Kohn, M. L., & Slomczynski, K. M. (1990). *Social structure and self-direction: A comparative analysis of the United States and Poland.* Cambridge, MA: Blackwell.

Kuhlen, R. G. (1940). Social change: A neglected factor in psychological studies of the life span. *School and Society, 52,* 14–16.

Mannheim, K. (1952) The problem of generations. In P. Kecskemeti (Ed.), *Essays in the sociology of knowledge* (pp. 276–322). Boston: Routledge & Kegan Paul. (Original work published 1927)

Mason, K. O., Mason, W. M., Winsborough, H. H., & Poole, W. K. (1973). Some methodological issues in cohort analysis of archival data. *American Sociological Review, 38,* 242–258.

Mason, W. M., & Fienberg, S. E. (1985). Cohort analysis in social research: Beyond the identification problem. New York: Springer-Verlag.

McArdle, J. J. (1986). Latent variable growth within behavior genetic models. *Behavior Genetics, 16,* 163–200.

McArdle, J. J. (1988). Dynamic but structural equation modeling of repeated measures data. In J. R. Nesselroade & R. B. Cattell (Eds.), *The handbook of multivariate experimental psychology* (Vol. 2, pp. 561–614). New York: Plenum Press.

McArdle, J. J. (1991). Structural models of developmental theory in psychology. *Annals of Theoretical Psychology, 7,* 139–160.

McArdle, J. J. (1994). Structural factor analysis experiments with incomplete data. *Multivariate Behavioral Research 29,* 409–454.

McArdle, J. J., & Anderson, E. (1990). Latent variable growth models for research on aging. In J. E. Birren & K. W. Schaie (Eds.), *Handbook of the psychology of aging* (3rd. ed., pp. 21–44). New York: Academic Press.

McArdle, J. J., Anderson, E., & Aber, M. (1987). Convergence hypotheses modeled and tested with linear structural equations. In *Proceedings of the 1987 Public Health Conference on Records and Statistics* (pp. 351–357). Hyattsville, MD: National Center for Health Statistics.

McArdle, J. J., & Bell, R. Q. (2000). An introduction to latent growth models for developmental data analysis. In T. D. Little, K. U. Schnabel, & J. Baumert (Eds.), *Modeling longitudinal and multilevel data: Practical issues, applied approaches and specific examples* (pp. 69–107). Mahwah, NJ: Erlbaum.

McArdle, J. J., & Epstein, D. (1987). Latent growth curves within developmental structural equation models. *Child Development, 58,* 110–133.

McArdle, J. J., Fisher, G. G., & Kadlee, K. M. (2007). Latent variable analyses of age trends of cognition in the Health and Retirement Study, 1992–2004. *Psychology and Aging, 22,* 525–545.

McArdle, J. J., & Hamagami, F. (2001). Latent difference score structural models for linear dynamic analyses with incomplete longitudinal data. In L. M. Collins & A. G. Sayer (Eds.), *New methods for the analysis of change* (pp. 137–175). Washington, DC: American Psychological Association.

McKlosky, K. A., & Reese, H. W. (1984). *Life-span developmental psychology—historical and generational effects.* New York: Academic Press.

Meredith, W. (1993). Measurement invariance, factor analysis and factorial invariance. *Psychometrika, 58,* 525–543.

Meredith, W., & Horn, J. L. (2001). The role of factorial invariance in modeling growth and change. In L. M. Collins & A. G. Sayer (Eds.), *New methods for the analysis of change* (pp. 204–240). Washington, DC: American Psychological Association.

Meredith, W., & Tisak, J. (1990). Latent curve analysis. *Psychometrika, 55,* 107–122.

Mirowsky, J., & Kim, J. (2007). Graphing age trajectories: Vector graphs, synthetic and virtual cohort projections, and cross-sectional profiles of depression. *Sociological Methods & Research, 35,* 497–541.

Mirowsky, J., & Ross, C. E. (2008). Education and self-rated health: Cumulative advantage and its rising importance. *Research on Aging, 30,* 93–122.

Miyazaki, Y., & Raudenbush, S. W. (2000). Tests for linkage of multiple cohorts in an accelerated longitudinal design, *Psychological Methods, 5,* 544–563.

Musgrove, F. (1977). *Margins of the mind.* London: Methuen.

Muthén, B. O., & Muthén, L. K. (2000). The development of heavy drinking and alcohol-related problems from ages 18 to 37 in a U.S. national sample. *Journal of Studies on Alcohol, 6,* 290–300.

Muthén, L. K., & Muthén, B. O. (2004). *Mplus: The comprehensive modeling program for applied researchers: User's guide* (Version 3.1) [Software]. Los Angeles: Author.

Neisser, U. (1997). Rising scores on intelligence tests. *American Scientist, 85,* 440–447.

Neisser, U. (1998). *The rising curve: Long term gains in IQ and related measures.* Washington, DC: American Psychological Association.

O'Brien, R. M. (2000). Age-period-cohort-characteristic models. *Social Science Research, 29,* 123–139.

Pampel, F. C. (1993). Relative cohort size and fertility: The socio-political context of the Easterlin effect. *American Sociological Review, 58,* 496–514.

Putnam, R. D. (2000). *Bowling alone: The collapse and revival of American community.* New York: Simon and Schuster.

Raudenbush, S. W., & Chan, W.-S. (1992). Growth curve analysis in accelerated longitudinal designs. *Journal of Research in Crime and Delinquency, 29,* 387–411.

Riley, M. W. (1973). Aging and cohort succession: Interpretations and misinterpretation. *Public Opinion Quarterly, 37,* 35–49.

Riley, M. W., Johnson, M., & Foner, A. (Eds.). (1972). *Aging and society: Vol. 3. A sociology of age stratification.* New York: Russell Sage Foundation.

Roscow, I. (1978). What is a cohort and why? *Human Development, 21,* 65–75.

Ryder, N. B. (1965). The cohort as a concept in the study of social change. *American Sociological Review, 30,* 843–861.

Salthouse, T. A. (1991). *Theoretical perspectives on cognitive aging.* Hillsdale, NJ: Erlbaum.

Schaie, K. W. (1959). Cross-sectional methods in the study of psychological aspects of aging. *Journal of Gerontology, 14,* 208–215.

Schaie, K. W. (1965). A general model for the study of developmental problems. *Psychological Bulletin, 64,* 92–107.

Schaie, K. W. (1970). A reinterpretation of age related changes in cognitive structure and functioning. In L. R. Goulet & P. B. Baltes (Eds.), *Life-span developmental psychology: Research and theory* (pp. 485–507). New York: Academic Press.

Schaie, K. W. (1983). The Seattle Longitudinal Study: A 21-year exploration of psychometric intelligence in adulthood. In K. W. Schaie (Ed.), *Longitudinal studies of adult psychological development* (pp. 64–135). New York: Guilford Press.

Schaie, K. W. (1984). Historical time and cohort effects. In K. A. McCloskey & H. W. Reese (Eds.), *Life-span developmental psychology: Historical and generational effects* (pp. 1–15). New York: Academic Press.

Schaie, K. W. (1989). Individual differences in rate of cognitive change in adulthood. In V. L. Bengtson & K. W. Schaie (Eds.), *The course of later life: Research and reflections* (pp. 65–85). New York: Springer.

Schaie, K. W. (1990). Intellectual development in adulthood. In J. E. Birren & K. W. Schaie (Eds.), *Handbook of the psychology of aging* (3rd. ed., pp. 291–309). San Diego, CA: Academic Press.

Schaie, K. W. (1994). The course of adult intellectual development. *American Psychologist, 49,* 304–313.

Schaie, K. W. (1996). *Intellectual development in adulthood: The Seattle Longitudinal Study.* Cambridge, England: Cambridge University Press.

Schaie, K. W. (2005). *Developmental influences on adult intelligence: The Seattle Longitudinal Study.* Oxford, England: Oxford University Press.

Schaie, K. W. (2008). Historical patterns and processes of cognitive aging. In S. M. Hofer & D. F. Alwin (Eds.), *Handbook of cognitive aging: Interdisciplinary perspectives* (pp. 368–383). Thousand Oaks, CA: Sage.

Schaie, K. W., & Hertzog, C. (1983). Fourteen-year cohort-sequential studies of adult intelligence. *Developmental Psychology, 19,* 531–543.

Schaie, K. W., Labouvie, G. V., & Barrett, T. J. (1973). Selective attrition effects in a fourteen-year study of adult intelligence. *Journal of Gerontology, 28,* 328–334.

Schaie, K. W., Willis, S. L., & Pennack, S. (2005). A historical framework for cohort differences in intelligence. *Research in Human Development, 2,* 43–67.

Schooler, C. (1987). Psychological effects of complex environments during the life span: A review and theory. In C. Schooler & K. W. Schaie (Eds.), *Cognitive functioning and social structure over the life course* (pp. 111–111). Norwood, NJ: Ablex.

Siegel, J. S., & Swanson, D. A. (2004). *The methods and materials of demography* (2nd ed.). New York: Elsevier.

Singer, J. D., & Willett, J. B. (2003). Applied longitudinal data analysis: Modeling change and event occurrence. London: Oxford University Press.

Stern, Y. (Ed.). (2007). *Cognitive reserve: Theory and applications.* New York: Taylor & Francis.

Stouffer, S. A. (1955). *Communism, conformity, and civil liberties.* Garden City, NY: Doubleday.

Thorvaldsson, V., Hofer, S. M., Hassing, L. B., & Johansson, B. (2008). Cognitive change as conditional on age heterogeneity in onset of mortality-related processes and repeated testing effects. In S. M. Hofer & D. F. Alwin (Eds.), *Handbook of cognitive aging: Interdisciplinary perspectives* (pp. 284–297). Thousand Oaks, CA: Sage.

Vaupel, J. W., & Yashin, A. I. (1985). Heterogeneity's ruses: Some surprising effects of selection on population dynamics. *The American Statistician, 39,* 176–185.

Weakliem, D., McQuillan, J., & Schauer, T. (1995). Toward meritocracy? Changing social-class differentials in intellectual stability. *Sociology of Education, 68,* 271–286.

Willett, J. B. (1989). Some results on reliability for the longitudinal measurement of change: Implications for the design of studies of individual growth. *Educational and Psychological Measurement, 49,* 587–602.

Willett, J. B., & Sayer, A. G. (1994). Using covariance structure analysis to detect correlates and predictors of individual change over time. *Psychological Bulletin, 116,* 363–381.

Willis, S. L., & Schaie, K. W. (2006). Cognitive functioning in the baby boomers: Longitudinal and cohort effects. In S. K. Whitbourne & S. L. Willis (Eds.), *The baby boomers grow up: Contemporary perspectives on midlife* (pp. 205–234). Mahwah, NJ: Erlbaum.

Wilson, J., & Gove, W. (1999). The intercohort decline in verbal ability: Does it exist? *American Sociological Review, 64,* 253–266.

Wirtz, W., & Howe, H., II. (Cochairs). (1977). *On further examination: Report of the advisory panel on the Scholastic Aptitude Test score decline.* New York: College Entrance Examination Board.

Yang, Y., Fu, W. J., & Land, K. C. (2004). A methodological comparison of age-period-cohort models: The intrinsic estimator and conventional generalized linear models. In R. M. Stolzenberg (Ed.), *Sociological methodology 2004* (pp. 75–110). Boston: Blackwell.

2

Factor Invariance, Measurement, and Studying Development Over the Life Span

John R. Nesselroade and Ryne Estabrook

The life-span orientation to the study of aging and other facets of developmental change (Baltes, 1987, 1997) includes a number of conceptual features that rely heavily on methodological advances incorporating a longitudinal perspective. These key conceptual elements include multidimensionality, multidirectionality, changing allocations of one's cognitive and physical resources, and differing ratios of gains to losses in the changes occurring with increasing age. The rigorous and systematic empirical study of these developmental phenomena places an immense burden not only on analysis and modeling capabilities but also on the behavioral and psychological measurement procedures and practices bearing directly on the collection of empirical data. Indeed, it does not overstate the case to argue that the scientific study of developmental change over the life span rests directly on the ability to measure behavioral and psychological changes. In turn, this implies being able to measure the same attributes in given individuals at different points in time.

Psychological change measurement in general has a long and somewhat troubled history (e.g., Bereiter, 1963; Cattell, 1966; Cronbach & Furby, 1970; Horn, 1972; McNemar, 1958, to cite only a few of a vast number of references). This is no less true of the history of measurement in the study of developmental phenomena—in which a critical emphasis on change is fundamental to the subject matter. One of the key concepts shaping the growth of measurement theory and practice in life-span developmental research has been the concept of factorial invariance (see, e.g., Baltes & Nesselroade, 1970; Hertzog & Schiae, 1986; Meredith, 1993; Millsap & Meredith, 2007; Nesselroade, 1970). It is to this topic that we initially turn.

Factorial Invariance and the Study of Developmental Change

For the measurement of change to be psychologically meaningful, the constituent measurements on which the change is defined must represent the same underlying qualities. This notion lies, for example, at the heart of what

This work was supported by The Institute for Developmental and Health Research Methodology at the University of Virginia.

Bereiter (1963) labeled the *unreliability–invalidity dilemma* and is strongly implicated in the influential criticisms by Cronbach and Furby (1970) of efforts to measure psychological change. One pertinent way to establish "sameness" relies on the demonstration of factorial invariance across the occasions of measurement involved in the computation of the changes (Nesselroade, 1970). To illustrate, consider the basic factorial specification equation that describes observed scores as linear combinations of the common factor scores and unique parts, that is,

$$a_{ji} = b_{jI}F_{Ii} + b_{jII}F_{IIi} + \ldots + b_{jk}F_{ki} + u_{ji,}$$

where a_{ji} represents the observed score for person i on variable a_j, the bs are factor loadings (regression-like weights) that specify the contributions of the unobserved factors or latent variables to the observed or manifest variables, the F_{pi} is person i's score on factor p, and u_{ji} is a unique part of person i's score on variable a_j composed of both an error of measurement and a true score component (specific factor score) that is completely uncorrelated with all of the other components of the model. Now, suppose person i is remeasured at a later time on a_j to yield $a_{ji'}$, where

$$a_{ji'} = b_{jI}F_{Ii'} + b_{jII}F_{IIi'} + \ldots + b_{jk}F_{ki'} + u_{ji'}$$

with the prime denoting the scores at the later occasion of measurement. The factor loadings (b_js) being the same for both the time t and the time t + 1 occasions of measurement represents the condition of factorial invariance,[1] which has direct implications for how one construes the nature of the observed changes. Subtracting the first occasion observed score from the second occasion observed score to obtain the change in amount—the difference score, d_{ji}—and rearranging terms yields

$$d_{ji} = a_{ji'} - a_{ji} = b_{jI}\left(F_{Ii'} - F_{Ii}\right) + b_{jII}\left(F_{IIi'} - F_{IIi}\right) + \ldots + b_{jk}\left(F_{ki'} - F_{ki}\right) + \left(u_{ji'} - u_{ji}\right)$$

according to which the difference in observed score (change) can be attributed to changes in the factor scores and in the unique parts. Thus, the condition of factorial invariance renders possible a straightforward interpretation of the nature of observed changes—that it is the individuals (represented by the factor scores) and not the nature of the measures (represented by the factor loadings) that are different from one time to another. Hence, the changes in the observed scores can be studied further as meaningful changes attributable to changes (development?) of individuals on the underlying constructs.

When factorial invariance does not hold (when the loadings are different from one occasion to the next), no such simplifying rearrangement of terms is possible. For example, suppose observed scores on the second occasion of measurement are described by

$$a_{ji'} = b_{jI}F_{Ii'} + b_{jII}F_{IIi'} + \ldots + b^*_{jk}F_{ki'} + u_{ji'}.$$

---

[1]Meredith (1993) called this weak factorial invariance. Interested readers should examine his further elaborations—strong and strict invariance.

Then, the observed difference is

$$d_{ji} = a_{ji'} - a_{ji} = b_{jI}F_{Ii'} - b_{jI}F_{Ii} + b^*_{jII}F_{IIi'} - b_{jII}F_{IIi} + \ldots + b^*_{jk}F_{ki'}$$
$$- b_{jk}F_{ki} + (u_{ji'} - u_{ji}),$$

which is a mishmash of information from both occasions with no simplifying characterization.[2]

Central to the strict representation of the factor analysis model are assumptions pertaining to the nature of various components of the model, including the unique variances. In the basic factor model, the unique variance is composed of two unrelated amounts—error variance and specific variance—and these unique factors are restricted to be uncorrelated with each other and with all other components of the model. These assumptions are a necessary part of creating "full blown" factorial invariance, allowing the model to be estimated and the factors (and changes) clearly interpreted. More general discussions of invariance (e.g., Meredith, 1993; Millsap & Meredith, 2007) attend to both factorial invariance as a broad conceptual tool and measurement invariance as a psychometric adjunct that relies heavily on factorial invariance for its definition and explication. Highly relevant are discriminations among levels of factorial invariance (configural, weak, strong, and strict) as they apply to measurement within a latent variable framework. For the latter three levels of invariance, the factor loadings are required to remain constant over comparison data. Strong invariance also requires the intercepts to be equal and strict invariance adds the further condition of equal unique variances.

Accommodating Idiosyncrasy in Studying Developmental Change

A dominant theme of this chapter—and one that will be systematically developed over the next sections—is the idea that both individuals and subgroups manifest idiosyncratic aspects of behavior that, although interesting from some perspectives, may well be irrelevant to the comparisons in which one is primarily interested (Nesselroade, Gerstorf, Hardy, & Ram, 2007). Indeed, such idiosyncratic aspects may be more than irrelevant—they may jeopardize the study of relationships by conflating qualitative differences with quantitative ones, thereby thwarting the efforts to demonstrate the kinds of invariant relationships described earlier as fundamental to the study of developmental change. Consider two aspects of this contention.

---

[2]However, if there is no change in the factor scores over time (i.e., if the F_{pi} and corresponding $F_{pi'}$ are equal), then the observed changes can be written as

$$a_{ji'} - a_{ji} = (b_{jI} - b_{jI})F_{Ii} + (b^*_{jII} - b_{jII})F_{IIi} + \ldots + (b^*_{jk} - b_{jk})F_{ki} + (u_{ji'} - u_{ji}),$$

signifying that the observed changes can be attributed to changes in the nature of the measures rather than changes in the individuals who are being measured. In passing, this latter development is a way to conceptualize stable traits of personality or ability (see the model presented by Harris, 1963), but it highlights primarily how what a given test measures may vary with the age of the participants, and it is most certainly not developmental in nature, given the stability of the trait scores over time. It will not be considered further here.

First, psychology involves the study of individuals, and individuals are somewhat idiosyncratic beings. Each of us has a unique life history of learning and conditioning, layered over a unique genotype. How any one of these peculiarities came about might be the focus of developmental investigation, but, at the same time, when we are asking the individual to be his or her own measuring instrument, for example, as in the case of self-report, we do not want the idiosyncrasies of the measurer to contaminate the evaluation of the measured. Even though two different individuals may "speak the same language," for instance, they still may understand and use the language system in an idiosyncratic fashion, that is, with somewhat different but overlapping semantic meaning. If some of those "flexible" words happen to be involved in the self-report process, then the measurements may well not lend themselves to meaningful aggregation as is attempted in the typical group data analysis (see, e.g., Kagan, 2007). Similarly, if accidents of history and experience condition particular responses (e.g., blushing, handwriting pressure, respiration rate) in somewhat different ways for different individuals, aggregating across those observable manifestations is problematic if they are employed as indicators of latent variables or psychological constructs.[3]

Second, the arguments just made apply to subgroups as well as individuals. Conducting group comparisons (e.g., males vs. females) on ostensibly the same manifest variables as indicators of latent variables can be equally problematic. Even worse, perhaps, pooling males and females in a single sample when such differences prevail can be completely misleading. Often, such pooling of structurally different subgroups may be inadvertent, but the rapid growth of "disaggregation" tools such as splines in cross-sectional regression that estimate different slopes for different score ranges on the predictors (e.g., Marsh & Cormier, 2001) and mixture modeling (e.g., McLachlan & Peel, 2000) testifies both to the frequency and to the increasing awareness of the deleterious effects of such unaccounted-for heterogeneity.

Despite issues relating to making meaningful subgroup comparisons, however, one cannot aspire to building a science of behavior and behavior development solely on basis of the individual. So, the larger question remains: How can one acknowledge and deal with idiosyncrasy and still focus on generality in the quest to establish lawful relationships concerning behavioral development across the life span? Perhaps an answer lies in the way we conceptualize and apply concepts of invariance in measuring behavioral and psychological attributes. We explore that possibility in the remainder of this chapter. We begin our examination with a more detailed look at some relevant properties of the factor model.

The Locus of Invariance

The search for invariant relationships is a sine qua non of science (Keyser, 1956). Determining what attributes remain invariant under which transformations is the general goal of scientific research. Because it is the factor loadings that rep-

---

[3]Such occurrences are likely to be much more common than we suspect. Cattell (1966) pointed out that even "obvious" cases of observed variables representing the "same" concepts can be reasonably questioned as in the case, for example, of the stature of a neonate versus that of an adult human. The former consists, in large part, of head size. This is not true of the adult so, in this case, human stature represents quite a different phenomenon at different ages.

resent the links between the observables and the unobservables, it is not surprising that much of the work in psychological measurement of the past century has been focused here. Abstract concepts are key elements of theory, and rendering abstractions accessible to empirical inquiry via testable hypotheses is critical for evaluating theory. As a direct path from the concrete to the abstract, the factor loadings have played a key role in validating measurement approaches through conceptions of factorial invariance. However, for reasons just discussed—that the individual is the proper unit of analysis but, for a given research question, one swathed in irrelevant idiosyncrasy—it seems timely to examine critically the traditional concept of factorial invariance as it applies to measurement concerns.

A proposal recently put forth by Nesselroade et al. (2007) explicitly recognizes the measurement dilemma created by the idiosyncratic aspects of behavior described earlier and provides a means to filter them out to clarify and enhance the generalized relationships of interest. The proposal rests on conceptions of factorial invariance but engages it at a more abstract level than is typically involved, including the discussion with which the present chapter began. Nesselroade et al. proposed invoking the factor model as the measurement model at both the first- and second-order levels simultaneously. Even higher levels might be incorporated, but that complexity is not necessary for the present discussion. *Second-order factors* are factors obtained by fitting the factor model to the intercorrelations of factors obtained by the usual confirmatory or exploratory methods. Obviously, obtaining second-order factors is a tacit recognition that the original factors are correlated with each other.

As was pointed out in the opening discussion of invariance and the measurement of change, it is at the level of the relationships between the observed variables and the unobserved factors—the factor loadings—that concerns with the concept of factorial invariance are generally focused. Instead of focusing on factor invariance at the first-order level, however, the proposal is to guarantee invariance at the second-order level by constraining the intercorrelations of the primary factors, rather than the factor loadings, to be invariant across comparison data sets. Instead of being constrained to be invariant over comparison data sets, the factor loadings are permitted to reflect idiosyncratic features, within the bounds of theoretical meaningfulness.

Because the factor intercorrelations are constrained to be invariant across comparison data sets, at the second-order level of analysis, the resulting factors will be perfectly invariant because the exact same matrix is being factor analyzed for all comparison groups. These ideas are illustrated in Figure 2.1, which depicts a single measurement space and factor spaces for two hypothetical individuals with somewhat idiosyncratic factor loading patterns and invariant factor intercorrelations.

By means of this approach, two vital matters are dealt with. First, invariance is identified but at a more abstract level than has typically been the case—the loadings of first-order factors on second-order ones. Second, idiosyncrasies are filtered out via the first-order factor loading patterns being allowed to reflect them, rather than being constrained to be invariant across comparison data sets. Of course, the whole line of reasoning rests on the proposition that the "same" factors can be identified from one data set to

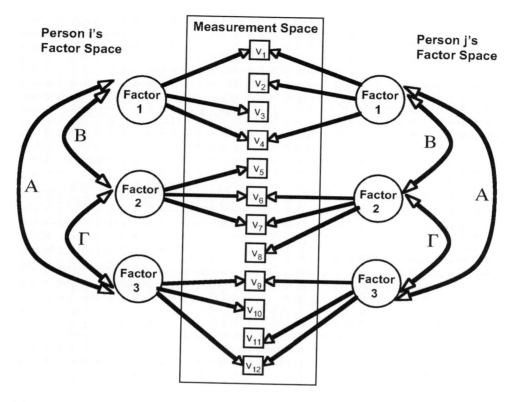

Figure 2.1. Schematic diagram of primary factors as idiographic filters defining invariant second-order factors by allowing different loading patterns on the measurement variables with invariant correlations among the factors. From "Idiographic Filters for Psychological Constructs," by J. R. Nesselroade, D. Gerstorf, S. A. Hardy, and N. Ram, 2007, *Measurement: Interdisciplinary Research and Perspectives, 5,* p. 225. Copyright 2007 by Taylor & Francis. Reprinted with permission.

another even if the loading patterns that link them to observables are not invariant in the traditional ways, provided the factors related to each other in the same way across data sets and the loading patterns plausibly represent the "same" factors.

To illustrate Nesselroade et al.'s proposal empirically, P-technique data from five participants were reanalyzed (for data details, see Lebo & Nesselroade, 1978; Nesselroade et al., 2007) and presented. P-technique involves fitting the factor model to data representing one individual's multivariate time series data (i.e., many variables measured repeatedly over many occasions of measurement). Essentially, the procedures involved fitting the five sets of P-technique data as a five-group model, allowing the factor patterns to reflect some individuality but keeping the factor intercorrelation matrices constrained to be identical for all five groups (participants). The resulting model fit was quite acceptable.

Table 2.1. Factor Loading Patterns for Five Participants on Well-Being Factor

Variable	Participant				
	1	2	3	4	5
Cheerful	.57	.91	.97	.71	1.32
Relaxed	.49	.88	.73	.68	2.00
Contented	.53	.79	.81	.55	1.41
At ease	.38	.51	.85	.57	1.25
Comfortable	.38	.33	.77	.40	.45
Happy	.55	.87	.96	.63	—
Glad	.51	.96	.84	.72	—
Pleased	.40	.96	.96	.64	—
Carefree	.35	—	.88	.45	1.38
Calm	.44	.38	.59	—	1.20
Friendly	—	—	—	—	1.15
Efficient	—	—	.75	—	—

Note.   Only variables with a salient loading for at least one participant are shown. From "Idiographic Filters for Psychological Constructs," by J. R. Nesselroade, D. Gerstorf, S. A. Hardy, and N. Ram, 2007, *Measurement: Interdisciplinary Research and Perspectives, 5,* p. 228. Copyright 2007 by Taylor & Francis. Reprinted with permission.

The outcome was interpreted as representing the same factors in the five groups even though the factor patterns were not invariant. "Sameness" rested on the patterns of interrelationships (correlations, in this case) being identical for all cases and the factor loading patterns showing plausible similarity to the theoretical expectations and to each other. To illustrate the situation concretely, the loading patterns of Well-Being and Social Affection are reproduced in Tables 2.1 and 2.2. The individuality reflected in the factor loading patterns was construed as the result of a filtering out of idiosyncratic information, for example, information associated with the self-report measurement process but not directly germane to the substantive structure of the day-to-day reports of the participants.

There is some precedent in the literature for resting the interpretations of factors on factor intercorrelations as compared with factor loading patterns. In their longitudinal factor analysis model, Corballis and Traub (1970) permitted both factor loadings and factor scores to vary over time but identified the "same" factors over time by resolving the factors so that one and only one factor at occasion two correlated with a given occasion one factor. Thus, there was a one-to-one matching on the basis of patterns of correlations between factors over time. Livson (1973) used canonical correlation to identify linear combinations of occasion one variables that correlated maximally with linear combinations of occasion two variables.

There are also precedents for resting the "sameness" of constructs on the interrelationships of the constructs instead of on the relationships between constructs and observable indicators. An example given by Nesselroade et al. (2007) concerned the relationship between area and volume in cylinders, cubes, and prisms. In all three cases, volume is the product of the cross-sectional area

Table 2.2. Factor Loading Patterns for Five Participants on Social Affection Factor

Variable	Participant				
	1	2	3	4	5
Warmhearted	.41	1.03	.86	.57	1.26
Kindly	.48	.84	.79	.54	1.29
Affectionate	.47	.66	.51	.69	1.21
Friendly	.52	.89	.74	.68	—
Forgiving	.27	.68	.75	.29	—
Excited	—	.51	—	.45	—
Grouchy	—	—	—	−.63	—
Happy	—	—	—	—	−.47
Pleased	—	—	—	—	1.44
Glad	—	—	—	—	1.39
Relaxed	—	—	—	—	1.18
Enthusiastic	—	—	—	—	−.86
	—	—	—	.43	—

Note. Only variables with a salient loading for at least one participant are shown. From "Idiographic Filters for Psychological Constructs," by J. R. Nesselroade, D. Gerstorf, S. A. Hardy, and N. Ram, 2007, *Measurement: Interdisciplinary Research and Perspectives, 5,* p. 228. Copyright 2007 by Taylor & Francis. Reprinted with permission.

and the length, but the cross-sectional areas of these different objects rest on different observables: radius, length and width, and altitude and base, respectively, for cylinders, cubes, and prisms.

In another arena entirely—disease constructs—it is the ability to discriminate among different diseases that may share some of the same symptoms (but not all), rather than the ability to measure the similarities (invariance) of their symptoms, that matters. Consider the concept of the *syndrome.* Typically, a syndrome includes a number of symptoms tending to occur together that reflect the presence of a disease or condition. However, a given case need not display all of the possible symptoms to be so diagnosed. Depression, for example, encompasses a number of symptoms, but no one depressed individual manifests every one of them. Still, the concept has considerable validity among health practitioners, especially since a linkage has been developed to physiological phenomena such as neurotransmitters.

J. W. Rowe (personal communication, January 13, 2008) distinguished between syndromes involving signs (e.g., fever) and symptoms (e.g., pain) reflecting an underlying disease process with the possibility of a definitive diagnosis resting on a biopsy or culture, for example, versus syndromes for which the diagnosis was not verifiable by a definitive test while the patient is alive. In either case, interindividual differences in signs and symptoms are common, and a given patient with the disease but lacking a cardinal component of the syndrome is labeled *atypical.* In the case of the clinical diagnosis based entirely on signs and symptoms, the "missing element" situation is somewhat murkier, but the patient may be treated with the same medications as the patient showing all the usual symptoms. When there are no definitive tests to confirm the presence of a specific pathology, as is generally the case in psychiatric diagnosis, it is not surprising that it may be difficult to reach consensus regarding diagnostic criteria.

In the case of construct validation in behavioral measurement, the construct has potentially many indicators, but no one gold standard provides a definitive measure of the construct. If there were, we would use it directly as a measure of the construct. Our argument for some individual flexibility in the way constructs are measured parallels the solution attempted in the case of medical syndromes.

Applications to Subgroups

The example used by Nesselroade et al. (2007) and discussed in the previous section was formulated in the context of individual level (P-technique) modeling, but that was primarily to emphasize the ability to recognize and accommodate idiosyncrasies that, while identifying the individual, may well be irrelevant to the scientific purpose of the investigator. The arguments would seem to apply equally well to the between-persons case. In fact, it may be more immediately compelling for the case of between-persons factors because of the much greater frequency of between-persons (R-technique) than within-person (P-technique) factor analyses in the literature.

To highlight how this conception of invariance might be applied to subgroups, we present the following example.[4] The Center for Epidemiologic Studies Depression Scale (CES-D; Radloff, 1977) was administered to 3,146 individuals ranging in age from 20 to 87 years in several studies carried out between 2001 and 2007 by the Salthouse laboratory. The scale used in this case is a 20-item self-report instrument with a four-point answer format. Participants rated the frequency of depressive feelings over the last week (see Table 2.3).

Preliminary item factor analyses of the scale yielded a three-factor solution (root mean square error of approximation [RMSEA] = 0.054) with one general depression factor loading moderately to high on approximately half of the items. A second factor loaded four positive affect items, and a third factor loaded items reflecting interpersonal interactions ("people were unfriendly" and "people disliked me"). The first two factors were negatively correlated ($r = -.67$), whereas the third (interpersonal) factor was positively related to the general factor ($r = .64$) and negatively related to the positive affect factor ($r = -.49$).

To illustrate more extensively the idea of subgroup idiosyncrasy in between-persons variability, we conducted both a traditional measurement invariance analysis and an invariance analysis as described earlier in this chapter. We split the sample into younger (age < 50, $N = 1,413$) and older ($N = 1,733$) subgroups, and first tested for subgroup differences in the relationships between the three factors by fitting the factor loading pattern described above to both age groups while allowing the factor covariance matrices to vary across the two groups. This model produced an RMSEA = .053, with the older group showing higher variances in all factors and stronger relationships among the factors, particularly those relationships involving the interpersonal factor.

---

[4]We are deeply indebted to our colleague, Tim Salthouse, for allowing us to use some of his recently collected data for illustrative purposes.

Table 2.3. CES-D Factor Loadings

Item	General factor younger	General factor older	Positive factor all	Interpersonal factor younger	Interpersonal factor older
Bothered	.409	.409	—	.253	.253
Poor appetite	.478	.478	—	—	—
Can't shake the blues	.613	.613	−.336	—	—
Just as good as others	—	—	.586	—	—
Trouble keeping my mind on task	.373	.876	—	.222	−.355
I felt depressed	.627	.627	−.397	—	—
Everything an effort	.303	1.052	—	.275	−.425
Hopeful about future	—	—	.725	—	—
Life a failure	.324	.324	−.395	.214	.324
I felt fearful	.471	.471	—	.313	.313
My sleep was restless	.303	.839	—	.218	−.447
I was happy	—	—	.911	—	—
I talked less than usual	.312	.312	—	.233	—
I felt lonely	.429	.429	−.173	.229	.229
People were unfriendly	—	—	.268	.846	.846
I enjoyed life	—	—	.885	—	—
I had crying spells	.733	.434	—	—	.289
I felt sad	.655	.655	−.206	.133	.133
People disliked me	—	—	—	.847	.847
Can't get "going"	.407	1.310	—	.251	−.728

Note. CES-D = Center for Epidemiologic Studies Depression Scale.

Along the lines discussed, we then fit a model that constrained the factor intercorrelation matrices to be equal across groups while permitting the factor loading patterns to vary in limited ways from one subgroup to the other. More specifically, the majority of the factor loadings (both the salient and nonsalient loadings) for 14 of the 20 items (48 of their 60 possible loadings) were constrained to be equal across groups. This included all of the items loaded on the positive affect factor and the items with the strongest loadings on the general ("can't shake the blues" and "felt sad") and interpersonal factors ("people were unfriendly" and "people disliked me"). However, 6 items were not constrained to equality across the groups.[5] The 6 items were "trouble keeping my mind on what I was doing," "everything was an effort," "sleep was restless," "talked less than usual," "had crying spells," and "could not get going." The difference was that for the younger group these 6 items loaded moderately (.3) on the general and the interpersonal factors, except for "crying" with a loading of .7 on the general factor. For the older group, the 6 items loaded strongly (.7–1.0) on the

---

[5]Choices of which items to be assigned a more relaxed fit status were based on the modification indices and guided by the principle of improving the fit the most with the smallest number of departures from invariant loadings.

general factor and negatively (0 to −.4) on the interpersonal factor. This model produced an RMSEA = .050.

Thus, on the basis of this analysis, it appears that the meaning of these 6 items was substantially different enough between the younger and older participants that they were not "measuring the same thing" and thus should not be regarded as though they were. Whether the differences in meaning between younger and older participants were semantic or statistical in nature is not clear. What is obvious, however, is that the responses on this subset of items were not directly comparable over age groups.

Our analysis illustrates an application of the logic of invariance that is typically missing in measurement considerations. What are objectively the same stimulus materials may not be interpreted the same way by different subgroups, and thus subgroup response differences may be qualitative in nature, rendering further comparisons questionable. Thus, a failure to demonstrate invariance across groups may be for reasons more complex than merely quantitative ones; it may be because of qualitative differences in the response patterns being compared. The procedure we have presented offers an approach to minimizing or negating the effects of such qualitative differences while permitting the investigator to infer invariance at a more abstract level. Cattell (1957) distinguished between surface and source traits with the former being clusters of correlated variables and the latter the underlying structural dimensions of personality. Our proposals bear some similarity to this notion by separating what might be considered surface "blemishes" in the correlations among variables from robust, invariant relationships at a deeper, more abstract level.

Tailoring the Observable Patterns of Constructs

When the factor intercorrelations are identical across groups, whether subgroups (R-technique) or individuals (P-technique), the factors derivable from them (e.g., second-order factors) will display metric invariance of the second-order factor loadings on the first-order factors. An interesting possibility that remains to be explored concerns the use of procedures, such as the Schmidt-Leiman transformation (Schmidt & Leiman, 1957), that define the invariant constructs directly on the observable variables as a way to articulate a "tailored" measurement framework for individuals or subgroups that respects their idiosyncrasies and yet links the abstract constructs to the observable variables in an operational way. Thus, by means of these or other transformations, one can identify an invariant, higher order structure that is tailored to the separate subgroups or individuals and then project this invariant, higher order structure directly onto the observed variables to obtain a (possibly) unique configuration of observables resting on an invariant abstract reference frame. The loading patterns of the observed variables directly on the second-order factors provide an individually tailored (filtered) set of relationships between observed variables and higher order constructs (e.g., second-order factors) with the latter having invariant properties across individuals or subgroups.

The measurement goal being discussed here is represented graphically in Figure 2.2 using a generalized stimulus–response paradigm. At the periphery

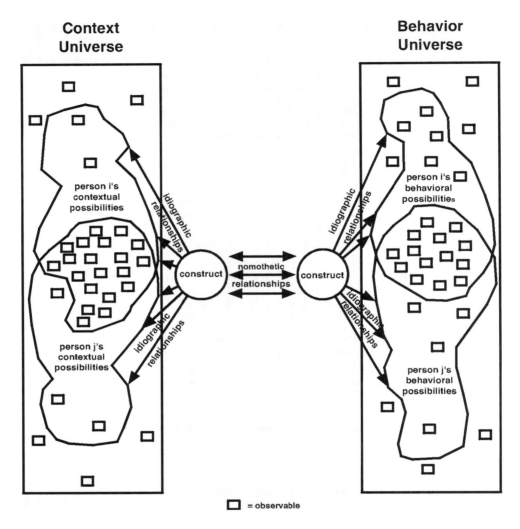

Figure 2.2. Building nomothetic relationships by means of idiographic filters illustrated within a generalized stimulus–response framework.

of the figure are located the context (stimuli) and behavior (response) universes. They lie outside the nomothetic space. Within the central confines of Figure 2.2 resides the lawful relationships of a nomothetic character. The key feature of Figure 2.2 is the mapping of the individual's unique contextual experiences and unique behavior patterns onto the nomothetic space. Nomothetic relationships drive the system, and idiographic information is prevented from degrading them.

These innovations promise some valuable measurement tools for the study of life-span development. Instead of having to rely on the observable variables to provide continuity to the measurement framework across substantial age ranges, continuity can be located at the level of constructs because of the capability of having constructs defined by different patterns of observable variables while maintaining a basis for arguing that the constructs are invariant. More will be said about this in the section to follow.

Some Implications for Studying Development Over the Life Span

The matters presented and discussed in this chapter and elsewhere (Nesselroade et al., 2007) seem to fly in the face of much current practice and thinking. The proposals certainly run roughshod over some of our more cherished notions regarding psychological measurement and psychometrics. Yet, for several reasons, we believe that these ideas represent an optimistic view of measurement from a life-span development perspective.

First, the proposals offer the possibility of measuring the same construct with different patterns of observable variables for different persons or subgroups (e.g., age levels). This paves the way to weight the choice of measurement instruments less in favor of using those measures that can contribute to a traditional invariant reference frame and more toward selecting the most appropriate measures for different ages, given one's substantive/theoretical considerations. This can be a major influence on instrument choice when the age range of one's sample of participants is very large. Obviously, there are various ways to deal with this matter, including trying to fit traditional measurement invariance models or the use of age-graded measurement instruments, but the proposal discussed here opens up rigorous possibilities for an integrated, yet specialized framework for both cross-sectional and longitudinal investigations.

Second, the proposals offer a rigorous, testable basis for employing abstractions such as *heterotypic continuity* (Kagan, 1980) in life span developmental theory. A very familiar reaction to concepts such as heterotypic continuity is that it seems like a good idea, but how does one do it in a convincing, rigorous fashion? From the standpoint of the approach being discussed here, the notion that constructs would be linked to different observable patterns depending on age or other subclass delimiters is a natural part of the discourse. A reviewer asked, How much can be accomplished by making theory-guided a priori measurement decisions versus empirical analysis that identifies variables behaving differently for different persons? The two certainly go hand in hand to some extent, but the empirical approach we propose provides a clear way to identify higher order invariance, if it does, indeed, obtain. Relying solely on a priori measurement decisions in designing a data collection can result in the kind of measurement problems faced by Block (1971), which led to the development of the California Q-sort as a way to blend disparate kinds of information into a common measurement framework.

Obviously, some scaling issues remain to be solved for these proposals to become commonplace in developmental research. But this seems a tractable goal and one worthy of vigorous pursuit. There is much to be gained in the scientific study of development across the life span if the measurement frameworks for theoretically important constructs can be tailored appropriately to different subgroups and occasions of measurement.

References

Baltes, P. B. (1987). Theoretical propositions of life-span developmental psychology: On the dynamics between growth and decline. *Developmental Psychology, 23,* 611–626.

Baltes, P. B. (1997). On the incomplete architecture of human ontogeny: Selection, optimization, and compensation as foundation of developmental theory. *American Psychologist, 52,* 366–380.

Baltes, P. B., & Nesselroade, J. R. (1970). Multivariate longitudinal and cross-sectional sequences for analyzing ontogenetic and generational change: A methodological note. *Developmental Psychology, 2,* 163–168.

Bereiter, C. (1963). Some persisting dilemmas in the measurement of change. In C. W. Harris (Ed.), *Problems in measuring change.* Madison, WI: University of Wisconsin Press.

Block, J. (1971). *Lives through time.* Berkeley, CA: Bancroft.

Cattell, R. B. (1957). Personality and motivation structure and measurement. New York: World Book.

Cattell, R. B. (1966). Patterns of change: Measurement in relation to state dimension, trait change, lability, and process concepts. In R. B. Cattell (Ed.), *Handbook of multivariate experimental psychology* (pp. 355–402). Chicago: Rand McNally.

Corballis, M. C., & Traub, R. E. (1970). Longitudinal factor analysis. *Psychometrica, 35,* 79–95.

Cronbach, L. J., & Furby, L. (1970). How should we measure "change"—Or should we? *Psychological Bulletin, 74*(1), 68–80.

Harris, C. W. (1963). Canonical factor models for the description of change. In C. W. Harris (Ed.), *Problems in measuring change* (pp. 138–155). Madison: University of Wisconsin Press.

Hertzog, C., & Schiae, K. W. (1986). Stability and change in adult intelligence: 1. Analysis of longitudinal covariance structures. *Psychology and Aging, 1*(2), 159–171.

Horn, J. L. (1972). State, trait, and change dimensions of intelligence. *British Journal of Educational Psychology, 42,* 159–185.

Kagan, J. (1980). Perspectives on continuity. In O. G. Brim & J. Kagan (Eds.), *Constancy and change in human development.* Cambridge, MA: Harvard University Press.

Kagan, J. (2007). A trio of concerns. *Perspectives on Psychological Science, 2,* 361–376.

Keyser, C. J. (1956). The group concept. In J. R. Newman (Ed.), *The world of mathematics* (Vol. 3, pp. 1538–1557). New York: Simon and Schuster.

Lebo, M. A., & Nesselroade, J. R. (1978). Intraindividual differences dimensions of mood change during pregnancy identified in five P-technique factor analyses. *Journal of Research in Personality, 12,* 205–224.

Livson, N. (1973). Developmental dimensions of personality: A life-span formulation. In P. B. Baltes & K. W. Schaie (Eds.), *Life-span developmental psychology: Personality and socialization* (pp. 97–122). New York: Academic Press.

Marsh, L. C., & Cormier, D. R. (2001). *Spline regression models.* Thousand Oaks, CA: Sage.

McLachlan, G., & Peel, D. (2000). *Finite mixture models.* New York: Wiley.

McNemar, Q. (1958). On growth measurement. *Educational and Psychological Measurement, 18,* 47–55.

Meredith, W. (1993). Measurement invariance, factor analysis and factor invariance. *Psychometrika, 58,* 525–543.

Millsap, R. E., & Meredith, W. (2007). Factorial invariance: Historical perspectives and new problems. In R. Cudeck & R. C. MacCallum (Eds.), *100 years of factor analysis* (pp. 131–152). Mahwah, NJ: Erlbaum.

Nesselroade, J. R. (1970). Application of multivariate strategies to problems of measuring and structuring long-term change. In L. R. Goulet & P. B. Baltes (Eds.), *Life-span developmental psychology: Research and theory* (pp. 193–207). New York: Academic Press.

Nesselroade, J. R., Gerstorf, D., Hardy, S. A., & Ram, N. (2007). Idiographic filters for psychological constructs. *Measurement: Interdisciplinary Research and Perspectives, 5,* 217–235.

Radloff, L. S. (1977). The CES-D scale: A self-report depression scale for research in the general population. *Applied Psychological Measurement, 1,* 385–401.

Schmidt, J., & Leiman, J. (1957). The development of hierarchical factor solutions. *Psychometrika, 22*(1), 53–61.

3

A Multilevel Factor Analysis Perspective on Intellectual Development in Old Age

Daniel Zimprich and Mike Martin

In the present chapter, we set out to examine what can be learned about intellectual development in old age from a multilevel factor analysis perspective. One of us was working with multilevel factor analysis procedures with respect to a data situation more representative of its typical applications so far, namely, individual and classroom data (cf. Härnqvist, Gustafsson, Muthén, & Nelson, 1994; Kuhlemeier, van den Bergh, & Rijlaarsdam, 2002; Muthén, 1991), in this case on adolescent self-esteem (cf. Zimprich, Perren, & Hornung, 2005). It occurred to us that this method of analyzing hierarchical multivariate data might be fruitfully transferred to examining data on intellectual development in old age. As is documented in an extensive literature on (univariate) multilevel models, longitudinal data are inherently hierarchical, with measurement occasions being nested within individuals (Bryk & Raudenbush, 1992; Goldstein, 1995; Hox, 1995). Using multilevel longitudinal models, it is possible to separate three different sources of variance existent in a variable that has been measured longitudinally: Variance that represents differences *between* persons, variance that represents changes *within* persons, and unsystematic residual or error variance. Extensions of multilevel models to multiple response variables by incorporating dummy-variables have been proposed (cf. MacCallum, Kim, Malarkey, & Kiecolt-Glaser, 1997). While such extensions allow for investigating bivariate correlated change in two variables (e.g., Zimprich, 2002a), they are not truly multivariate in nature; that is, they are not suited for modeling the amount of shared variance in more than two variables at the same time.

By contrast, in multilevel factor analysis, the amount of shared variance among more than two variables can be examined on both levels (person and measurement occasion) simultaneously. Thus, multilevel factor analysis allows for separating five different sources of variance in a longitudinally measured variable (cf. McDonald, 1993): *Unique* variance that represents differences *between* persons unshared with other variables, *common* variance that reflects differences *between* persons shared with other variables, *unique* variance that represents changes *within* persons unshared with other variables, *common* variance that reflects changes *within* persons shared with other variables, and unsystematic residual or error variance (cf. Hox, 1995). By definition, shared or common variance exists if two (or more) variables either load on the same factor or on different, but correlated factors. The focus of a substantive multilevel factor analysis may then be on the between-person factor structure, on the within-person factor structure, on the structure at both levels or on the comparison of factor structures at both levels (Longford & Muthén, 1992). Although, with respect to cognition, a number of studies have focused on the factor structure of differences between persons, the within-person factorial structure has, to the best of our knowledge, rarely been examined (e.g., Horn, 1972). From a developmental perspective, however, the within-person factorial structure is of major importance, because those variables that load on the same common factor change together over time. That is, the within-person structure sheds light on coupled or correlated longitudinal change within persons.

The aim of the present chapter is to model the within-person structure of intelligence and compare it to the between-person structure. Specifically, the goal of the empirical illustration (see later in this chapter) was to examine whether cognitive differences between persons and changes within persons can be mapped along the same set of dimensions (cf. Nesselroade, 1984). If so, this would imply that cross-sectional differences between persons and longitudinal changes within persons form a *functional unity*—a term introduced by Cattell (1950) to describe a psychological construct that can be studied either in comparisons of different persons or in comparisons over occasions in observing a given person. This issue is of relevance not just from the perspective of transferring a statistical analysis method to a new domain of data. To the contrary, we noticed that applying multilevel factor analysis to cognitive aging data has the potential to shed light on some pressing methodological and substantive issues of (cognitive) aging research, such as how cognitive age trends in the population are linked to individual cognitive changes (e.g., Hofer, Flaherty, & Hoffman, 2006).

Factor Analysis and the Data Box

Starting with a methodological perspective, in conjunction with cognitive aging research, two of Cattell's data box techniques have been used for the most part (Cattell, 1988). The majority of research has been conducted using R-technique, which examines *cross-sectional* relationships among a set of variables measured in a sample of individuals. Despite a number of well-known limitations of R-technique (cf. Hofer & Sliwinski, 2001), it prevails in research on intellectual development in old age (e.g., Verhaeghen & Salthouse, 1997). Pertaining to factor analysis, it has been applied to cross-sectional cognitive aging data mainly with two goals in mind. First, the examination of cognitive differentiation or dedifferentiation in old age has been a focus, be it cross-sectionally (e.g., Baltes & Lindenberger, 1997) or longitudinally by comparing cross-sectional relations among variables across several measurement occasions (cf. Anstey, Hofer, & Luszcz, 2003a). Second, R-technique factor analysis has been used to investigate the amount of cross-sectionally shared age-related variance among a set of cognitive variables in order to determine the generality versus specificity of age-related differences in cognitive abilities (e.g., Salthouse & Czaja, 2000). However, as Hofer et al. (2006) demonstrated, the shared age-related variance in age-heterogeneous samples is influenced by individual differences in cognitive abilities and the similarity of cross-sectional age gradients of cognitive abilities, which complicates strong conclusions about cognitive aging (cf. Hofer & Sliwinski, 2001; Zimprich, 2002b). Similarly, Nesselroade (1984) argued that "from the standpoint of the developmentalist, R-technique per se generates one of the least interesting data sets" (p. 277).

Unlike R-technique, differential R-technique or dR-technique involves the examination of relationships among a set of change or difference scores derived from at least two measurements of a set of variables in a sample of individuals. As such, dR-technique requires longitudinal data. In early applications, difference scores were calculated on the manifest level (e.g., Nesselroade & Cable, 1974). With the introduction of (latent) growth curve models (e.g., McArdle & Anderson, 1990) and latent change models (McArdle & Nesselroade, 1994), changes or differences are calculated on the latent level and, hence, less contaminated by measurement error. Hitherto, dR-technique has been employed most often with respect to single variables or two variables at once (Anstey, Hofer, & Luszcz, 2003b; Sliwinski, Hofer, & Hall, 2003; Zimprich, 2002a; Zimprich & Martin, 2002). Attempts to model the shared variance among a larger number of cognitive changes or difference variables—usually by applying factor analysis to produce a so-called factor-of-curves model (McArdle, 1988)—are less common. Hultsch, Hertzog, Dixon, and Small (1998), using data from the Victoria Longitudinal Study, specified a common factor model of cognitive change for a number of measures of intellectual abilities (see also Hertzog, Dixon, Hultsch, & MacDonald, 2003). Zimprich (2000b) modeled a common change factor of cognitive variables using data from the Bonn Longitudinal Study on Aging (Lehr & Thomae, 1987) and the Interdisciplinary Longitudinal Study on Adult Development (cf. Allemand, Zimprich, & Hertzog, 2007). More recently, Christensen et al. (2004) fitted a common factor of changes in cognitive variables to data from the Canberra Longitudinal Study. Note that, although based on change or difference scores, the goals of dR-technique are usually cross-sectional in nature because focus is on differences *between* persons with regard to changes within persons (see Sliwinski & Buschke, 1999). Although dR-technique has led to new insights into the process of cognitive aging by providing the possibility to examine between-person intellectual changes or development, an open question remains regarding what the structure of within-person changes or development looks like.

Cattell (1988) put forward the P-technique to answer questions such as this. P-technique involves the longitudinally based examination of covariances among a number of variables as they vary across a number of occasions within individual persons. The rationale underlying P-technique is that occasion-to-occasion scores of an individual may change as a function of time. To the extent that common or shared influences affect the change in different variables, an individual's changes in these variables will covary across the occasions of measurement. Note that such intraindividual changes can have two different sources: a change of a trait, that is, long-term or lasting change, and a change of states, that is, short-term or transient fluctuations (cf. Horn, 1972; Nesselroade, 1991). In the present chapter, we focus on the first source of intraindividual change, namely, long-term changes in cognitive abilities as a result of aging. This is not to say that fluctuations in cognitive abilities do not exist, but rather that compared with the developmental change occurring during longer time spans (e.g., several years), the relative contribution of fluctuations is small. The multivariate structure of intraindividual changes in a number of variables within a person can be examined by applying factor analysis to P-technique data. Whereas there were and continue to be applications of P-technique factor analysis for the purpose of determining shared intraindividual change (e.g., Cattell, Cattell, & Rhymer, 1947; Nesselroade, 2007; Zevon & Tellegen, 1982), a major problem is that it remains unclear how to generalize or extrapolate from the results obtained in one individual to groups of individuals or, let alone, whole populations. To overcome this problem, Nesselroade and Ford (1985) suggested using replicated, multivariate, single-subject designs, the results of which may then be combined as described in Nesselroade and Molenaar (1999). However, the requirements of such procedures are demanding. Moreover, their focus is on time-lagged relationships among a large number of measurements, which are of secondary interest in the present context.

We suggest an alternative way, which could be considered a *generalized* P-technique as it is implemented in the within-part of the multilevel factor analysis model (McDonald, 1993; Muthén, 1991). That is, we propose to analyze within-person change data pooled over a number of individuals (cf. Horn, 1972). Apart from the fact that doing so overcomes problem of generalizability of single P-technique factor analysis, the multilevel factor analysis model offers another noteworthy advantage. As Nesselroade (1984, p. 276) noted, in Cattell's data box the P- and R-techniques represent theoretically orthogonal approaches, that is, they are (logically) independent. That is, in principle, the structure of between-person differences in cognition can be completely different from the according within-person change structure. The assumption of orthogonality is exactly what the multilevel factor analysis model is based upon—as is exemplified in more detail in the Statistical Modeling section in this chapter (Hox, 1995; McDonald, 1993; Muthén, 1991). By simultaneously modelling both R- and P-technique features of longitudinal data and comparing factor analyses on both levels (persons and measurement occasions), multilevel factor analysis allows for understanding the relationship between cognitive changes within persons and differences in cognition between persons (Longford & Muthén, 1992). To summarize, from a methodological perspective the multilevel factor analysis model offers a straightforward way to empirically deal with the issue of how results from R- and P-technique factor analysis correspond.

The Structure of Cognitive Aging

Turning to the substantive issues of cognitive aging, one of the most popular hierarchical models of intelligence is the model of fluid and crystallized abilities developed by Cattell (e.g., 1988) and Horn (e.g., 1988). This model postulates a set of related, broad dimensions of ability, the two most prominent of which are fluid ability (Gf) and crystallized ability (Gc). Both Gf and Gc involve abstraction, concept formation and perception, and education of relations. However, whereas Gf is involved in tasks that are new, Gc is shown in familiar tasks, mostly with verbal-conceptual content. Moreover, whereas Gf is thought to represent influences of biological factors and incidental learning on intellectual development, Gc is interpreted as reflecting educational and experiential influences. From the other broad ability dimensions included in the Gf–Gc model (cf. Horn & Hofer, 1992), information processing speed (Gs) was included in the present study. Briefly, Gs represents the quickness of identifying elements of a stimulus pattern and processes them. By contrast to many other structural models of intelligence, the Gf–Gc model is also based on developmental findings, that is, part of the evidence for different broad ability dimensions comes from the different developmental trajectories these abilities exhibit. A number of studies have demonstrated that, whereas Gf, on average, tends to decline after a peak in early adulthood, Gc remains relatively stable into old age (Horn, 1988; Schaie, 2005). Processing speed typically shows the most pronounced decline into old age (Verhaeghen & Salthouse, 1997).

Although the Gf–Gc model has proven useful in describing the structure of cognitive ability variables with respect to intellectual performance differences between persons (cf. Horn, 1988), it has hardly ever been tested with regard to within-person changes of intellectual performance. An exception is a study conducted by Horn (1972), who gathered data on 16 cognitive variables in 106 individuals across 10 measurement occasions within 5 consecutive days. He found that fluid intelligence, crystallized intelligence, broad visualization, and broad fluency captured the differences in intelligence between persons. At the within-persons level, factors were very similar to those between persons, as indexed by congruence coefficients between .74 and .95. However, the common variance of the four factors was considerably lower at the within-persons level, where commonality estimates averaged .29 (as opposed to .73 between persons). Because factors were extracted orthogonally applying varimax criteria, they were assumed to be uncorrelated, and, instead, cross-loadings of variables were allowed. This assumption lowered the computational burden considerably—an issue of relevance in the early 1970s—but might be considered inadequate in light of the Gf–Gc model, which comprises correlated factors. Still, it appears as if there is substantial overlap among short-term changes (or performance fluctuations) in a number of indicators of intelligence.

The structure of within-person cognitive changes as obtained by applying factor analysis to P-technique data is not only relevant regarding short-term cognitive changes. Based on the developmental assumptions of the Gf–Gc model, one would expect that long-term changes (or development) in a variety of cognitive performance variables were associated. More generally, this touches on the issue of shared or correlated changes in intelligence within persons, which is important for any thorough description and understanding of cognitive aging (Baltes & Nesselroade, 1973; Buss, 1974).[1] To be more specific, using R-technique and factor analysis, it has been demonstrated that cross-sectional age differences in processing speed are strongly associated with age differences in other cognitive variables (Salthouse, 2001; Salthouse & Czaja, 2000), which led to the assumption that a decline in processing speed may be a cause of decline in other cognitive abilities (Salthouse, 1996). As an alternative explanatory variable of aging

---

[1]By analogy to classic research on intelligence, the issue of correlated change in intelligence may be regarded as searching for a "positive manifold" among developmental changes of intelligence.

declines in cognitive and sensory functioning, a common cause has been proposed and examined (Baltes & Lindenberger, 1997). It thus seems as if, cross-sectionally, cognitive variables share a large amount of age-related variance.

By contrast, dR-technique shows that, although longitudinal changes in processing speed and other cognitive variables are bivariately related, the correlation is lower than what would have been expected based on R-technique (Hultsch et al., 1998; Zimprich, 2002a; Zimprich & Martin, 2002). For sensory functioning, the discrepancy between R- and dR-technique is even more pronounced: Changes in sensory functioning show weak relations with changes in cognitive variables, at best (Anstey et al., 2003b; Zimprich, 2002b). Eventually, the status of processing speed as an explanatory variable of within-person cognitive changes was investigated by Sliwinski and Buschke (1999). They found that associations between within-person processing speed changes and changes in cognitive variables (P-technique) were much lower than associations between age-related differences in processing speed and cognition. Sliwinski, Hofer, and Hall (2003) reported a similar finding. However, whereas for dR-technique data there have been attempts to simultaneously model the amount of shared variance in a number of variables—although with different results (cf. Christensen et al., 2004; Hultsch et al., 1998; Zimprich, 2002b)—with respect to P-technique no such multivariate models have been investigated, at least not regarding long-term changes.

Cognitive gerontopsychology, therefore, appears to be puzzled by a paradox: Although the aim of many developmental models is to describe and explain within-person changes, empirical findings are mainly based on interindividual differences data, be they in the form of R- or dR-technique (cf. Borsboom, Mellenbergh, & van Heerden, 2003). This point has been made several times in the literature, usually accompanied by a proposal of factor analysis of P-technique data as a viable way to overcome this discrepancy (Baltes & Nesselroade, 1973; Nesselroade, 2007; Nesselroade & Ford, 1985; Zevon & Tellegen, 1982). With the invention of multilevel factor analysis (Longford & Muthén, 1992; McDonald, 1993) and its implementation in standard software (e.g., Muthén & Muthén, 2004), it is now straightforward to simultaneously conduct factor analyses at different levels of data—a fact that has been acknowledged in conjunction with hierarchical data in, for example, education (e.g., Härnqvist et al., 1994; Zimprich et al., 2005), but not so in conjunction with P-technique and developmental data. This is where the present chapter is intended to fill the gap in examining both the between- and within-person structure of a number of indicators of fluid intelligence, crystallized intelligence, and processing speed.

An Empirical Example

The potential benefits of multilevel factor analysis as a statistical tool to gain new insights into multivariate cognitive aging is demonstrated using data that were collected in the Bonn Longitudinal Study on Aging (BOLSA; Lehr & Thomae, 1987), an eight-occasion German longitudinal study conducted between 1965 and 1984. BOLSA started in 1965 with a sample of 221 men and women drawn randomly in the Western part of Germany. The sample consisted of two cohorts, 108

(49%) participants born between 1890 and 1895, and 113 (51%) participants born between 1900 and 1905. At first measurement occasion, the average age was 67.7 years (*SD* = 4.9, range = 59–77); 47% of the sample were female.

Part of the testing protocol of BOLSA was the German version of the Wechsler Adult Intelligence Scale (WAIS), except for the Vocabulary subtest (Wechsler, 1982). At T2 (1966), the WAIS was not included, while at T8 (1984) only selected subtests of the WAIS (Information, Similarities, Picture Completion, Block Design, Digit Symbol) were administered. From the initial sample of 221 participants, only 34 (15%) participated at all, including the eighth measurement occasion. Attrition was monotone in the sense that once a participant dropped out, she did not return at later measurement occasions. Thomae and Lehr (1987) noted that most participants left the study because of health reasons or because they had died (Lehr, Schmitz-Scherzer, & Zimmermann, 1987). More specifically, dropout until the fifth measurement occasion in 1976 was due to the following reasons: 85 (62%) participants had died, 30 (22%) were too ill to continue, 15 (10%) could not be contacted, and 8 (6%) refused to continue. Attrition was related to age, gender, and intellectual performance level at first measurement occasion. To illustrate, those who dropped out before the fifth measurement occasion (*n* = 138, 40% female) differed significantly from those who continued to participate (*n* = 83, 58% female) at T1 in that they were older (67.4 years vs. 65.9 years) and had a lower average intellectual performance level (Wechsler-IQ 101 vs. 110). In what follows, we use the available data from all 221 participants, for whom—if the second measurement occasion, at which the WAIS had not been administered, is discarded—there were 3.88 measurements, on average, corresponding to an average longitudinal follow-up time of almost 7 years. In total, there were 859 individual observations. Note that by including all available data, we assumed that data were missing at random (Little & Rubin, 1989). The cognitive abilities analyzed were crystallized intelligence, fluid intelligence, and processing speed.

Crystallized intelligence was measured using four subtests of the German version of the WAIS (Wechsler, 1982): (a) Information (IN), which consists of 25 questions about common knowledge; (b) Comprehension (CO), which contains 10 questions requiring abstract reasoning or judgment; (c) Similarities (SI), which involves finding a unifying theme in each of 12 word pairs; and (d) Picture Completion (PC), which consists of 15 picture cards with missing features.

Fluid intelligence was also measured using four subtests of the German WAIS (Wechsler): (a) Block Design (BD), which demands arrangement of 16 colored blocks to match patterns; (b) Picture Arrangement (PA), which contains seven card sets requiring correct story order; (c) Object Assembly (OA), which consists of three puzzles in pieces requiring assembly; and as a fourth indicator, (d) PC was used. PC was thus specified as being a marker of both crystallized intelligence and fluid intelligence. Previous analyses of the BOLSA data had shown that PC, although originally specified as a marker of Gf, had a cross-loading on Gc (Zimprich, 2002b). Similarly, McGrew (1997) has argued that PC might also be considered an indicator of Gc, because to find a missing feature of a given object, a certain familiarity with that object is required.

Processing speed was measured using a subtest of the German WAIS and a psychomotor task: (a) Digit Symbol Substitution (DS), which requires using a code table of numbers paired with symbols in order to fill in as many correct symbols under the numbers of the answer sheet as possible within 90 seconds, and (b) Complex Choice Reaction Time (RT) as assessed by the Vienna Determination Apparatus. Participants had to respond correctly and as quickly as possible to different visual color signals and/or to differently pitched tones by pressing hand and foot pedals.

Statistical Modeling

Repeated measurements represent a typical two-level situation in which measurements are nested within persons (Hox, 1995). Consider a multivariate repeated measures situation, in which there are $i = 1, \ldots, N$ individuals (Level 2) and within each individual i, there are p variables measured across $j = 1, \ldots, T_i$ occasions (Level 1). Let $\mathbf{y}_{ij}$ denote the $p \times 1$ vector of variables measured in individual i at occasion j. Suppose that the vector of observed variables is composed as (cf. Cronbach & Webb, 1975)

$$\mathbf{y}_{ij} = \mu + \mathbf{x}_i + \mathbf{z}_{ij},$$

where μ is a $p \times 1$ vector of overall means, $\mathbf{x}_i$ is a $p \times 1$ vector of latent random variables varying across the N individuals, that is, *between* persons, and $\mathbf{z}_{ij}$ is a $p \times 1$ vector of latent random variables varying across the T_i measurement occasions of individual i, that is, *within* persons. More specifically, the $\mathbf{x}_i$ represent person-specific deviations from the overall means, while the $\mathbf{z}_{ij}$ represent time-specific deviations from the person-specific mean. It is assumed that $\mathbf{x}_i$ and $\mathbf{z}_{ij}$ are mutually independent. The observed data $\mathbf{y}_{ij}$ and $\mathbf{y}_{ik}$ (k in $1, \ldots, T_i$, $k \neq j$), however, are not independent due to the presence of $\mathbf{x}_i$. Suppose that

$$\mathbf{x}_i = \mathbf{L}\mathbf{f}_i + \mathbf{d}_i,$$

where $\mathbf{L}$ is the $p \times q$ matrix of factor loadings at the between-person level, $\mathbf{f}_i$ is a $q \times 1$ vector of factor scores at the between-person level with distribution $N(\mathbf{0}, \mathbf{F})$, and $\mathbf{d}_i$ is a $p \times 1$ vector of residuals at the between-person level with distribution $N(\mathbf{0}, \mathbf{D})$. Assuming that $\text{cov}(\mathbf{f}_i, \mathbf{d}_i) = \mathbf{0}$, the between-person covariance structure $\Sigma_{\mathbf{x}_i}$ of $\mathbf{x}_i$ is given as

$$\Sigma_{\mathbf{x}_i} = E\left(\mathbf{x}_i\,\mathbf{x}_i'\right) = \mathbf{L}\mathbf{F}\mathbf{L}' + \mathbf{D}.$$

Moreover, suppose that

$$\mathbf{z}_{ij} = \mathbf{M}\mathbf{g}_{ij} + \mathbf{e}_{ij},$$

where $\mathbf{M}$ is the $p \times r$ matrix of factor loadings at the within-person level, $\mathbf{g}_{ij}$ is an $r \times 1$ vector of factor scores at the within-person level with distribution $N(\mathbf{0}, \mathbf{G})$, and $\mathbf{e}_{ij}$ is a $p \times 1$ vector of residuals at the within-person level with distribution $N(\mathbf{0}, \mathbf{E})$. Assuming that cov $(\mathbf{g}_{ij}, \mathbf{e}_{ij}) = \mathbf{0}$, the within-person covariance structure $\Sigma_{\mathbf{x}_{ij}}$ of $\mathbf{z}_{ij}$ is

$$\Sigma_{\mathbf{z}_{ij}} = E\left(\mathbf{z}_{ij}\, \mathbf{z}'_{ij}\right) = \mathbf{MGM'} + \mathbf{E}.$$

The covariance matrix $\Sigma_{\mathbf{y}_{ij}}$ of the manifest variable vector $\mathbf{y}_{ij}$ is then equal to (cf. McDonald, 1993)

$$\Sigma_{\mathbf{y}_{ij}} = \Sigma_{\mathbf{x}_i} + \Sigma_{\mathbf{z}_{ij}} = \mathbf{LFL'} + \mathbf{D} + \mathbf{MGM'} + \mathbf{E} \qquad (1)$$

The between part of Equation 1 is to be interpreted in line with conventional factor analysis, that is, the between-factors and the between-residuals refer to cross-sectional interindividual differences. The within part in Equation 1, however, differs from standard factor analysis in that it reflects the associations among intraindividual changes. Here, factors are to be interpreted in terms of shared within-person change in intellectual performance due to the passage of time. Specifically, variables that load on the same within-person factor exhibit correlated or coupled change over time. Moreover, variables loading on different but correlated factors also show coupled change, although usually to a lesser extent. Assuming for simplicity that both the between- and within-factor models are congeneric, such that a variable loads on one factor only (Horn & McArdle, 1992), according to Equation 1 the variance of the vth (v in $1, \ldots, p$) observed variable y_v loading on the fth (f in $1, \ldots, q$) between-person factor and on the gth (g in $1, \ldots, r$) within-person factor can be decomposed into

$$\sigma^2_{y_v} = l_v^2 \sigma_f^2 + \sigma_{d_v}^2 + m_v^2 \sigma_g^2 + \sigma_{e_v}^2 \qquad (2)$$

Using Equation 2, the intraclass correlation coefficient r_{ic}, that is, the proportion of between-person variance in relation to the total variance (cf. Koch, 1983), for variable y_v is

$$r_{ic_v} = \frac{l_v^2 \sigma_f^2 + \sigma_{d_v}^2}{\sigma_{y_v}^2} \qquad (3)$$

The definition of the intraclass correlation coefficient shows that it is contaminated by measurement error. Muthén (1991) proposed a "true" intraclass correlation coefficient, which makes use of the factor-analytic decomposition of the observed variance into a systematic and a residual part and gives the error-free proportion of between-person variance, namely,

$$\hat{\rho}_{ic_v} = \frac{l_v^2 \sigma_f^2}{l_v^2 \sigma_f^2 + m_v^2 \sigma_g^2} \qquad (4)$$

By contrast to the ordinary intraclass correlation coefficient, the true intraclass correlation coefficient is a model-based quantity depending on factor loadings and factor variances, which may take on different values depending on the model used to estimate it.

Note that the general model as expressed in Equation 1 allows for cross-level parameters, that is, some elements in {**L, F, D**}, the between-person or Level 2 matrices, may be equal to some of the elements in {**M, G, E**}, the within-person or Level 1 matrices. For example, in many applications of two-level factor analysis, an issue of interest is whether the number of columns of **L** and **M** is equal, that is, $q = r$, or whether between-person and within-person factor loadings are equal, that is, **L** = **M** (cf. Mehta & Neale, 2005).

The comparison of loading matrices is common in another branch of factor analysis, namely, the examination of measurement invariance (Meredith & Horn, 2001). However, whereas in measurement invariance, research factor loading and other matrices are compared across subgroups of persons (e.g., Zimprich, Allemand, & Hornung, 2006), in the present context we compared factor solutions between and within persons. However, because means or intercepts are not estimated at both levels, only configural invariance (zero elements of pattern matrices in the same locations), weak measurement invariance (equality of factor loadings), and strict measurement invariance (equality of residual variances) can be meaningfully compared across levels of analysis (cf. Muthén & Satorra, 1995).

All analyses were conducted using Mplus (Muthén & Muthén, 2004). The absolute goodness-of-fit of models was evaluated using the χ^2-test and the root mean square error of approximation (RMSEA). In addition, we report the standardized root mean square residual (SRMR), which indicates the standardized difference between the observed covariances and predicted covariances. In our analyses, we calculated the SRMR for both the between- and the within-person covariance matrix. For both the RMSEA and the SRMR, values less than .08 indicate an acceptable fit, whereas values less than .05 indicate good model fit (Hu & Bentler, 1999). In comparing the relative fit of nested models, we used the χ^2-difference test. Because of its dependency on sample size, we complemented it by calculating 90% RMSEA confidence intervals for the models estimated (MacCallum, Browne, & Sugawara, 1996). Because the RMSEA is virtually independent of sample size, the comparison of RMSEA confidence intervals, that is, whether they do or do not overlap, provides an effective, alternative method of assessing relative fit of nested models.

Results

We checked raw data for departures from both univariate and multivariate normality. Apart from the indicator of complex choice reaction time, skewness and kurtosis estimates of the cognitive variables did not exceed 1 or –1. The distribution of RT was negatively skewed ($g_1 = -1.6$) and leptokurtic ($g_2 = 4.1$). To improve the distributional properties of the choice reaction time task, we applied a Box-Cox transformation (Box & Cox, 1964) with its parameter λ set to 2.3. The resulting variable RT was T-transformed with a mean of 50 and a standard deviation of 10. Afterward, skewness and kurtosis of the transformed variable (RT) were in the normal range.

Table 3.1. Descriptive Statistics of Variables

Variable	Mean	Between standard deviation	Within standard deviation	Intraclass correlation	"True" intraclass correlation[a]
Information[b]	15.17	4.31	1.92	.839	0.929
Comprehension[b]	14.26	2.34	2.14	.547	0.897
Similarities[b]	15.34	3.95	2.53	.712	0.899
Picture completion[b]	10.45	1.87	1.50	.610	0.869
Block design[b]	20.20	6.23	3.56	.757	0.847
Picture arrangement[b]	9.91	3.15	2.88	.546	0.832
Object assembly[b]	17.40	2.51	2.57	.490	0.778
Digit symbol[b]	29.46	7.97	5.03	.718	0.835
Choice reaction time[c]	50.00	7.34	6.80	.540	0.667
Age	71.91	4.25	4.86	.434	—

[a]Estimates are based on Model 4. [b]Taken from the Wechsler Adult Intelligence Scale.
[c]Box-Cox-transformed variable, see text.

Descriptive statistics of the nine manifest cognitive variables and age are displayed in Table 3.1. Of interest is the size of standard deviations between and within persons. For the majority of the cognitive variables, the between-person standard deviations were larger than the standard deviations within persons. Consequently, the intraclass correlations of the cognitive variables were consistently high. On average, the intraclass correlation was .64, ranging from .49 for PA to .84 for IN. Hence, the larger part (64%) of the total variance was between persons. Contrasted with other applications of multilevel statistical models, in which, for example, individual differences are modeled at Level 1 and classroom differences are modeled at Level 2 (e.g., Zimprich et al., 2005), this represents a comparatively high value. Compared with previous findings from multilevel modeling of cognitive aging data, however, these values are in the range of what is typically found (e.g., Sliwinski et al., 2003). From a substantive point of view, this implies that for most cognitive variables the amount of individual differences at cross-section outweighed the amount of individual differences in longitudinal age changes. However, that interindividual differences were more pronounced than intraindividual changes also reflects design features of the study, in case of BOLSA, the inclusion of two age cohorts.

The intraclass correlation of age deserves special mention: According to its value, approximately 43% of the total age variance was between persons, which is due to the design of BOLSA with its inclusion of two birth cohorts. In turn, the larger part (57%) of the total age variance was longitudinal, that is, variance that reflects the passage of time—up to 19 years, at least for 34 persons of the original sample. Hence, the intraclass correlation of age includes a mixture of influences, since it reflects, in part, the study design, the longitudinal time span covered, and the rate of attrition in BOLSA. Table 3.2 contains the between-person and within-person sample correlations. In general, between-person correlations among the cognitive variables were much larger than the corresponding within-person correlations. Specifically, whereas between-person correlations amounted to .62, on average, the mean within-person correlation was .20. In

Table 3.2. Between-Person and Within-Person Correlations

	IN	CO	SI	PC	BD	PA	OA	DS	RT	Age
IN	—	.829	.845	.752	.548	.656	.477	.592	.433	.145
CO	.208	—	.828	.732	.454	.678	.456	.486	.367	.103
SI	.283	.128	—	.690	.514	.669	.540	.586	.543	−.027*
PC	.213	.128	.210	—	.656	.789	.647	.647	.530	−.155
BD	.278	.193	.244	.226	—	.653	.744	.767	.558	−.088*
PA	.205	.107	.100	.189	.252	—	.607	.628	.523	−.108*
OA	.173	.018	.156	.192	.249	.146	—	.630	.505	−.062*
DS	.229	.121	.166	.176	.383	.227	.259	—	.709	−.219
RT	.154	.148	.167	.092	.333	.221	.184	.381	—	−.385
Age	−.258	−.279	−.181	−.228	−.469	−.331	−.178	−.449	−.578	—

Note.   Above main diagonal: between-person correlations. Below main diagonal: within-person correlations. IN = Information subtest of the Wechsler Adult Intelligence Scale (WAIS); CO = WAIS Comprehension; SI = WAIS Similarities; PC = WAIS Picture Completion; BD = WAIS Block Design; PA = WAIS Picture Arrangement; OA = WAIS Object Assembly; DS = WAIS Digit Symbol; RT = Choice Reaction Time (transformed).
*Correlations in italics are not statistically significant at $p < .05$.

terms of an effect size metric, cognitive variables shared, on average, 38% of variance between persons, whereas within persons they had only 4% in common. There are several possible reasons for this discrepancy. On lower levels of analysis, random errors and performance fluctuations may not cancel out as they tend to do on higher levels of analysis, which might have attenuated the within-person correlations in the present analysis. Similarly, whereas within-person correlations were based on approximately four observations (3.93) per person, the between-person correlations relied on 221 different observations. We elaborate on these issues in the Discussion and Conclusions section. Interpreted substantively, these results demonstrate that shared cross-sectional, between-person age differences in intellectual performance were more pronounced than shared longitudinal, within-person age changes in intellectual performance.

Regarding the between- and within-person correlations of the cognitive variables with age, the opposite picture emerged. Whereas between persons the average correlation of the intellectual performance variables with age was −.09, at the within-person level it was −.32. This implies that the amount of cross-sectional age-related differences in intellectual performance is outweighed by the amount of age-changes in intellectual performance.[2] In particular, while for IN and CO correlations with age were positive between persons, they were negative within persons, representing a dissociation of processes between and within persons.

Two-level factor modeling started with Model 0, a baseline model of complete independence of variables at both the between- and within-level of analysis. As can be seen from Table 3.3, Model 0 did not achieve an acceptable fit,

---

[2]As an aside, we note that the finding of age correlations being stronger at the within-person level than at cross-section may be taken as an indication that the data contained meaningful information about within-person *changes* and not just within-person performance fluctuations.

Table 3.3. Summary of Model Fitting Procedure

Model	χ^2	df	$\Delta\chi^2$	Δdf	RMSEA	RMSEA 90% CI	SRMR between	SRMR within
Model 0	2046.69*	72			.180	.173–.186	.510	.190
Model 1	948.22*	63	1098.47*	9	.129	.121–.136	.206	.190
Model 2	726.46*	59	221.76*	4	.115	.108–.123	.048	.190
Model 3	148.85*	50	577.61*	9	.048	.039–.057	.048	.041
Model 4	103.14*	46	45.71*	4	.038	.028–.048	.048	.024
Model 5	117.25*	53	14.11	7	.038	.029–.047	.052	.032
Model 6	122.67*	56	9.42	3	.037	.028–.046	.054	.034

Note. Model 0 = baseline model of no covariances; Model 1 = one common factor at the between-level; Model 2 = three common factors at the between-level; Model 3 = Model 2 plus one common factor at the within-level; Model 4 = Model 2 plus three common factors at the within-level; Model 5 = model of pattern invariance at the between- and within-level; Model 6 = Model 5 plus equal factor correlations at the between- and within-level. RMSEA = root mean square error of approximation; SRMR = standardized root mean square residual.
*$p < .01$.

indicating that there were systematic associations among variables at either the between- or within-level, or both. Because the SRMR values indexed a misfit at both levels of analyses, one might conclude that at both levels there were relations among variables unaccounted for in Model 0. However, the fact that the SRMR value was much larger at the between-level (.510) than at the within-level (.190) implied that, in accordance with Table 3.2, associations among variables were much more pronounced between persons.

Next, in Model 1, one common factor at the between-person level was specified, whereas, as in Model 0, at the within-person level only variances were estimated. Table 3.3 shows that, although absolute model fit was still not acceptable, compared with Model 0 the relative fit had increased considerably. Specifically, as one would expect given the two-level nature of the data, the SRMR value remained unaltered at the within-level, whereas at the between-level it improved, although it did not yet reach an acceptable level.

Subsequently, in Model 2, at the between-person level a model of three correlated factors of crystallized intelligence (IN, CO, SI, and PC as indicator variables), fluid intelligence (PC, BD, PA, and OA as indicator variables), and processing speed (DS and RT as indicator variables) was imposed. As before, absolute model fit was not yet acceptable, but as indexed by the χ^2-difference it had improved substantively in comparison with Model 1. Specifically, the SRMR value for the between-level, which was in the range of a well-fitting model, indicated that a three-factor model described between-person differences in intelligence better than a one-factor model as in Model 1 did. In light of the acceptable fit at the between-level, we decided to retain the three-factor model of crystallized intelligence, fluid intelligence, and processing speed as adequately capturing differences in intellectual performance between persons.

Afterward, in extending Model 2, a common factor was specified at the within-person level in Model 3. Table 3.3 shows that doing so led to a well-fitting model as judged by the RMSEA and the SRMR values. Specifically, whereas the SRMR of the between-level was unchanged—as one would expect given that the between-person model remained unaltered—the SRMR of the within-level decreased notably, indicating an improved fit to the data at the within-level compared with Model 2.

In the next model (Model 4), analogous to the between-person level, at the within-person level a three-factor model was imposed. Model fit was further improved and, as judged by the $\Delta\chi^2$-value, was significantly better than that of Model 3. Whether this statistically significant difference in model fit was also important from a perspective of practical significance remains open because the RMSEA confidence intervals of Models 3 and 4 overlapped considerably. From a conceptual point of view, however, we regarded Model 4 as superior to Model 3, even more so because it exhibited a smaller SRMR for the within part, which represents the focus of the present study. Hence, we arrived at a three-factor model of crystallized intelligence, fluid intelligence, and processing speed at both the between- and within-person level that described interindividual differences and intraindividual changes in intellectual performance. We used the parameters estimates from Model 4 to calculate true intraclass correlation coefficients as given by Equation 4. Results are shown in Table 3.1, last column. As one would expect, once the unreliability of manifest indicators was taken into account, intraclass correlation coefficients had increased. In addition, they were much more homogeneous, both within factors and across factors.

In Model 5, the hypothesis of cross-level pattern invariance was tested by constraining factor loadings on both levels of analysis to be equal. As shown in Table 3.3, Model 5 did achieve a good fit, which, compared with Model 4, did not represent a statistically significant decrement in fit. Hence, the hypothesis of equal factor loadings appeared tenable. This implies that factors were equally scaled at the between-person and the within-person level, allowing for a direct comparison of factor variances and covariances at both levels. Such a comparison bears the advantage that, as opposed to individual indicator variables, factors represent the intellectual abilities of interest on a more general level. As it turned out, the between-person variance of the crystallized intelligence factor was approximately 10 times as large as its counterpart at the within-person level (15.72 vs. 1.49). For the fluid intelligence factor, interindividual differences were five times as pronounced as intraindividual changes (28.04 vs. 5.61). Eventually, the between-person variance of the processing speed factor outweighed its within-person variance by approximately the factor 3.7 (37.19 vs. 10.18). Another way to display the relation of between- and within-person factor variances is to calculate intraclass correlations on the latent variable level, which amounted to .91 (crystallized intelligence), .83 (fluid intelligence), and .79 (processing speed).

The large differences of variances on the between- and within-person levels rendered a test of equality of factor variances across levels dispensable. Hence, a comparison of factor covariances also appeared inappropriate. To still compare associations at both levels, in Model 6 we constrained factor correlations to be equal between persons and within persons. Table 3.3 reveals that Model 6 evinced a more than acceptable fit, which, in addition, did not differ significantly from that of Model 5 at the 1% level. Hence, once the fact that factor variances differed considerably between and within persons was taken into account, the

Table 3.4. Parameter Estimates at the Between- and Within-Level (Based on Model 6)

	Factors		
Factor loadings	Gc	Gf	Gs
IN	1.00 (0.92) *0.63*		
CO	0.54 (0.90) *0.31*		
SI	0.91 (0.91) *0.44*		
PC	0.22 (0.47) *0.18*	0.16 (0.46) *0.26*	
BD		1.00 (0.85) *0.67*	
PA		0.49 (0.81) *0.41*	
OA		0.39 (0.82) *0.37*	
DS			1.00 (0.93) *0.72*
RT			1.18 (0.78) *0.47*
Factor variances	15.29 *1.49*	26.72 *5.84*	36.71 *9.76*
Factor covariances			
Gc	—	14.39 (.71)	14.08 (.59)
Gf	*2.10 (.71)*	—	26.96 (.86)
Gs	*2.27 (.59)*	*6.50 (.86)*	—

Note. Parameter estimates on the within-person level of analysis are in italics. Standardized parameter estimates are given in parentheses. Gc = crystallized ability; Gf = fluid ability; Gs = information processing speed; IN = Information subtest of the Wechsler Adult Intelligence Scale (WAIS); CO = WAIS Comprehension; SI = WAIS Similarities; PC = WAIS Picture Completion; BD = WAIS Block Design; PA = WAIS Picture Arrangement; OA = WAIS Object Assembly; DS = WAIS Digit Symbol; RT = Choice Reaction Time (transformed).

correlations among factors were of equal size at both levels of analysis. On the basis of both model fit and parsimony, Model 6 appeared to score best, which is why we accepted it as adequately reflecting between-person differences and within-person changes in intelligence in old age. Parameter estimates based on Model 6 are given in Table 3.4.[3] On the basis of Model 6, it is possible to calculate the amount of shared between-person differences and the amount of shared within-person change, either for the manifest indicators or for the latent factors. For example, although CO and SI shared 67% of variance regarding differences between persons, they had only 2% common variance with respect to within-person changes. More generally, the amount of shared variance among the Gc indicators was, on average, 43% between persons but only 3% within persons. Similarly, Gf indicators shared 31% variance between persons and 4% variance within persons. Eventually, the two Gs indicator variables had 53% variance in common on Level 2 but 11% on Level 1. These numbers clearly demonstrate that for the manifest variables between-person relationships far outweigh within-person relationships—a fact that is apparent from Table 3.2. A different picture, however, emerges regarding shared variance among factors: Both between and

---

[3]For reasons of completeness, Model 6 was re-estimated with the linear age effects partialled from the nine manifest indicators both between and within persons. For this modified model, $\chi^2 = 136.73$, $df = 56$, RMSEA = .041 (90% CI .032–.050), $SRMR_{between}$ = .054, $SRMR_{within}$ = .034, showing that fit decreased only slightly. In addition, factor loadings were virtually the same as in Model 6, indicating that cross-sectional age differences and age changes had not led to inflated associations among the indicator variables.

within persons, crystallized intelligence shared 50% of variance with fluid intelligence and 35% of variance with processing speed. Gf and Gs, in turn, had 74% variance in common. Hence, different from the manifest variables, latent variables were as strongly related between persons, reflecting cross-sectional ability differences, and within persons, reflecting longitudinal ability changes.

Discussion and Conclusions

In his contribution to the life span developmental psychology conferences held at Virginia University in the early 1970s, K. Warner Schaie (1973) stated that "much of the literature . . . has little to offer to our understanding of aging *within* individuals. This literature merely reports how individuals who differ in chronological age also differ on other dimensions at a given point in time" (p. 253). Despite a few exceptions, for example, John Nesselroade's (1984) research program dedicated to idiographic methodology and P-technique (e.g., see also Lebo & Nesselroade, 1978; Nesselroade & Ford, 1985; Nesselroade & Molenaar 1999), this situation does not appear to have changed very much during the last 30 years. As one possible means to overcome this state of affairs, in this chapter we suggested the multilevel factor analysis model, even more so since it is readily implemented in major statistical software (e.g., Muthén & Muthén, 2004). We presented a two-level factor analysis of intellectual development in old age, with within-person changes modeled at Level 1 and between-person differences at Level 2. As we outlined in the introduction, one may consider the within-part of the multilevel factor model as a generalized P-technique factor analysis (cf. Horn, 1972).

We started with an examination of the amount of variance between persons versus within persons of nine cognitive variables by calculating intraclass correlations. It turned out that for almost all variables, between-person differences were more pronounced than within-person changes, especially for those indicators designated to measure crystallized intelligence. The results thus reflect what is known about fluid and crystallized intelligence and processing speed (cf. Horn, 1988; Hultsch et al., 1998; Schaie, 2005; Verhaeghen & Salthouse, 1997): Whereas crystallized intelligence may remain stable into old age, which implies no or small within-person changes, fluid intelligence and, especially, processing speed, usually show a marked longitudinal decline, which implies more pronounced within-person changes. Of course, apart from the age-sensitivity of variables that were included in an investigation, intraclass correlations also reflect the study design: By incorporating two age cohorts, between-person differences were increased relative to within-person age changes—although for age itself, intriguingly, within-person changes (up to 19 years) were larger then between-person differences.

In comparing between-person and within-person relationships among the nine cognitive variables, we found that correlations were much stronger between persons than within persons. Such a finding is not unusual for cognitive aging data (cf. Sliwinski & Buschke, 1999; Sliwinski et al., 2003), implying that commonalities among cognitive variables are much larger at cross-section than within persons. This also means that interindividual differences are more homogenous than intraindividual changes in intelligence. Probably, this is due to stable individual differences that, by their nature, persist over time, while such stable characteristics are held constant in the estimation of longitudinal age effects, where every individual may be considered as serving as his or her own control. This is to say that cross-sectional differences capture age-related differences and a large proportion of variance that is unrelated to age. By contrast, although the longitudinal follow-up time does not exclusively reflect the effects of aging, but also, for example, the influences of repeated testing, the within-person changes are a comparatively pure measure of the aging process. Thus, two different data-generating mechanisms are compared in looking at between-person and within-person correlations among cognitive variables. However, these two processes collapse in a certain sense if one acknowledges that, in part, cross-sectional differences also reflect the outcome of differential development, which is characterized by less homogenous within-person change processes (cf. Borsboom et al., 2003; Hofer et al., 2006).

Subsequently, a series of multilevel factor models was estimated, from which a number of new findings regarding change in cognitive abilities emerged. First, in Model 3, the fact that one common factor at the within-person level could be established at all showed that there was coupled or correlated change in cognitive variables. Subsequently, in Model 4, which was the best-fitting model tested here, we demonstrated that the between-person and the within-person factor models were configurally the same (Horn & McArdle, 1992). Specifically, on both levels of analysis three correlated factors represented fluid intelligence, crystallized intelligence, and processing speed. This implies that interindividual differences and intraindividual changes in intelligence as measured by nine indicator variables could be mapped along the same three dimensions—although "the same" at this stage of analysis meant conceptually the same set of dimensions. Extending Model 4, in Model 5 we found that factor loadings were equal both between persons and within persons, implying weak cross-level measurement invariance (cf. Mehta & Neale, 2005; Meredith & Horn, 2001). Weak measurement invariance means that the relationships of the indicator variables to their respective factors were equal regarding differences between persons and changes within persons. Hence, factors were identically scaled, that is, they had the same unit of measurement, which allowed for direct comparisons of factor variances and covariances across levels. Doing so revealed that factor variances were much larger between persons than within persons, showing that cross-sectional differences outweighed longitudinal changes in intelligence, even more so in crystallized intelligence.

Note that another implication of equal pattern matrices at the between-person and the within-person level is that for variables that load on one factor only (congeneric model), those variables loading on the same factor have the same true intraclass correlation, which only depends on the between- and within-person factor variances. To see this, observe that if $l_v = m_v = 1$, Equation 4 becomes

$$\hat{\rho}_{ic_v} = \frac{l_v^2 \sigma_f^2}{l_v^2 \sigma_f^2 + l_v^2 \sigma_g^2} = \frac{l_v^2 \sigma_f^2}{l_v^2 \left(\sigma_f^2 + \sigma_g^2 \right)} = \frac{\sigma_f^2}{\sigma_f^2 + \sigma_g^2} \qquad (4)$$

Although Muthén (1991) suggested the true intraclass correlation coefficient, and although Muthén and Satorra (1995, pp. 290–291) discussed the equality of between- and within-parameter matrices, this implication of weak cross-level measurement invariance in congeneric models has, to our knowledge, not been mentioned to date.[4] From a substantive perspective equal true intraclass correlations appear reasonable: Theoretically, those variables measuring the same underlying factor should have the same ratio of true between-person variance in comparison to the total true variance—with this ratio being independent of the actual scaling of variables.

In addition to weak cross-level measurement invariance, we found in Model 6 that factor correlations were of equal size at both levels of analysis. That is, correlations between individual differences in crystallized intelligence, fluid intelligence, and processing speed were the same as correlations between intraindividual changes in crystallized intelligence, fluid intelligence, and processing speed. Note that we compared factor correlations instead of factor covariances because factor variances were highly different. The finding that factor loadings were equal and that the (standardized) relationships among factors were equal between and within persons may be taken as a first indication that, borrowing from Cattell's (1950) terminology, these three factors of intelligence form a *functional unity*. That is, not only do the correlated factors Gf, Gc, and Gs capture ability differences between persons, but according to the within-person model, they also capture ability change over time. The amount of shared variance of the manifest indicators differed considerably between and within persons, with the latter being much lower—a finding that has been reported in the literature previously (e.g., Horn, 1972; Slwiniski et al., 2003). However, the amount of shared variance was equal between and within persons with respect to factors (Gf–Gc: 50%; Gf–Gs: 74%; Gc–Gs: 35%). That is, the associations among cross-sectional differences between persons in fluid intelligence, crystallized intelligence, and processing speed were of the same size as were the associations among longitudinal changes within persons in these three broad ability factors. Thus, once analyses are conducted on the latent level and are, thus, less contaminated by measurement error and/or random fluctuations of performance, cross-sectional and longitudinal relationships might converge (cf. Borsboom et al., 2003), although, certainly, statistical power is an issue here (cf. MacCallum et al., 1996).

One might object that the associations among within-person intelligence changes might themselves be subject to change over time, as might the between-person relations, whereas we (implicitly) assumed that the structure of change within persons and differences between remains stable. That is, it might be that changes become less or more strongly related over time, which would give rise to a developmental process of intraindividual dedifferentiation (cf. Anstey, Hofer, & Luszcz, 2003a; Baltes & Lindenberger, 1997). Although beyond the scope of the present chapter, it would be possible to examine intraindividual dedifferentiation using multilevel factor analysis by dividing the available measurement

---

[4]For noncongeneric models, where manifest indicators may load on more than one factor, equal "true" intraclass correlation coefficients can only emerge if in addition to $\mathbf{L} = \mathbf{M}$ it also holds that $\mathbf{F} = \mathbf{G}$, i.e., that factor (co)variances are equal.

occasions into two or more distinct phases and then compare the change corre-lations during, say, phase one with the change correlations in phase two. Such an endeavor, however, depends heavily on the number of measurement occasions available. With the BOLSA data used herein, for example, splitting the longitu-dinal time span into two phases would have meant relying on as few as three or four measurement occasions as a basis for the within-person model.

Another issue regarding the structure of within-person cognitive changes is that we implicitly assumed that the structure is the same for every partici-pant. Similar to functional unity, Molenaar (2004) recently introduced the term *ergodicity,* which means (asymptotic) equivalency of the structure of *inter*individ-ual variation and *intra*individual variation in any single person. As interpreted here, ergodicity is more restrictive than functional unity, because it requires that all individuals exhibit the same structure of cognitive changes as the struc-ture arrived at for cognitive differences. To see the difference to a functional unity, note that because P-technique data were pooled across individuals, we can not expect that the Gf/Gc/Gs model to describe intraindividual change holds for all individuals. What is even worse, however, is that we cannot safely assume that the model holds for the majority of individuals or even a single individual. One could, in principle, investigate the within-person factorial structure of every individual and test for its equality across persons by treating every individual as a single group in a multilevel multiple groups factor analy-sis (cf. Muthén & Muthén, 2004). A somewhat different and more elaborated approach would address the issue of between-person differences in the within-person structure of cognitive changes by treating factor loadings, factor vari-ances, and factor covariances as random and, thus, varying across individuals. Such a model, although it has been used in a simplified version by McArdle and Hamagami (1996), is statistically underdeveloped at present, however. Alternatively, the use of so-called definition variables might help in modeling individually varying effects of intraindividual change (Mehta & Neale, 2005).

Whereas the question of temporal stability and between-person differences in the within-person structure of cognitive changes is directly linked to the multi-level factor analysis model, there are more general limitations in measuring and modeling change (cf. Hertzog, Lindenberger, Ghisletta, & Oertzen, 2006). First, one could argue that many psychological measures are not well-suited to reliably detect small changes. That is, in case of minimal true performance changes, it is virtually impossible to separate change from measurement error (e.g., Cohen & Cohen, 1983). A possible remedy would be to examine less stable abilities and/or to cover longer longitudinal time spans. Thus, our results should be interpreted within the limits of accuracy that psychometric intelligence measures can offer. Second, as with all applications of multilevel data analysis techniques, for multilevel factor analysis the sample size at both the between- and within-person level is of importance. Although Hox and Maas (2001) demon-strated that, especially when intraclass correlations are low, sample size repre-sents a critical issue mainly for the accuracy of the between-person model, these findings can not directly be transferred to the longitudinal situation we faced. In their simulation study, the authors focused on intraclass correlations between .25 and .50, that is, more variance on Level 1, while in our study intra-class correlations were much stronger, indicating more variance on Level 2. We suspect such strong intraclass correlations to pose problems for the accuracy of the within-person model, although simulation studies in this respect are lacking. Thus, for our focus on the within-person model, a larger sample size within persons, that is, more measurement occasions, would have been preferable. A larger sample size within persons also might have increased within-person indicator variable correlations and, hence, the statistical power to detect differences between the interindividual differences and intraindividual changes models (cf. MacCallum et al., 1996). This is because the comparatively low relationships at Level 1 probably contributed to the feasibility of finding weak cross-level measurement invariance. Third, we assumed that attrition was noninformative in the sense that data on cognitive abilities were comparable for those with complete data and those for whom only incomplete data were available (cf. Little & Rubin, 1989). To be more specific, as opposed to studies that focus on mean changes and, thus, rely on the assumption that mean changes are comparable for participants with different dropout patterns, we implicitly assumed that within-person correlations were equal. In principle, one could transfer the different modeling techniques which aim at assessing the tenability of the missing-at-random assumption to the multilevel situation (cf. Diggle, Heagerty, Liang, & Zeger, 2002; also see chap. 13, this volume), but doing so was beyond the scope of the present chapter. Moreover, approaches that involve splitting the sample into subgroups (e.g., Hedeker & Gibbons, 1997) would require a larger sample than the BOLSA one.

These methodological limitations notwithstanding, what can be learned about cognitive aging from a multilevel factor analysis perspective? A fundamental question of cognitive aging research is whether and, if so, to what extent cognitive abilities change or develop together over time (e.g., Baltes & Nesselroade, 1973; Buss, 1974). In terms of the multilevel factor analysis model, this question may be addressed by examining the structure of cognitive development in old age at the within-person level. Hitherto, information regarding within-person coupled cognitive change has been available in terms of bivariate correlated change (Sliwinski & Buschke, 1999; Sliwinski et al., 2003). A truly multivariate approach, however, has been absent to date. The key insight provided by the analyses presented herein is that interindividual differences and intraindividual changes in intelligence in old age exhibit high similarity in terms of structure: They coincided in terms of factor loadings and factor correlations among Gf, Gc, and Gs. In turn, they differed in the amount of factor variances—a fact that is strongly influenced by the study design.

Note that the commonalities of the between- and within-person structure we have found may have several implications. First and foremost, similar to the endeavors of Botwinick (1977), who showed that cross-sectional and longitudinal findings regarding average cognitive age changes can converge, we have demonstrated that cross-sectional and longitudinal correlations among cognitive abilities appear to converge. Second, inasmuch correlations might represent a common cause, one might argue that our results represent a necessary condition for the supposition that the same cause (or causal structure) leads to both interindividual differences and intraindividual change (Pearl, 2000; cf. Zimprich, 2002b). That is, in the same way that cognitive development in old age within persons is driven by a common cause (or causal structure), the cause might act or have already acted to produce differences between persons. However, as outlined earlier, the multilevel factor analyses presented herein might be refined in many respects and, hence, represent but a first step into examining multivariate within-person change. In that sense, the present study only scratched the surface of the capabilities the multilevel factor model offers as an analytical framework for measuring and structuring between-person differences and within-person changes in intelligence in old age. We expect to see more of this kind of analysis in the future, given their suitability and significance for developmental research.

References

Allemand, M., Zimprich, D., & Hertzog, C. (2007). Cross-sectional age differences and longitudinal age changes of personality in middle adulthood and old age. *Journal of Personality, 75,* 323–358.

Anstey, K. J., Hofer, S. M., & Luszcz, M. A. (2003a). Cross-sectional and longitudinal patterns of de-differentiation in late-life cognitive and sensory function: The effects of age, ability, attrition and occasion of measurement. *Journal of Experimental Psychology: General, 132,* 470–487.

Anstey, K. J., Hofer, S. M., & Luszcz, M. A. (2003b). A latent growth curve analysis of late life cognitive and sensory function over eight years: Evidence for specific and common factors underlying change. *Psychology and Aging, 18,* 714–726.

Baltes, P. B., & Lindenberger, U. (1997). Emergence of a powerful connection between sensory and cognitive functions across the adult life span: A new window to the study of cognitive aging? *Psychology and Aging, 12,* 12–21.

Baltes, P. B., & Nesselroade, J. R. (1973). The developmental analysis of individual differences on multiple measures. In J. R. Nesselroade & H. W. Reese (Eds.), *Life-span developmental psychology—Methodological issues* (pp. 219–251). New York: Academic Press.

Borsboom, D., Mellenbergh, G. J., & van Heerden, J. (2003). The theoretical status of latent variables. *Psychological Review, 110,* 203–219.

Botwinick, J. (1977). Intellectual abilities. In J. E. Birren & K. W. Schaie (Eds.), *Handbook of the psychology of aging* (pp. 580–605). New York: Van Nostrand Reinhold.

Box, G. E. P., & Cox, D. R. (1964). An analysis of transformations (with discussion). *Journal of the Royal Statistical Society, 26,* 211–252.

Bryk, A. S., & Raudenbush, S. W. (1992). *Hierarchical linear models.* Newbury Park, CA: Sage.

Buss, A. R. (1974). A general developmental model for interindividual differences, intraindividual differences, and intraindividual changes. *Developmental Psychology, 10,* 70–78.

Cattell, R. B. (1950). *Personality.* New York: McGraw-Hill.

Cattell, R. B. (1988). The data box—Its ordering of total resources in terms of possible relational systems. In J. R. Nesselroade & R. B. Cattell (Eds.), *Handbook of multivariate experimental psychology* (2nd ed., pp. 69–130). New York: Plenum Press.

Cattell, R. B., Cattell, A. K. S., & Rhymer, R. M. (1947). P-technique demonstrated in determining psychophysiological source traits in a normal individual. *Psychometrika, 12,* 267–288.

Christensen, H., Mackinnon, A., Jorm, A. F., Korten, A., Jacomb, P., Hofer, S. M., & Henderson, S. (2004). The Canberra Longitudinal Study: Design, aims, methodology, outcomes, and recent empirical investigations. *Aging, Neuropsychology, and Cognition, 11,* 169–195.

Cohen, J., & Cohen, P. (1983). *Applied multiple regression/correlation analysis for the behavioral sciences.* Hillsdale, NJ: Erlbaum.

Cronbach, L. J., & Webb, N. M. (1975). Between-class and within-class effects in a reported aptitude × treatment interaction: Reanalysis of a study by G. L. Anderson. *Journal of Educational Psychology, 67,* 717–727.

Diggle, P. J., Heagerty, P., Liang, K.-Y., & Zeger, S. L. (2002). *Analysis of longitudinal data* (2nd ed.). Oxford, England: Oxford University Press.

Goldstein, H. (1995). *Multilevel statistical models* (2nd ed.). London: Arnold.

Härnqvist, K., Gustafsson, J.-E., Muthén, B. O., & Nelson, G. (1994). Hierarchical models of ability at individual and class levels. *Intelligence, 18,* 165–187.

Hedeker, D., & Gibbons, R. D. (1997). Application of random-effects pattern-mixture models for missing data in longitudinal studies. *Psychological Methods, 2,* 64–78.

Hertzog, C., Dixon, R. A., Hultsch, D. F., & MacDonald, S. W. S. (2003). Latent change models of adult cognition: Are changes in processing speed and working memory associated with changes in episodic memory? *Psychology and Aging, 18,* 755–769.

Hertzog, C., Lindenberger, U., Ghisletta, P., & Oertzen, T. (2006). On the power of multivariate latent growth curve models to detect correlated change. *Psychological Methods, 11,* 244–252.

Hofer, S. M., Flaherty, B. P., & Hoffman, L. (2006). Cross-sectional analysis of time-dependent data: Problems of mean-induced association in age-heterogeneous samples and an alternative method based on sequential narrow age-cohorts. *Multivariate Behavioral Research, 41,* 165–187.

Hofer, S. M., & Sliwinski, M. J. (2001). Understanding ageing—An evaluation of research designs for assessing the interdependence of ageing-related changes. *Gerontology, 47,* 341–352.

Horn, J. L. (1972). State, trait, and change dimensions of intelligence. *British Journal of Educational Psychology, 42,* 159–185.

Horn, J. L. (1988). Thinking about human abilities. In J. R. Nesselroade & R. B. Cattell (Eds.), *Handbook of multivariate experimental psychology* (2nd ed., pp. 645–685). New York: Plenum Press.

Horn, J. L., & Hofer, S. M. (1992). Major abilities and development in the adult period. In R. J. Sternberg & C. A. Berg (Eds.), *Intellectual development* (pp. 44–99). Cambridge, England: Cambridge University Press.

Horn, J. L., & McArdle, J. J. (1992). A practical and theoretical guide to measurement invariance in aging research. *Experimental Aging Research, 18,* 117–144.

Hox, J. J. (1995). *Applied multilevel analysis.* Amsterdam: TT-Publikaties.

Hox, J. J., & Maas, C. J. M. (2001). The accuracy of multilevel structural equation modeling with pseudobalanced groups and small samples. *Structural Equation Modeling, 8,* 157–174.

Hu, L. T., & Bentler, P. M. (1999). Cutoff criteria for fit indexes in covariance structure analysis: Conventional criteria versus new alternatives. *Structural Equation Modeling, 6,* 1–55.

Hultsch, D. F., Hertzog, C., Dixon, R. A., & Small, B. J. (1998). *Memory change in the aged.* Cambridge, England: Cambridge University Press.

Koch, G. G. (1983). Intraclass correlation coefficient. *Encyclopedia of Statistical Sciences, 4,* 212–217.

Kuhlemeier, H., van den Bergh, H., & Rijlaarsdam, G. (2002). The dimensionality of speaking and writing: A multilevel factor analysis of situational, task and school effects. *British Journal of Educational Psychology, 72,* 467–482.

Lebo, M. A., & Nesselroade, J. R. (1978). Intraindividual differences in dimensions of mood change during pregnancy identified in five P-technique factor analyses. *Journal of Research in Personality, 12,* 205–224.

Lehr, U., Schmitz-Scherzer, R., & Zimmermann, E. J. (1987). Vergleiche von Überlebenden und Verstorbenen in der Bonner Gerontologischen Längsschnittstudie (BOLSA) [Comparisons of survivors and deceased in the Bonn Gerontological Longitudinal Study (BOLSA)]. In U. Lehr & H. Thomae (Eds.), *Formen seelischen Alterns—Ergebnisse der Bonner Gerontologischen Längsschnittstudie* (pp. 228–249). Stuttgart: Enke.

Lehr, U., & Thomae, H. (Eds.). (1987). *Formen seelischen Alterns—Ergebnisse der Bonner Gerontologischen Läangsschnittstudie* [Forms of mental aging—Results of the Bonn Gerontological Longitudinal Study]. Stuttgart: Enke.

Little, R. J. A., & Rubin, D. B. (1989). The analysis of social science data with missing values. *Sociological Methods and Research, 18,* 292–326.

Longford, N. T., & Muthén, B. O. (1992). Factor analysis for clustered observations. *Psychometrika, 57,* 581–597.

MacCallum, R. C., Browne, M., & Sugawara, H. M. (1996). Power analysis and determination of sample size for covariance structure modeling. *Psychological Methods, 2,* 130–149.

MacCallum, R. C., Kim, C., Malarkey, W. B., & Kiecolt-Glaser, J. K. (1997). Studying multivariate change using multilevel models and latent curve models. *Multivariate Behavioral Research, 32,* 215–253.

McArdle, J. J. (1988). Dynamic but structural equation modeling of repeated measures data. In J. R. Nesselroade & R. B. Cattell (Eds.), *Handbook of multivariate experimental psychology* (pp. 561–614). New York: Plenum Press.

McArdle, J. J., & Anderson, E. (1990). Latent variable growth models for research on aging. In J. E. Birren & K. W. Schaie (Eds.), *Handbook of the psychology of aging* (3rd ed., pp. 310–319). San Diego, CA: Academic Press.

McArdle, J. J., & Hamagami, F. (1996). Multilevel models from a multiple group structural equation perspective. In G. A. Marcoulides & R. E. Schumacker (Eds.), *Advanced Structural Equation Modeling* (pp. 89–124). Mahwah, NJ: Erlbaum.

McArdle, J. J., & Nesselroade, J. R. (1994). Using multivariate data to structure developmental change. In H. W. Reese & S. H. Cohen (Eds.), *Lifespan developmental psychology: Methodological contributions* (pp. 223–267). Hillsdale, NJ: Erlbaum.

McDonald, R. P. (1993). A general model for two-level data with responses missing at random. *Psychometrika, 58,* 575–585.

McGrew, K. S. (1997). Analysis of the major intelligence batteries according to a proposed comprehensive Gf-Gc framework. In D. P. Flanagan, J. L. Genshaft, & P. L. Harrison (Eds.), *Contemporary intellectual assessment—Theories, tests, and issues* (pp. 151–174). New York: Guilford Press.

Mehta, P. D., & Neale, M. C. (2005). People are variables too: Multilevel structural equation modeling. *Psychological Methods, 10,* 259–284.

Meredith, W., & Horn, J. L. (2001). The role of factorial invariance in modeling growth and change. In L. M. Collins & A. G. Sayer (Eds.), *New methods for the analysis of change* (pp. 203–240). Washington, DC: American Psychological Association.

Molenaar, P. C. M. (2004). A manifesto on psychology as idiographic science: Bringing the person back into scientific psychology, this time forever. *Measurement, 2,* 201–218.

Muthén, B. O. (1991). Multilevel factor analysis of class and student achievement components. *Journal of Educational Measurement, 28,* 338–354.

Muthén, B. O., & Satorra, A. (1995). Complex sample data in structural equation modeling. *Sociological Methodology, 25,* 267–316.

Muthén, L. K., & Muthén, B. O. (2004). *Mplus user's guide* (Version 3) [Software]. Los Angeles: Muthén & Muthén.

Nesselroade, J. R. (1984). Concepts of intraindividual variability and change: Impressions of Cattell's influence on lifespan developmental psychology. *Multivariate Behavioral Research, 19,* 269–286.

Nesselroade, J. R. (1991). The warp and the woof of the developmental fabric. In R. Downs, L. Liben, & D. S. Palermo (Eds.), *Visions of aesthetics, the environment, and development: The legacy of Joachim F. Wohlwill* (pp. 213–240). Hillsdale, NJ: Erlbaum.

Nesselroade, J. R. (2007). Factoring at the individual level: Some matters for the second century of factor analysis. In R. Cudeck & R. C. MacCallum (Eds.), *Factor analysis at 100: Historical developments and future directions* (pp. 249–264). Mahwah, NJ: Erlbaum.

Nesselroade, J. R., & Cable, D. G. (1974). "Sometimes it's okay to factor difference scores"—The separation of state and trait anxiety. *Multivariate Behavioral Research, 9,* 273–281.

Nesselroade, J. R., & Ford, D. H. (1985). P-technique comes of age—Multivariate, replicated, single-subject designs for research on older adults. *Research on Aging, 7,* 46–80.

Nesselroade, J. R., & Molenaar, P. C. M. (1999). Pooling lagged covariance structures based on short, multivariate time series for dynamic factor analysis. In R. C. Hoyle (Ed.), *Statistical strategies for small sample research* (pp. 223–250). Thousand Oaks, CA: Sage.

Pearl, J. (2000). *Causality: Models, reasoning, and inference.* Cambridge, England: Cambridge University Press.

Salthouse, T. A. (1996). The processing-speed theory of adult age differences in cognition. *Psychological Review, 103,* 403–428.

Salthouse, T. A. (2001). Structural models of the relations between age and measures of cognitive functioning. *Intelligence, 29,* 93–115.

Salthouse, T. A., & Czaja, S. J. (2000). Structural constraints on process explanations in cognitive aging. *Psychology and Aging, 15,* 44–55.

Schaie, K. W. (1973). Methodological problems in descriptive developmental research on adulthood and aging. In J. R. Nesselroade & H. W. Reese (Eds.), *Life-span developmental psychology—Methodological issues* (pp. 253–280). New York: Academic Press.

Schaie, K. W. (2005). *Developmental influences on adult intelligence.* Oxford, England: Oxford University Press.

Sliwinski, M. J., & Buschke, H. (1999). Cross-sectional and longitudinal relationships among age, cognition, and processing speed. *Psychology and Aging, 14,* 18–33.

Sliwinski, M. J., Hofer, S. M., & Hall, C. (2003). Correlated and coupled cognitive change in older adults with and without clinical dementia. *Psychology and Aging, 18,* 672–683.

Verhaeghen, P., & Salthouse, T. A. (1997). Meta-analyses of age-cognition relations in adulthood: Estimates of linear and nonlinear age effects and structural models. *Psychological Bulletin, 122,* 231–249.

Wechsler, D. (1982). *Handanweisung zum Hamburg–Wechsler–Intelligenztest für Erwachsene (HAWIE)* [Instruction manual for the Hamburg–Wechsler–Intelligence Test for Adults (HAWIE)]. Bern: Huber.

Zevon, M. A., & Tellegen, A. (1982). The structure of mood change: An idiographic nomothetic analysis. *Journal of Personality and Social Psychology, 43,* 111–122.

Zimprich, D. (2002a). Cross-sectionally and longitudinally balanced effects of processing speed on intellectual abilities. *Experimental Aging Research, 28,* 231–251.

Zimprich, D. (2002b). *Kognitive Entwicklung im Alter—Die Bedeutung der Informationsverarbeitungsgeschwindigkeit und sensorischer Funktionen für den kognitiven Alterungsprozess.* [Cognitive development in old age—On the significance of processing speed and sensory functioning for cognitive aging]. Hamburg, Germany: Dr. Kovac.

Zimprich, D., Allemand, M., & Hornung, R. (2006). Measurement invariance of the abridged sense of coherence scale in adolescents. *European Journal of Psychological Assessment, 22,* 280–287.

Zimprich, D., & Martin, M. (2002). Can longitudinal changes in processing speed explain longitudinal age changes in fluid intelligence? *Psychology and Aging, 17,* 690–695.

Zimprich, D., Perren, S., & Hornung, R. (2005). A two-level confirmatory factor analysis of a modified Rosenberg self-esteem scale. *Educational and Psychological Measurement, 65,* 465–481.

4

The Search for Structure: The Temperamental Character of the Temperament and Character Inventory

Scott B. Maitland, Lars Nyberg, Lars Bäckman, Lars-Göran Nilsson, and Rolf Adolfsson

Methodological and measurement concerns have always been critical issues in developmental psychology. First, the foundations of measurement include the use of valid and reliable measures before turning to the goal of most developmental research—the study of change in behavior over time (Baltes, Reese, & Nesselroade, 1988; Hofer & Sliwinski, 2006; Schaie, 2005; Schaie & Hofer, 2001). Second, factor analytic techniques are used to ensure that constructs are psychometrically sound and represent the data appropriately. Finally, beyond simply ensuring that a measurement model fits the data well, the extension to multigroup factor models to test whether measures mark the same constructs across comparison groups is crucial (i.e., measurement equivalence/invariance (ME/I; Baltes et al., 1988; Bollen, 1989; Horn & McArdle, 1992; Horn, McArdle, & Mason, 1983; Labouvie, 1980; Meredith, 1993; Thurstone, 1947; Vandenberg & Lance, 2000). The Seattle Longitudinal Study (SLS) has been exemplary in employing these approaches to the study of human aging in a variety of substantive areas (e.g., Hertzog & Schaie, 1986, 1988; Maitland, Intrieri, Schaie, & Willis, 2000; Schaie, 1996, 2005; Schaie, Dutta, & Willis, 1991; Schaie, Maitland, Willis, & Intrieri, 1998; Schaie & Parham, 1976; Schaie, Willis, & Caskie, 2004; Schaie, Willis, Jay, & Chipuer, 1989).

Scott B. Maitland completed graduate training with K. Warner Schaie on the SLS and has been fortunate to collaborate with the Betula Project (BP; Nilsson, 1997, 1999; Nilsson et al., 2004). The general developmental model (Schaie, 1965) and other methodological contributions by Schaie (see Schaie,

The Betula Study is funded by the Bank of Sweden Tercentenary Foundation (1988-0082:17; J2001-0682), Swedish Council for Planning and Coordination of Research (D1988-0092, D1989-0115, D1990-0074, D1991-0258, D1992-0143, D1997-0756, D1997-1841, D1999-0739, B1999-474), Swedish Council for Research in the Humanities and Social Sciences (F377/1988-2000), the Swedish Council for Social Research (1988-1990: 88-0082, and 311/1991-2000), and the Swedish Research Council (345-2003-3883, 315-2004-6977).

1996, 2005) were influential in the design of the BP. The current chapter uses key tenets of psychometric measurement and analysis to examine the underlying structure and ME/I of the Temperament and Character Inventory (TCI), a widely used measure of personality, in data from the BP.

Regardless of the particular theory, model, or analytic approach used, the underlying structure of personality remains a contentious issue. Some of the difficulties in defining personality echo the historic debates in life-span development and developmental methodology, such as whether personality remains stable or changes over time, strategies for measuring constancy versus change, and ensuring that scales are measuring the same constructs in comparison groups or over time. Numerous studies have addressed these concerns in relation to the major conceptions of personality structure (e.g., Neuroticism-Extraversion-Openness Personality Inventory [NEO-PI]; Costa & McCrae, 1994, 1997), but the findings are often mixed across studies. For example, support for the general structure of the NEO-PI and Neuroticism-Extraversion-Openness Five-Factor Inventory (NEO-FFI; or components thereof) has been reported (e.g., Allemand, Zimprich, & Hertzog, 2007; Mroczek, Spiro, & Griffin, 2006; Reise, Smith, & Furr, 2001; Small, Hertzog, Hultsch, & Dixon, 2003), but other studies have documented weaknesses that may be related to methodology (e.g., Borsboom, 2006; Church & Burke, 1994; McCrae, Zonderman, Costa, Bond, & Paunonen, 1996; Vassend & Skrondal, 1995, 1997).

The lack of concordance among studies may be attributable to a number of factors, including sample differences, differences in data collection procedures, different versions of a measure being used, and the analytic methods used to test models. In addition, the measures used as markers of a theoretical model are expected to map onto that theory yet success varies greatly. Mroczek et. al (2006) discussed the tendency for research on personality development to focus on change or stability in means or rank orders of individuals within distributions. Whereas group or individual fluctuations in traits are of interest, one should not ignore the importance of ensuring that the underlying structure of any measure is upheld before issues about mean-level change are addressed (Baltes & Nesselroade, 1970; Kogan, 1990; Labouvie, 1980; regarding NEO-PI, see Reise et al., 2001). Recognizing the importance of measurement and structural invariance in personality research, in this chapter we address methodological issues in defining the underlying structure of personality using the TCI as an exemplar.

Temperament, Character, and the Temperament and Character Inventory Model

What are temperament and character, and what role do they play in personality? Ralph Waldo Emerson stated that "temperament is the iron wire on which the beads are strung" (1844b) and that "character is that which can do without success" (1844a). Recently, Cloninger and colleagues (Cloninger, 1987; Cloninger, Przybeck, Svrakic, & Wetzel, 1994; Cloninger, Svrakic, & Przybeck, 1993) developed a seven-factor model of temperament (novelty seeking, harm avoidance, reward dependence, and persistence) and character (self-directedness, cooperativeness, and self-transcendence) traits that map onto their psychobiological model of personality (see Figure 4.1). *Temperament* reflects automatic emotional responses, with some genetic basis, that are moderately heritable and stable across the life span. *Character* refers to self-concepts and individual differences in goals and values and is expected to mature throughout life. The temperament and character factors were developed independently of one another. Three Temperament dimensions (i.e., Novelty Seeking, Harm Avoidance, and Reward Dependence) were proposed in earlier work and measured by the Tridimensional Personality Questionnaire (TPQ; Cloninger, 1987). Later work showed that a Persistence factor could be created from a subscale previously thought to be part of Reward Dependence (Cloninger & Przybeck, 1991; Nixon & Parsons, 1989). The resulting four-factor model of temperament was useful but proved unable to determine whether someone has a personality disorder. Therefore, Cloninger et al. (1993) generated three additional factors (i.e., Self-Directedness, Cooperativeness, and Self-Transcendence) labeled as components of "character" for this purpose. Subsequent theoretical discussion of the TCI model conceptualized temperament and character as elements of an integrated structure for understanding personality (e.g., Cloninger et al., 1993). Cloninger et. al suggested that temperament and character should be modeled separately because the relationship between the two constructs is assumed to be nonlinear. However, a strong justification for this latter point has not been made, especially from a methodological or measurement perspective. The virtues of adopting the integrated model versus examining the two components separately may leave researchers who employ the TCI confused about how best to proceed.

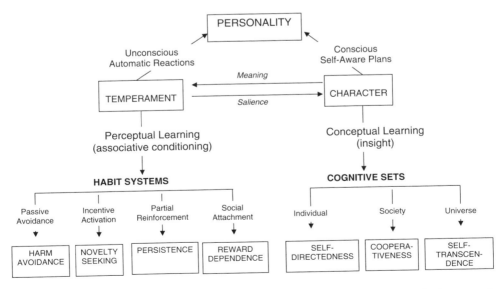

Figure 4.1. A hierarchical model of personality based on the work of Cloninger and colleagues. From C. R. Cloninger's 1993 lecture notes. Reprinted with permission.

Widespread Use of the Temperament and Character Inventory

The TCI model or individual TCI factors have been widely used in a variety of studies (e.g., Gusnard et al., 2003; Hansenne, Delhez, & Cloninger, 2005; Paulus, Rogalsky, Simmons, Feinstein, & Stein, 2003; Suhara et al., 2001; Svrakic, Whitehead, Przybeck, & Cloninger, 1993). In fact, the TCI has been adopted worldwide and for widely varied applications. A recent report (Pelissolo et al., 2005) stated that the TCI has been reported in almost 400 published studies, and searches conducted for this chapter found over 1,000 citations using the PsycINFO search engine. The measure has been translated into at least 18 different languages to date. There are three major versions of the TCI (Versions 8, 9, and TCI–R), with Versions 8 and 9 having the same 226 items that map onto the seven Temperament and Character factors, but different additional items are not used for modeling purposes (i.e., perceptual aberration/dissociation items). Therefore, TCI Versions 8 and 9 are comparable for use in modeling the TCI. Whereas versions 8 and 9 use a true–false response format, the TCI–R uses a 5-point Likert scale, and the items are not directly comparable to Versions 8 or 9 (i.e., 28 items from Versions 8 and 9 were deleted, and 37 new items were added). Additionally, the Junior Temperament and Character Inventory (JTCI) was developed for use with young adults. Finally, another reason for the widespread popularity of the TCI is use of the dimensions in clinical settings for diagnostic purposes. Arguably, however, for diagnoses to be valid the structure of the underlying dimensions should display appropriate psychometric properties including validity, reliability and replicability, and generalizability.

Statistical Modeling of the Temperament and Character Inventory

Modern multivariate methods are helpful when examining constructs like the TCI because they can test how well data map onto the conceptual model. However, a matter of initial concern is the issue of the appropriate level of analysis. First, there is often a discrepancy between results produced by exploratory versus confirmatory methodologies (Borsboom, 2006; Church & Burke, 1994; Vassend & Skrondal, 1995, 1997). Most of the factor analytic studies of the TCI have used exploratory methods such as principal components analysis (PCA) or exploratory factor analysis (EFA; e.g., Brändström, Richter, & Nylander, 2003; Cloninger et. al., 1993; Hansenne et al., 2005). Several studies used confirmatory factor analysis (CFA) to test the underlying structure of the Tridimensional Personality Questionnaire (TPQ), the three-factor precursor of the larger TCI model, with mixed results (for supporting results, see Bagby, Parker, & Joffe, 1992; Sher, Wood, Crews, & Vandiver, 1995; for results failing to support the TPQ factor structure, see Earleywine, Finn, Peterson, & Pihl, 1992; Waller, Lilienfeld, Tellegen, & Lykken, 1991).

When factor analysis is reported, most studies employing exploratory methods typically conclude that the TCI constructs were measured appropriately. However, difficulties replicating the proposed factor structure have been reported even when exploratory methods were used (Ball, Tennen, & Kranzler, 1999;

Herbst, Zonderman, McCrae, & Costa, 2000). Herbst et al. (2000) used PCA and found evidence for fewer than seven factors using TCI Version 9, and subscales of each of the seven factors that failed to consistently load on the expected factor. Herbst et al. concluded there was no supporting evidence for the temperament and character model. Ball et al. (1999) also used exploratory methods and noted a lack of support for a seven-factor solution, instead reporting four factors as best fitting TCI Version 8. Both PCA and maximum likelihood EFA of our data, not reported in detail here, suggested that a six-factor solution best fit the data and showed contamination across factors as was reported in the two studies described earlier (Maitland, Nyberg, et al., 2004).

Mulaik (1988) suggested that the conclusions of EFA are never complete without a subsequent CFA. Furthermore, warnings about the inappropriate use of PCA when confirmatory methods are warranted and the lack of replicability of exploratory findings with confirmatory methods in personality data deserve attention (e.g., Borsboom, 2006; Church & Burke, 1994; Vassend & Skrondal, 1995, 1997). Therefore, we next examine studies using confirmatory methods to model the TCI. Although they did not provide a detailed description of their analyses, Schmeck, Goth, Poustka, and Cloninger (2001) found support for both the temperament and character models of the JTCI using CFA. However, Gana and Trouillet (2003) used CFA to examine 25 different TCI (Version 8) measurement models, including both item and facet analysis, and concluded that none of the models provided compelling fit to the data, thereby rejecting the factor structure of the TCI as defined in the literature. Similarly, Ball et al. (1999) stated that neither item-level CFA nor post hoc exploratory analyses on the TCI items supported the association of items with their subscales (Version 8). Additionally, Tomita et al. (2000) reported mixed results when applying CFA to the Japanese version of the TCI (125 items, 4-point scale). They found four temperament and three character factors; however, not all items loaded appropriately, and model fit was questionable. These inconsistent results raise questions about the widespread use of the TCI. Specifically, it remains unclear whether factor-analytic results, in general, and confirmatory factor results, in particular, support the temperament and character constructs.

Furthermore, like any complex measure, the level of analysis of the TCI is critical because different choices may lead to disparate results. One framework for evaluation of models of personality examines the level of aggregation or disaggregation of items (Bagozzi & Edwards, 1998; Bagozzi & Heatherton, 1994). Within the factor-analytic literature, the related method of item parceling has been widely debated (e.g., Little, Cunningham, Shahar, & Widaman, 2002). The three most common reasons item parceling is conducted are to gain more stable estimates and stronger variable-to-sample-size ratios and to handle smaller samples (Bandalos, 2002; Bandalos & Finney, 2001). However, the literature is undecided about the appropriate methods and decision-making process.

Finally, once evidence suggests a model fits well to the data, and a best fitting model is determined, ME/I should be addressed across comparison groups. Exploratory work has generally used measures of congruence to examine similarity between factor structures. Confirmatory methods allow more rigorous evaluations of equivalence for all estimated parameters in factor models. The importance of determining that underlying measurement structures are invariant before making quantitative comparisons has been emphasized in a variety of domains (e.g., Baltes et al., 1988; Hertzog & Nesselroade, 2003; Horn & McArdle, 1992; Labouvie, 1980; Maitland, Dixon, Hultsch, & Hertzog, 2001; Maitland et al., 2000; Maitland, Herlitz, Nyberg, Bäckman, & Nilsson, 2004; Nyberg et al., 2003; Schaie et al., 1998; Vandenberg & Lance, 2000). Within studies in developmental psychology, invariance is most often tested between sexes, age groups, and/or over time to examine change in the construct of interest. Without evidence for measurement invariance, there is reason to doubt that the same construct has been measured across groups and therefore to exercise caution about making subsequent mean-level comparisons.

In summary, first, few studies have used CFA to test the seven factors of the full TCI model (for exceptions, see Gana & Trouillet, 2003; Tomita et al., 2000). Second, and further complicating the question of how well the TCI fits across studies, is the question of whether researchers model item data or the facets or subscale scores from the TCI to test factor structures. Indeed, Cloninger and colleagues model facets (e.g., Cloninger et al., 1993; Hansenne et al., 2005), whereas item analysis of the TCI is relatively rare in the literature (for TPQ examples, see Cannon, Clark, Keeka, & Keefe, 1993; Parker, Bagby, & Joffe, 1996; for TCI examples, Gana & Trouillet, 2003; Tomita et al., 2000). Regardless of which version is examined, analysis of TCI items proves an onerous task because TCI Version 8 (as used in our analyses) and Version 9 each have 226 items creating the seven TCI factors. Ball et al. (1999) suggested that many studies avoid item analysis because of the large N required for the optimal subject-to-variable ratio. Additionally, they suggest that factor analyzing facets to create factors is "fairer" to a measure constructed from a rationale approach. Cloninger himself suggested that using psychometric methods to examine TCI structure may fail, as these methods were not used to develop the model. Alternatively, employing the facets in analyses presumes that all items actually map onto their hypothesized constructs—a potentially risky proposition.

Third, despite the implicit presence of second-order factors in the TCI model (i.e., items to facets, facets to TCI factors (or) facets to factors, first-order factors to higher order Temperament and Character factors), few studies have tested whether the seven TCI factors represent the constructs they were designed to measure in this manner (for exceptions, see Gana & Trouillete, 2003; Maitland, Nyberg, et al., 2004; and Tomita et al., 2000). A likely explanation for the lack of second-order factor models may be the prevalence of studies using exploratory methods, which precludes the ability to test such models. Moreover, when using confirmatory methods, one would generally not test for second-order factors unless strong evidence confirms that the first-order factors fit the data well.

Finally, knowledge of whether measurement instruments mark the under-lying constructs consistently between comparison groups or over time is crucial for all comparative work. However, to date, ME/I using confirmatory factor methods has not been reported for the TCI. Therefore, the question of how well the TCI model fits to data may have different answers even within the same measurement instrument and data set depending on the methodological deci-sions made by researchers. The literature reveals both supportive and negative results from previous attempts to determine how well the theoretical model proposed by Cloninger and colleagues fits the data collected using the TCI (for supportive results, see Cloninger et al., 1993; Hansenne et al., 2005; for a lack of support, see Ball et al., 1999; Gana & Trouillet, 2003; Herbst et al., 2000).

One objective of this chapter is to discuss how, even within the same data set, different levels of support are found depending on the statistical method used to examine the data and the level of analysis (i.e., item analysis vs. analysis of facets) employed. We present results examining the structure of the TCI from a large population-based study of adults in Sweden (Nilsson, 1999; Nilsson et al., 1997, 2004), using CFA and structural equation modeling to test TCI models at different levels of aggregation or disaggregation (i.e., item analysis vs. modeling facets; Bagozzi & Edwards, 1998; Bagozzi & Heatherton, 1994). The importance of level of analysis and how it relates to item parceling (e.g., Little et al., 2002) is also discussed. Interpretation and implications of results are provided accompanied by a discussion of the tension between applications of psychometric methods to measures of personality compared with the clinical or practical utility of those measures.

To address these concerns, we report tests of the factor structure of TCI using CFA and at multiple levels of analysis including (a) item-level analyses and (b) facet/subscale analysis of the TCI. We then extend the results of the best fitting confirmatory models to examine ME/I across sexes, providing one of the first tests of invariance for the TCI.

Analyzing Temperament and Character Inventory Data From the Betula Project

Analyses based on facets included 2,423 participants ages 35 to 90 (1,093 women, 1,330 men). However, only 1491 participants (792 women and 699 men, ages 34–91) had item data available for analysis; therefore, item analyses are reported on this smaller sample of community-dwelling adults from the BP (Nilsson, 1999; Nilsson et al., 1997, 2004). The majority of participants in the BP report themselves as healthy (Nilsson et al., 1997). The Swedish translation of TCI Version 8 was administered as part of larger testing sessions, lasting between 1.5 and 2 hours (Nilsson, 1999; Nilsson et al., 1997, 2004). TCI Version 8 has 226 items used to create the seven factors. The response format for all items was true–false, and the answers were coded using Cloninger's key for creating scale scores. The Swedish version replicates the English version well, with means, standard deviations, distribution of scores, and relationships within and between scales and subscales within expected ranges (Brändström et al., 1998).

The temperament scales include Novelty Seeking (NS; 4 facets), Harm Avoidance (HA; 4 facets), Reward Dependence (RD; 3 facets), and Persistence (P; 1 facet with 8 items). Facets for NS are defined as NS1 (Exploratory Excitement, 11 items), NS2 (Impulsiveness, 10 items), NS3 (Extravagance, 9 items), and NS4 (Disorderliness, 10 items). HA facets include HA1 (Worry and Pessimism, 11 items), HA2 (Fear of Uncertainty, 7 items), HA3 (Shyness with Strangers, 9 items), HA4 (Fatigability and Asthenia, 8 items). RD is marked by RD1 (Sentimentality, 10 items), RD3 (Attachment, 8 items), and RD4 (Dependence, 6 items). The RD2 scale (aka Persistence) was part of RD until additional factor analyses suggested it was a distinct factor.

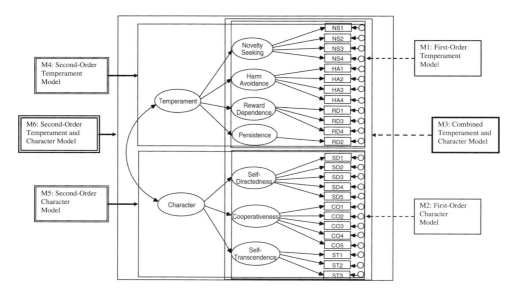

Figure 4.2. Illustration of facet models. Two correlated second-order factors (Temperament and Character) and seven first-order factors are displayed, whereas many of the models tested Temperament and Character independently.

Character scales include Self-Directedness (SD; 5 facets), Cooperativeness (CO; 5 facets), and Self-Transcendence (ST; 3 facets). Facets for SD include SD1 (Responsibility, 8 items), SD2 (Purposefulness, 8 items), SD3 (Resourcefulness, 5 items), SD4 (Self-Acceptance, 11 items), and SD5 (Congruent Second Nature, 12 items). Facets for CO include C1 (Social Acceptance, 8 items), C2 (Empathy, 7 items), C3 (Helpfulness, 8 items), C4 (Compassion and Revenge, 10 items), and C5 (Integrated Conscience, 9 items). Finally, facets for ST include ST1 (Self-Forgetfulness, 11 items), ST2 (Transpersonal Identity, 9 items), and ST3 (Spiritual Acceptance, 13 items).

P is the only factor that is not multiply marked in facet analysis (see Figure 4.2).

Confirmatory Factor Analyses

Models were tested using AMOS 7 (Arbuckle, 2006). Analyses were conducted on covariance matrices with results of the final models reported as standardized estimates for ease of interpretation. Factor scaling was accomplished by fixing one item for each factor to a value of 1.0. Where applicable, second-order factors were scaled using the same procedure. The chi-square difference test ($\Delta\chi^2$; Jöreskog & Sörbom, 1987) was used to compare nested models. The critical value used for all comparisons was $p < .01$.

Model fit was evaluated by examining the following fit indexes: (a) model χ^2, (b) goodness of fit index (GFI; Jöreskog & Sörbom, 1987), (c) nonnormed fit index (NNFI; Bentler & Bonnett, 1980), (d) comparative fit index (CFI; Bentler,

1990), and (e) root mean square error of approximation (RMSEA; Steiger, 1990). Models were determined to fit well if consensus of these fit indexes met or exceeded generally accepted levels. These accepted values include ≥.9 for GFI, NNFI, and CFI values and for the RMSEA, which indicates the amount of error variance per degree of freedom in the model, values smaller than .05 indicate a good fit, and values up to .08 represent a mediocre fit (Browne & Cudeck, 1993). More recently, Hu and Bentler (1999) suggested that a cutoff of less than .06 indicated adequate fit.

Results for Item Analyses

With regard to item analyses, results are reported across two levels of analyses. First, models were specified that used items to model a unitary factor for each construct (i.e., all ST items loading onto a single ST factor; see left side of Figure 4.3). The unitary factor provides a nested model for comparison purposes to the multiple factors described as part of the TCI model. Second, the items were loaded onto facets as defined in the TCI literature and facets were

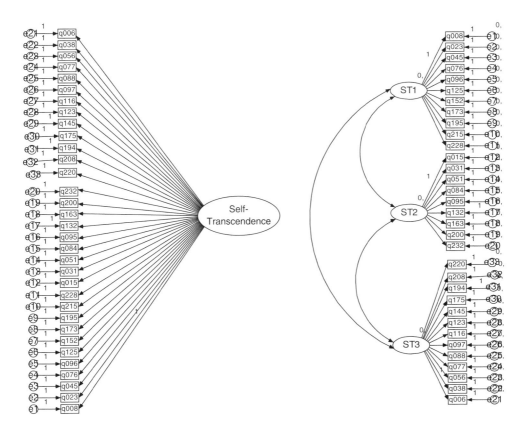

Figure 4.3. Example of a unidimensional item analysis model and a multiple factor item analysis for Self-Transcendence.

allowed to correlate (see right side of Figure 4.3). These analyses help to determine how well item analyses reproduce the underlying dimensions expected from the TCI model. We also report analyses based on the 25 facets of TCI. We conducted separate analyses for the temperament and character factors as recommended by Cloninger and colleagues (Cloninger et al., 1993, 1994; Hansenne et al., 2005). Results for simultaneous models of temperament and character were presented in Maitland, Nyberg, et al. (2004).

All models were examined with 1,491 participants. As can be seen from Tables 4.1 and 4.2, item factor analysis resulted in poor to moderate fit across all seven TCI dimensions regardless of the level of analysis employed. Among temperament factors, the NS and HA models were rejected and did not approach reasonable fit. Models for NS showed nonsignificant factor loadings, and the percentage of factor loadings greater than .4 (provided as an indicator of strength of relationship between the items and factors) was below 50% for all NS models. However, HA showed stronger factor loadings (all estimates were statistically significant), and over 60% of loadings were above the .40 cutoff. The pattern of results suggested that the multiple facets fit better than a single, unitary dimension. Whereas results suggest model fit could be improved, the results for the RD and P models were significantly better than those for NS and HA. GFI and RMSEA values are within acceptable levels, whereas the CFI is well below normal cutoff values. Additionally, both RD and P models, as specified in the literature, demonstrated one nonsignificant factor loading, and approximately 50% of all loadings were larger than the .40 cutoff.

Regarding the Character models (see Table 4.2), none of the item analyses demonstrated acceptable fit without further modification; however, the same pattern of model fit was noted with models based on multiple facets fitting better than a unitary factor. Regardless of level of measurement, the SD model had a number of nonsignificant factor loadings, yet over 50% of loadings exceeding .40. CO showed weaker factor loadings overall, with only 24% of items exceeding .40, although only a single loading was nonsignificant. The RMSEA values were good for CO, and the GFI might reach acceptable levels (i.e., > .90) by deleting items from this factor. Finally, the ST results were not acceptable with regard to model fit indexes, yet all factor loadings were statistically significant, and almost 60% of the loadings exceeded the .40 cutoff for the three-factor model as defined by Cloninger.

In summary, the results of item analyses for each of the seven TCI factors, including a unitary model and a multifactor model based on Cloninger's work, resulted in unacceptable model fit and rejection of the models as adequately fitting data collected with TCI. Many TCI factors had nonsignificant loadings suggesting that culling of items to improve fit is necessary. Regardless of the level of analysis, factors accounted for a small proportion of reliable variance in all models. Whereas modeling item data proved a complex task, the information garnered suggests two possible courses of action: (a) Because the large number of items leads to poorer model fit, some form of aggregation should be considered, or (b) Conduct item-level analyses and reformulate the structure of the TCI on that basis. The former approach is preferable because we want to evaluate the TCI model as it is most widely employed. Therefore, we switch from item analyses to models that use the 25 facets defined by Cloninger as a

Table 4.1. Temperament and Character Inventory (TCI) Item Analysis—Temperament Models

TCI dimension	df	χ^2	GFI	CFI	RMSEA	90% CI of RMSEA	Range of factor loadings	% of loadings > .40
Novelty Seeking (40 items)								
One-factor model	740	5475.87	.789	.401	.066	.064–.067	.001–.543(6)	18%
Four-factor model	735	3966.93	.835	.591	.054	.053–.056	.003–.636(3)	40%
Harm Avoidance (35 items)								
One-factor model	560	6217.23	.733	.524	.082	.080–.084	.122–.655(0)	37%
Four-factor model	554	5386.45	.756	.593	.077	.075–.078	.145–.719(0)	60%
Reward Dependence (24 items)								
One-factor model	252	2228.98	.861	.450	.073	.070–.075	.001–.690(11)	21%
Three-factor model	249	1377.65	.920	.686	.055	.052–.058	.070–.699(1)	50%
Persistence (8 items)								
One-factor model	20	113.10	.981	.884	.056	.046–.066	.085–.598(1)	50%

Note.   GFI = goodness of fit index; CFI = comparative fit index; RMSEA = root mean square error of approximation; CI = confidence interval.

Table 4.2.　Temperament and Character Inventory (TCI) Item Analysis—Character Models

TCI dimension	df	χ^2	GFI	CFI	RMSEA	90% CI of RMSEA	Range of factor loadings	% of loadings > .40
Self-directedness (44 items)								
One-factor model	819	5591.27	.796	.478	.063	.061–.064	.006–.491(10)	27%
Five-factor model	810	4413.53	.840	.606	.055	.053–.056	.001–.604(5)	52%
Cooperativeness (42 items)								
One-factor model	819	4203.15	.837	.480	.053	.051–.054	.016–.519(2)	14%
Five-factor model	809	3620.24	.854	.568	.048	.047–.050	.145–.719(1)	24%
Self-transcendence (33 items)								
One-factor model	495	4929.87	.771	.585	.078	.076–.080	.070–.697(2)	42%
Three-factor model	492	4137.46	.821	.659	.071	.069–.073	.105–.709(0)	58%

Note. GFI = goodness of fit index; CFI = comparative fit index; RMSEA = root mean square error of approximation; CI = confidence interval.

starting point for determining whether aggregation helps to improve fit of the TCI. Development of the TCI–R has the potential to result in better model fit.

Confirmatory Factor Analysis of Facets for Temperament

All temperament factors were modeled together (i.e., 4 factors defined by 12 temperament facets; model M1 in Figure 4.2) resulting in less than acceptable fit: $\chi^2 = 1301.80$, $df = 51$, $p < .001$, GFI = .92, CFI = .76, RMSEA = .10. Clearly, factor loadings for RD1 and RD4 were weak. Squared multiple correlations (SMC) ranged from 0 to .61 (averaging 28% of the variance in subscales accounted for by the latent factors). Factor correlations were mixed, ranging from $r = .09$ (between P and RD) to $r = .68$ (between RD and NS). Results are shown in Figure 4.4. For legibility SMCs have been moved next to each box marking a facet.

Confirmatory Factor Analysis of Facets for Character

All character factors were modeled simultaneously (i.e., 3 factors defined by 13 character facets; model M2 in Figure 4.2), and this model revealed mixed results: $\chi^2 = 977.53$, $df = 51$, $p < .001$, GFI = .94, CFI = .81, RMSEA = .09. Figure 4.5 shows the results from this model. Again, SMCs have been moved next to each box marking a facet for legibility. Whereas the GFI is strong, the CFI (and other similar measures of model fit) and RMSEA did not reach acceptable levels. Two factor loadings were at or below .40 (CO5, SD4). SMC ranged from .11 to .50, with an average of .32 for this model. Factor correlations ranged from $r = -.15$ (between SD and ST) to $r = .50$ (between CO and SD).

Summary of Aggregated Models

The lack of support for models tested, regardless of the level of analysis, suggested that the TCI models defined by Cloninger and colleagues are not acceptable without further modification. Item analysis for each TCI factor suggested that the multiple dimensions described by Cloninger fit better than a unitary factor model; however, model fit was still suboptimal. However, support was found for the analysis of facets over item data. Model fit was consistently better for the former, although models still showed signs of stress. Combining these results with our goal of examining sex invariance for TCI, we next examined how to modify separate Temperament and Character models to make these comparisons.

Reduced Temperament Model and Sex Invariance

Given the lack of fit for item analyses, we focused on modifying our facet analyses to improve model fit for purposes of testing sex invariance. Examining modification indexes from the four-factor Temperament model that resulted from

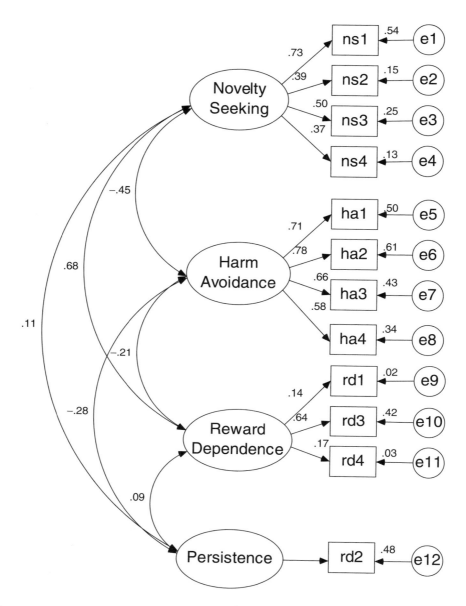

Figure 4.4. Standardized results for Temperament model (facet analysis).

modeling facets, the easiest solution for improving model fit appears to be removing the RD and P factors (thereby eliminating all RD subscales). The reduced model, comprising NS and HA factors, resulted in improved fit $\chi^2 = 426.00$, $df = 19, p < .001$, GFI = .96, CFI = .90, RMSEA = .09. GFI and CFI were acceptable, whereas RMSEA was still inflated. Additional fit indexes showed similar results, with adjusted GFI = .92, although the NNFI = .85. Factor loadings were all statistically significant and ranged from .45 to .78. The correlation between

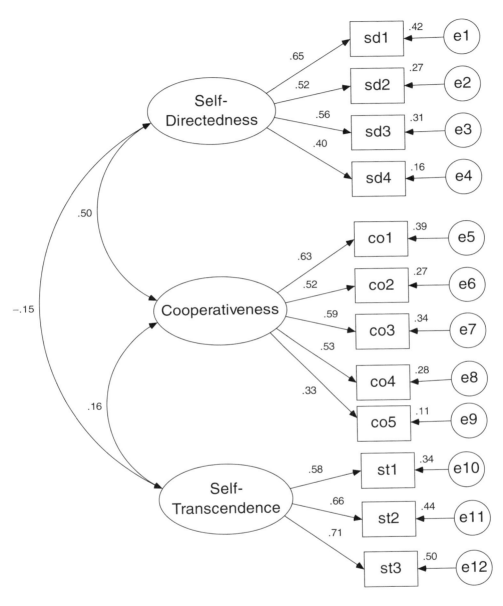

Figure 4.5. Standardized results for Character model (facet analysis).

NS and HA was negative and significant $r = -.39$. Extending this model to examine sex invariance requires an initial test of the configural model, allowing all parameters to be freely estimated for men and women. It reveals $\chi^2 = 444.06$, $df = 38$, $p < .001$, GFI = .97, CFI = .90, RMSEA = .07. Fit is comparable to the model reported above, with slight improvement in RMSEA. The test for weak metric invariance, whereby factor loadings are constrained to be equivalent across sexes, was found to be plausible: $\chi^2 = 452.16$, $df = 44$, $p < .001$, GFI = .96,

CFI = .90, RMSEA = .06; $\Delta\chi^2$ = 8.09, df = 6, p = .231. Thus, the factor loadings for the Temperament model composed of the NS and HA factors demonstrated measurement equivalence. Additional evidence showed that the factor variance and covariances in the model could be constrained to be equivalent between sexes: χ^2 = 452.88, df = 47, p < .001, GFI = .95, CFI = .90, RMSEA = .06; $\Delta\chi^2$ = .73, df = 3, p = .867. A further test of equivalence of residuals in the model was not supported. Sex invariance results are shown in Figure 4.6.

Reduced Character Model and Sex Invariance

Examining modification indexes from the three-factor Character model (modeled on facets) fails to reveal any simple solutions for model improvement. The strongest modification indexes suggest cross-loading of facets onto additional factors (e.g., allow the SD2 facet to load onto the ST factor), or suggest correlating residual terms, not within factors but for facets that load onto different factors (e.g., correlating residuals for C5 and ST1 or correlating residuals for C4 and ST3). Without an acceptable rationale for making such changes, we

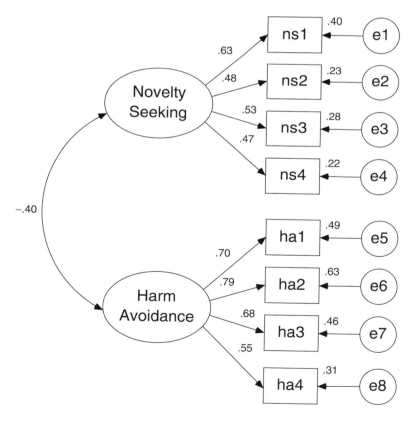

Figure 4.6. Standardized results for test of sex invariance of Temperament model (facet analysis). Results demonstrated that factor loadings and factor variances/covariances were equivalent across sexes.

decided to test for sex invariance in the three-factor Character model without modifications. Results for the configural model, allowing all parameters to estimate separately for men and women, resulted in: $\chi^2 = 1026.11$, $df = 102$, $p < .001$, GFI = .93, CFI = .81, RMSEA = .06. GFI and RMSEA are acceptable, whereas CFI is too low. Factor loadings were all statistically significant and ranged from .30 to .70 for men, and from .37 to .72 for women. The correlation between SD and CO was moderate and significant $r = -.46$ for women and $r = -.57$ for men.

The test for weak metric invariance, whereby factor loadings are constrained to be equivalent across sexes, was not found to be plausible: $\chi^2 = 1060.22$, $df = 111$, $p < .001$, GFI = .93, CFI = .80, RMSEA = .06; $\Delta\chi^2 = 34.12$, $df = 9$, $p = .001$. Therefore, the factor loadings for the Character model failed to meet the requirements for sex invariance. As is usual practice in ME/I testing, more stringent constraints were not tested. The lack of sex invariance means that measurement properties of the TCI Character model differ for men and women. Results are shown in Figure 4.7, with the model for women on the left and results for men on the right. Examining parameter estimates for the Character model does not reveal much discrepancy in values for men and women. Factor loadings could be tested for differences using tests of partial measurement invariance (e.g., Byrne, Shavelson, & Muthén, 1989), helping to determine how many factor loadings may be constrained compared with those that require different estimates across sexes. Without evidence that at least the majority of the factor loadings could be constrained to equality across men and women, comparison of means for the Character factors between these groups should be conducted with caution.

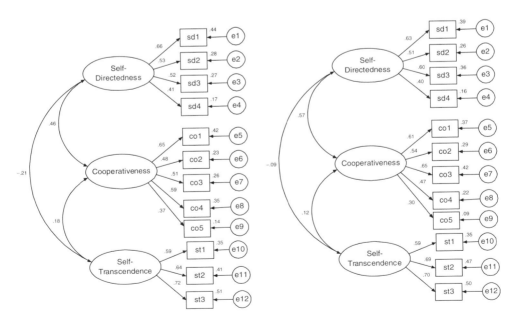

Figure 4.7. Standardized results for test of sex invariance for Character model (facet analysis). Separate results reported for women (left) and men (right) based on a lack of evidence for invariance.

Discussion of Modeling Results

Our results represent one of the few efforts to determine whether the seven TCI factors map onto the two theoretical constructs, temperament and character, using confirmatory methods. Combining results from item analysis, unique to this report and uncommon in the TCI literature, with second-order factor models and simultaneous models of temperament and character, provides a comprehensive view of the many potential levels of analysis of the TCI. Results provide limited support for the TCI model regardless of whether we modeled Temperament and Character items to facets or facets to factors. We did find better support for models conducted on facets when compared to item analysis, which would be expected given that too many items in analyses can result in poorer fit (e.g., Bandalos, 2002; Bandalos & Finney, 2001; Little et al., 2002).

Additionally, separate models for temperament and character appeared to fit better than combined models with all seven TCI factors. As reported by Herbst et al. (2000), the patterns of correlations in which all seven factors are modeled together raise concerns. Of particular note, correlations between the Temperament and Character factors are stronger than correlations within each of these domains. Cloninger et al. (1993) suggested that the relationship between temperament and character is nonlinear, and hence the two models should remain distinct. The strong correlations between the Temperament and Character factors argue against this notion of separation, although the best method for modeling the relationship between these constructs remains unknown. Certainly, if temperament has a stronger hereditary basis, as suggested in this psychobiological model, it should precede character. However, most published studies of the TCI have been cross-sectional, therefore not allowing one to test temporal ordering. Even with longitudinal data, it is assumed that both temperament and character are likely to continue to evolve, regardless of the age of respondents or the time of measurement.

Whereas the results reported here fail to support the TCI model in its entirety, we do find evidence that particular factors meet the rigorous psychometric standards employed here. The TCI model should not be taken at face value and—without additional efforts to modify the items, facets, and factor structure—caution is warranted concerning the use of the model's components. Additionally, we did find evidence of sex invariance for the reduced Temperament model, whereas the model for Character did not show evidence of measurement equivalence for men and women. These preliminary results regarding ME/I require further testing and replication. More studies testing comparing the TCI 8/9 with the TCI–R would be beneficial (Brändström et al., 2003). Evaluation of the TCI–R for model fit and ME/I across common comparisons (i.e., sex, age groups, over time, etc.) is also needed to determine whether the changes made to the questions and response format result in stronger evidence for the use of TCI–R in comparative work.

It is also interesting that regardless of whether exploratory or confirmatory methods were used, most studies have taken a firm stand, stating either that the TCI model fits their data well (e.g., Schmeck et al., 2001) or that there is no evidence the model exists (e.g., Ball et al., 1999; Herbst et al., 2000). Very few studies have suggested support for components of the model, even if the model as a whole fails to meet levels of acceptable fit. Tomita et al. (2000) provided one example of mixed evidence even though it uses the Japanese version of the TCI. This study evaluated TCI data at different levels of aggregation and conducted factor modification to try to improve fit where weaknesses were noted. The researchers suggested that TCI does map onto four temperament and three character factors; however, these factors were not entirely as predicted. Similar to our own results, Tomita et al. found that analysis of TCI facets provided better fit than did item analyses. It is also possible that only particular TCI factors demonstrate ME/I rather than relying on wholesale acceptance or rejection that results from traditional tests of equivalence of factor loadings (for a discussion of partial measurement invariance, see Byrne et al., 1989).

Psychometric Properties Versus Clinical Utility

It is clear that mixed evidence for the underlying structure of the TCI has been shown; however, an additional measure of the usefulness of a tool such as the TCI is how well it performs in practice. After all, Cloninger et al. (1993) and Svrakic et al. (1993) suggested that the TCI is a more complete characterization of personality and provides better differential diagnosis of personality disorders than does the NEO-FFI. When the subject of interest is not the TCI model as a whole but rather the relevance of key factors or facets to clinical work with clients in treatment, one might reach different conclusions about the TCI's value. Cloninger and other clinicians have validated components of the TCI by examining how well it informs diagnostic judgments when compared with other clinically validated measures (e.g., Suhara et al., 2001; Svrakic et al., 1993). The clinical value of the TCI in the evaluation of a patient is limited. The TCI is generally applied in practice as a method of obtaining additional information or support for a clinical diagnosis of a certain personality disorder or clusters of personality disorders. Therefore, we recommend administering the TCI in a remitted state. Even then, the instrument cannot be used alone, without a comprehensive clinical interview for a proper diagnosis of personality disorder, with low SD/CO supporting lack of mature development, and HA, NS, and RD giving some suggestion to a particular personality cluster (i.e., A, B, or C). In psychotherapy the personality profile can be of value because self-evaluation is an important part of psychotherapeutic process. Furthermore, profiling HA, NS, and RD could give valuable information about the basis of maladaptive behavior in various settings (e.g., in relation to other people).

Recommendations

The evidence from the Betula data, combined with that of the previous studies described, suggests mixed support for the TCI. Particular facets or TCI factors have been shown to fit reasonably well. For example, when modeled together, NS and HA fit reasonably well in our data, and from a purely psychometric standpoint, these factors could be recommended for use, whether as part of a larger study of personality or for clinical purposes. In addition, these same constructs also demonstrated sex invariance, thereby providing additional confidence in the ability to use NS and HA for comparative work. However, other TCI facets and factors (e.g., RD and P using TCI Version 8) demonstrated relatively poor psychometric properties, and caution is warranted when using these measures.

Conclusions

Most studies, including our own, whether providing supporting or contradictory evidence for TCI, were conducted on older versions of the measure. Employing many of the key tenets of measurement theory, Cloninger has continued to address criticism by developing new versions of the TCI, and the evidence is starting to accumulate as to how well these modifications have addressed earlier criticisms or suggestions for improving the model. Early reports on the TCI–R suggest stronger psychometric properties, including a better fit to the suggested underlying factor structure using exploratory methods (Brändström et al., 2003). However, confirmatory studies are necessary to provide stronger evidence beyond the preliminary, exploratory results reported to date. Additional tests of ME/I should be conducted to provide further evidence that the TCI, regardless of version used, provides comparable results across groups being compared. More critical from the perspective of developmental methodology is the dearth of longitudinal ME/I results for TCI data, precluding one from differentiating stability or change of the measurement instrument from developmental processes within individuals.

References

Allemand, M., Zimprich, D., & Hertzog, C. (2007). Cross-sectional age differences and longitudinal age changes in personality in middle adulthood and old age. *Journal of Personality, 75,* 323–358.

Arbuckle, J. L. (2006). *Amos 7.0* [Computer software]. Chicago: Smallwaters.

Bagby, R. M., Parker, J. D., & Joffe, R. T. (1992). Confirmatory factor analysis of the Tridimensional Personality Questionnaire. *Personality and Individual Differences, 13,* 1245–1246.

Bagozzi, R. P., & Edwards, J. R. (1998). A general approach for representing constructs in organizational research. *Organizational Research Methods, 1,* 45–87.

Bagozzi, R. P., & Heatherton, T. F. (1994). A general approach for representing multifaceted personality constructs: Application to state self esteem. *Structural Equation Modeling, 1,* 35–67.

Ball, S., Tennen, H., & Kranzler, H. (1999). Factor replicability and validity of the temperament and character inventory in substance dependent patients. *Psychological Assessment, 11,* 514–524.

Baltes, P. B., & Nesselroade, J. R. (1970). Multivariate longitudinal and cross-sectional sequences for analyzing ontogenetic and generational change: A methodological note. *Developmental Psychology, 2,* 163–168.

Baltes, P. B., Reese, H. W., & Nesselroade, J. R. (1988). *Life-span developmental methodology: Introduction to research methods.* Hillsdale, NJ: Erlbaum.

Bandalos, D. L. (2002). The effects of item parceling on goodness-of-fit and parameter estimate bias in structural equation modeling. *Structural Equation Modeling, 9,* 78–102.

Bandalos, D. L., & Finney, S. J. (2001). Item parceling issues in structural equation modeling. In G. A. Marcoulides & R. E. Schumacker (Eds.), *New developments and techniques in structural equation modeling* (pp. 269–296). Mahwah, NJ: Erlbaum.

Bentler, P. M. (1990). Fit indices, LaGrange multipliers, constraint changes, and incomplete data in structural models. *Multivariate Behavioral Research, 25,* 163–172.

Bentler, P. M., & Bonnett, D. G. (1980). Significance tests and goodness-of-fit in the analysis of covariance structures. *Psychological Bulletin, 88,* 588–600.

Bollen, K. A. (1989). *Structural equations with latent variables.* New York: Wiley.

Borsboom, D. (2006). The attack of the psychometricians. *Psychometrika, 71,* 425–440.

Brändström, S., Richter, J., & Nylander, P.-O. (2003). Further development of the temperament and character inventory. *Psychological Reports, 93,* 995–1002.

Brändström, S., Schlette, P., Przybeck, T. R., Lundberg, M., Forsgren, T., Sigvardsson, S., et al. (1998). Swedish normative data on personality using the Temperament and Character Inventory. *Comprehensive Psychiatry, 39,* 122–128.

Browne, M. W., & Cudeck, R. (1993). Alternative ways of assessing model fit. In K. A. Bollen & J. S. Long (Eds.), *Testing structural equation models* (pp. 136–162). Newbury Park, CA: Sage.

Byrne, B. M., Shavelson, R. J., & Muthén, B. (1989). Testing for the equivalence of factor covariance and mean structures: The issue of partial measurement invariance. *Psychological Bulletin, 105,* 456–466.

Cannon, D. S., Clark, L. A., Keeka, J. K., & Keefe, C. K. (1993). A reanalysis of the Tridimensional Personality Questionnaire (TPQ) and its relation to Cloninger's Type 2 alcoholism. *Psychological Assessment, 5,* 62–66.

Church, A. T., & Burke, P. T. (1994). Exploratory and confirmatory tests of the Big Five and Tellegen's three- and four-dimensional models. *Journal of Personality and Social Psychology, 66,* 93–114.

Cloninger, C. R. (1987). A systematic method for clinical description and classification of personality. *Archives of General Psychiatry, 50,* 573–588.

Cloninger, C. R., & Przybeck, T. R. (1991). The Tridimensional Personality Questionnaire: U.S. normative data. *Psychological Reports, 69,* 1047–1057.

Cloninger, C. R., Przybeck, T. R., Svrakic, D. M., & Wetzel, R. (1994). *The Temperament and Character Inventory (TCI): A guide to its development and use.* St. Louis, MO: Washington University, Center for Psychobiology of Personality.

Cloninger, C. R., Svrakic, D. M., & Przybeck, T. R. (1993). A psychobiological model of temperament and character. *Archives of General Psychiatry, 50,* 975–990.

Costa, P. T., Jr., & McCrae, R. R. (1994). Set like plaster? Evidence for the stability of adult personality. In T. F. Heatherton & J. L. Weinberger (Eds.), *Can personality change?* (pp. 21–40). Washington, DC: American Psychological Association.

Costa, P. T., Jr., & McCrae, R. R. (1997). Longitudinal stability of adult personality. In R. Hogan, J. Johnson, & S. Briggs (Eds.), *Handbook of personality psychology* (pp. 269–290). San Diego, CA: Academic Press.

Earleywine, M., Finn, P. R., Peterson, J. B., & Pihl, R. O. (1992). Factor structure and correlates of the Tridimensional Personality Questionnaire. *Journal of Studies on Alcohol, 53,* 233–238.

Emerson, R. W. (1844a). Character. In *Essays: Second series.*

Emerson, R. W. (1844b). Experience. In *Essays: Second series.*

Gana, K., & Trouillet, R. (2003). Structure invariance of the Temperament and Character Inventory (TCI). *Personality and Individual Differences, 35,* 1483–1495.

Gusnard, D. A., Ollinger, J. M., Shulman, G. L., Cloninger, C. R., Price, J. L., Van Essen, D. C., & Raichle, M. E. (2003). Persistence and brain circuitry. *PNAS, 100,* 3479–3484.

Hansenne, M., Delhez, M., & Cloninger, C. R. (2005). Psychometric properties of the temperament and character inventory—revised (TCI–R) in a Belgian Sample. *Journal of Personality Assessment, 85,* 40–49.

Herbst, J. H., Zonderman, A. B., McCrae, R. R., & Costa, P. T. (2000). Do the dimensions of the Temperament and Character Inventory map a simple genetic architecture? Evidence from molecular genetics and factor analysis. *American Journal of Psychiatry, 157,* 1285–1290.

Hertzog, C., & Nesselroade, J. R. (2003). Assessing psychological change in adulthood: An overview of methodological issues. *Psychology and Aging, 18,* 639–657.

Hertzog, C., & Schaie, K. W. (1986). Stability and change in adult intelligence: 1. Longitudinal covariance structures. *Psychology and Aging, 1,* 159–171.

Hertzog, C., & Schaie, K. W. (1988). Stability and change in adult intelligence: 2. Simultaneous analysis of longitudinal means and covariance structures. *Psychology and Aging, 3,* 122–130.

Horn, J. L., & McArdle, J. J. (1992). A practical and theoretical guide to measurement invariance in aging research. *Experimental Aging Research, 18,* 117–144.

Horn, J. L., McArdle, J. J., & Mason, R. (1983). When is invariance not invariant: A practical scientist's look at the ethereal concept of factor invariance. *Southern Psychologist, 1,* 179–188.

Hu, L., & Bentler, P. M. (1999). Cutoff criteria for fit indexes in covariance structure analysis: Conventional criteria versus new alternatives. *Structural Equation Modeling, 6,* 1–55.

Jöreskog, K. G., & Sörbom, D. (1987). *LISREL 7. A Guide to the Program and Applications.* Chicago: SPSS.

Kogan, N. (1990). Personality and aging. In J. E. Birren & K. W. Schaie (Eds.), *Handbook of the psychology of aging* (3rd ed., pp. 330–346). San Diego, CA: Academic Press.

Labouvie, E. W. (1980). Identity versus equivalence of psychological measures and constructs. In L. W. Poon (Ed.), *Aging in the 1980s: Psychological issues* (pp. 493–502). Washington, DC: American Psychological Association.

Little, T. D., Cunningham, W. A., Shahar, G., & Widaman, K. F. (2002). To parcel or not to parcel: Exploring the question, weighing the merits. *Structural Equation Modeling, 9,* 151–173.

Maitland, S. B., Dixon, R. A., Hultsch, D. F., & Hertzog, C. (2001). Well-being as a moving target: Measurement equivalence of the Bradburn Affect Balance Scale. *The Journals of Gerontology: Series B. Psychological Sciences and Social Sciences, 56,* P69–P77.

Maitland, S. B., Herlitz, A., Nyberg, L., Bäckman, L., & Nilsson, L.-G. (2004). Selective sex differences in declarative memory. *Memory and Cognition, 32,* 1160–1169.

Maitland, S. B., Intrieri, R. C., Schaie, K. W., & Willis, S. L. (2000). Gender differences and changes in cognitive abilities across the adult life span. *Aging, Neuropsychology, and Cognition, 7,* 32–53.

Maitland, S. B., Nyberg, L., Forsgren, T., Bäckman, L., Nilsson, L.-G., & Adolfsson, R. (2004, November). *Conceptual and confirmatory analysis of the Temperament and Character Inventory.* Paper presented at the Annual Scientific Meetings of The Gerontological Society of America, Washington, DC.

McCrae, R. R., Zonderman, A. B., Costa, P. T., Jr., Bond, M. H., & Paunonen, S. B. (1996). Evaluating replicability of factors in the Revised NEO Personality Inventory: Confirmatory factor analysis versus Procrustes rotation. *Journal of Personality and Social Psychology, 70,* 552–566.

Meredith, W. (1993). Measurement invariance, factor analysis, and factorial invariance. *Psychometrika, 58,* 525–543.

Mroczek, D. K., Spiro, A., & Griffin, P. W. (2006). Personality and aging. In J. E. Birren & K. W. Schaie (Eds.), *Handbook of the Psychology of Aging* (pp. 363–377). Burlington, MA: Elsevier Academic Press.

Mulaik, S. A. (1988). Confirmatory factor analysis. In J. R. Nesselroade & R. B. Cattell (Eds.), *Handbook of multivariate experimental psychology* (2nd ed., pp. 259–288). New York: Plenum Press.

Nilsson, L.-G. (1999). *Aging, dementia, and memory.* In L.-.G Nilsson & H. J. Markowitsch (Eds.), *Cognitive neuroscience of memory* (pp. 147–162). Göttingen: Hogrefe & Huber.

Nilsson, L.-G., Bäckman, L., Erngrund, K., Nyberg, L., Adolfsson, R., Bucht, G., et al. (1997). The Betula prospective cohort study: Memory, health, and aging. *Aging, Neuropsychology, and Cognition, 4,* 1–32.

Nilsson, L.-G., Adolfsson, R., Bäckman, L., de Frias, C. M., Molander, B., & Nyberg, L. (2004). Betula: A prospective cohort study on memory, health, and aging. *Aging, Neuropsychology, and Cognition, 11,* 134–148.

Nixon, S. J., & Parsons, O. A. (1989). Cloninger's tridimensional theory of personality: Construct validity in a sample of college students. *Personality and Individual Differences, 10,* 1261–1267.

Nyberg, L., Maitland, S. B., Rönnlund, M., Bäckman, L., Dixon, R. A., Wahlin, Å., & Nilsson, L.-G. (2003). Selective adult age differences in an age-invariant multifactor model of declarative memory. *Psychology and Aging, 18,* 149–160.

Parker, J. D. A., Bagby, R. M., & Joffe, R. T. (1996). Validation of the biosocial model of personality: Confirmatory factor analysis of the Tridimensional Personality Questionnaire. *Psychological Assessment, 8,* 139–144.

Paulus, M. P., Rogalsky, C., Simmons, A., Feinstein, J. S., & Stein, M. B. (2003). Increased activation in the right insula during risk-taking decision making is related to harm avoidance and neuroticism. *Neuroimage, 19,* 1439–1448.

Pelissolo, A., Mallet, L., Baleyte, J.-M., Michel, G., Cloninger, C. R., Allilaire, J.-F., & Jouvent, R. (2005). The Temperament and Character Inventory—Revised (TCI–R): Psychometric characteristics of the French version. *Acta Psychiatrica Scandinavica, 112,* 126–133.

Reise, S. P., Smith, L., & Furr, R. M. (2001). Invariance of the NEO-PI–R neuroticism scale, *Multivariate Behavioral Research, 36,* 83–110.

Schaie, K. W. (1965). A general model for the study of developmental problems. *Psychological Bulletin, 64,* 91–107.

Schaie, K. W. (1996). *Intellectual development in adulthood: The Seattle Longitudinal Study.* New York: Oxford.

Schaie, K. W. (2005). *Developmental influences on adult intelligence: The Seattle Longitudinal Study.* New York: Oxford University Press.

Schaie, K. W., Dutta, R., & Willis, S. L. (1991). The relationship between rigidity-flexibility and cognitive abilities in adulthood. *Psychology and Aging, 6,* 371–383.

Schaie, K. W., & Hofer, S. M. (2001). Longitudinal studies in research on aging. In J. E. Birren & K. W. Schaie (Eds.), *Handbook of the psychology of aging* (5th ed., pp. 53–77). San Diego, CA: Academic Press.

Schaie, K. W., Maitland, S. B., Willis, S. L., & Intrieri, R. C. (1998). Longitudinal invariance of adult psychometric ability factor structures across seven years. *Psychology and Aging, 13,* 8–20.

Schaie, K. W., & Parham, I. A. (1976). Stability of adult personality traits: Fact or fable? *Journal of Personality and Social Psychology, 34,* 146–158.

Schaie, K. W., Willis, S. L., & Caskie, G. I. L. (2004). The Seattle Longitudinal Study: Relation between personality and cognition. *Aging, Neuropsychology, and Cognition, 11,* 304–324.

Schaie, K. W., Willis, S. L., Jay, G., & Chipuer, H. (1989). Structural invariance of cognitive abilities across the adult life span: A cross-sectional study. *Developmental Psychology, 25,* 652–662.

Schmeck, K., Goth, K., Poustka, F., & Cloninger, R. C. (2001). Reliability and validity of the Junior Temperament and Character Inventory. *International Journal of Methods in Psychiatric Research, 10,* 172–182.

Sher, K. J., Wood, M. D., Crews, T. M., & Vandiver, P. A. (1995). The Tridimensional Personality Questionnaire: Reliability and validity studies and derivation of a short form. *Psychological Assessment, 7,* 195–208.

Small, B. J., Hertzog, C., Hultsch, D. F., & Dixon, R. A. (2003). Stability and change in adult personality over 6 years: Findings from the Victoria longitudinal study. *The Journals of Gerontology: Series B. Psychological Sciences and Social Sciences, 58,* P166–P176.

Steiger, J. H. (1990). Structural model evaluation and modification: An interval estimation approach. *Multivariate Behavioral Research, 25,* 173–180.

Suhara, T., Yasuno, F., Sudo, Y., Yamamoto, M., Inoue, M., Okubo, Y., et al. (2001). Dopamine D2 receptors in the insular cortex and the personality trait of novelty seeking. *Neuroimage, 13,* 891–895.

Svrakic, D. M., Whitehead, C., Przybeck, T. R., & Cloninger, C. R. (1993). Differential diagnosis of personality disorders by the seven-factor model of temperament and character. *Archives of General Psychiatry, 50,* 991–999.

Thurstone, L. L. (1947). *Multiple factor analysis.* Chicago: University of Chicago Press.

Tomita, T., Aoyama, H., Kitamura, T. Sekiguchi, C., Murai, T., & Matsuda, T. (2000). Factor structure of psychobiological seven-factor model of personality: A model revision. *Personality and Individual Differences, 29,* 709–727.

Vandenberg, R. J., & Lance, C. E. (2000). A review and synthesis of the measurement invariance literature: Suggestions, practices, and recommendations for organizational research. *Organizational Research Methods, 2,* 4–69.

Vassend, O., & Skrondal, A. (1995). Factor analytic studies of the NEO Personality Inventory and the five-factor model: The problem of high structural complexity and conceptual indeterminacy. *Personality and Individual Differences, 19,* 135–147.

Vassend, O., & Skrondal, A. (1997). Validation of the NEO Personality Inventory and the five-factor model: Can findings from exploratory and confirmatory factor analysis be reconciled? *European Journal of Personality, 11,* 147–166.

Waller, N. G., Lilienfeld, S. O., Tellegen, A., & Lykken, D. T. (1991). The Tridimensional Personality Questionnaire: Structural validity and comparison with the Multidimensional Personality Questionnaire. *Multivariate Behavioral Research, 26,* 1–23.

5

Convergence Between Cross-Sectional and Longitudinal Studies: Cohort Matters

Elizabeth M. Zelinski, Robert F. Kennison, Amber Watts, and Kayan L. Lewis

Although there are many more longitudinal studies of aging today than in the recent past, they remain relatively rare. An examination of research papers published in *Psychology and Aging* in 2006 indicates that about 5% of the articles were based on longitudinal designs. Thus, most of what we know about change in aging is still based on cross-sectional studies, which are subject to cohort differences that may inflate estimates (e.g., Hofer, Berg, & Era, 2003; Sliwinski, Hofer, & Hall, 2003). Longitudinal studies, of course, directly measure change, but age effects may be underestimated because of selection, attrition, and retest. However, the use of statistical methods that circumvent these problems has become the norm in longitudinal analyses. For example, with use of the maximum likelihood algorithm in model estimation and inclusion of data from all available cases (see Hertzog & Nesselroade, 2003), an increasing number of longitudinal studies confirm findings of age changes with retest-only samples (e.g., Ghisletta & Lindenberger, 2003). Yet, by including participants from widely differing ages and therefore birth cohorts, these studies may violate the convergence assumption (Hertzog & Nesselroade, 2003; McArdle & Bell, 2000), which posits that results of cross-sectional and longitudinal analyses are similar and therefore can be combined. Thus, even longitudinal studies may produce magnified estimates of age change if they ignore cohort differences (e.g., McArdle, Ferrer-Caja, Hamagami, & Woodcock, 2002).

In this chapter, we use data from the Long Beach Longitudinal Study (LBLS) to examine two requirements of convergence: that data are metrically invariant (McArdle & Bell, 2000; see also Nesselroade & Estabrook, chap. 2, this volume) and that there are no attrition, practice, or cohort effects that may affect outcomes across designs (Hertzog & Nesselroade, 2003). First, we evaluate the effects of attrition, dropout, and retest on the invariance of covariance

The Long Beach Longitudinal Study is an ongoing study conducted at the Andrus Gerontology Center, University of Southern California, funded by National Institute on Aging Grants R01 AG10569 and T32 AG00156.

structures. Second, we test the effects of cohort and age at the level of means on cognitive change and on participation in activities that are likely to increase mental and physical fitness.

Long Beach Longitudinal Study

We begin by describing the LBLS. The timeline, sample sizes, and data collection plan are shown in Figure 5.1. The LBLS was started by K. Warner Schaie in 1978. His goal at the time was to obtain normative data for the Schaie-Thurstone Adult Mental Abilities Test (STAMAT; Schaie, 1985) from a sample of 65 adults ages 28 to 33 and 518 ages 55 to 84 that was independent of the Seattle Longitudinal Study (SLS; Schaie, 2006). Besides the STAMAT, a 20-item list of common English nouns for a free recall test and a brief essay for a text recall test were administered. Follow-ups are designated in Figure 5.1 by an arrow between the boxes representing the panel and sample size at each occasion. The figure shows that 264 individuals repeated these tasks 3 years later (Zelinski, Gilewski, & Schaie, 1993).

In 1994–1995, Zelinski extended the study by retesting 106 participants from the original sample, 13 years after the 1981 retest (Zelinski & Burnight, 1997; Zelinski & Stewart, 1998), indicated in Figure 5.1 by the break in the arrow between the second and third boxes. This first group, as shown in Figure 5.1, is referred to as Panel/Cohort 1 in this chapter. Zelinski also added a new panel of 630 participants ages 30 to 97 and included multiple indices of list recall, text recall, working memory, perceptual speed, and vocabulary for structural equation modeling. Assessments of language, autobiographical memory, personality, depression, health, health behaviors, and other measures were also incorporated into the LBLS (see Zelinski & Lewis, 2003). One third of the new sample, referred to as Panel/Cohort 2, included individuals over age 80. Three years later, 42 members of Panel/Cohort 1 and 352 members of Panel/Cohort 2

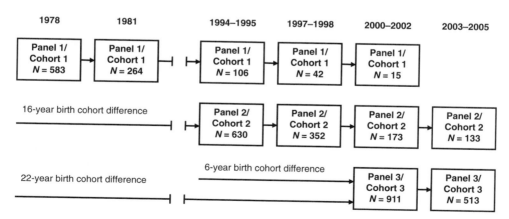

Figure 5.1. Testings and sample sizes of Long Beach Longitudinal Study panels. Some data from Zelinski, Gilewski, and Schaie (1993), Zelinski and Burnight (1997), and Zelinski and Lewis (2003).

were retested. In 2000–2002, 15 members of Panel/Cohort 1 and 173 members of Panel/Cohort 2 completed the 1994–1995 measures, as well as several tests extending the ability battery to indices of executive function. A third sample, Panel/Cohort 3, of 911 men and women ages 30 to 98, was recruited during the 2000–2002 time frame, again with about a third of the participants over the age of 80. Three years later, 133 members of Panel/Cohort 2 and 513 members of Panel/Cohort 3 were retested. The attrition rates are similar to those of SLS.

The guiding principle for the extensive and broad selection of measures for the LBLS is that cognitive aging is a largely contextual phenomenon. Individual differences in abilities and changes in those abilities over adulthood are associated not only with cognitive mechanisms but also with sociodemographic phenomena such as birth cohort, or gender, and within-individual characteristics, including health, affect, self-efficacy, personality, and other variables that impact health (see chap. 1, this volume). Clearly, the design and measurement approach of LBLS is very much inspired by SLS (Schaie, 2006). Indeed, besides the original ability measures used by Schaie, the Life Complexity Inventory (LCI; Gribbin, Schaie, & Parham, 1980) has been included in all testings. One of the many benefits of including these measures in this "second generation" study is that independent and direct comparisons can be made with SLS to replicate findings and to generalize across longitudinal samples.

Studies of Invariance

We have evaluated the question of convergence between cross-sectional and longitudinal findings with respect to the covariance structure of variables over age and time in LBLS (Lewis & Zelinski, 2008; Zelinski & Lewis, 2003). The developmental theory is that abilities are integrated, or highly correlated early in life, become more specialized in adolescence (Garrett, 1946), then neo-integrate or dedifferentiate in old age (Baltes, Cornelius, Spiro, Nesselroade, & Willis, 1980). Dedifferentiation would be predicted because age-related declines in abilities, reflecting reduced cognitive efficiency, would increase correlations (Deary, Egan, Gibson, Austin, Brand, & Kellaghan, 1996). Findings of dedifferentiation have been interpreted as suggesting that cognitive declines with age are due to a unitary process, such as slowing (Salthouse, 1996) or declines in neuromodulation (Li, 2002; see also Salthouse & Craik, 2000).

However, an evaluation of extant findings examining age changes and age differences in correlations between factors (Zelinski & Lewis, 2003) suggested that there was no evidence for a strong theory of dedifferentiation, which would predict that separate ability factors in adulthood would collapse into a single g factor (a general intelligence factor) in old age. Weaker models of dedifferentiation, suggesting increased factor variances and covariances in older adults, had some support. In the Zelinski and Lewis (2003) article, we observed that cross-sectional studies were more likely than longitudinal ones to produce evidence that factor variability and relationships increased with age. This suggests less than complete convergence across designs, perhaps because selection issues affect both types of designs (Horn & Donaldson, 1976), and attrition and retest may affect relationships between variables (e.g., Nesselroade, 1986).

Zelinski and Lewis (2003) examined age differences and changes in relationships between factors representing text and list recall, speed, working memory, and vocabulary. We compared three wide age ranges, with approximately 200 participants each, in multigroup covariance structure analyses with the 1994 data of Panel/Cohort 1 and Panel/Cohort 2; we combined the panels because test scores from those individuals participating in the 1994 testing did not vary either structurally or at the level of means. We evaluated measurement invariance in this study to test the dedifferentiation hypothesis.

Metric invariance, the equality or proportionality of the factor pattern matrices and factor loadings, indicates that the same construct is being measured at different times and with different people (Horn & McArdle, 1992; see also chap. 2, this volume). Configural invariance is observed when manifest variables load on the same factors across age, but the loadings vary in magnitude. Metric or configural invariance is required to assess whether differences in covariances or correlations between factors occur. Increases in factor covariances with age suggest weak dedifferentiation. Although theories of structural changes suggest that changes in factor covariances should be comprehensive with complete dedifferentiation across all factors (e.g., Reinert, 1970), partial changes, with some variances and covariances differing across age and time, can suggest nonunitary processes underlying age changes. For example, Hultsch, Hertzog, Dixon, and Small (1998) suggested that if age changes in speed cause changes in working memory, correlations among latent variables representing those constructs should increase. Relationships among latent variables that are less strongly related to the age changes in speed, such as vocabulary, should not.

Zelinski and Lewis (2003) found that their measurement model was metrically invariant, with identical parameters (Meredith & Horn, 2001) for cross-sectional factor loadings from people ages 30 to 64 and those ages 65 to 74. There were some differences in the loadings of the 75- to 97-year-olds, indicating configural invariance, with manifest variables loading on the same factors (Meredith & Horn, 2001). In subsequent analyses, the metric loadings for the two younger groups and the configural (freely estimated) loadings for the older group were used. Multiple group factor analyses using full information modeling compared the partially invariant measurement model across the three age groups in 1994–1995 with those retested in 1997–1998 with respect to relationships among the five factors and their variability. Another set of multiple group analyses across the three age groups compared only those who were retested at both occasions. Both sets of analyses indicated that identical factor variability and relationships did not degrade fit more than models allowing freely estimated parameters for the six groups. Thus, the only evidence for a cross-sectional difference was in the factor loadings for the old-old group. It is important to note, however, that not all loadings were larger in the oldest group; of 14 loadings, 6 were numerically larger, 7 were smaller, and 1 was the same. Although the longitudinal and cross-sectional findings were otherwise invariant, it could also be argued that a 3-year retest cannot capture the equivalent change implicit in the age ranges examined in this study. The lack of difference in factor relationships and variability across the cross-sectional age groups suggested that dedifferentiation may not be either as widespread or as substantial as claimed (e.g., Salthouse & Craik, 2000).

In the interest of replicating our findings, we analyzed more extensive longitudinal sequences and tested the hypothesis that cross-sectional data are more likely to show dedifferentiation because those who eventually drop out have more negative characteristics, including poorer performance, which would be reflected in greater variability and relationships between factors. The presence of near-term eventual dropouts could thus bias the structure of data in cross-sectional samples so that apparent dedifferentiation is observed for the entire group (Anstey, Hofer, & Luszcz, 2003a, 2003b). Lewis and Zelinski (2008) studied changes in relationships across latent variables up to four occasions and directly compared dropouts and retested individuals. This study examined a path model of list and text recall with predictors of latent speed, working memory, vocabulary, and age. The model was fit with the 1994–1995 data from the combined Panels/Cohorts 1 and 2, that is, from the same participants of the 2003 publication.

Results of the path analysis indicated that age was a significant covariate of speed, working memory, and vocabulary, and an independent predictor of list recall. Age was only an indirect predictor of text recall. Although both speed and working memory predicted vocabulary, they did not predict either latent recall variable. Finally, speed and working memory predicted list recall, but only working memory predicted text recall. These results suggested that there were independent predictors of each type of recall, following other work showing that different verbal memory tasks (cued recall, free recall, recognition) were represented by latent task-specific factors and predictors (e.g., Hedden, Lautenschlager, & Park, 2005). The findings also supported conclusions that speed does not account for all of the variance in list memory (e.g., Ferrer, Salthouse, McArdle, Stewart, & Schwartz, 2005; Salthouse, 2004), and, furthermore, that it was not directly related to text recall.

The next step was to test invariance of the factor relationships and their variability in the model. The parameter comparisons made with multigroup analyses are shown in Figure 5.2, using brackets to indicate the groups and data samples used in specific analyses. In the interest of replication, data from participants of Panel/Cohort 3 of LBLS were compared with those of the combined first two panels/cohorts with respect to the measurement model of Zelinski and Lewis (2003), with the comparison illustrated in section (a) of Figure 5.2. The models were metrically invariant across samples and did not differ in factor *SD*s and correlations. Full information modeling was subsequently used to compare the path model between first two times of measurement of the combined first two panels, and of the third panel, replicating the 3-year longitudinal analysis of the 2003 study with a new sample, seen in the comparisons in section (b) of Figure 5.2 and over the four times of measurement, that is, over 9 years, for Panels/Cohorts 1/2, seen in section (c) of Figure 5.2.

A second set of analyses examined invariance in the path model between dropouts and retested individuals at their respective Time 1 (Time 3 for Panel/Cohort 1) testing, comparing the Time 2 (Time 4 for Panel/Cohort 1) retested and Time 2 permanent dropout group for the combined Panels/Cohorts 1 and 2, and replicated with Panel 3. This is shown as (d) in Figure 5.2 and as (e) in Figure 5.2 over Times 1 and 2 (Times 3 and 4 for Panel/Cohort 1) for the Time 3 (Time 5 for Panel/Cohort 1) retested and Time 3 permanent dropout group of Panels/Cohorts 1/2.

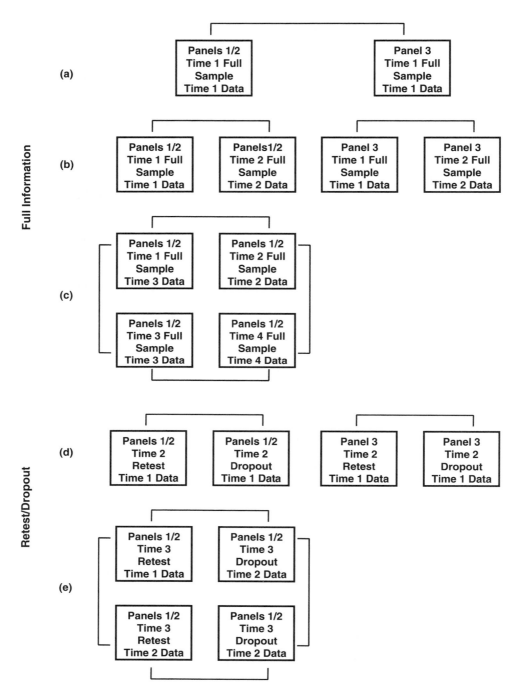

Figure 5.2. Comparisons for tests of invariance. Brackets indicate the groups whose parameters are compared in specific analyses. Comparisons (a), (b), and (c) used all available data, and (d) and (e) compared retest and dropout groups.

Results were remarkably uniform: The most stringent model of invariance held over all of the comparisons. There was little evidence of dedifferentiation for samples associated with attrition, dropout, or retest. This is contrary to the hypothesis that selection might affect relationships between variables (Nesselroade, 1986) and supports the observation that dropout may be linked to stable individual differences rather than to within-individual processes (e.g., Anstey et al., 2003a; Sliwinski & Buschke, 1999; Wilson et al., 2002).

These findings are consistent with the literature. When correlations of latent variables are tested for significant changes over age, generally less than 20% of the relationships tested are significantly larger over time or age, regardless of design or of conclusions regarding dedifferentiation (e.g., Anstey et al., 2003a; Hertzog & Bleckley, 2001; Hultsch et al., 1998; Schaie, Maitland, Willis, & Intrieri, 1998), though there are exceptions (e.g., de Frias, Lövdén, Lindenberger, & Nillson, 2007). Latent growth models have also been used to test correlations in slopes of change. Results thus far do not either confirm consistent or strong slope correlations in the direction of increasing relationships, suggesting no or weak dedifferentiation (e.g., Anstey et al., 2003b; Ferrer et al., 2005; Hertzog, Dixon, Hultsch, & MacDonald, 2003; Lövdén, Ghisletta, & Lindenberger, 2004; Wilson et al., 2002; Zimprich & Martin, 2002; see also chap. 3, this volume).

However, dynamic analyses evaluating leading-lagging relationships between variables suggest dedifferentiation of fluid and crystallized abilities in elderly adults (Ghisletta & de Ribaupierre, 2005; Ghisletta & Lindenberger, 2003). The few studies evaluating dynamic changes in abilities earlier in life do not support the predicted patterns that should occur from childhood to early adulthood (e.g., Ferrer & McArdle, 2004) or over the course of childhood into late adulthood (McArdle, Hamagami, Meredith, & Bradway, 2000). It is thus difficult to interpret the aging findings within a life-span developmental framework at this time.

The studies of invariance with LBLS support the convergence assumption at the structural level because findings with cross-sectional full information samples did not differ from those of the longitudinal samples. An increasing number of studies making similar comparisons confirm these findings (e.g., Australian Longitudinal Study of Aging [ALSA], Anstey et al. 2003b; Berlin Aging Study [BASE], Ghisletta & Lindenberger, 2003). Like the LBLS, these studies involve longitudinal intervals that are substantially shorter than the age ranges studied. For example, the age span in the Berlin Aging Study is 34 years and for ALSA it is 38 years, whereas the maximum longitudinal interval for both studies is 8 years. Studies have not systematically evaluated cohort differences, which may affect correlational relationships, as they do means, and this is undoubtedly due to the scarcity of longitudinal studies with sufficient data for cohort-sequential analyses.

Cohort and Ability

Cohort effects have been ignored in the vast majority of studies that make inferences about age changes at the level of means (e.g., Salthouse, 2004; see also chap. 1, this volume). Yet increases of 1.5 *SD* in reasoning for 19-year-olds tested in 1950 and 1980 indicate substantial improvements in intellectual ability between people born in 1931 and those born in 1951 (Flynn, 1987). Although the Flynn effect, at first blush, appears to be a relatively recent development, the SLS has demonstrated cohort improvements in people born in 1910 compared with those born in 1896 (e.g., Schaie, 2006). It is quite likely that cohort differences in abilities have arisen over the past 100 years. The apparent dramatic rise in fluid intelligence reported by Flynn is probably an epiphenomenon associated with the sampling of the ability measurements—that is, cohort change is incremental and cumulative (see also Flynn, 2003; Raven, 2000). This has major implications for the assumption of cross-sectional studies that the baseline level of abilities in adults of widely different ages is equivalent. However, positive cohort changes have not been ubiquitous (Schaie, 2006; see also chap. 1, this volume). For example, relatively small cohort improvements have been observed in crystallized abilities (e.g., Raven, 2000).

Both the increase in fluid abilities and the relative stability of crystallized ones over cohorts suggest that cultural environments drive differential cohort-specific changes in intellectual abilities. It has been suggested that the transformation toward a more highly educated, urban population in the first half of the 20th century (e.g., Williams, 1998), and the conversion from verbal to visual processing modes in the second half (e.g., Greenfield, 1998; also see later in this chapter) drove some of the increase in reasoning. Over the last few decades, educational practices in mathematics curricula have moved toward training more fluid-like abilities that improve working memory capacity and frontal functioning (Blair, Gamson, Thorne, & Baker, 2005). This may generalize to performance on ability tests.

Other changes in the cultural milieu have had less positive results for ability scores. One explanation for the relative stability in vocabulary is the historical shift from the practice of reading literature, which promotes knowledge of an advanced lexicon and complex decontextualized grammatical forms, to that of watching movies and television, which are more visual, contextual media. This shift promotes development of basic vocabulary and contextualized grammatical structures (e.g., Greenfield, 1998). More recently born cohorts show greater improvements in basic than advanced vocabulary (Bowles, Grimm, & McArdle, 2005), supporting Greenfield's account.

Because transformations in the intellectual environment have occurred over many decades, cohort effects may account for some of the age differences observed in cross-sectional cognitive-aging studies, but the size and direction of those effects may vary with the type of ability studied (Schaie, 2006).

Zelinski and Kennison (2007) tested hypotheses of age and cohort differences in patterns of cognitive aging in LBLS in a sequential design. We examined the longitudinal performance of individuals whose baseline ages were 55 to 82. We compared performance between Panel/Cohort 1 and Panel/Cohort 2, organizing the data with a time lag approach, so that the age at the first evaluation (1978 or 1994) was equivalent for both groups, although participants in the first panel/cohort were born about 16 years earlier than those of the second, as shown in Figure 5.1. The members of Panel/Cohort 1 were born between 1893 and 1923, and those of Panel/Cohort 2 were born between 1908 and 1940. Overlapping birth years were not confounded because of the time lag between panels/cohorts. Data were structured over age. This reduced estimation problems resulting from the 13-year retest interval for Panel/Cohort 1 between their second and third testing. All other retest intervals were approximately 3 years. It was expected that the relative size of panel/cohort effects would vary, with larger effects for reasoning, list and text recall, and space—the more fluid-like abilities—and with smaller ones for vocabulary—a more crystallized-like ability.

To facilitate comparison of age and cohort effects on the five abilities, data were Rasch scaled to score ranges of 0 to 100. Rasch scaling recalibrates data to intervals, meets the assumptions of interval level scaling for multivariate modeling, and makes it possible to make direct contrasts across variables (see Zelinski & Gilewski, 2003; Zelinski & Kennison, 2007).

Latent growth models (McArdle & Bell, 2000) were fit to the data, which were configured to 3-year age "buckets" to increase the number of observations for the ages studied (e.g., Bowles et al., 2005). Covariates of attrition in LBLS, including baseline age, cohort, gender, and education, were evaluated prior to modeling, following recommendations that inclusion of predictors of dropout in full information, maximum-likelihood analysis reduces selection bias by adjusting age estimates (e.g., Kennison & Zelinski, 2005). However, the only independent predictors were baseline age and cohort membership, which were directly modeled. Two-piece linear growth functions were estimated. The knot point was centered at age 74, with one linear function representing the young-old age range, with ages below 74, and the other, the old-old range, with ages above 74. This roughly corresponded to the young-old/old-old age distinction of Neugarten (1975). The age parameters represented 6-year effects because other possible scalings of age did not produce uniformly identifiable solutions across analyses of the five measures.

The magnitude of age declines, seen as ds in Table 5.1, varied among tasks over the ages of 56 to 74, with the largest 6-year effects for reasoning, followed by list recall. Smaller significant declines were observed for text recall, space, and vocabulary. Declines were larger after age 74, with reasoning and vocabulary showing significantly greater declines than list and text recall and space. The STAMAT vocabulary test, used in this analysis, has a strong speed component (e.g., Hertzog, 1989), and longitudinal speed declines probably account for much of the old-old decline on vocabulary.

Average 16-year birth cohort effects at the intercept of age 74 indicated that effect sizes varied by task: They were moderate for list recall and reasoning with d = .42 and .33, respectively; smaller for space (.29) and text recall (.19); and almost 0 for vocabulary (.03). These values, except for vocabulary, com-

Table 5.1. Six-Year Age Effect Sizes (d) With and Without Effects of Cohort

Ability test	Without cohort		With cohort	
	Young-old	Old-old	Young-old	Old-old
Reasoning	.45	.71	.37	.49
List recall	.43	.38	.30	.11
Text recall	.50	.41	.34	.12
Space	.50	.65	.38	.42
Vocabulary	.25	.51	.12	.43

Note. Data from Zelinski and Kennison (2007).

pared favorably with the effect sizes estimated for 14-year cohort improvements for the same variables and birth cohorts evaluated by Schaie (2006). List recall had significantly larger panel/cohort effects than any other task, and reasoning, in turn, had significantly larger effects than the remaining three tasks, which did not differ from one another. Thus, as predicted, cohort differences varied across measures, with larger increases for the more fluid-like measures than the crystallized-like one.

Including cohort in the latent growth model reduced the observed age d values seen in Table 5.1 from 20% to 52% for the young-old, and from 18% to 71% for the old-old. Although cohort was a significant covariate for those tests traditionally showing large age differences, it did not eliminate all of the age effects, as proposed elsewhere (e.g., Raven, 2000). Only 3 of the 10 age slopes in this study, that is, vocabulary for the young-old, and list and text recall for the old-old, did not differ from 0 as a result of including cohort in the analyses.

This study was the first to quantify relative cohort differences across fluid-like and crystallized-like tasks in older adults that parallel the conclusions for children and young adults (e.g., Flynn, 2003). The effects of cohort on list recall were the largest of all observed, and this suggests that estimates of recall from cross-sectional studies may be more affected by cohort than other abilities. Reasoning scores were also affected by cohort and by the other tests to a lesser degree. Thus, the convergence assumption may be differentially violated depending on the measures studied. This study compared those born from before the turn of the 20th century through the early 1920s with those born between the 1st decade of the 20th century through the beginning of World War II. Flynn's (1987) earlier-born cohort samples were of individuals born within the Panel/Cohort 2 birth period, so his findings are for the comparison of the pre–World War II generation with the postwar cohort, who are believed to have experienced a more intellectually stimulating environment than previous generations. It is possible that size and therefore impact of cohort effects may be greater for cohorts born subsequent to the ones we tested.

If the hypothesis of cultural reinforcement of abilities is correct, differential patterns in cohort effects on abilities may not be restricted to the 20th century. Depending on what cognitive processes are reinforced, cohort differences for some abilities may increase, decrease, or become asymptote. This implies that continual cohort sequential evaluations are necessary to separate age from cohort effects to inform the validity of the convergence assumption.

Cohort and Activities

Moving from studies of abilities to those of leisure activities, we examined the role of age changes and cohort differences in activity participation. Longitudinal analyses of older adult samples suggest that there are declines of both mental and physical fitness activities (e.g., Hultsch, Hertzog, Small, & Dixon, 1999), although Schaie (2006) reported no 7-year declines in retest-only SLS participants. No studies, to our knowledge, have considered whether age-matched cohorts born nearly a generation apart have different longitudinal activity trajectories.

Like abilities, there is good reason to assume that there are cohort differences in mental and physical fitness activity in older adults. Agahi and Parker

(2005) found 10-year time-lag increases in activity participation. Verbrugge, Gruber-Baldini, and Fozard (1996) observed increases from the 1960s to the 1990s and longitudinal age declines in the Baltimore Longitudinal Study of Aging in physical fitness activities. The most obvious explanation for cohort increases in leisure participation is a decrease in required hours of work time over the past century (e.g., Verbrugge et al., 1996). The introduction of new technologies has not only decreased the amount of time spent in domestic duties but also has provided new sources of education, communication, and leisure entertainment. Acceptance of older adulthood in recent decades as a more active phase of life and of personal responsibility for maintaining health and well-being has also become more prevalent (Lalive D'Epinay, Maystre, & Bickel, 2002).

Using responses to the Life Complexity Inventory (LCI; Gribbin et al., 1980), we focused on items associated with mental and physical fitness pursuits. After eliminating items with very low prevalence of responses and low intercorrelations, we selected a set of items likely to reflect mental and physical fitness activity factors for further analysis.

In the LCI, participants are asked to estimate the number of hours per week spent engaging in a list of activities. The open-ended responses can be quite variable, are likely to produce differential findings in working and retired individuals, and are censored because there are a limited number of hours per week. To eliminate measurement issues associated with the estimation of hours spent in specific activities, responses were converted to binary (categorical) scales. Thus, if a person had indicated any amount of time spent on a particular activity, that response was scored as a 1; a zero or no response was coded as 0. If the activity section of the questionnaire had not been filled out at all, it was treated as missing for that individual. The left side of Table 5.2

Table 5.2. Means, Thresholds, and Factor Loadings of Mental and Physical Fitness Activities

Activity factor	Mean/ proportion[a] (SD)		Threshold	SE	Loadings	SE
Factor	Panel/ Cohort 1	Panel/ Cohort 2	Invariant over panels/cohorts			
Baseline N	399	521				
Mental fitness						
Educational	.28 (.45)	.42 (.49)	0.94	.16	= 1	0
Cultural	.30 (.46)	.41 (.49)	0.88	.13	0.89	3.96
Going out to movies	.12 (.32)	.31 (.47)	1.28	.11	0.31	3.06
Self-improvement	.28 (.45)	.39 (.49)	0.87	.10	0.62	4.44
Volunteering	.32 (.47)	.41 (.49)	0.62	.08	0.39	3.98
Writing/correspondence	.59 (.49)	.68 (.47)	−0.22	.07	0.30	3.20
Physical fitness						
Fitness	.40 (.49)	.60 (.49)	0.43	.11	= 1	0
Participant sports	.28 (.45)	.24 (.43)	0.69	.08	0.31	2.99
Walking	.67 (.47)	.81 (.40)	0.47	.09	0.80	3.46
Outdoor hobbies	.38 (.49)	.50 (.50)	0.35	.07	0.46	3.62

[a]Means also represent the proportion of people reporting any participation in the activity because of categorical (0,1) coding.

shows the items analyzed. One item not in the table (reading) had been elimi-
nated from further analyses because 100% of the responses were 1, making it
uninformative.

The 10 items in Table 5.2 were hypothesized to represent two factors of
mental and physical fitness activities and analyzed with categorical factor
analysis, using the Mplus 4.2 program (Muthén & Muthén, 2006). All models
used the specifications described next. The estimation algorithm was a robust
weighted-least squares method, coded in Mplus as weighted least squares means
and variance (WLSMV). This estimator is impervious to sample size, normality
of latent response distribution, and model complexity (Flora & Curran, 2004).
This algorithm also computes a variance-adjusted χ^2 test statistic that uses a
full weight matrix. This statistic has been shown to be accurately distributed
as chi-square, with degrees of freedom estimated from both the data and the
model specification (see Flora & Curran, 2004; Muthén & Muthén, 2006). The
theta parameterization option of Mplus was used because of its relevance to
invariance studies for ordered-categorical data (see Milsap & Yun-Tein, 2004).
We proceeded with the time lag data organized as in the Zelinski and Kennison
(2007) study, that is, with the age range of 55 to 82 and 16-year cohorts defined
as Panels/Cohorts 1 and 2 of LBLS. The baseline analysis included responses
from Panel/Cohort 1 at Time 1 (1978).

The one-factor solution had a reasonable fit, with χ^2 (29, $N = 399$) = 55, root
mean square error of approximation (RMSEA) = .048, and comparative fit
index (CFI) = .931. However, a two-factor solution with correlated mental and
physical fitness activity factors was a significant improvement in fit, χ^2 (28,
$N = 399$) = 39, RMSEA = .031, and ΔCFI = .040, with the variance-adjusted
$\Delta\chi^2 = 13$, $\Delta df = 1$. Invariance testing of the model between Panels/Cohorts 1 and
2 at their respective Time 1 data collection then proceeded, following the principles for multiple group analyses of ordered-categorical measures proposed by
Milsap and Yun-Tein (2004) and for longitudinal analyses by Meredith and
Horn (2001). All analyses constrained the thresholds of manifest items to be
identical across all groupings. To test a configural model with equal factor patterns across cohorts, constraints for ordered-categorical analyses not used in
common-factor models were required for identification of the congeneric (simple
structure) two-factor model. These included a reference variable for each factor
with a loading fixed at 1, and its unique variance also set at 1. The remaining factor loadings and uniquenesses were free across groups. This model fit well, with
χ^2 (58, $N = 399$, Panel/Cohort 1; 521, Panel/Cohort 2) = 86, RMSEA = .033, and
CFI = .965.

The test of metrically invariant loadings involved constraining the loadings of both panels/cohorts as identical, leaving uniquenesses free. The model
was a good fit, with χ^2 (60, $N = 399$, Panel/Cohort 1; 521, Panel/Cohort 2) = 90,
ΔRMSEA = .000, and ΔCFI = .003, and the variance-adjusted $\Delta\chi^2 = 8$, $\Delta df = 1$.
The panel/cohort-invariant thresholds and factor loadings and their respective
SEs are shown in the right columns of Table 5.2. The 3-year invariance of the
Time 1/Time 2 models was tested within panels/cohorts for replication. In both
cohorts, metric invariance was observed, with no significant loss of fit over their
respective configural models, with χ^2 (57, $N = 399$, Time 1; 274, Time 2) = 100,
RMSEA = .047, and ΔCFI = −.004, and the variance-adjusted $\Delta\chi^2 = 10$, $\Delta df = 5$, for

Panel/Cohort 1, and χ^2 (59, $N = 521$, Time 1; 340, Time 2) = 86, RMSEA = .033, and ΔCFI = .003, and the variance-adjusted $\Delta\chi^2 = 5$, $\Delta df = 5$, for Panel/Cohort 2. Thus, the two activity factors were shown to be metrically invariant across panels and over two testings.

Items for each of the activity scores were then scaled into 0 to 100 Rasch scores over panels and all test occasions for comparison of age and cohort effects in the longitudinal analyses. A multilevel approach was used to model cohort differences over age on each activity factor using the full information maximum likelihood algorithm. The unconditional analyses, with no covariates, were used to establish the age basis functions. The intercept for all models was set at age 71.7, the mean age of the sample. The model for mental fitness activities showed no systematic improvement in fit with either linear, quadratic, or two-piece linear effects relative to a model representing level effects only. However, Table 5.3 shows that linear effects were significantly different from 0 in the unconditional model, with decreases over age in mental fitness activities, and so the linear model was selected for further analysis despite its being less parsimonious. A quadratic model fit best for physical activities, with significant linear and quadratic age declines in participation. The linear model for mental fitness scores and the quadratic one for physical fitness scores, respectively, tested cohort effects.

The numerical results for the unconditional and conditional models are shown in Table 5.2. There was no effect of cohort at the intercept for mental fitness activities. However, there was a significant negative interaction of cohort and the linear effect, suggesting that Panel/Cohort 1 declined more steeply in participation. These results are depicted in the left panel of Figure 5.3. The age declines reported here confirm other studies of longitudinal reductions in cognitively challenging activities (e.g., Hultsch et al., 1999). These findings differ

Table 5.3. Unconditional and Conditional Growth Coefficients and Standard Errors in Longitudinal Analyses of Activities

Parameters	Mental fitness		Physical fitness	
	Unconditional	Conditional	Unconditional	Conditional
	Age effect			
Level[a]	36.69 (0.77)	36.82 (0.77)	40.57 (0.93)	40.51 (0.94)
Linear	−0.19 (0.08)	−0.17 (0.08)	−0.40 (0.08)	−0.38 (0.09)
Quadratic	—	—	−0.06 (0.02)	−0.05 (0.02)
	Cohort effect			
Level	—	−0.09 (0.39)	—	1.13 (0.47)
Linear	—	−0.08 (0.04)	—	−0.08 (0.05)
Quadratic	—	—	—	−0.02 (0.01)
	Variance components			
Level	327.24 (27.20)	323.73 (27.00)	242.62 (33.12)	241.94 (33.20)
Linear	0.10 (0.23)	0.09 (0.24)	0.95 (0.55)	0.94 (0.55)
Quadratic	—	—	0.01 (0.01)	0.00 (0.01)
Error	308.57 (19.7)	306.56 (19.61)	359.56 (21.51)	357.49 (21.42)

Note. Standard errors are listed in parentheses.
[a]The intercept at age 71.7.

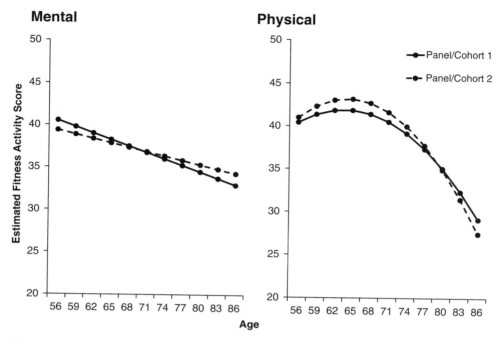

Figure 5.3.   Estimated fitness activity scores over age by panel/cohort. The intercept is at age 71.7.

from those of SLS, in which no 7-year longitudinal changes in a retest-only sample were detected for an educational/cultural measure that includes three of the items used in our mental fitness factor. However, because our analyses were full information, and the items differed, the longitudinal effects are not directly comparable.

Despite no cohort differences at the intercept, the interaction of cohort with linear decline is intriguing. On the one hand, the result might suggest that recent emphases on the importance of mentally stimulating activities in old age or continuing increases in the intellectual stimulation of the environment have enhanced participation in the more recent cohort. On the other hand, the interaction may not be significant if different intercepts are tested.

For physical fitness activities, results were somewhat different. There were significant effects at the intercept, with Panel/Cohort 2 members at age 71.7 more likely to report participation. The right panel of Figure 5.3 shows the estimated scores over age for each panel/cohort. Like the Victoria Longitudinal Study (Hultsch et al., 1999) participation in physical fitness activities did show effects of age that indicated increasing and accelerating declines. There were also cohort effects in favor of the more recently born cohort (e.g., Verbrugge et al., 1996).

Taken together, our findings suggest that there may be differential effects of cohort on the two activities studied. In the analyses of activities, we were able to compare results relevant to the question of whether convergence is more likely to occur at the level of the covariance structure or of the means of variables.

We did find that the two cohorts studied did not differ in structure, but did differ in means. Unfortunately, latent variable analyses could not be used on the abilities tested by Zelinski and Kennison (2007), as only one indicator per ability was measured for Panel/Cohort 1 at Time 1, so the generality of cohort-invariant factors is unknown for our cognitive measures.

Summary and Conclusions

Findings from LBLS suggest that convergence may hold for structural comparisons, that is, of the relationships between latent variables and their variability (see also Hertzog & Nesselroade, 2003), though this conclusion may be premature because cohort differences in abilities have not been evaluated at the structural level. At the level of means, direct comparisons of cohort differences indicate that cohort does matter—even over slightly less than a generation, we observed differences in mean levels of performance and activity participation in individuals matched on age, and those differences varied with the measure used. We have demonstrated that cohort effects do not exist only in abilities; we have also found them in participation in activities in the same samples. In both cases, the differences vary in size. Thus, convergence may be violated both within and between different classes of measures.

The majority of the studies investigating the relationships between age and abilities and age and activity participation have not had the data to test cohort or generational effects or possible differential longitudinal changes in cohorts. Yet cohort effects are not only important for current models of age changes, they are a moving target for future studies. With the baby boom generation at the cusp of old age, we argue that it is critical to assess cohort effects in this group, which has enjoyed unprecedented levels of education, health, and prosperity. However, we do not assume that cohort effects will be uniformly positive (e.g., Schaie, 2006, see also chap. 1, this volume) or historically consistent if cultural reinforcement of abilities and activities changes. They may also change with survival into very old age (see Zelinski & Kennison, 2007; chap. 1, this volume). Nevertheless, it is important that we develop models of aging within the larger context of these changes.

References

Agahi, N., & Parker, M. G. (2005). Are today's older people more active than their predecessors? Participation in leisure-time activities in Sweden in 1992 and 2002. *Ageing & Society, 25,* 925–941.

Anstey, K. J., Hofer, S. M., & Luszcz, M. A. (2003a). Cross-sectional and longitudinal patterns of dedifferentiation in late-life cognitive and sensory function: The effects of age, ability, attrition, and occasion of measurement. *Journal of Experimental Psychology: General, 132,* 470–487.

Anstey, K. J., Hofer, S. M., & Luszcz, M. A. (2003b). A latent growth curve analysis of late-life sensory and cognitive function over 8 years: Evidence for specific and common factors underlying change. *Psychology and Aging, 18,* 714–726.

Baltes, P. B., Cornelius, S. W., Spiro, A., Nesselroade, J. R., & Willis, S. (1980). Integration versus differentiation of fluid/crystallized intelligence in old age. *Developmental Psychology, 16,* 625–635.

Blair, C., Gamson, D., Thorne, S., & Baker, D. (2005). Rising mean IQ: Cognitive demand of mathematics education for young children, population exposure to formal schooling, and the neurobiology of the prefrontal cortex. *Intelligence, 33,* 93–106.

Bowles, R. P., Grimm, K. J., & McArdle, J. J. (2005). A structural factor analysis of vocabulary knowledge and relations to age. *The Journals of Gerontology: Series B. Psychological Sciences and Social Sciences, 60,* P234–P241.

Deary, I. J., Egan, V., Gibson, G. J., Austin, E. J., Brand, C. R., & Kellaghan, T. (1996). Intelligence and the differentiation hypothesis. *Intelligence, 23,* 105–132.

De Frias, C. M., Lövden, M., Lindenberger, U., & Nilsson, L.-G. (2007). Revisiting the dedifferentiation hypothesis with longitudinal multi-cohort data. *Intelligence, 35,* 381–392.

Ferrer, E., & McArdle, J. J. (2004). An experimental analysis of dynamic hypotheses about cognitive abilities and achievement from childhood to early adulthood. *Developmental Psychology, 40,* 935–952.

Ferrer, E., Salthouse, T. A., McArdle, J. J., Stewart, W. F., & Schwartz, B. S. (2005). Multivariate modeling of age and retest in longitudinal studies of cognitive abilities. *Psychology and Aging, 20,* 412–422.

Flora, D. B., & Curran, P. J. (2004). An empirical evaluation of alternative methods of estimation for confirmatory factor analysis with ordinal data. *Psychological Methods, 9,* 466–491.

Flynn, J. R. (1987). Massive IQ gains in 14 nations: What IQ tests really measure. *Psychological Bulletin, 101,* 171–191.

Flynn, J. R. (2003). Movies about intelligence: The limitations of *g. Psychological Science, 12,* 95–99.

Garrett, H. E. (1946). A developmental theory of intelligence. *American Psychologist, 1,* 372–378.

Ghisletta, P., & de Ribaupierre, A. (2005). A dynamic investigation of cognitive dedifferentiation with control for retest: Evidence from the Swiss Interdisciplinary Longitudinal Study on the oldest-old. *Psychology and Aging, 20,* 671–682.

Ghisletta, P., & Lindenberger, U. (2003). Age-based structural dynamics between perceptual speed and knowledge in the Berlin Aging Study: Direct evidence for ability dedifferentiation in old age. *Psychology and Aging, 18,* 696–713.

Gribbin, K., Schaie, K. W., & Parham, I. A. (1980). Complexity of lifestyle and maintenance of intellectual abilities. *Journal of Social Issues, 36,* 47–61.

Greenfield, P. M. (1998). The cultural evolution of IQ. In U. Neisser (Ed.), *The rising curve: Long-term gains in IQ and related measures* (pp. 81–123). Washington, DC: American Psychological Association.

Hedden, T., Lautenschlager, G., & Park, D. C. (2005). Contributions of processing ability and knowledge to verbal memory tasks across the adult life-span. *Quarterly Journal of Experimental Psychology, 58A,* 169–190.

Hertzog, C. (1989). Influences of cognitive slowing on age differences in intelligence. *Developmental Psychology, 25,* 636–651.

Hertzog, C., & Bleckley, M. K. (2001). Age differences in the structure of intelligence: Influences of information processing speed. *Intelligence, 29,* 191–217.

Hertzog, C., Dixon, R. A., Hultsch, D. F., & MacDonald, S. W. S. (2003). Latent change models of adult cognition: Are changes in processing speed and working memory associated with changes in episodic memory? *Psychology and Aging, 18,* 755–769.

Hertzog, C., & Nesselroade, J. R. (2003). Assessing psychological changes in adulthood: An overview of methodological issues. *Psychology and Aging, 18,* 639–657.

Hofer, S. M., Berg, S., & Era, P. (2003). Evaluating the interdependence of aging-related changes in visual and auditory acuity, balance, and cognitive functioning. *Psychology and Aging, 18,* 285–205.

Horn, J. L., & Donaldson, G. (1976). On the myth of intellectual decline in adulthood. *American Psychologist, 31,* 701–719.

Horn, J. L., & McArdle, J. J. (1992). A practical and theoretical guide to measurement invariance in aging research. *Experimental Aging Research, 18,* 117–144.

Hultsch, D. F., Hertzog, C., Dixon, R. A., & Small, B. J. (1998). *Memory change in the aged.* Cambridge, England: Cambridge University Press.

Hultsch, D. F., Hertzog, D., Small, B. J., & Dixon, R. A. (1999). Use it or lose it? Engaged lifestyle as a buffer of cognitive decline in aging. *Psychology and Aging, 14,* 245–263.

Kennison, R. F., & Zelinski, E. M. (2005). Estimating age change in 7-year list recall in AHEAD: The roles of independent predictors of missingness and dropout. *Psychology and Aging, 20,* 460–475.

Lalive D'Epinay, C. J., Maystre, C., & Bickel, J. (2002). Aging and cohort changes in sports and physical training from the golden decades onward: A cohort study in Switzerland. *Society & Leisure, 24,* 453–481.

Lewis, K. L., & Zelinski, E. M. (2008). *Effects of attrition and practice on resource models of list and text recall: A test of the dedifferentiation hypothesis.* Unpublished manuscript.

Li, S.-C. (2002). Connecting the many levels and facets of cognitive aging. *Current Directions in Psychological Science, 11,* 38–43.

Lövdén, M., Ghisletta, P., & Lindenberger, U. (2004). Cognition in the Berlin Aging Study (BASE): The first 10 years. *Aging, Neuropsychology and Cognition, 11,* 104–133.

McArdle, J. J., & Bell, R. Q. (2000). An introduction to latent growth models for developmental data analysis. In T. D. Little & K. U. Schnabel (Eds.), *Modeling longitudinal and multilevel data: Practical issues, applied approaches, and specific examples* (pp. 69–281). Mahwah, NJ: Erlbaum.

McArdle, J. J., Ferrer-Caja, E., Hamagami, F., & Woodcock, R. W. (2002). Comparative longitudinal structural analyses of the growth and decline of multiple intellectual abilities over the life span. *Developmental Psychology, 38,* 115–142.

McArdle, J. J., Hamagami, F., Meredith, W., & Bradway, K. P. (2000). Modeling the dynamic hypotheses of Gf-Gc theory using longitudinal life-span data. *Learning and Individual Differences, 12,* 53–79.

Meredith, W., & Horn, J. (2001). The role of factorial invariance in modeling growth and change. In L. M. Collins & A. G. Sayer (Eds.), *New methods for the analysis of change* (pp. 201–240). Washington, DC: American Psychological Association.

Milsap, R., & Yun-Tein, J. (2004). Assessing factorial invariance in ordered-categorical measures. *Multivariate Behavioral Research, 39,* 479–515.

Muthén, L. K., & Muthén, B. O. (2006). *Mplus user's guide* (Version 4.0) [Software]. Los Angeles: Author.

Nesselroade, J. R. (1986). Selection and generalization investigations of interrelationships among variables: Some commentary on aging research. *Educational Gerontology, 2,* 395–402.

Neugarten, B. L. (1975). The future and the young-old. *Gerontologist, 15,* 4–9.

Raven, J. (2000). The raven's progressive matrices: Change and stability over culture and time. *Cognitive Psychology, 41,* 1–48.

Reinert, G. (1970). Comparative factor analytic studies of intelligence throughout the human life span. In L. R. Goulet & P. B. Baltes (Eds.), *Life-span developmental psychology* (pp. 467–484). New York: Academic Press.

Salthouse T. A. (1996). The processing-speed theory of adult age differences in cognition. *Psychological Review, 103,* 403–428.

Salthouse, T. A. (2004). What and when of cognitive aging. *Current Directions in Psychological Science, 13,* 140–144.

Salthouse, T. A., & Craik, F. I. M. (2000). Closing comments. In F. I. M. Craik & T. A. Salthouse (Eds.), *The handbook of aging and cognition* (pp. 689–703). Mahwah, NJ: Erlbaum.

Schaie, K. W. (1985). Schaie-Thurstone Adult Mental Abilities Test. Palo Alto, CA: Consulting Psychologists Press.

Schaie, K. W. (2006). *Developmental influences on adult intelligence.* Oxford, England: Oxford University Press.

Schaie, K. W., Maitland, S. B., Willis, S. L., & Intrieri, R. C. (1998). Longitudinal invariance of adult psychometric ability factor structures across 7 years. *Psychology and Aging, 13,* 8–20.

Sliwinski, M., & Buschke, H. (1999). Cross-sectional and longitudinal relationships among age, cognition, and processing speed. *Psychology and Aging, 14,* 18–33.

Sliwinski, M. J., Hofer, S. M., & Hall, C. (2003). Correlated and coupled cognitive change in older adults with and without clinical dementia. *Psychology and Aging, 18,* 672–683.

Verbrugge, L. M., Gruber-Baldini, A. L., & Fozard, J. L. (1996). Age differences and age changes in activities: Baltimore Longitudinal Study of Aging. *The Journals of Gerontology: Series B. Psychological Sciences and Social Sciences, 51,* S30–S41.

Williams, W. M. (1998). Are we raising smarter children today? School- and home-related influences on IQ. In U. Neisser (Ed.), *The rising curve: Long-term gains in IQ and related measures* (pp. 125–154). Washington, DC: American Psychological Association.

Wilson, R. S., Beckett, L. A., Barnes, L. L., Schneider, J. A., Bach, J., Evans, D. A., et al. (2002). Individual differences in rates of change in cognitive abilities of older persons. *Psychology and Aging, 17,* 179–193.

Zelinski, E. M., & Burnight, K. P. (1997) Sixteen-year longitudinal and time-lag changes in memory and cognition in older adults. *Psychology and Aging, 12,* 503–523.

Zelinski, E. M., & Gilewski, M. J. (2003). Effects of demographic and health variables on Rasch scaled cognitive scores. *Journal of Aging and Health, 15,* 435–464.

Zelinski, E. M., Gilewski, M. J., & Schaie, K. W. (1993). Individual differences in cross-sectional and three-year longitudinal memory performance across the adult lifespan. *Psychology and Aging, 8,* 176–186.

Zelinski, E. M., & Kennison, R. F. (2007). Not your father's test scores: Cohort reduces psychometric aging effects. *Psychology and Aging, 22,* 546–557.

Zelinski, E. M., & Lewis, K. L. (2003). Adult age differences in multiple cognitive functions: differentiation, dedifferentiation, or process-specific change? *Psychology and Aging, 18,* 727–745.

Zelinski, E. M., & Stewart, S. (1998). Individual differences in 16-year memory changes. *Psychology and Aging, 13,* 622–630.

Zimprich, D., & Martin, M. (2002). Can longitudinal changes in processing speed explain longitudinal age changes in fluid intelligence? *Psychology and Aging, 17,* 690–695.

Part II

Cognitive, Social, and Psychological Development in Adulthood

6

How Those Who Have, Thrive: Mechanisms Underlying the Well-Being of the Advantaged in Later Life

Carmi Schooler and Leslie J. Caplan

The interconnections among sociological, psychological, and biological level phenomena seem to be such that "those who have" (i.e., those who are relatively advantaged psychologically and/or in their positions in their society's social structures) are likely to see their relative advantages increase over the life course, compared with "those who have not." In this chapter, we provide evidence supporting this assertion and describe a variety of processes by which the advantages of psychological and social privilege accrue over time.

Described at the most general level, the processes underlying the ways that "those who have" thrive seem simplistic. Over the life course, social advantages often lead to further social advantages; psychological advantages lead to further psychological advantages. Furthermore, social advantages often translate into psychological advantages; reciprocally, psychological advantages often lead to social advantages. Rarely does an initial psychological or sociological advantage lead to a psychological or sociological disadvantage (as occurred in the Chinese Cultural Revolution or the French Revolution). Since the positive effects of earlier advantages would seem to accumulate, and possibly multiply, over the life course, the differences between those whose histories tended to be characterized by relative advantage versus relative disadvantage would increase over time. Such differences would therefore be greatest late in life.

As noted, the underlying theory is simplistic; the devil is in the details. In this chapter, we try to provide some of these. Basing our discussion on both the research of our unit—the Section on Socioenvironmental Studies (SSES) of the National Institute on Mental Health Intramural Research Program—and other relevant empirical research, we describe some possible mechanisms that may underlie these social-structural disparities in well-being. These mechanisms include (a) some of the reciprocal causal processes through which initial differences in psychological functioning and social status increase over the

This chapter was coauthored by an employee of the United States government as part of official duty and is considered to be in the public domain. Any views expressed herein do not necessarily represent the views of the United States government, and the author's participation in the work is not meant to serve as an official endorsement.

life course; (b) some of the reciprocal interrelationships among social status, physical health, and psychological well-being that seem to lead to increased disparities over the life course; and (c) the causes and consequences of socioeconomic status-related (SES-related) beliefs about the degree of control over life circumstances.

Before discussing these substantive issues, we present a series of interlocking definitions that, taken together, represent a working conceptualization of social structure. We do so because social structure, an aspect of reality that is often overlooked in psychological research (Schooler, 2007), plays a central role in our hypotheses and conclusions. These definitions are adaptations of, and extrapolations from, the noted sociologist Robert Merton's (1957) general schema and are well within the mainstream of sociological thought (for an extended theoretical discussion, see Schooler, 1994):

- *Status:* A position in a social system occupied by designated actors (i.e., individuals or social organizations) that consists of a set of roles that define the incumbents' expected patterns of interrelationships with incumbents of related statuses.

  Statuses may be ranked hierarchically in terms of the interrelated concepts of (a) prestige, (b) unequal distribution of relatively scarce social resources and unequal opportunity for acquiring them, and (c) *power*—the ability to induce others to fulfill one's goals.

  When statuses are considered in terms of such a hierarchical perspective, the term *social status* is frequently used (social status is particularly difficult to assess in retired people). When the emphasis is on (b)—for example, the unequal distribution of resources—the term *socioeconomic status* (SES) is frequently used.
- *Social class:* Often used almost interchangeably with the term *social status.*

  Most sociologists who deal with stratification, however, distinguish between the two. They reserve the use of the term *social class* to reflect the types of societal divisions envisaged by Marx. Thus, Kohn and Slomczynski (1990) described social classes as "groups defined in terms of their relationship to ownership and control over the *means of production* [italics added], and their control over the labor power of others" (p. 2). The definition is readily expanded to also include ownership and control over the *means of distribution.*
- *Social structure:* The patterned interrelationships among a set of individual and organizational statuses, as defined by the nature of their interacting roles.
- *Culture:* A historically determined set of *denotative* (what is), *normative* (what should be), and *stylistic* (how done) beliefs, shared by a group of individuals who have undergone a common historical experience and participate in an interrelated set of social structures.

  The definition could include the institutional, instrumental, and material embodiments of these beliefs.
- *Society or sociocultural system:* A set of persons and social positions that possesses both a culture and a social structure.

Research on Reciprocal Causal Processes Increasing Initial Psychological and Social Status Differences

In an earlier article, part of the Penn State Conference series on Social Structures and Aging (Schooler & Caplan, in press), we provided three examples from our own research of reciprocal causal processes that contribute to the increasing disparity over the life course between the initially relatively advantaged and unadvantaged. These examples involve the patterns of causal interconnections among (a) social status, occupational self-direction, and intellectual functioning; (b) social status, occupational self-direction, and self-directed orientations toward oneself and others; and (c) social status, intellectually demanding leisure time activities, and intellectual functioning. We review these findings here and also discuss the relationships between socioeconomic status, on the one hand, and the psychological characteristics of intellectual functioning and self-directed orientation, on the other.

Social Status, Occupational Self-Direction, and Intellectual Functioning

There is a fair amount of evidence demonstrating the existence of a correlation between older individuals' levels of intellectual functioning and the intellectual demandingness of the tasks they perform (for a review, see Mulatu & Schooler, 2007). The core problem is discerning the direction of causal effects that underlie this correlation. Any given correlation between relatively high levels of cognitive function and participation in a particular cognitively demanding activity can be, on the one hand, the result of dealing with the cognitive demands imposed by that activity. On the other hand, such a correlation may be the result of having characteristics that increase the likelihood of selecting, or being selected, to engage in and stay engaged that activity. At its most basic level, the question is how much of such a correlation is the result of the effect of the characteristics of the environment on the characteristics of the individual, and how much of the correlation is the result of the plausible reciprocal effect of the characteristics of the individual on the environment?

We deal with this issue by using reciprocal-effects structural equation modeling (for full discussions of our use of this method, see Schooler, Mulatu, & Oates, 1999, 2004). The data come from the 1974 and 1994 waves of the SSES longitudinal study. The sample of 706 respondents is essentially a representative sample of men who were working in civilian jobs in the United States in 1964, who were under 65 years of age in 1974, and their wives (for full descriptions of the sample, see Schooler, Mulatu, & Oates, 1999, 2004). The analyses are based on all of the respondents who were working in both 1974 and 1994. Figure 6.1 presents the results of an age-based, multigroup reciprocal-effects model depicting the positive reciprocal effects between Occupational Self-Direction (a status-related occupational characteristic that includes autonomy on the job and occupational complexity) and Intellectual Flexibility (a measure that correlates highly [$r = .87$] with a psychometrically derived measure indexing general cognitive functioning). The multigroup nature of the model permits us to ascertain

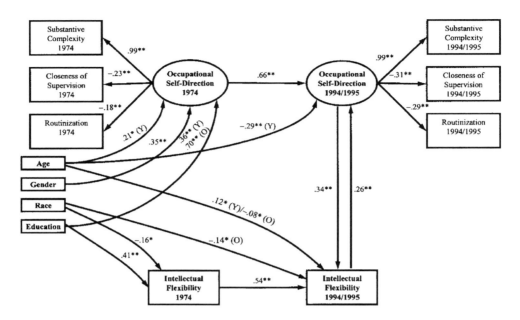

Figure 6.1. Multigroup reciprocal effects model of occupational self-direction and intellectual flexibility. Paths marked by Y or O show significant paths for the younger or older groups, respectively. χ^2 ($df = 83$, $N = 244$) = 75.83, $p = .699$; $\chi^2/df = .91$; comparative fit index = 1.00; root mean square error of approximation = .000. Adapted from "Effects of Occupational Self-Direction on the Intellectual Functioning and Self-Directed Orientations of Older Workers: Findings and Implications for Individuals and Societies," by C. Schooler, M. S. Mulatu, and G. Oates, 2004, *American Journal of Sociology, 110,* p. 187. In the public domain.
*$p < .05$. **$p < .01$.

that there is no significant difference between the effects of occupational self-direction on the older and effects on the younger half of the respondents (median age = 57 years; Schooler, Mulatu, & Oates, 2004). Indeed, earlier findings about the greater effects of substantively complex work on intellectual functioning in older adults compared with younger adults (Schooler, Mulatu, & Oates, 1999) suggest that, if anything, the intellectual functioning of older adults may be more positively affected by cognitively demanding environmental conditions than is the intellectual functioning of younger adults. The positive reciprocal relationship between Occupational Self-Direction and Intellectual Flexibility indicates that workers of lower social status are particularly likely to be caught in a negative loop. The relatively low status, non-self-directed jobs that they are likely to get, in part because of their relatively low levels of cognitive functioning (Farkas, England, Vicknair, & Kilbourne, 1997), are likely to lead to lower levels of intellectual functioning. These, in turn, lead to further decreases in the likelihood of their obtaining higher status jobs and thereby to a downward career spiral. The reverse is true for those who start out functioning relatively well intellectually; their work careers are relatively more likely to spiral upwards. Through these processes, initial cognitive and socioeconomic differences are intensified as people age throughout their work careers.

Social Status, Occupational Self-Direction, and Self-Directed Orientations Toward Oneself and Others

We have also described the reciprocal effects between occupational self-direction and self-directed orientation (a psychological characteristic reflecting beliefs in the importance of autonomy; Schooler, Mulatu, & Oates, 2004). Once again, the data come from the 1974 and 1994 waves of the SSES longitudinal study. The results, depicted in Figure 6.2, demonstrate the existence of at least moderate-sized reciprocal effects between Occupational Self-Direction and Self-Directed Psychological Orientation, thereby supporting the hypothesis that dealing with cognitively demanding complex environments increases the value placed on self-direction and autonomy (Schooler 1984, 1990). The findings also show that there is no significant difference between older and younger groups in the magnitude of these effects. In doing so, they support the hypothesis that the "lessons" people

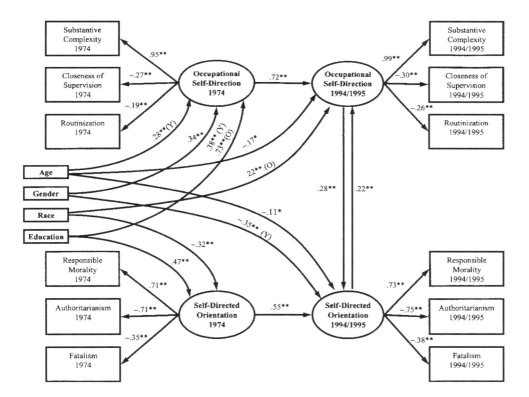

Figure 6.2. Multigroup reciprocal effects model of occupational self-direction and self-directed orientation. Paths marked by Y or O show significant paths for the younger or older groups, respectively. χ^2 (df = 188, N = 244) = 133.85, p = .999; χ^2/df = .71; comparative fit index = 1.00; root mean square error of approximation = .000. Adapted from "Effects of Occupational Self-Direction on the Intellectual Functioning and Self-Directed Orientations of Older Workers: Findings and Implications for Individuals and Societies," by C. Schooler, M. S. Mulatu, and G. Oates, 2004, *American Journal of Sociology, 110,* p. 185. In the public domain.
*p < .05. **p < .01.

learn from their work are unaffected by how old they are. As is the case for self-directed job conditions, intellectual flexibility and social status, the pattern of relationships among self-directed job conditions, self-directed orientations, and social status suggests the existence of a feedback loop that will, over time, magnify initial differences in all of these characteristics. Those in higher social status positions and from relatively higher social status backgrounds tend to have higher levels of self-directed orientations (e.g., Kohn & Schooler, 1983). Having such self-directed orientations, in turn, contributes to the likelihood that people will obtain relatively high status, self-directed jobs (Kohn & Schooler, 1983). Thus, through the perpetuation of this loop throughout their careers, people who early in life hold jobs likely to be linked to having self-directed orientations (e.g., high status jobs) are likely to have careers leading to jobs with increasingly higher social status and income; the reverse is likely to be true of people who hold jobs linked to having non-self-directed orientations early in life.

Social Status, Intellectually Demanding Leisure Time Activities, and Intellectual Functioning

We have reported similar positive reciprocal effects between cognitively demanding leisure time activities and intellectual functioning (Schooler & Mulatu, 2001). Figure 6.3 shows our latent Cognitive Leisure Activities Factor. The significant reciprocal effects between Intellectual Flexibility and Cognitive Leisure Activities are depicted in Figure 6.4. These reciprocal effects occur both among those working and not working and persist even when the effects of health, exercise, and work status are controlled. They are analogous to the reciprocal relationship between substantively complex self-directed work and intellectual functioning. Furthermore, the model reveals a significant path from SES to Intellectual Flexibility, even with earlier Intellectual Flexibility controlled. This indicates that Intellectual Flexibility leads to an increase in Cognitive Leisure

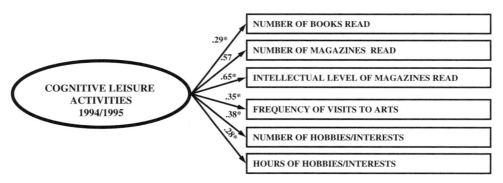

Figure 6.3. Measurement model of cognitive leisure activities from full-information model. Adapted from "The Reciprocal Effects of Leisure Time Activities and Intellectual Functioning in Older People: A Longitudinal Analysis," by C. Schooler and M. S. Mulatu, 2001, *Psychology and Aging, 16,* p. 472. In the public domain.
*$p < .001$.

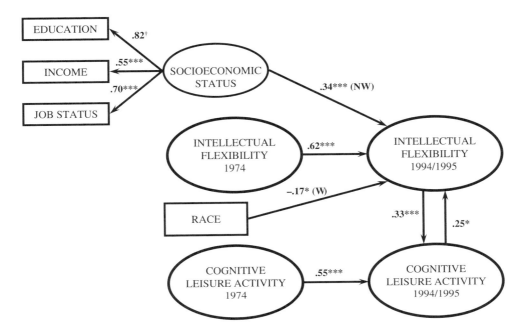

Figure 6.4.   Longitudinal (1974–1994) reciprocal effects model of cognitive leisure activity and intellectual flexibility (paths constrained to be equal for working and nonworking participants). † = reference variables whose ± values cannot be computed. Adapted from "The Reciprocal Effects of Leisure Time Activities and Intellectual Functioning in Older People: A Longitudinal Analysis," by C. Schooler and M. S. Mulatu, 2001, *Psychology and Aging, 16,* p. 473. In the public domain.
*p < .05. **p < .01. ***p < .001.

Activities. More important, it indicates that because SES directly affects Intellectual Flexibility, high SES indirectly increases the likelihood that individuals will engage in Cognitive Leisure Activities—and, in doing so, high SES increases the likelihood that they will benefit intellectually from such activity.

Direct Examination of the Relationship Between Psychological and Socioeconomic Characteristics

Each of the above examples provides evidence suggesting the general validity of our hypotheses about the cumulative advantages deriving from initially higher levels of social or psychological capital. Each example provides strong evidence for the proposition that differences between the initially advantaged and the disadvantaged (in terms either of psychological characteristics, such as intellectual functioning and self-directed values, and/or of social status) should increase over time.

To test this general hypothesis directly, we conducted several sets of analyses. In the first set, we used median splits to divide our sample into two halves, either on the basis of 1974 Intellectual Flexibility or 1974 Self-Directed Orientation. We then compared family incomes in 1974 with family incomes in 1994 (in estimated 1974 dollars, using logarithmic transformations of family income in thousands of dollars to normalize the distributions). We found that although income generally decreased over time throughout the sample, the decrease was less for individuals who were either high in Intellectual Flexibility (see Figure 6.5) or high in Self-Directed Orientation (see Figure 6.6). In a parallel set of analyses, we divided the sample in terms of their 1974 levels of income and examined whether the initial differences in Intellectual Flexibility and Self-Directed orientation increased over time. Although the results for Self-Directed Orientation exhibited the divergence we expected, the predicted pattern was not statistically significant for either psychological variable. Nevertheless, our findings do provide significant support for the relative increase, in the long term, of fiscal advantages related to earlier levels of intellectual functioning and self-directed values. In another set of analyses, we used a different measure of socioeconomic status. We created a latent variable, Financial Status 1994, whose indicators were family income, total assets, and whether the individual owned his or her own home. We then examined the effects of 1974 Intellectual Flexibility on 1994 Financial Status, while controlling for 1974 family income. Individuals who were higher in Intellectual Flexibility in 1974 (as determined by median split) had higher Financial Status 20 years later than those who had been lower in Intellectual Flexibility (see Table 6.1). We also conducted a

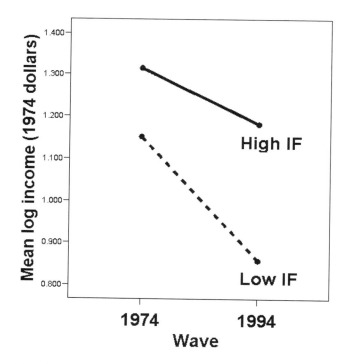

Figure 6.5.   Mean log (income) as a function of 1974 intellectual flexibility (IF). $p = .002$.

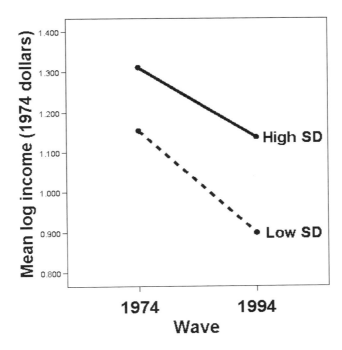

Figure 6.6. Mean log (income) as a function of 1974 self-directed (SD) orientation.
$p < .001$.

parallel analysis, comparing the Financial Status 1994 of people who were
either high or low in Self-Directed Orientation in 1974 (again determined by
median split), again controlling for family income in 1974. Similar to the previous results, individuals who were higher in Self-Directed in 1974 had higher
Financial Status in 1994 than those who had been lower in Self-Directed
Orientation (see Table 6.1). Although we have succeeded in demonstrating only

Table 6.1. Mean Financial Status 1994 Factor Scores (Net of 1974 Family Income)
as a Function of 1974 Self-Direction and 1974 Intellectual Flexibility

Factor	Financial status 1994 factor score
As a function of self-direction	
Self-direction	
High self-direction	.506
Low self-direction	−.469
(difference significant, $p < .01$)	
As a function of intellectual flexibility	
Intellectual flexibility	
High intellectual flexibility	.810
Low intellectual flexibility	−.765
(difference significant, $p < .01$)	

the cumulative effects of initial psychological differences on later financial well-being, these results provide at least partial empirical support for the theoretically based proposal that the reciprocal effects between psychological advantages and status-based advantages lead to increasing disparities over time. In this case, this phenomenon is demonstrated by the fact that the financial advantage of individuals with higher intellectual functioning or higher self-directed orientation increases over a 20-year time period.

Social Status, Physical Health, and Psychological Well-Being

Many different research literatures describe the physical and psychological health advantages that accompany high social status. Among the most directly relevant to our present concerns is the extensive literature examining the interrelationships between social structure and health. One common finding is that relatively poor social-structural position is related to relatively poor mental and physical health (Adler, Marmot, McEwan, & Stewart, 1999; Marmot, Ryff, Bumpass, Shipley, & Marks, 1997). Intriguingly, the relationship is so regularly linear that it has been described as a gradient in which health status apparently improves with every increment of SES (Adler & Ostrove, 1999; Marmot, 1999; Seeman & Crimmins, 2001).

A variety of mechanisms have been postulated to explain these socioeconomic disparities in health. Many studies have concluded that SES-related health disparities are, at least in part, the result of lower-SES individuals having less access to good medical care (e.g., Fiscella, Franks, Gold, & Clancy, 2000) and other health-promoting products and services (House, 2001). The gradient may also be attributable in part to documented SES differences in distress (e.g., McLeod & Kessler, 1990; Seeman & Crimmins, 2001; Stansfield, Head, & Marmot, 1998). Lantz, House, Mero, and Williams (2005) found that stress and life event measures accounted for SES differences in functional limitations. The research in the general area of allostatic load (for a review, see McEwen, 2000) indicates that the negative physiological effects of psychological stress build up over the life span. This research also links such physiological burden, induced by psychological stress, to low social status, suggesting that the negative physiological effects of a life history of low social status accumulate with age.

It does not take too much theoretical imagination to realize that within every pair of variables in this triumvirate of psychological distress, physical health, and social-structural status, each variable in the pair may plausibly both affect and be affected by the other. A limitation of all of the research that we have discussed examining the interrelationships among the pairs of variables in the triumvirate is that none has attempted to analytically disentangle these hypothetically plausible effects.

A goal of the analysis reported by Mulatu and Schooler (2002) was to estimate the possible reciprocal effects among social status, psychological distress, and physical health. The data are from the 1974 and 1994 waves of the SSES longitudinal study described previously. Health in 1974 was based on ratings of responses to questions about the impacts of any serious illnesses or injuries the respondent had had in the past year or of any physical health conditions that limited their activities. Health in 1994 was indexed by a latent factor based on three variables: the number of physical illnesses with which the respondent was diagnosed, the number of types of medication prescribed, and self-reported health. Psychological Distress was measured by a second-order latent factor indexed by the first order factors of Anxiety and Self-Deprecation, based on respondents' interview responses.

With one exception, the model presented in Figure 6.7 is basically the same as that in Mulatu and Schooler (2002, Figure 4). The exception is the addition of a path from SES 1974 to Psychosocial Distress. In an ideal world, this would be modeled in terms of reciprocal effects between the two variables. We do not, however, have the identification necessary to do so. We have nevertheless included this one-way path from SES 1974 to Psychosocial Distress because doing so provides a somewhat more complete, although not as unquestionably specified, representation of the potential effects of SES. The path's inclusion

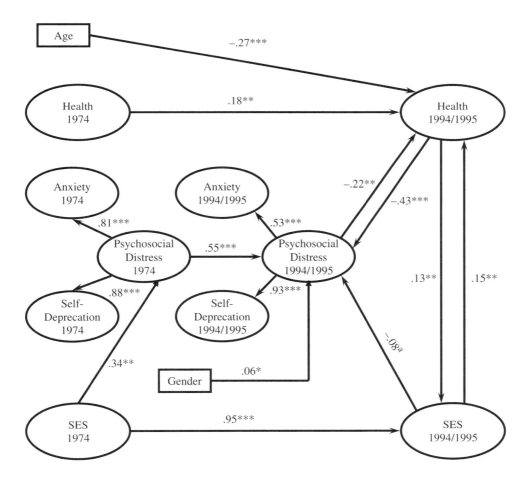

Figure 6.7. Longitudinal (1974–1994) reciprocal effects model of health and socioeconomic status (SES).
[a]$p < .10$.
*$p < .05$. **$p < .01$. ***$p < .001$.

does not affect the other model estimates. The findings indicate that Health and Psychosocial Distress have significant reciprocal effects on each other, with the effect of Health on Psychosocial Distress (−.43) being twice that of Psychosocial Distress on Health. There is also evidence in Mulatu and Schooler (2002) and in the model shown in Figure 6.7 that low SES also directly increases Psychosocial Distress. Even taking these causal pathways into account, health and SES continue to have significant reciprocal effects on each other.

Furthermore, as can be seen from Table 6.2, when direct and indirect effects from this model are taken into account, 1974 SES has substantial and significant total effects on 1994 Health (.23) and Psychosocial Distress (.37). Psychosocial Distress also has a significant total effect on Health (.14), as does Health on Psychosocial Distress (.09). If we look only at the 1994 variables of SES, Health and Psychosocial Distress, we find that these variables have significant effects on each other. The effect of Health on Psychosocial Distress is the largest (−.50), the effect of Psychosocial Distress on Health (−.25) being next largest, and the other effects being greater than .15. The effect of SES on Health is at least partially mediated by Psychosocial Distress; conversely, the effect of SES on Psychosocial Distress is at least partially mediated by Health. The overall pattern of these results indicates that over time, those who were initially relatively healthy, wealthy, and happy become relatively even more so and that initial advantages (or disadvantages) in any one of these generally desired characteristics led to later advantages (or disadvantages) in the others.

Socioeconomic Status, Control Beliefs, and Well-Being

SES-related beliefs about the degree of control one has over one's circumstances are central to the connection between SES and a variety of aspects of well-being, including emotional well-being, health, and disability. Furthermore, to the extent that low-SES individuals have less control over their lives, one would expect levels of perceived control to decrease cumulatively over the course of a lifetime.

People from less advantaged groups experience more stress and more stress-related problems and distress than do those of advantaged groups (Kubzansky, Berkman, & Seeman, 2000; Pearlin, 1989; Thoits, 1995; Turner & Roszell, 1994).

Table 6.2. Total Effects and Total Indirect Effects: Socioeconomic Status (SES), Health, and Psychosocial Distress (Standardized Coefficients)

Effects	Total	Total indirect
Effects from SES 1994 to Health 1994	0.193**	0.041*
Effects from SES 1994 to Psychosocial Distress 1994	−0.169**	−0.085**
Effects from Psychosocial Distress 1994 to Health 1994	−0.249*	−0.029
Effects from Health 1994 to Psychosocial Distress 1994	−0.496***	−0.069**

$*p < .05. **p < .01. ***p < .001.$

This is almost certainly a result of, in part, the greater number and severity of life difficulties low-SES individuals must face; such difficulties include not only relatively rare crisis-like life events, but, more important, the "persistent and recurrent stressors" that characterize the life of individuals from low-SES strata (Aneshensel, 1992, p. 20). In addition, even when faced with an equal level of environmental stress, individuals from disadvantaged groups are more likely than those from more advantaged groups to experience emotional distress in response to such life difficulties (e.g., Gallo & Matthews, 2003).

Given the likelihood of facing more usual and unusual stressors than higher SES individuals, it is not surprising that lower SES individuals are less likely than higher SES individuals to believe that they have control over their lives. This tendency is reflected in group differences in a number of variables related to control beliefs, such as self-confidence, fatalism, mastery, and self-efficacy (Bailis, Segal, Mahon, Chipperfield, & Dunn, 2001; Galanos, Strauss, & Pieper, 1994; Mirowsky & Ross, 1990; Ross & Mirowsky, 1989; Thoits, 1995; for general discussions of control-related concepts, see Caplan & Schooler, 2003; Lachman, 1986; Rodin, Timko, & Harris, 1985). Lower levels of perceived control are also associated with lower levels of SES components, such as lower educational level (Galanos et al., 1994; Lachman & Weaver, 1998; Ross & Mirowsky, 2002; Wolinsky & Stump, 1996), and lower income (Ross & Mirowsky, 2002).

Socioeconomic Status, Perceived Control, and Coping

These differences in control beliefs among different SES groups have implications for coping with life's stressors. Coping strategies are commonly divided into two classes: problem-focused and emotion-focused coping (e.g., Folkman & Lazarus, 1980; Lazarus, 1999; Lazarus & Folkman, 1984). *Problem-focused strategies* involve defining and solving the relevant problem; *emotion-focused strategies,* in contrast, include a variety of strategies aimed at lessening emotional distress. It is often hypothesized that people who believe that life events, or at least their current problem, can be controlled may be more likely to engage in problem-focused coping strategies (Aldwin, 1991; Folkman, 1984; Folkman & Lazarus, 1980; Holahan & Moos, 1987; Pearlin & Schooler, 1978; Ross & Mirowsky, 1989; Thoits, 1995). A particular specification of this general hypothesis is the goodness-of-fit hypothesis, which posits that the probability of choosing problem-focused coping, and its efficacy, are higher when the problematic life situation is appraised as more controllable. Conversely, the likelihood and efficacy of emotion-focused coping are hypothesized to be greater when problems are appraised as less controllable. There is empirical support for this hypothesis (Conway & Terry, 1992; Forsythe & Compas, 1987; Vitaliano, DeWolfe, Maiuro, Russo, & Katon, 1990; Zakowski, Hall, Klein, & Baum, 2001).

Given that SES is related to control beliefs, and that control beliefs are related to coping strategies, one might expect that SES would be related to the choice of coping strategies. Thus, it is not surprising that higher SES individuals are more likely to engage in problem-focused coping and less likely to engage in emotion-focused coping than are lower SES individuals (Billings & Moos, 1985; Pearlin & Schooler, 1978; Ross & Mirowsky, 1989), although such reports of SES-related group differences are not universal (Menaghan & Merves, 1984; Thoits, 1995).

With these findings in mind, we conducted an analysis to investigate all three of these relations (SES and control beliefs, control beliefs and coping strategy, SES and coping strategy) simultaneously (Caplan & Schooler, 2007). We examined the effects of SES on problem-focused and emotion-focused approaches to coping and whether those effects were mediated by two types of general control beliefs, fatalism and self-confidence, in the context of financial stress and strain. We also examined the degree to which these two coping strategies were elicited by stress, as well as their efficacy in decreasing psychosocial distress.

Using the data from the 1994 sample of the SSES longitudinal study, we found that lower SES was linked to greater use of Emotion-Focused Financial Coping and lesser use of Problem-Focused Financial Coping. Lower socioeconomic status was also related to higher levels of Fatalism, and lower levels of Self-Confidence, our two measures of perceived control. Most important, the effects of SES on the use of Problem-Focused Financial Coping appears to have been mediated by these two measures of perceived control (Self-Confidence, Fatalism). In fact, when Self-Confidence and Fatalism were introduced into the model as mediator variables, the effects of SES on Problem-Focused Financial Coping disappeared entirely. The effect of SES on Emotion-Focused Financial Coping was not so mediated; see Table 6.3. Furthermore, Problem-Focused Financial Coping was elicited by Financial Stress and decreased Psychosocial Distress. In contrast, Emotion-Focused Financial Coping was not elicited by Financial Stress and actually increased Psychosocial Distress. These results suggest that low SES may decrease people's control beliefs, which in turn decrease the likelihood of choosing effective financial coping processes—resulting in double disadvantage. These cumulating disadvantages would seem to serve to magnify initial SES differences in psychological well-being.

Socioeconomic Status, Perceived Control, and Disability

As people age, the probability of physical disability increases (e.g., Verbrugge & Jette, 1994). The probability of disability is also inversely related to socioeconomic status (Minkler, Fuller-Thomson, & Guralnik, 2006), following a gra-

Table 6.3. Effects of 1974 Socioeconomic Status (SES) on Financial Coping Styles in 1994 (Standardized Path Coefficients)

Model	SES → Problem-focused financial coping 1994/1995	SES → Emotion-focused financial coping 1994/1995
Without fatalism and self-confidence as mediators	.15*	−.26***
With fatalism and self-confidence as mediators	−.01, n.s.	−.27***

Note. Data from Caplan and Schooler (2007).
*p < .05. **p < .01. ***p < .001.

dient similar to the socioeconomic health gradient discussed in the previous section. Such SES differences in disability may be related to SES differences in control beliefs and coping in several ways. First, the literature on coping, control beliefs, and SES suggest that lower SES individuals might have more difficulty than higher SES individuals in dealing with the onset of disability, as they might have with other serious stressors. Smith, Langa, Kabeto, and Ubel (2005) examined the decreases in subjective well-being experienced by individuals of relatively high or relatively low wealth soon after the onset of a disability. They found that the negative impact of disability onset was greater for individuals below the median for wealth than for those above the median. They suggested that wealth (or some related social status-related characteristic) serves as a buffer in people's experience of disability, presumably due to SES differences in coping capacity or resources in the face of adversity.

Second, differences in control beliefs might affect the actual occurrence of disability itself. It is important to remember that illness and pathology are not the same as disability. Current research emphasizes that disability involves the interaction between the person and the environment. Thus, Verbrugge and Jette (1994) defined *disability* as "a gap between personal capability and environmental demand" (p. 1). For example, the degree to which older individuals with osteoarthritis of the knee are disabled (i.e., have difficulty in normal activities and roles) will depend not just on pathology but on a number of environmental factors: the nature and efficacy of medical interventions, the availability of environmental supports, changes in activities and lifestyle, environmental demands, and psychological resources.

In addition, psychological characteristics that reflect lower degrees of actual or perceived control are associated with higher degrees of disability. Decreased fatalism (or increased mastery) is associated with lower degrees of disablement (Femia, Zarit, & Johansson, 1997; Simonsick, Guralnik, & Fried, 1999). Similarly, higher levels of self confidence-related constructs, particularly self-efficacy, are associated with lower levels of disablement (Kempen Sanderman, Miedema, Meyboom-de Jong, & Ormel, 2000; Mendes de Leon, Seeman, Baker, Richardson, & Tinetti, 1996; Rejeski, Miller, Foy, Messier, & Rapp, 2001).

How might perceived control influence whether an individual becomes disabled? One useful perspective, derived from the Verbrugge and Jette model, was suggested by Femia, Zarit, and Johansson (2001). They proposed that psychological, or "internal" resources "can strongly influence the relationship between personal capability and environmental demand by either increasing personal capability, reducing the environmental demand, or both" (p. P13). There are a number of ways in which perceived control might help increase personal capability. It may (a) enable people to engage in more adaptive coping strategies, (b) contribute to motivational factors for engaging in health- or rehabilitation-related behaviors, or (c) increase the use of environmental supports or interventions.

In another analysis of the SSES longitudinal study data set, we examined the interrelationships among income (a component of SES), three psychological variables (fatalism, self-confidence, and intellectual resources), and the subsequent development of illness and disability 20 years later (Caplan & Schooler, 2003); see Figure 6.8. Higher family incomes in 1974 were associated with lower Fatalism in 1974 and higher Self-Confidence in 1974 (for Fatalism, $r = -.22$,

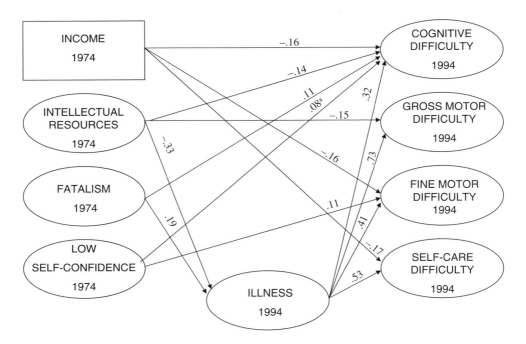

Figure 6.8. Relations between 1974 characteristics (fatalism, self-confidence, intellectual resources, and income) and four aspects of ADL/IADL disability in 1994. ADL = activities of daily life; IADL = instrumental activities of daily life. Adapted from "The Roles of Fatalism, Self Confidence and Intellectual Resources in the Disablement Process in Older Adults," by L. J. Caplan and C. Schooler, 2003, *Psychology and Aging, 18,* p. 556. In the public domain.

$p < .01$; for Self-Confidence, $r = .27$, $p < .01$). Results indicated that greater Fatalism in 1974 predicted greater difficulty in everyday cognitive tasks, as well as illness, in 1994. Higher Self-Confidence in 1974 was associated with lesser degrees of Cognitive Difficulty and Fine Motor Difficulty in 1994. These effects of perceived control held even though 1994 Illness was controlled (the results were also unchanged when 1974 illness was included in the model). Although these effects of SES-related control beliefs were relatively small, they were impressive given that they covered a 20-year time interval.

Implications for the Role of Perceived Control

These findings contribute to an important literature regarding the effects of perceived control on well-being. First, they are consistent with findings of other investigators that demonstrate the importance of SES differences in perceived control as critical in understanding other SES psychological differences. For example, SES differences in perceived control have been suggested as a mediating factor in the relations between SES and a variety of measures of psychological well-being (Gallo, Bogart, Vranceanu, & Matthews, 2005; Mirowsky & Ross, 1990; Turner, Lloyd, & Roszell, 1999).

Second, they may be relevant to discussions of the SES gradient in health. A number of investigators have suggested that status differences in stress, or in perceived control, may explain at least part of that gradient (Bailis et al., 2001; Cohen, Kaplan, & Salonen, 1999; Gallo & Matthews, 2003; Mulatu & Schooler, 2002; Taylor & Seeman, 1999). If this is the case, then researchers need to better understand not just the relation between social status and health, but also the relations among social status, control, and stress.

Most critical to the central point in this chapter is the possibility that differences in perceived control between "those who have" and "those who have not" may accumulate over time. To the extent that individuals from less advantaged groups actually do experience less real control over their lives, their perceived control might be expected to decrease over time. In contrast, the perceived control of the more advantaged groups might be expected to increase. Consequently, one might expect to see increased disparities in both psychological and physical well-being.

Conclusion

In this chapter, we have described processes through which "those who have" earlier in life thrive later in life. We have detailed mechanisms through which early differences in psychological functioning and social status become even greater over the life course. We have described reciprocal interrelationships among social status, physical health, and psychological well-being that similarly lead to increased disparities over the life course. We have depicted ways in which SES-related beliefs about the degree of control over life circumstances can affect one's financial coping strategies as well as one's ability to effectively carry out daily life activities when one grows older.

In doing so, we have provided evidence of interconnections among social-structural, psychological, and biological level phenomena indicating the variety of ways in which individuals who are initially advantaged in one of these spheres tend, with the passage of time, to become relatively more advantaged, not only in that sphere, but in the other spheres as well. Figure 6.9 provides a graphic illustration of the types of causal connections that we have good reason to believe exist among the types and levels of phenomena discussed here (for an extended theoretical discussion of levels of phenomena and their plausible reciprocal interconnections, see Schooler, 1991, 1994). In the figure, we have added another class of phenomena that we have not previously specified—social/interpersonal—that we believe represents a level that should be taken into consideration. The number of potential interlevel causal connections we portray is obviously daunting. Nevertheless, arguments can be made and plausible examples be given for every direction of effect portrayed—with many of these effects being mechanisms underlying the comparatively greater well-being of the initially advantaged later in life. In this chapter, we have been able to only skim the surface. We hope, however, that the examples we provide will convince others of the complexity of the web of causal interconnections underlying "how those who have, thrive."

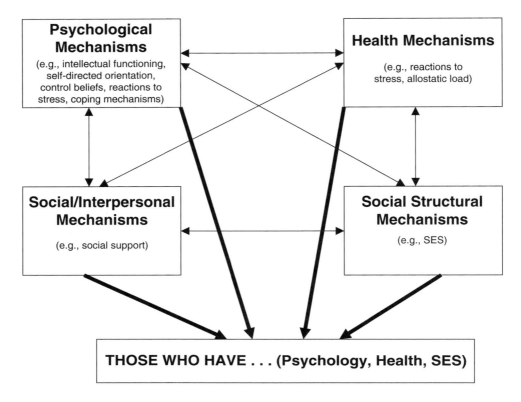

Figure 6.9.   A schematic depiction of mechanisms that may underlie the notion that "those who have, thrive."

References

Adler, N. E., Marmot, M., McEwan, B. S., & Stewart, J. (Eds.). (1999). *Annals of the New York Academy of Sciences: Vol. 896. Socioeconomic status and health in industrialized nations.* New York: New York Academy of Sciences.

Adler, N. E., & Ostrove, J. M. (1999). Socioeconomic status and health: What we know and what we don't. In N. E. Adler, M. Marmot, B. S. McEwan, & J. Stewart (Eds.), *Annals of the New York Academy of Sciences: Vol. 896. Socioeconomic status and health in industrialized nations* (pp. 3–15). New York: New York Academy of Sciences.

Aldwin, C. M. (1991). Does age affect the stress and coping process? Implications of age differences in perceived control. *The Journals of Gerontology: Series B. Psychological Sciences and Social Sciences, 46,* P174–P180.

Aneshensel, C. S. (1992). Social stress: Theory and research. *Annual Review of Sociology, 18,* 15–38.

Bailis, D. S., Segall A., Mahon, M. J., Chipperfield, J. G., & Dunn E. M. (2001). Perceived control in relation to socioeconomic and behavioral resources for health. *Social Science & Medicine, 52,* 1661–1676.

Billings, A. G., & Moos, R. H. (1985). Psychosocial processes of remission in unipolar depression: Comparing depressed patients with matched community controls. *Journal of Consulting and Clinical Psychology, 53,* 314–325.

Caplan, L. J., & Schooler, C. (2003). The roles of fatalism, self confidence and intellectual resources in the disablement process in older adults. *Psychology and Aging, 18,* 551–561.

Caplan, L. J., & Schooler, C. (2007). Socioeconomic status and financial coping strategies: The mediating role of perceived control. *Social Psychology Quarterly, 70,* 63–78.

Cohen, S. A., Kaplan, G. A., & Salonen, J. T. (1999). The role of psychological characteristics in the relation between socioeconomic status and perceived health. *Journal of Applied Social Psychology, 29,* 445–468.

Conway, V. J., & Terry, D. J., (1992). Appraised controllability as a moderator of the effectiveness of different coping strategies: A test of the goodness of fit hypothesis. *Australian Journal of Psychology, 44,* 1–7.

Farkas, G., England, P., Vicknair, K., & Kilbourne, B. S. (1997). Cognitive skill, skill demands of jobs, and earnings among young European American, African American, and Mexican American workers. *Social Forces, 74,* 913–938.

Femia, E. E., Zarit, S. H., & Johannsson, B. (1997). Predicting change in activities of daily living: A longitudinal study of the oldest old in Sweden. *The Journals of Gerontology: Series B. Psychological Sciences and Social Sciences, 52,* P294–P302.

Femia, E. E., Zarit, S. H., & Johansson, B. (2001). Predicting change in activities of daily living: A longitudinal study of the oldest old in Sweden. *The Journals of Gerontology: Series B. Psychological Sciences and Social Sciences, 52,* P12–P23.

Fiscella, K., Franks, P., Gold, M. R., & Clancy, C. M. (2000). Inequality in quality: Addressing socioeconomic, racial, and ethnic disparities in health care. *Journal of the American Medical Association, 283,* 2579–2584.

Folkman, S. (1984). Personal control and stress and coping processes: A theoretical analysis. *Journal of Personality and Social Psychology, 46,* 839–852.

Folkman, S., & Lazarus, R. S. (1980). An analysis of coping in a middle-aged community sample. *Journal of Health and Social Behavior, 21,* 219–239.

Forsythe, C. J., & Compas, B. E. (1987). Interaction of cognitive appraisals of stressful events and coping: Testing the goodness of fit hypothesis. *Cognitive Therapy and Research, 11,* 473–485.

Galanos, A. N., Strauss, R. P., & Pieper, C. F. (1994) Sociodemographic correlates of health beliefs among Black and White community dwelling elderly individuals. *International Journal of Aging and Human Development, 38,* 339–350.

Gallo, L. C., Bogart, L. M., Vranceanu, A. M., & Matthews, K. A. (2005). Socioeconomic status, resources, psychological experiences, and emotional responses: A test of the reserve capacity model. *Journal of Personality and Social Psychology, 88,* 386–399.

Gallo, L. C., & Matthews, K. A. (2003). Understanding the association between socioeconomic status and physical health: Do negative emotions play a role? *Psychological Bulletin, 129,* 10–51.

Holahan, C. J., & Moos, R. H. (1987). Personal and contextual determinants of coping strategies. *Journal of Personality and Social Psychology, 52,* 946–955.

House, J. S. (2001). Relating social inequalities in health and income. *Journal of Health Politics, Policy and Law, 26,* 523–532.

Kempen, G. I., Sanderman, R., Miedema, I., Meyboom-de Jong, B., & Ormel, J. (2000). Functional decline after congestive heart failure and acute myocardial infarction and the impact of psychological attributes: A prospective study. *Quality of Life Research, 9,* 439–450.

Kohn, M. L., & Schooler, C. (1983). *Work and personality: An inquiry into the impact of social stratification.* Norwood, NJ: Ablex.

Kohn, M. L., & Slomczynski, K. M. (1990). *Social structure and self-direction.* London: Blackwell.

Kubzansky, L. D., Berkman, L. F., & Seeman, T. E. (2000). Social conditions and distress in elderly persons. *The Journals of Gerontology: Series B. Psychological Sciences and Social Sciences, 55,* P238–P246.

Lachman, M. E. (1986). Locus of control in aging research: A case for multidimensional and domain-specific assessment. *Psychology and Aging, 1,* 34–40.

Lachman, M. E., & Weaver, S. L. (1998). Sociodemographic variations in the sense of control by domain: Findings from the MacArthur studies of midlife. *Psychology and Aging, 13,* 553–562.

Lantz, P. M., House, J. S., Mero, R. P., & Williams, D. R. (2005). Stress, life events, and socioeconomic disparities in health: Results from the Americans' Changing Lives Study. *Journal of Health and Social Behavior, 46,* 274–288.

Lazarus, R. S. (1999). *Stress and emotion: A new synthesis.* New York: Springer.

Lazarus, R. S., & Folkman, S. (1984). *Stress, appraisal, and coping.* New York: Springer.

Marmot, M. (1999). Epidemiology of socioeconomic status and health: Are determinants within countries the same as between countries? In N. E. Adler, M. Marmot, B. S. McEwan, & J. Stewart (Eds.), *Annals of the New York Academy of Sciences: Vol. 896. Socioeconomic status and health in industrialized nations* (pp. 16–29). New York: New York Academy of Sciences.

Marmot, M., Ryff, C. D., Bumpass, L. L., Shipley, M., & Marks, N. F. (1997). Social inequalities in health: Next questions and converging evidence. *Social Science Medicine, 44,* 901–910.

McEwen, B. S. (2000). Allostasis and allostatic load: Implications of neuropsychopharmacology. *Neuropsychopharmacology, 22,* 108–124.

McLeod, J. D., & Kessler, R. C. (1990). Socioeconomic status differences in vulnerability to undesirable life events. *Journal of Health and Social Behavior, 31,* 162–172.

Menaghan, E. G., & Merves, E. S. (1984). Coping with occupational problems: The limits of individual efforts. *Journal of Health and Social Behavior, 25,* 406–423.

Mendes de Leon, F., Seeman, T. E., Baker, D. I., Richardson, E. D., & Tinetti, M. E. (1996). Self-efficacy, physical decline, and change in functioning in community-living elders: A prospective study. *The Journals of Gerontology: Series B. Psychological Sciences and Social Sciences, 51,* S183–S190.

Merton, R. K. (1957). *Social theory and social structure.* New York: The Free Press.

Minkler, M., Fuller-Thomson, E., & Guralnik, J. M. (2006). Gradient of disability across the socioeconomic spectrum in the United States. *New England Journal of Medicine, 355,* 695–703.

Mirowsky, J., & Ross, C. E. (1990). Control or defense? Depression and the sense of control over good and bad outcomes. *Journal of Health and Social Behavior, 31,* 71–86.

Mulatu, M. S., & Schooler, C. (2002). Causal connections between SES and health: Reciprocal effects and mediating mechanisms. *Journal of Health and Social Behavior, 43,* 22–41.

Mulatu, M. S., & Schooler, C. (2007). Environmental complexity and intellectual functioning in older people. In F. Columbus (Ed.), *Psychology of aging* (pp. 89–114). Hauppauge, NY: Nova Science.

Pearlin, L. I. (1989). The sociological study of stress. *Journal of Health and Social Behavior, 30,* 241–256.

Pearlin, L. I., & Schooler, C. (1978). The structure of coping. *Journal of Health and Social Behavior, 19,* 2–21.

Rejeski, W. J., Miller, M. E., Foy, C., Messier, S., & Rapp, S. (2001). Self-efficacy and the progression of functional limitations and self-reported disability in older adults with knee pain. *The Journals of Gerontology: Series B. Psychological Sciences and Social Sciences, 56,* S261–S265.

Rodin, J., Timko, C., & Harris, S. (1985). The construct of control: Biological and psychosocial correlates. *Annual Review of Gerontology & Geriatrics, 5,* 3–55.

Ross, C. E., & Mirowsky, J. (1989). Explaining the social patterns of depression: Control and problem-solving—or support and talking? *Journal of Health and Social Behavior, 30,* 206–219.

Ross, C. E., & Mirowsky, J. (2002). Age and the gender gap in the sense of personal control. *Social Psychology Quarterly, 65,* 125–145.

Schooler, C. (1984). Psychological effects of complex environments during the life span: A review and theory. *Intelligence, 8,* 259–281.

Schooler, C. (1990). Psychosocial factors and effective cognitive functioning through the life span. In J. E. Birren & K. W. Schaie (Eds.), *Handbook of the psychology of aging* (pp. 347–358). Orlando, FL: Academic Press.

Schooler, C. (1991). Interdisciplinary lessons: The two social psychologies from the perspective of a psychologist practicing sociology. In C. W. Stephan, W. G. Stephan, & T. F. Pettigrew (Eds.), *The future of social psychology: Defining the relationships between sociology and psychology* (pp. 71–81). New York: Springer-Verlag.

Schooler, C. (1994). A working conceptualization of social structure: Mertonian roots and psychological and sociocultural relationships. *Social Psychology Quarterly, 57,* 262–273.

Schooler, C. (2007). Culture and social structure: The relevance of social structure to cultural psychology. In S. Kitayama & D. Cohen (Eds.), *Handbook of cultural psychology* (370–390). New York: Guilford Press.

Schooler, C., & Caplan, L. J. (in press). Those who have, get: Social structure, environmental complexity, intellectual functioning and self-directed orientations in the elderly. In K. W. Schaie & R. Abeles (Eds.), *Social structures and aging individuals: Continuing challenges.* New York: Springer.

Schooler, C., & Mulatu, M. S. (2001). The reciprocal effects of leisure time activities and intellectual functioning in older people: A longitudinal analysis. *Psychology and Aging, 16,* 466–482.

Schooler, C., Mulatu, M. S., & Oates, G. (1999). The continuing effects of substantively complex work on the intellectual functioning of older workers. *Psychology and Aging, 14,* 483–506.

Schooler, C., Mulatu, M. S., & Oates, G. (2004). Effects of occupational self-direction on the intellectual functioning and self-directed orientations of older workers: Findings and implications for individuals and societies. *American Journal of Sociology, 110,* 161–197.

Seeman, T., & Crimmins, E. (2001). Social environment effects on health and aging: Integrating epidemiological and demographic approaches and perspectives. In M. Weinstein, A. I. Hermalin, & M. A. Soto (Eds.), *Annals of New York Academy of Sciences: Vol. 954. Population health and aging: Strengthening the dialogue between epidemiology and demography* (pp. 88–117). New York: New York Academy of Sciences.

Simonsick, E. M., Guralnik, J. M., & Fried, L. P. (1999). Who walks? Factors associated with walking behavior in disabled older women with and without self-reported walking difficulty. *Journal of the American Geriatrics Society, 47,* 672–680.

Smith, D. M., Langa, K. M., Kabeto, M. U., & Ubel, P. A. (2005). Health, wealth, and happiness: Financial resources buffer subjective well-being after the onset of a disability. *Psychological Science, 16,* 663–666.

Stansfeld, S. A., Head, J., & Marmot, M. (1998). Explaining social class differences in depression and well-being. *Social Psychiatry and Psychiatric Epidemiology, 33,* 1–9.

Taylor, S. E., & Seeman, T. E. (1999). Psychosocial resources and the SES-health relationship. In N. E. Adler, M. Marmot, B. S. McEwan, & J. Stewart (Eds.), *Annals of New York Academy of Sciences: Vol. 896. Socioeconomic status and health in industrialized nations* (pp. 210–255). New York: New York Academy of Sciences.

Thoits, P. A. (1995). Stress, coping, and social support processes: Where are we? What next? *Journal of Health and Social Behavior, 35,* 53–79.

Turner, R. J., Lloyd, D. A., & Roszell, P. (1999). Personal resources and the social distribution of depression. *American Journal of Community Psychology, 27,* 643–672.

Turner, R. J., & Roszell, P. (1994). Psychosocial resources and the stress process. In W. R. Avison & I. H. Gotlib (Eds.), *Stress and mental health: Contemporary issues and prospects for the future* (pp. 179–209). New York: Plenum Press.

Verbrugge, L. M., & Jette, A. M. (1994). The disablement process. *Social Science & Medicine, 38,* 1–14.

Vitaliano, P. P., DeWolfe, D. J., Maiuro, R. D., Russo, J., & Katon, W. (1990). Appraised changeability of a stressor as a modifier of the relationship between coping and depression: A test of the hypothesis of fit. *Journal of Personality and Social Psychology, 59,* 582–592.

Wolinsky, F. D., & Stump, T. E. (1996). Age and the sense of control among older adults. *The Journals of Gerontology: Series B. Psychological Sciences and Social Sciences, 51,* S217–S220.

Zakowski, S. G., Hall, M. H., Klein, L. C., & Baum, A. (2001). Appraised control, coping, and stress in a community sample: A test of the goodness-of-fit hypothesis. *Annals of Behavioral Medicine, 23,* 158–165.

7

The Rise and Fall of Control Beliefs in Adulthood: Cognitive and Biopsychosocial Antecedents and Consequences of Stability and Change Over 9 Years

Margie E. Lachman, Christopher B. Rosnick, and Christina Röcke

There is robust evidence that a sense of control is a key marker of successful aging (Rowe & Kahn, 1998) and low control may be a risk factor for poor aging-related outcomes (Lachman, 2006). Those who have a greater sense of control show better physical and psychological functioning (Krause, 2007; Krause & Shaw, 2003; Lachman, 2005; 2006). Sense of control can be assessed as a general or domain-specific construct. General control indicates the extent to which one believes outcomes in one's overall life are tied to one's own actions or abilities. Beliefs about controllability may vary also across domains, with the possibility that expectations are higher in some domains than in others. With regard to cognitive functioning, those who believe they have some control over their memory show better memory performance, and this is particularly the case for older adults (Lachman & Andreoletti, 2006). Although much of the work has been cross-sectional and correlational, there is longitudinal evidence that those who have higher control beliefs improve more on cognitive tests with practice, and they are less likely to show aging-related declines in cognitive functioning over time (Caplan & Schooler, 2003). Little is known about whether control beliefs are related to changes in key domains such as subjective well-being and physical health.

On average, there is strong evidence that the sense of control decreases with aging. This evidence is based primarily on cross-sectional work but also on

This research was supported by a grant from the National Institute on Aging (PO1-AG020166) to conduct a longitudinal follow-up of the Midlife in the United States investigation. The authors thank Chandra Murphy for her able assistance with data analysis and manuscript preparation and the editors for their constructive comments on our manuscript. They express gratitude to K. Warner Schaie for inspiring them and countless other scholars and students from multiple generations and for providing them with the conceptual and methodological tools to pursue the challenges and rewards of life-span developmental psychology.

some longitudinal studies (Krause & Shaw, 2003; Lachman & Firth, 2004; Lachman & Weaver, 1998; Mirowsky, 1995). Given the benefits of a high sense of control for affect and action, whether or not veridical (Thompson, 1999), a decline in perceived control with aging could have a negative impact on well-being. In the work presented in this chapter, we seek a better understanding of the nature of longitudinal changes in the sense of control as well as the antecedents and consequences of such change. The methodological approaches we use are highly influenced by and derived from the life-span developmental methodologies developed and promoted by Schaie (1996, 2005) and his colleagues (e.g., Baltes, Lindenberger, & Staudinger, 2006; Baltes, Reese, & Nesselroade, 1977).

On the basis of cross-sectional studies, older adults seem to maintain their overall sense of mastery (beliefs about one's ability or self-efficacy) perhaps because they adjust the salient domains or the standards that they use to define their competence (Bandura, 1997). With aging, we see mainly a loss of perceived control associated with an increasing acknowledgment of the constraints and limitations due to uncontrollable factors or to reduced contingency between actions and outcomes (Lachman & Firth, 2004). In this chapter, we focus on subjective conceptions of control rather than actual or objective levels of control, which are difficult to assess for factors such as cognitive and health. These expectancies for control, or lack thereof, have implications for affect and action whether or not they are veridical (Lachman, 2006).

Although a majority in the United States may believe that the decrements associated with aging are preventable or modifiable, there are many adults, especially in later life, who believe declines are largely inevitable or irreversible. There is a great deal of evidence that such individual differences in control beliefs are associated with key aging outcomes (Rowe & Kahn, 1998). It has consistently been found that a high sense of control is associated with being happy, healthy, wealthy, and wise. On the basis of cross-sectional findings from the first wave of the Midlife in the United States (MIDUS) study national sample, those with a higher sense of control had greater life satisfaction and a more optimistic view of adulthood; they reported that things were going well, and they expected them to either stay that way or to get even better in the future (see Lachman & Firth, 2004). We also have found that persons with higher control were less depressed and had better self-rated health, fewer chronic conditions, and less severe functional limitations. There are wide individual differences in multiple components of perceived control (self-efficacy or competence, contingency or constraints), and such appraisals are related to behaviors and outcomes, including use of adaptive compensatory memory strategies (Lachman, 2006).

As for the developmental course of sense of control, on the basis of cross-sectional work (Lachman & Weaver, 1998), cross-sectional evidence exists (Lachman & Firth, 2004) that some aspects of perceived control do not vary by age (e.g., health, contribution to others), others increase with age (e.g., work, finances, marriage), and some show patterns of decline by age (e.g., children and sex life). Little work, however, has examined changes in perceived control and whether these changes vary by age. We also were interested in identifying the psychosocial antecedents and consequences of changes in control beliefs.

Whereas previous cross-sectional studies have mainly shown that higher control is associated with better health and well-being and domain-related adaptive functioning (Lachman & Weaver, 1998), we also were interested in identifying what factors predict maintenance of the sense of control in the face of aging-related losses and declines in functioning. Based on previous work (Krause, 2007), we expected that having high quality social relationships with anticipated support would be associated with greater maintenance of control beliefs. It has been suggested that having close supportive relationships provides conditions conducive to developing a sense of mastery and effectance because it promotes a sense that one will have encouragement or help if needed (Antonucci & Jackson, 1987).

In this chapter, we address the following questions, inspired and motivated by the extensive life-span developmental methodological innovations by Schaie (2005) over the past 5 decades: What aspects of the sense of control show changes, and which are stable over a 9- to 10-year period? Are there age/cohort differences in change patterns? To what extent are there individual differences in intraindividual change? Which biopsychosocial factors associated with successful aging are related to differential patterns of change in control beliefs? Do changes in control beliefs predict changes in life satisfaction?

The Midlife in the United States Study (MIDUS)

The participants for this research were from the MIDUS survey of adults. Telephone interviews and mail surveys were conducted in 1995–1996 and 2004–2006. A national probability sample of households in the 48 contiguous states with at least one telephone was selected initially in 1995–1996 (MIDUS I) using random digit dialing and conducted by the John D. and Catherine T. MacArthur Foundation Research Network on Successful Midlife Development (Brim, Ryff, & Kessler, 2004). The sample of 7,120 noninstitutionalized adults was stratified in advance by gender and age to achieve an equal gender distribution and an age distribution with the greatest number between 40 and 60. An average of 9 years (range of 8 to 10 years) later, approximately 70% of the original sample ($n = 4,967$) agreed to participate in the second wave. In the analyses, we used the maximum number available for each variable. At baseline the ages ranged from 24 to 75. At Time 2 the mean age was 55.47 years ($SD = 12.44$, range 32 to 84). For analysis purposes, the sample was divided into five age groups with the age span comparable to the 9-year interval for the two waves of data: 32 to 44, 45 to 54, 55 to 64, 65 to 74, and 75 to 84. Women comprised 53.3% of sample. There were 37% with a 4-year college degree or higher. Average health rating on a 5-point scale from poor to excellent was 3.54 ($SD = 1.02$).

As expected, there was evidence for positive selection. The longitudinal sample was slightly older at baseline than the dropouts ($M = 47.15$, $SD = 12.3$ vs. $M = 45.53$, $SD = 13.71$ years of age). The longitudinal sample was also more likely to have a college degree (36.6% vs. 24.1%), had a higher percentage of women (55.1% vs. 47.7%), and had better self-rated health on a 5-point scale (longitudinal $M = 3.64$, $SD = .93$; dropout $M = 3.41$, $SD = 1.04$).

Multidimensional Assessment of Control Beliefs

The MIDUS included multiple indicators of control beliefs. This enabled us to assess both general and domain-specific aspects of control.

Sense of Control

Two multi-item general control constructs were measured in MIDUS: personal mastery (e.g., "I can do just about anything I really set my mind to"; "Whether or not I am able to get what I want is in my own hands") and perceived constraints (e.g., "There is little I can do to change the important things in my life"; "I often feel helpless in dealing with the problems of life"; Lachman & Weaver, 1998; Pearlin & Schooler, 1978). Participants rated all 12 items on a 7-point scale ranging from 1 (*strongly agree*) to 7 (*strongly disagree*). In some of the analyses reported in the sections on antecedents of control beliefs and relationship to life satisfaction, we used an overall measure of general control, which was computed by averaging across the reverse-scored items belonging to the mastery subscale and across the (non-reverse-scored) items belonging to the perceived constraints subscale for all participants who provided valid responses for at least half of the items (Cronbach's alpha = .84, .86, at Time 1 and Time 2, respectively).

Domain-specific control beliefs were assessed for the following domains: children, health, contribution to the well-being of others, work, finances, sex life, and marriage or partner relationship. Participants were asked, "Using a 0–10 scale where 0 means *no control at all* and 10 means *very much control,* how would you rate the amount of control you have over your _____ these days?"

Selective Attrition

As would be expected, there was some evidence for selective attrition in relation to the perceived control variables. We compared the Time 1 control responses for those who remained in the longitudinal sample over the 10 years versus those who dropped out. We found evidence that the survivors were positively selected on the following variables: perceived constraints, health control, control over finances, work, and contributions to others. The differences between survivors and dropouts were typically more pronounced among the oldest age cohorts.

Measurement of Biopsychosocial and Cognitive Factors Related to Successful Aging

The MIDUS contains a rich battery of measures covering a broad range of domains relevant to successful aging. This includes assessments of personality, health, social relationships, and cognitive ability (Lachman, Röcke, Rosnick, & Ryff, 2008).

Personality Traits

Personality was measured with a list of 30 attributes derived from existing trait rating inventories (see Lachman & Weaver, 1997). Respondents were asked to indicate how well each of the items described them on a 4-point scale from 1 (*a lot*) to 4 (*not at all*). Items were recoded so that a greater number indicated a higher score on each trait. The five traits assessed included agreeableness (e.g., helpful, warm), extraversion (e.g., outgoing, talkative), neuroticism (e.g., moody, worrying), openness to experience (e.g., creative, adventurous), and conscientiousness (e.g., organized, responsible). The pattern of findings was very similar across these factors (i.e., extraversion, agreeableness, openness and conscientiousness were positively related to sense of control, whereas neuroticism was negatively related to sense of control). Thus, an overall personality composite was created in the present study for reasons of parsimony by averaging across all items (after reverse-scoring all items except those belonging to the neuroticism subscale) so that a higher score would indicate a more positive overall personality profile (see Musek, 2007; Röcke & Lachman, in press). The term *positive personality profile* is based on previous research showing that neuroticism tends to be associated with a higher standing on negative affect and stress, among others, whereas the other factors, such as extraversion, tend to be related to greater positive affect and health (Costa & McCrae, 1980). Internal consistency for the personality scale was high at both time points (Cronbach's alpha = .84 and .85 at Time 1 and Time 2, respectively).

Health

The health measure was computed on the basis of three indicators: (a) the number of daily activities for which participants experienced health-related limitations (e.g., lifting or carrying groceries, walking more than a mile), (b) the number of health problems they had experienced or been treated for in the past 12 months (e.g., asthma, thyroid disease, migraine headaches; overall, 29 health problems were rated), and (c) the frequency of experiencing each of 9 physical symptoms during the past 30 days (e.g., lower backaches, trouble getting to sleep or staying asleep, sweating a lot). Given that the relationships with other variables were similar for the separate measures of health and that they were moderately correlated, for parsimony we combined them into a composite score. These indicators were standardized, averaged, and reverse-scored so that a higher score reflects better health (Cronbach's alpha = .70 and .71 for Time 1 and Time 2, respectively).

Social Relationship Quality

Two aspects of the quality of social relationships with family (including spouse) and friends were assessed in the MIDUS study: social support and social strain. Social support scales for family, spouse, and friends included four items each (e.g., "How much do your family/spouse/friends care about you?" "How much can you open up to your family/spouse/friends if you need to talk about your worries?"). Responses were made on a 4-point scale ranging from 1 (*a lot*) to 4 (*not at all*). Social strain scales for family, spouse, and friends also consisted of four items each (e.g., "How often do your family/spouse/friends make too many demands on you?" "How often do your family/spouse/friends get on your nerves?") rated on a 4-point scale ranging from 1 (*often*) to 4 (*never*). For the purpose of the present study, a social relations composite score was computed by averaging across all reverse-scored social support items and all non-reverse-scored social strain items. We chose to average across the different relationship types because of moderate to high levels of intercorrelation and to retain participants in the sample who were not married and thus unable to provide a spouse-related rating. Internal consistency for the composite score was high (Cronbach's alpha = .87 at Time 1 and Time 2).

Cognitive Ability

Several indicators of cognitive ability were assessed at the longitudinal follow-up of the MIDUS study using the Brief Test of Adult Cognition by Telephone (Lachman & Tun, 2008). The test includes measures of episodic verbal memory (immediate and delayed), working memory span, verbal fluency, inductive reasoning, and speed of processing. A composite score (the average of standardized z-scores) of these tests was used in the present study as an overall indicator of cognitive mechanics with Cronbach's alpha of .72 (for details, see Lachman & Tun, 2008).

We also included the following demographic variables in our regression models: age, gender, and educational level attained.

Changes in Control Beliefs

We first examined changes over the 9 to 10 years in all general and domain-specific control beliefs. We used analysis of variance with Age (5) by Time (2) with repeated measures on time. Age groups at Time 2 were 32 to 44, 45 to 54, 55 to 64, 65 to 74, and 75 to 84. We also examined gender and educational attainment differences. Because there was little variation in change in relation to these variables, we do not present these findings. As expected, there were main effects of both gender and education, but these have been reported elsewhere (Lachman & Weaver, 1998).

General Control

We found personal mastery decreased for the youngest and the two oldest age cohort groups (see Figure 7.1). Perceived constraints increased over the 9- to 10-year period for the youngest and oldest age groups, but all of the middle age groups decreased in constraints (see Figure 7.2).

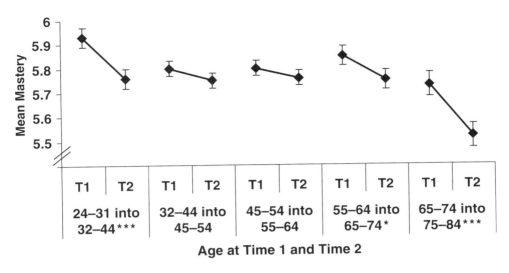

Figure 7.1. Changes in personal mastery by age over 9 years.
*p < .05. ***p < .001.

Domain-Specific Control Beliefs

We also examined changes in domain-specific control (see Figures 7.3 through 7.9). Control over children showed declines for the two youngest age groups. Control over health decreased for the oldest group. Control over contributions to others decreased for the oldest age group, but increased for the youngest group. Work control increased for the 55- to 64- and 65- to 74-year-olds, but

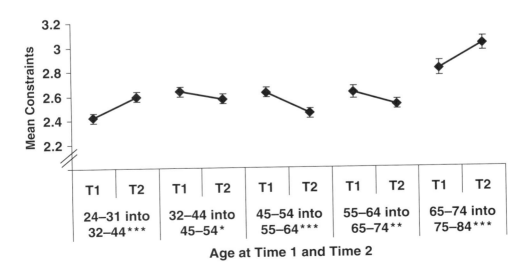

Figure 7.2. Change in perceived constraints by age over 9 years.
*p < .05. **p < .01. ***p < .001.

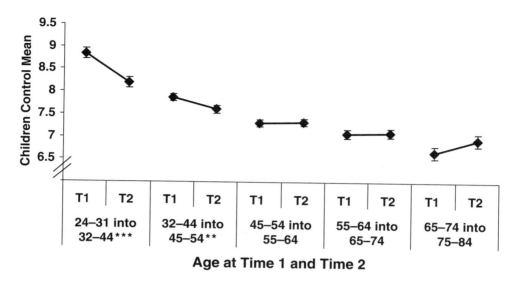

Figure 7.3. Change in control over children by age over 9 years. **$p < .01$. ***$p < .001$.

declined for the 75- to 84-year-olds. We compared these results for those who were working and not working. The same effects were found when we removed those who were not working (e.g., the retired) from the analysis. Control over finances increased over time for the two youngest groups. In contrast, control over sex declined over time for all ages. For marriage control the middle-age group (those moving from range 45–54 into range 55–64) increased over time. For this analysis we included only those who were married or in a marriage-like relationship at both occasions.

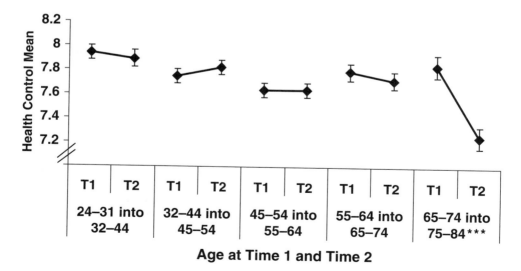

Figure 7.4. Change in control over health by age over 9 years. ***$p < .001$.

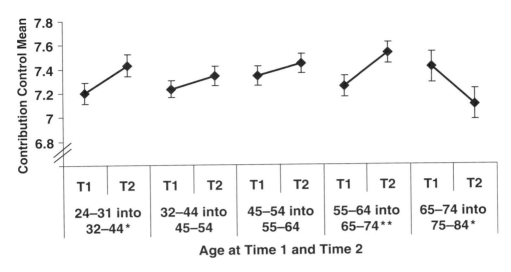

Figure 7.5. Change in control over contributions to others by age over 9 years. *p < .05. **p < .01.

Antecedents of Changes in Control Beliefs:
Interindividual Differences in Change

Given the importance of a sense of control for successful aging, we were interested in identifying the key components of functioning associated with changes in control beliefs in multiple domains. We conducted multiple regressions with the Time 2 control variables as the dependent variable, and the Time 1 control measures included in the first step to create residualized change. Age, educa-

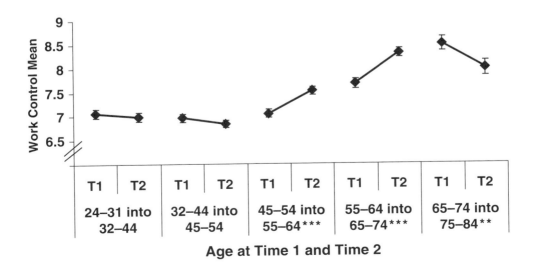

Figure 7.6. Change in control over work by age over 9 years. **p < .01. ***p < .001.

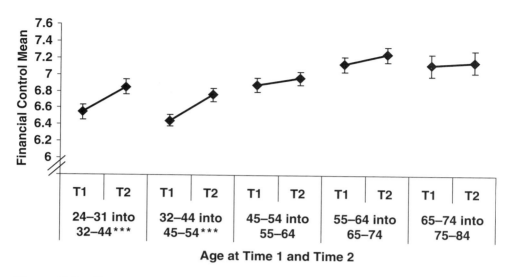

Figure 7.7.   Change in control over finances by age over 9 years.
***$p < .001$.

tion, and gender were also entered. Next, we included the following composite measures as predictors: health, personality, social relations, and cognitive functioning. These measures were computed as the mean of the Time 1 and Time 2 scores, although for cognitive functioning only Time 2 data were available. This approach allowed us to examine predictors of interindividual differences in control maintenance versus changes based on the average functioning across the 9-year interval of the study. Age was a significant predictor of changes in control over health, finances, work, children, and marriage. We also found that

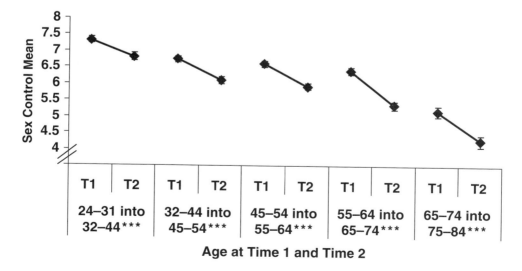

Figure 7.8.   Change in control over sex by age over 9 years.
***$p < .001$.

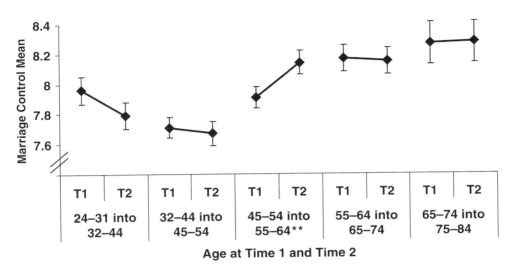

Figure 7.9. Change in control over marriage by age over 9 years.
$**p < .01$.

changes in control were predicted by biopsychosocial factors associated with successful aging. Those who increased in mastery had better health, a more adaptive personality profile, and better quality of social relations, but cognition was not related, and there were no age interactions ($R^2 = .32$). Those who increased in perceived constraints had poorer health, less adaptive personality profiles, poorer quality social relations, and lower levels of cognitive functioning ($R^2 = .43$). We also found a significant Age × Cognition interaction. Those who had higher cognitive resources showed smaller increases inconstraints, but this effect was only found for middle-age and older adults (see Figure 7.10).

Change in control over health was positively predicted by health and a personality profile ($R^2 = .25$). Work ($R^2 = .18$) and finances ($R^2 = .20$) control change was positively predicted by health, personality, and social relations. Changes in control over contributions to others ($R^2 = .12$) and control over children ($R^2 = 18$) were positively predicted by personality, social relations, and cognition. Sex-life control ($R^2 = .21$) change was positively predicted by health, personality, and social relations. And marriage control ($R^2 = .26$) change was positively predicted by social relations and the personality composite. Overall, the results suggest there are interindividual differences in changes for control, and those who have better health, a more adaptive personality profile, greater social support, and better cognitive functioning showed less decline in their sense of control across key life domains. Although we tested the model with change in control as the dependent measure, and assumed that the other variables are antecedents of change, it is not possible with only two occasions of measurement to adequately test reciprocal models. In future research we hope to have collected a third wave of MIDUS data and plan to model multidirectional dynamic relationships as would be expected based on cognitive–behavioral theory (Bandura, 1997).

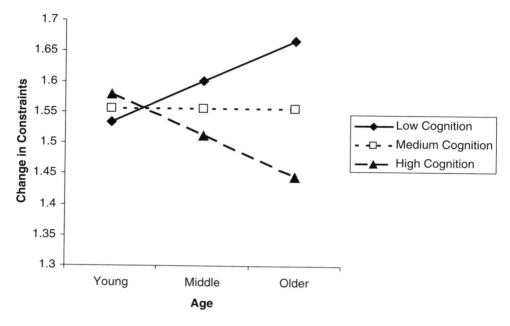

Figure 7.10. Age by cognition interaction for changes in perceived constraints (for age and cognition, low is 1 *SD* below the mean, medium is the mean, and high is 1 *SD* above the mean).

Relationship of Control Beliefs to Life Satisfaction

In past work we found that those who have higher control are more satisfied with their lives; they are more likely to think things are good and that they will stay that way or even get better (Lachman & Firth, 2004; Röcke & Lachman, in press). We were interested to see if control beliefs would be related to changes in life satisfaction, over and above other variables known to be associated with life satisfaction level and change (e.g., health, social support). Although, on average, life satisfaction was relatively stable, there were individual differences in change over the 9 years. We examined the relationship between control beliefs and life satisfaction change and compared the relationship with other factors. We conducted hierarchical multiple regression analyses with Time 2 life satisfaction as the dependent variable, and Time 1 life satisfaction was entered as a predictor at the first step to examine residualized change. The predictors were age, education level, gender, general control (combined mastery and constraints), cognitive mechanics, health, and social relations. All predictors were significant except education. When unique variance was examined, control beliefs ($\Delta R^2 = .05$) showed the strongest independent contribution after initial level of life satisfaction ($\Delta R^2 = .06$). The other predictors in order of unique variance explained are social relationships ($\Delta R^2 = .03$), health ($\Delta R^2 = .01$), age ($\Delta R^2 = .006$), and cognition ($\Delta R^2 = .003$) Education was not significant ($\Delta R^2 = .000$). Altogether the predictors accounted for 40% of the variance in life satisfaction change, with initial level of life satisfaction contributing 22% of the variance. We com-

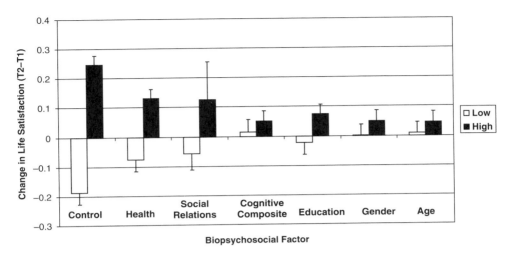

Figure 7.11. Biopsychosocial factors in relation to changes in life satisfaction. Low and high groups are based on median splits. For gender, low = men and high = women. For education, low = no college degree; high = college degree or higher. Error bars represent one standard error of the mean.

puted median splits on all predictor variables and plotted the group differences in Figure 7.11.

Next, we examined whether changes in control as well as in health and social support were related to changes in life satisfaction. We computed change score groups for the biopsychosocial variables: general control, health, and social support using quartiles, with the middle 50% of the distribution classified as *stable,* and those in the bottom quartile as *decliners,* and those in the top quartile as *increasers.* We conducted separate analysis of variance with each of the biopsychosocial change variables (decrease, stable, increase) and age group (young, middle, old), education (college, no college) and gender (male, female) as independent variables. The dependent variable was the change score for life satisfaction (Time 2 – Time 1). For cognition, we had only one occasion of data so we computed three groups on the basis of the distribution at Time 2, bottom 25%, middle 50%, and top 25%. Here and in Figure 7.12, we report only the main effects for change in biopsychosocial variables. Those who showed declines in control beliefs, health, and supportive social relations were more likely to show declines in life satisfaction. Level of cognitive functioning, which was only available at Time 2, was also related to life satisfaction change. In Figure 7.12, we show that those who had the lowest levels of cognition were more likely to decline in life satisfaction, suggesting poor cognition is a risk factor for psychological well-being in later life.

Discussion

The sense of control plays a central role in the maintenance and optimization of psychological and physical health in adulthood and old age and has been identified as a key indicator of successful aging (Krause, 2007; Lachman, 2006; Rowe &

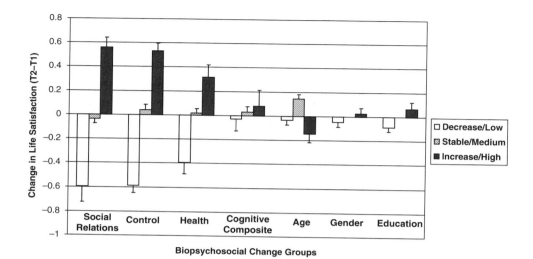

Figure 7.12. Changes in biopsychosocial factors in relation to changes in life satisfaction. For cognition and age, the values do not represent change but rather low (bottom 25%), medium (middle 50%), and high (top 25%) at Time 2. For age, low = 32 to 49, medium = 50 to 69, and high = 70 to 85. For gender, low = men and high = women. For education, low = no college degree and high = college degree or higher. Error bars represent one standard error of the mean.

Kahn, 1998). Adults who have a lower sense of control may be at increased risk of a wide range of negative behavioral, affective, and functional outcomes, including higher levels of depression, anxiety, and stress and the use of fewer health protective behaviors and compensatory memory strategies, and they have poorer health and memory functioning. Yet, little is known about the developmental course of control beliefs in adulthood. Moreover, it is likely that those who are aging successfully are more likely to maintain or even boost their sense of control over time. These reciprocal models will need to be tested in future studies that have more than two occasions of measures. In the present study, we set out to investigate the extent and nature of changes in the sense of control in adulthood assessed on two occasions over a 9-year period. Inspired by Schaie's (1996, 2005) large body of life-span developmental work and methodological innovations, we were interested in average change trajectories as well as interindividual differences in patterns of change. First, we considered average change over 9 to 10 years in different aspects of control beliefs. We found age/cohort differences in the extent and direction of change. Moreover, the nature of change varied as a function of type of control dimension. We investigated what biopsychosocial factors predict regarding who is able to maintain a sense of control in the face of aging-related losses in multiple domains. We were interested in identifying the protective and risk factors for a changing sense of control in adulthood. Finally, we examined the implications of changes in control beliefs for satisfaction with life.

The results show a complex picture of change trajectories for the sense of control as a function of dimension (e.g., mastery vs. constraints) and domain (e.g., children, health). There is evidence for stability but also for a rise and fall in some aspects of control. For a number of domains (contributions to others, work, children, health), we found differential patterns of change by age/cohort. Thus, adulthood is characterized by a combination of ups and downs in the sense of control across different domains of life. Across adulthood, it would be desirable to maintain a favorable balance of gains and losses across domains, so that on average there are more domains that increase or show maintenance of a sense of control compared with those in which losses are predominant (Baltes, Lindenberger, & Staudinger, 2006). Or perhaps it is not the number of domains that is critical. What may be important is to maintain control in the domains that are most meaningful or central for the individual, as Krause (2007) has suggested. In future work it will be interesting to determine whether control is more likely to be maintained in those domains that are most salient for the individual. The psychological and physical consequences of declines in the most important domains of life would be expected to be greater than for less central domains (Krause, 2007). It is also possible that adaptation could be facilitated by selection of domains in which control is most feasible. As suggested by the model of selective optimization with compensation (Baltes et al., 2006), successful aging can be achieved by making choices to focus or invest efforts in those areas which would be most fruitful and satisfying.

The general sense of personal mastery showed significant declines over time in the youngest and oldest two groups. Those in the middle maintained their levels of mastery over the 9 to 10 years. One way that mastery may be maintained is that middle-age adults become skilled at knowing their strengths (Lachman, 2004). They may identify the areas in which they excel, and this can boost their overall sense of mastery and protect them against declines in general personal mastery when failures or losses are experienced. There is also evidence that mastery is formed and maintained by experiencing challenges and experiencing oneself as an effective agent in the face of adversity (Pearlin, Nguyen, Schieman, & Milkie, 2007). Although past work has found this trend for older adults, we are not aware of earlier work finding this loss of mastery in those moving from their late 20s and early 30s into their early 30s and 40s. This may be a particularly vulnerable group as they are faced with multiple life transitions in the work and family domains. It also could be a period effect (Schaie, 2005) due to the occurrence of major events such as 9/11, economic downturn, or the Iraq War during the period of the study between 1994–1995 and 2004–2006, which could have a particularly devastating effect on the sense of control for those transitioning into adulthood.

We also found significant change in perceived constraints. The youngest and oldest groups both showed an increase in constraints. It is also striking that those in midlife look the best with regard to perceived constraints. The middle-age groups experienced a decrease in constraints over the 10-year period, and they had the highest level of control captured by the lowest level of perceived constraints. Those in midlife may be able to minimize constraints due to increasing experience in dealing with the stresses and strains of work and family life. This picture is consistent with the view that midlife is a period of peak competence (Lachman, 2004). With regard to control over children, there is a clear downward pattern in control across the life span, but it was only the two youngest groups moving from mid-20s through mid-50s who experienced significant declines over the 10 years. This likely reflects an adaptive process of children becoming more independent and self-sufficient as they get older. Nevertheless, a loss of control over one's children is a uniform experience across adulthood.

An interesting pattern was revealed for health control. Consistent with previous cross-sectional data (Lachman & Firth, 2004; Lachman & Weaver, 1998), we found no significant longitudinal changes in health control up to the early seventies. However, during the transition of the oldest group from the mid-60s and 70s into the mid-70s and 80s, there was evidence for declines in health control. Generally, adults feel there are things they can do to control their health, at least until old old age (i.e., after 75 years). This is consistent with the widespread belief in the U.S. that there are things we can do to maintain our health, even if we do not necessarily do them (Lachman, 2005, 2006). Nevertheless, in late life, as losses accumulate and reserve capacity diminishes, the sense that one can do things to control health also begins to decline.

For contributions to others' well-being, there was an increase in control for the youngest adults and the young old, but the oldest group showed a steep decline. This may reflect a shift from a focus on generativity and giving to others to a period in which help from younger members of the family and society is directed toward the older adult rather than the other way around (Lachman, 2004). Work control increased in midlife but showed a decline in late life, which is likely tied to issues related to mandatory retirement or the need to leave the workforce due to health problems and limitations. Financial control increased in early midlife, during the time that adults typically establish themselves in their careers, and remained stable thereafter. Control over sex showed marked decline for all ages. In past cross-sectional work, we found a similar pattern and found also that sex control was positively related to frequency of sexual relations (Lachman & Weaver, 1998). The decline in perceived control over sex could be tied to decreases in sexual relations due to physical health changes, stresses, and pressures associated with juggling work and family responsibilities, or marital/partner problems. Nevertheless, perceived control over marriage relationship increased, but only for those in midlife. Findings of improved marital relations in midlife are often attributed to the timing of grown children leaving the home (Lachman, 2004). Many of these longitudinal changes are consistent with the cross-sectional changes noted in earlier studies (e.g., Lachman & Firth, 2004). Note that in Figures 7.1 to 7.9, the longitudinal change examined over 10 years is highly comparable to the 10 years between age groups; thus it is possible to look at the degree of convergence of cross-sectional and longitudinal patterns by comparing the points from Time 1 to Time 2 with the age group differences within time periods. In many cases the Time 1 and Time 2 points match up across age/cohorts, indicating similarities between cross-sectional and longitudinal patterns.

When looking at antecedents of changes in control beliefs, we found a number of significant predictors, although the specific ones varied by control dimension. Consistent with findings by Krause (2007), we found that those who have greater anticipated social support are more likely to maintain a sense of control. Also, those who have a more adaptive personality profile and better health and cognitive functioning show smaller declines in control over time. We found that increases in constraints were associated with an interaction of cognition and age.

For young adults, the level of cognition was not related to change. However, for middle-age and older adults, those who had low levels of cognition had greater increases in constraints. Those older adults with higher cognition showed the lowest level of increased constraints. Thus, cognitive resources seem to be protective in terms of minimizing a loss of control in middle and older adulthood.

Control beliefs also play a salient role in maintaining life satisfaction in adulthood. Those who had higher levels of control beliefs were more likely to maintain or increase in life satisfaction over time. Also, health and social relations were positively related to life satisfaction changes. Moreover, when we examined changes in these predictors we found that for those who increased their social support, control beliefs and health were more likely to increase in life satisfaction. This suggests that psychosocial factors play a major contributing role in the maintenance or improvement in life satisfaction. In contrast, demographic factors such as age, gender, and education do not contribute as much to variations in life satisfaction.

Conclusion

The sense of control over one's life in general and within specific domains of life is considered a key indicator of successful aging (Rowe & Kahn, 1998). Consistent with much of the cross-sectional literature, we found evidence for declines in the sense of control over time in a national sample of adults in the United States studied over a 9- to 10-year period. In many cases, the 10-year cross-sectional differences map directly onto the 10-year change data. Average patterns of change show both gains and losses across different dimensions of control, and these patterns also vary by age cohort group. Those in midlife look particularly strong in terms of reporting the lowest levels of perceived constraints and showing declines over time. In contrast, those in later life not only experienced increases in perceived constraints but also declines in health control. We also found a surprising pattern in which the youngest age cohorts, moving from mid-20s and early 30s into mid-30s and early 40s, showed a significant decline in mastery and increase in constraints. Further work is needed to disentangle the possible sources of these changes and to what extent they are due to period effects.

We also investigated individual differences in control beliefs and identified significant antecedents of changes in control. We found that maintaining a sense of control in adulthood is tied to key biopsychosocial factors. Specifically, we found that those who have a more adaptive personality profile, better quality of social relationships, better health, and higher cognitive functioning were more likely to maintain or increase control beliefs in general and in multiple domains. Finally, control beliefs also play a significant role for maintaining life satisfaction in later life in the face of increasing losses. A high sense of control over one's life was associated with greater increases in life satisfaction across adulthood. Moreover, those who showed increases in control beliefs were more likely to show increases in life satisfaction. Control beliefs contributed to life satisfaction changes in conjunction with health and social support. Overall, the results suggest that a sense of control is a key protective factor for subjective well-being in the face of declining health and other losses in later life.

References

Antonucci, T. C., & Jackson, J. S. (1987). Social support, interpersonal efficacy, and health: A life course perspective. In L. L. Carstensen & B. A. Edelstein (Eds.), *Handbook of clinical gerontology* (pp. 291–311). New York: Pergamon.

Baltes, P. B., Lindenberger, U., & Staudinger, U. M. (2006). Lifespan theory in developmental psychology. In R. M. Lerner & W. Damon (Eds.), *Handbook of child psychology: Vol. 1. Theoretical models of human development* (6th. ed., pp. 569–664). Hoboken, NJ: Wiley.

Baltes, P. B., Reese, H. W., & Nesselroade, J. R. (1977). *Lifespan developmental psychology: Introduction to research methods*. Belmont, CA: Wadsworth.

Bandura, A. (1997). *Self-efficacy: The exercise of control*. New York: Freeman.

Brim, O. G., Ryff, C. D., & Kessler, R., (Eds.). (2004). *How healthy are we?: A national study of well-being at midlife*. Chicago: University of Chicago Press.

Caplan, L. J., & Schooler, C. (2003). The roles of fatalism, self-confidence, and intellectual resources in the disablement process in older adults. *Psychology and Aging, 18,* 551–561.

Costa, P. T., Jr., & McCrae, R. R. (1980). Influence of extraversion and neuroticism on subjective well-being: Happy and unhappy people. *Journal of Personality and Social Psychology, 38,* 668–678.

Krause, N. (2007). Age and decline in role-specific feelings of control. *The Journals of Gerontology: Series B. Psychological Sciences and Social Sciences, 62,* S28–S35.

Krause, N., & Shaw, B. A. (2003). Role-specific control, personal meaning, and health in late life. *Research on Aging, 25,* 559–586.

Lachman, M. E. (2004). Development in midlife. *Annual Review of Psychology, 55,* 305–331

Lachman, M. E. (2005, January). Aging under control? *Psychological Science Agenda*. Retrieved January 11, 2005, from http://www.apa.org/science/psa/sb-lachman.html

Lachman, M. E. (2006). Perceived control over aging-related declines: Adaptive beliefs and behaviors. *Current Directions in Psychological Science, 15,* 282–286.

Lachman, M. E., & Andreoletti, C. (2006). Strategy use mediates the relationship between control beliefs and memory performance for middle-aged and older adults. *The Journals of Gerontology: Series B. Psychological Sciences and Social Sciences, 61,* P88–P94.

Lachman, M. E., & Firth, K. M. P. (2004). The adaptive value of feeling in control during midlife. In O. G. Brim, C. D. Ryff, & R. Kessler (Eds.), *How healthy are we? A national study of well-being at midlife* (pp. 320–349). Chicago: University of Chicago Press.

Lachman, M. E., Röcke, C., Rosnick, C., & Ryff, C. D. (2008). Realism and illusion in Americans' temporal views of their life satisfaction: Age differences in reconstructing the past and anticipating the future. *Psychological Science, 9,* 889–897.

Lachman, M. E., & Tun, P. A. (2008). Cognitive testing in large-scale surveys: Assessment by telephone. In S. M. Hofer & D. F. Alwin (Eds.), *Handbook on cognitive aging: Interdisciplinary perspectives* (pp. 506–523). Thousand Oaks, CA: Sage.

Lachman, M. E., & Weaver, S. L. (1997). *The Midlife Development Inventory (MIDI) Personality Scales: Scale construction and scoring*. Unpublished technical report, Brandeis University, Waltham, MA.

Lachman, M. E., & Weaver, S. L. (1998). Sociodemographic variations in the sense of control by domain: Findings from the MacArthur Studies of Midlife. *Psychology and Aging, 13,* 553–562.

Mirowsky J. (1995). Age and the sense of control. *Social Psychology Quarterly, 58,* 31–43.

Musek, J. (2007). A general factor of personality: Evidence for the Big One in the five-factor model. *Journal of Research in Personality, 41,* 1213–1233.

Pearlin, L. I., & Schooler, C. (1978). The structure of coping. *Journal of Health and Social Behavior, 19,* 2–21.

Pearlin, L. I., Nguyen, K. B., Schieman, S., & Milkie, M. A. (2007). The life-course origins of mastery among older people. *Journal of Health and Social Behavior, 48,* 164–179.

Röcke, C., & Lachman, M. E. (in press). Perceived trajectories of past, present, and future life satisfaction: Patterns, correlates and 10-year change in young, middle-aged and older adults. *Psychology and Aging*.

Rowe, J. W., & Kahn, R. L. (1998). *Successful aging*. New York: Random House.

Schaie, K. W. (1996). *Intellectual development in adulthood: The Seattle Longitudinal Study*. New York: Cambridge University Press.

Schaie, K. W. (2005). *Developmental influences on adult intelligence: The Seattle Longitudinal Study*. New York: Oxford University Press.

Thompson, S. C. (1999). Illusions of control: How we overestimate our personal influence. *Current Directions in Psychological Science, 8,* 187–190.

8

Use It or Lose It: An Old Hypothesis, New Evidence, and an Ongoing Controversy

Christopher Hertzog

One of the more interesting and difficult questions regarding aging is the extent of malleability or plasticity in cognitive development over the adult life span. Few scientists question that there is a causal relation between biological aging mechanisms, as they affect the central nervous system, and some aspects of cognitive function. What are at stake, however, are two important issues. First, to what extent do observed age differences and age changes in cognitive tasks reflect the effects of neurobiological aging as opposed to other influences such as environmental context (e.g., Hertzog, 2008; Hess, 2005)? Second, do people's behaviors influence the course of their own cognitive development? Stine-Morrow (2007) posed this question in terms of how people's life choices influence their cognitive development in adulthood.

This chapter focuses on this second issue. I shall use the generic term *cognitive enrichment* to capture the concept that individuals' actions can influence their cognitive status in old age (see Hertzog, Kramer, Wilson, & Lindenberger, in press, for further discussion of these ideas). The chapter begins with a discussion of the current societal prevalence of the idea that lifestyles influence cognitive development in adulthood. Next, I outline three different types of mechanisms that could affect cognitive enrichment. I then review the current controversy regarding evidence for and against cognitive enrichment effects.

The "Use It or Lose It" View of Aging and Cognition

Scientific and general societal views on how peoples' behaviors influence their cognitive status in adulthood and old age have evolved considerably over the course of the last 50 years. Whereas the dominant stereotype in the early 20th century about cognitive function in old age was one of senility and inevitable decline, it is far more common to view cognitive function as a direct consequence of one's lifestyle. The adage "use it or lose it" may reflect in general a lay

This chapter was supported by a grant from the National Institute on Aging, one of the National Institutes of Health (R37-AG13148).

representation of a well-known principle of skill acquisition and maintenance—namely, that only by deliberate practice can a skill be acquired and then maintained at its highest levels of execution (Ericsson & Charness, 1994). A good example is the ability to comprehend and speak a language first acquired in adolescence or later. There is an astonishing degree of savings in passive recognition vocabulary in a second language with the passage of long periods of time (e.g., Bahrick, 1984). However, speaking the language is a different matter. Without consistent use, speaking fluency decays rapidly. Not using the language causes one to lose proficiency with it. Likewise, complex motor skills, such as playing golf or tennis, drop in proficiency if not practiced. In effect, one could argue that this concept has been generalized to include the idea that using one's cognitive machinery will prevent age-related loss in its integrity.

What about aging and cognitive functioning? As opposed to the dominant stereotype of senility, the current prevailing attitude is that use it or lose it is in fact directly relevant to the problem of maintaining levels of cognitive function in old age. In one study, my colleagues and I asked younger and older adults to take a test of memory—free recall of a list of words—and then to respond to questions about their performance on the test, and memory experiences in everyday life, using a structured interview method (Hertzog, McGuire, Horhota, & Jopp, 2008). We transcribed the interview and then used a qualitative coding scheme to classify people's responses with respect to implicit theories about control over memory. In what ways do people have, or not have, control over their memories? What are the means by which such control could be achieved? Younger adults were more likely to mention metacognitive factors (see Hertzog & Hultsch, 2000), such as knowing about how memory works, using strategies to help them remember, and so on. Their approach involved strategic management of memory in task contexts. Older adults were more likely to make statements consistent with the idea that practicing and using memory helped to maintain it. One respondent stated explicitly that he routinely practiced retrieving information to make sure that his memory would work when he needed it. Older adults were also more likely to state that their control over memory derived from maintaining an active mind, including activities such as doing crossword puzzles, brain teasers, and other mental exercise. In short, older adults were more likely than younger adults to believe that how they behave has a major impact on how well they can maintain cognitive functioning as they grow old.

These beliefs of older adults do not arise in a social vacuum and are probably not merely a reflection of learning, through direct or indirect experience, that mental activity helps to maintain function. Instead, these beliefs seem to reflect a major societal shift in beliefs and attitudes about aging and cognition that has occurred over the past 30 years. They are consistent with arguments made in the popular press, in the publications and Web postings of the Alzheimer's Association, the American Association of Retired Persons, and other organizations concerned with the well-being and welfare of older adults.

The use it or lose it belief is also consistent with arguments made by some scientists who study the aging process and how it affects cognition. Evidence concerning the benefits of an intellectually engaged lifestyle has been accumulating over the last 50 years, although there is still considerable debate whether the evidence supports the cognitive enrichment hypothesis. Many scientists have discussed the idea in books, articles, or statements intended for the general public. In effect, the scientific community is speaking and the public is listening.

K. Warner Schaie is one scientist who has consistently challenged the stereotype of cognitive decline and argued that cognitive abilities are malleable throughout adulthood. Based in part on results from the Seattle Longitudinal Study (SLS), Schaie has argued strongly for the position that intellectually engaging activities promote enhancement and maintenance of cognitive functioning. His position on this issue was perhaps first and best crystallized in an article on the "myth of intellectual decline" (Baltes & Schaie, 1974) that provoked a great deal of controversy and scientific debate at the time (e.g., Botwinick, 1977; Horn & Donaldson, 1976). His argument and evidence evolved with the introduction of a training component to the SLS in collaboration with Sherry Willis (Schaie & Willis, 1986) in which they demonstrated training improvements in persons with prior history of cognitive decline in psychometric test performance. In his 2005 book on the SLS, Schaie stated,

> I conclude that the onset of intellectual decline is often postponed for individuals who live in favorable environmental circumstances, as would be the case for those persons characterized by a high socioeconomic status. These circumstances include above-average education, histories of occupational pursuits that involve high complexity and low routine, and the maintenance of intact families. Likewise, risk of cognitive decline is lower for persons with substantial involvement in activities typically available in complex and intellectually stimulating environments. Such activities include extensive reading, travel, attendance at cultural events, pursuit of continuing education activities, and participation in clubs and professional associations. (p. 421)

In this case, Schaie is arguing that risk of cognitive decline depends on the degree of cognitive complexity created by one's lifestyle at work and at play.

Warner has also given interviews to members of the press in which he has argued for the benefits of mental exercise. I found one such interview on the Web:

> People who maintain their mental abilities tend to seek out activities that require thinking and decision-making. For example, playing bridge is probably a lot better for you than playing bingo, unless you're playing 25 bingo cards and have to remember them all. If you feel that you are beginning to have trouble thinking of the right word, crossword puzzles are a great exercise. (Schaie, as quoted in Schardt, 1997)

The implication of Schaie's position in the interview is clear. If you want to maintain a cognitive skill, practice it. If you do, you won't lose it.

In fact, one encounters in various guises both of these views on cognitive enrichment in the general literature, as well as a third view: the benefits of continued intellectual engagement for acquisition of new knowledge. I turn now to a brief description and discussion of each of the three types of cognitive enrichment effects.

Cognitive Enrichment as Deliberate
Practice of Cognitive Skills

Note that the premise of Schaie's interview statement is that practicing specific cognitive skills will help maintain those skills in adulthood and old age. This idea of deliberate practice as a means of attaining and achieving expertise is also grounded in studies on training cognitive performance of older adults (e.g., Ball et al., 2002; Willis et al., 2006) that show that performance improvements are possible with training. When Willis, Baltes, and colleagues (see Baltes & Willis, 1982) first argued for the plasticity of cognitive function in adulthood, basing their argument on training studies, their arguments met with considerable skepticism and controversy. For instance, training studies were dismissed as "training the test" rather than as evidence for plasticity of the cognitive mechanisms in question. Critics of the plasticity argument suggested that training improvements in older adults were uninteresting without the "proper" young adult controls to determine whether older adults benefited more than younger adults. Today, in 2009, results of the rigorous, large-scale training studies that have been conducted over the past decades suggest that training effects are not occurring only at the level of the test (e.g., Schaie, Willis, Hertzog, & Schulenberg, 1987). However, these studies do still indicate that these improvements typically have a narrow span of transfer to other cognitive tasks (cf. Edwards et al., 2002, 2005).

What is the implication of narrow transfer of training for cognitive enrichment effects? The answer seems to be that one needs to practice the skills one wants to keep. For example, working with addition and subtraction will help with balancing a checkbook. (One might hasten to add: only if you balance your checkbook by hand and not with a computer program!) Indeed, Schaie's work on cohort effects in cognition suggests that, if anything, there are cohort differences in the simple numerical skills—with older adults tending to have high levels of skill—that could be a consequence of cohort difference in the reliance on those skills for everyday tasks (e.g., Schaie, 2005). Such effects do not prevent age-related changes in performance on psychometric tests of numerical facility, but that may be more a reflection of age-related slowing of information-processing speed than loss of numerical skill per se (e.g., Hertzog, 1989).

Presumably, Schaie would extend the argument of practice-based enhancement to a wide variety of cognitive skills and mechanisms that are studied by cognitive psychologists. For example, practicing tasks high in working memory demands (holding information in a short-term store while working with it; Baddeley, 1986) would maintain the functional capacity of working memory. Older adults are known to have difficulty in resisting the effects of interference during cognitive tests (e.g., the build up of proactive interference during learning tasks using similar items in repeated trials; Kliegl & Lindenberger, 1993). People high in working memory capacity show more resistance to interference within and outside the working memory task (Lustig, May, & Hasher, 1999; Rosen & Engle, 1998). Perhaps repeated practice with working memory tasks would facilitate resistance to these types of interference effects, a phenomenon that might produce a broader gradient of transfer to other cognitive tasks. In fact, recent work involving training of executive control functions suggests that training aspects of cognitive control that are relevant to complex task environments increase the likelihood of transfer of training to different, untrained cognitive tasks (e.g., Basak, Boot, Voss, & Kramer, in press; Dahlin, Stigsdotter-Neely, Larsson, Bäckman & Nyberg, 2008; Jennings, Webster, Kleykamp, & Dagenbach, 2005; see Hertzog et al., in press, for a review). Transfer, from this perspective, is best when one trains cognitive skills required in a wide array of controlled-processing tasks.

Knowledge Accumulation and Adult Development

An alternative type of cognitive enrichment is based on concepts of knowledge accumulation and on the benefits of knowledge and expertise on complex cognition. As noted in Baltes and Baltes's (1990) metatheory on life-span development, individuals occupy specific niches or roles through processes of selection and optimization. They choose what to do with their lives, and these choices have consequences for the kinds of skills they learn and the knowledge and expertise they develop (Rybash, Hoyer, & Roodin, 1986). Ackerman and his colleagues have likewise argued that development in adulthood is characterized by the accumulation of specialized knowledge that enhances function in one's occupation and other life roles (Ackerman, 2000; Ackerman & Rolfhus, 1999; Beier & Ackerman, 2005). This type of positive change with increasing age and experience is consistent with the concept of crystallized intelligence (Cattell, 1971; Horn, 1989), but it goes well beyond the kinds of knowledge measured by typical psychometric tests of vocabulary tests or tests of world knowledge that characterize standardized tests of crystallized knowledge (e.g., McGrew, 1997). The knowledge people gain with life experience is not merely declarative knowledge about the world but also includes tacit procedural knowledge about how to achieve goals in social contexts (Cianciolo et al., 2006; Wagner & Sternberg, 1985).

Knowledge accumulation matters for maintaining cognitive function in actual life precisely because most cognition in the real world involves application of what one knows to solve problems that are different but generically familiar. People learn how to work in teams to achieve goals. They learn strategies that enable them to perform at high levels in specific contexts and how to adapt strategic approaches to tailor their behavior to situational demands. From this point of view, the types of cognitive processes and mechanism studied by cognitive psychologists, which often show normative decline in old age, are less relevant to understanding effective cognitive functioning in the workplace and other environments because of the importance of building and using knowledge. Older adults function well in familiar work environments, despite changes in memory or other cognitive mechanisms, because they have relevant experience with typical problem structures in their work environments, and they can rely on knowledge about what works and what does not work to achieve relevant goals. Maintaining high levels of function require, from this perspective, building and maintaining active access to knowledge that is relevant to a problem and can be used efficiently in real time to solve that problem.

For example, Masunaga and Horn (2000) showed that strategic reasoning in a complex game, Go, required flexible reasoning in the context of knowledge about game scenarios and situations. Masunaga and Horn referred to knowledge-imbued reasoning as something like grounded fluid intelligence and contrasted it to fluid intelligence as measured by performance on the relatively context-free, unfamiliar reasoning problems used in psychometric tests of fluid ability. Standard fluid ability alone could not predict much of the variance in reasoning during a game of Go, and it overestimated age effects on performance among experienced players (Masunaga & Horn, 2001). Older experts often outperform young novices in complex tasks because rapidly accessed and utilized knowledge trumps raw reasoning power (Hertzog, 2008). In Baltes's (1987) terms, pragmatics can be far more important than the mechanics of cognition for successful thinking in the natural ecology.

Broad-Spectrum Benefits of an Engaged Lifestyle

The specificity-of-practice and knowledge-accumulation hypotheses can be contrasted with another type of cognitive enrichment effect stated by older adults in the Hertzog et al. (2008) study on perceptions of control over memory, that is, the general benefits of a cognitively engaged lifestyle. In this case, the hypothesis is that leading an intellectually active life has broad and general benefits for cognitive function. Indeed, the broadest construal of the hypothesis is that behaviors such as good nutritional practice, physical exercise, and social engagement benefit cognition. Such effects could be mediated by enhancing the function of the central nervous system, the substrate of all behavior and cognition (for a review, see Hertzog et al., in press). Physical fitness can lead to increased blood flow to the brain and even to the growth of new neurons and new interconnections among neurons (e.g., through the process of synaptogenesis).

By this account, intellectually engaging activities could be part of a larger profile of an active, involved individual whose zest for life leads to continuing enrichment of many aspects of psychological and physical function. Included in that pattern of active life-engagement is a style of engaging with the world that enhances cognition—seeking new ideas, new information, and new experiences. Proponents of a positive psychology of aging would argue that individuals produce their own developmental patterns of cognition in adulthood and old age by the way in which they lead their lives. Well-adjusted, goal-directed, self-enhancing individuals create an abundant life that results in a positive cascade of benefits for the mind, its neuronal substrate, and its varied functions, including cognition.

Salthouse's Contrarian View

Salthouse (2006) argued that there is little compelling evidence to support the claim that mental exercise forestalls cognitive decline. He debunked the use it or lose it hypothesis as unproven at best and, at worst, largely unsupported by available empirical evidence. His arguments included several points. First, he argued that the hypothesis should be tested by demonstrating different cross-sectional curves mapping age onto cognitive function. That is, individuals who engage in intellectually stimulating activities should show less cognitive decline, and this effect should result in shallower average chronological age slopes in cross-sectional data, relative to their peers who do not engage in such activities. He found no statistically significant evidence of Age × Activity interactions in several of his own cross-sectional data sets.

Second, he questioned the validity of self-reports of activities relevant to cognitive enrichment effects. He noted that in his own data, people report an implausibly large number of hours of relevant activities. Third, he criticized studies by Schooler and colleagues (e.g., Schooler, Mulatu, & Oates, 1999) that contributed some of the supporting evidence for cognitive enrichment effects. The critique focused in large part on the validity of Schooler's measures of cognitive ability.[1]

To play on the bard, I write this section to praise Salthouse, not to bury him. Salthouse's contrarian view of cognitive enrichment effects is important precisely because the current Zeitgeist is running so strongly in the other direction. It is useful for the field to have a gadfly, one well-respected for his many contributions to our science, who questions a generally accepted viewpoint. This characterization in itself may be too extreme because it is an open question whether the cognitive enrichment hypothesis can be characterized as having been generally accepted by the scientific community, even though it is a widely held concept in society at large. Indeed, in the interest of full disclosure, I must note that Salthouse's (2006) closing statement echoes an argument my colleagues and I (Hertzog, Hultsch, & Dixon, 1999) made several years earlier concerning what we then termed the *engagement hypothesis* (i.e., that living a cognitively engaged lifestyle would maintain cognitive functioning):

> We argue that the current evidence for the engagement hypothesis is less than definitive. Naturally, we would endorse and recommend to adults of all ages that they engage in intellectually stimulating activities, that they function as fully informed citizens of society, and that they take on and solve difficult and challenging problems in their everyday lives. We would do so because we endorse the view that intellectual engagement and an active personal and social life are a component of quality of life and, in older adults, one possible indication of successful aging (Rowe & Kahn, 1998). Older adults, like anyone else, should do crossword puzzles and other activities if they find them entertaining and enjoyable. Whether they should consider such activities to be the analog of aerobic exercise for their cortex, and therefore solve puzzles in order to foster maintenance of their cognitive functioning, is still very much a matter of debate. (Hertzog et al., 1999, p. 533)

Salthouse (2006) put it this way:

> Although my professional opinion is that at the present time the mental-exercise hypothesis is more of an optimistic hope than an empirical reality, my personal recommendation is that people should behave as if it were true. That is, people should continue to engage in mentally stimulating activities because even if there is not yet evidence that it has beneficial effects in slow-

---

[1]For further discussion of this point, see Schooler (2007) along with Salthouse's (2007) rejoinder.

ing the rate of age-related decline in cognitive functioning, there is no evidence that it has any harmful effects, the activities are often enjoyable and thus may contribute to a higher quality of life, and engagement in cognitively demanding activities serves as an existence proof—if you can still do it, you know that you haven't lost it. (pp. 84–85)

Actually, neither Salthouse (2006) nor Hertzog et al. (1999) claimed that cognitive enrichment effects did not exist. Rather, both papers argued that the evidence was inconclusive and that more compelling evidence was needed. Salthouse (2006, 2007) raised a rather high standard of evidence that would be needed to convince him of the validity of the mental exercise hypothesis. I explain my own current views on that issue later in this chapter. They have changed somewhat on this subject, for several reasons.

I do argue, however, that Salthouse's own empirical evidence against the broad-spectrum cognitive enrichment hypothesis is itself unconvincing for several reasons. First, Salthouse, Berish, and Miles (2002) actually found an Age × Activity interaction in cross-sectional data for a composite vocabulary test (a measure of crystallized intelligence). Salthouse (2006) dismissed it as a simple effect of knowledge acquisition. Perhaps so, but that is a form of cognitive enrichment, and these results suggest that acquisition of new knowledge is occurring across the life span for those who are intellectually active (see also Bowles, Grimm, & McArdle, 2005). The effects might have been larger if person-specific measures of life experience and expertise had been assessed, as in Ackerman's (2000) work.

Second, Salthouse et al. (2002) failed to find a relationship of their total activity measure to cross-sectional age trends on three other cognitive composite variables: spatial ability, reasoning, and episodic memory. However, their activity scale showed very low correlations with cognition in general. The problem with a general activity scale, even one that weights activities as a function of theoretically expected cognitive stimulation, is that many activities have negligible or even negative relations to cognitive functioning. Studies using the Victoria Longitudinal Study (VLS) activity questionnaire suggest stronger relations of factorially defined subsets of activities to cognition than were detected by Salthouse et al. (see Hultsch, Hammer, & Small, 1993; Hultsch, Hertzog, Small, & Dixon, 1999; Jopp & Hertzog, 2007), especially when latent variable analysis is used to correct for the measurement error one finds in specific activity items (see also Schooler, 2007).[2] The problem may lie in part with Salthouse's questionnaire and the adequacy of its representation (content validity) of cognitively stimulating activities. The questionnaire also asked people to estimate the number of hours per week they engaged in specific activities, which may have encouraged the kind of over-reporting described at length in Salthouse (2006), thereby reducing the construct validity of their measure. The frequency rating scale used by Hultsch et al. (1993) may be more immune to

---

[2]Jopp and Hertzog (2007) found stronger cross-sectional activity-cognition relations with the Victoria Longitudinal Study activity questionnaire but also failed to detect cross-sectional Age × Activity interactions in predicting cognitive abilities, including measures of inductive reasoning in a cross-sectional sample of about 300 persons.

distorted estimates at the upper end of the scale. Admittedly, more work is certainly needed to demonstrate and enhance the validity of self-reported activities that are relevant to cognitive enrichment effects.

Third, Salthouse (2006) also showed aggregate data from some of his previous studies evaluating relations of crossword puzzle experience (in this context, a proxy for long-term cognitive exercise) to reasoning and vocabulary. He plotted age trends in these two cognitive variables as a function of highest or lowest quartiles of self-reported experience doing puzzles. Note that crossword puzzle activity is only one possible component of a cognitively engaged lifestyle that could influence age changes in fluid intelligence measures like reasoning. Nevertheless, the cross-sectional trends suggested a small Age × Puzzle Experience interaction effect for the reasoning test (see Salthouse, 2006, Figure 6). The sample slopes for age appeared to be shallower for more experienced puzzlers, even though the difference in these slopes wasn't statistically reliable. Given that continuous variable interactions are difficult to detect in moderated regression analysis (McClelland & Judd, 1993), the problem could be one of low statistical power, even though Salthouse used a large aggregate sample of more than 1,000 persons. As McClelland and Judd (1993) pointed out, the problem is not merely one of obtaining a large sample but also of adequate sampling of bivariate extremes to identify the interaction (i.e., sampling sufficient numbers of high activity vs. low activity persons at each age level in the cross-section). Salthouse accepted the null hypothesis of zero Age × Activity interaction effects without conducting a post hoc power analysis on his interaction effects.

There is good reason to believe that cross-sectional Age × Activity interaction effects on cognition will have very small effect sizes, even when it is the case that changes in cognitive function are reliably associated with levels of cognitively stimulating activities. Cross-sectional variance can be decomposed into three parts: (a) variance due to individual differences in the variable at the age of onset (e.g., mean age 25); (b) variance due to the mean cross-sectional trend (slope); and (c) variance due to individual differences in change over the life span, realized at the age at which different persons are sampled. Some persons will have aged from 25 to 50, some from 25 to 75, and so on. When two variables are correlated in cross-sectional data, correlations due to sources (a) and (b) above will dominate, because individual differences in rates of change are typically small relative to the individual differences in young adulthood and average changes in the population (e.g., Hertzog & Schaie, 1986, 1988). Although many longitudinal studies show that there are individual differences in cognitive change in midlife and old age (e.g., Hertzog, Dixon, Hultsch, & MacDonald, 2003), it is still the case that stability of individual differences over long periods of time in these same studies is relatively high. Regarding activities and cognition, the proportion of cross-sectional variance associated with individual differences in cognitive change for persons differing in cognitively enriching activities can be quite low because of the dominance of mean cross-sectional trends in cognition and activities as well as age-consistent ability-activity relations (Hofer, Flaherty, & Hoffman, 2006; Lindenberger, von Oertzen, Ghisletta, & Hertzog, 2008; for additional discussion of this issue, see Hertzog et al., in press). To put it crudely, no one expects a cognitively active and engaged lifestyle to make an Einstein out of a used car salesman, nor would one expect one active and one inactive identical twin to show radically different profiles of cognitive ability. Given the importance of genetic and ontogenetic influences on adult cognition, cognitive enrichment effects will be, by any reasonable standard, small effects associated with subtle ordinal interactions. Given this expectation, doubting the existence of cognitive enrichment effects by accepting the null hypothesis is a hazardous exercise.

Fourth and finally, cross-sectional data are not well-suited for examining the cognitive enrichment hypothesis, for reasons other than the small effect size problem just noted. One reason concerns whether the Age × Activity interaction is the right criterion for judging enrichment effects (Hertzog et al., in press; Schooler, 2007). Another reason is the potential methodological confound of differential selection of participants into studies from different parts of the adult life span. Low levels of physical and social activity may be differentially associated with morbidity and mortality in late middle-age and old age, progressively changing the composition of the surviving population at older ages. Conversely, the most active middle-age individuals may refuse to participate in psychological studies because of issues of time commitment. The combination of these two forces (refusal in active middle-age adults; morbidity and mortality of inactive older adults) would attenuate the Age × Activity interactions Salthouse insists are the critical evidence for cognitive enrichment effects.

I argue that longitudinal data, even though they have their own problems, are a more compelling means to evaluate the cognitive enrichment hypothesis, mainly because one can evaluate intraindividual changes in cognition as a function of prior activity levels.

Longitudinal Evidence for Maintenance and Enhancement of Cognitive Function

Over the past 30 years, a wealth of longitudinal data have supported the idea that a cognitively active lifestyle enriches cognitive function and produces less cognitive decline than is observed in persons who are not cognitively active. Some of the data come from the SLS (e.g., Gribbin, Schaie, & Parham, 1980; Schaie, 2005). Much of the recent evidence comes from large-scale epidemiological studies that use large, representative samples in prospective longitudinal designs (e.g., Wilson et al., 2005; see Hertzog et al., in press, for a review). Data from other major longitudinal studies also support variants of the cognitive enrichment hypothesis (e.g., Albert et al., 1995; Hultsch et al., 1999; MacKinnon, Christensen, Hofer, Korten, & Jorm, 2003; Small & McEvoy, 2008). The evidence comes in many different forms, with many different ways of measuring activity or an engaged lifestyle, and by using many different statistical models that are possible for analyzing longitudinal data (see Hertzog & Nesselroade, 2003).

I briefly illustrate some of the findings of the Hultsch et al. (1999) study from the VLS, which used a latent change approach (McArdle & Nesselroade, 1994) to examine a structural regression model. It assessed relations of change in cognition to level and change in cognitively stimulating activities. Figure 8.1 shows the major results, in which both prior level of self-reported activities and change in activities over a 6-year interval predicted change in verbal working

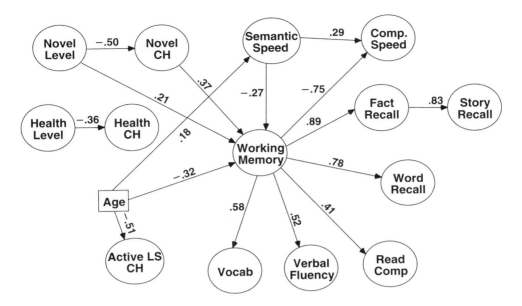

Figure 8.1. Structural equation model depicting relationships among latent changes in contextual variables and latent changes in cognitive variables. Novel = novel information processing; level = status of variable at Time 1; CH = latent change from Time 1 to Time 3; comp = comprehension; Active LS = active lifestyle; vocab = vocabulary. Reprinted from "Use It or Lose It: Engaged Lifestyle as a Buffer of Cognitive Decline in Aging," by D. F. Hultsch, B. J. Small, C. Hertzog, and R. A. Dixon, 1999, *Psychology and Aging, 14,* p. 258. Copyright 1999 by the American Psychological Association.

memory, which in turn predicted 6-year change in other cognitive constructs. These outcomes indicate that individuals who engage in cognitively stimulating activities (characterized by a set of items Hultsch et al. termed *novel information processing*) manifest less cognitive change than individuals who do not. Note that level and change in self-reported health, as measured by typical Likert-rating items, did not predict cognitive change in these data. Such a finding might indicate that the VLS is a positively selected sample, with a truncated range of health problems. Be that as it may, this result indicated it cannot be the case that the effect of intellectual engaging activities is merely an outcome of subjective health status. The linkage between subjective health and actual physical health status also makes it unlikely the cognitive enrichment effect can be reduced to changes in general physical health.

Any causal model based on correlational data is inevitably subject to the argument that the model fits the data but is not actually a reflection of the specific causal effects incorporated in the model. One needs to rule out rival hypotheses, perhaps in the form of competing models. All one can really conclude from results, like the ones in Figure 8.1, is that the data are consistent with the claim of causal flow represented by the model, given acceptable model fit. One can then proceed to interpret the magnitude of the regression coefficients, subject to the assumption that the model is an accurate approximation to reality.

In fact, Hultsch et al. (1999) also estimated an alternative model, shown in Figure 8.2. It suggests that changes in activity in old age are an outcome of general cognitive decline, as defined by a higher order factor of 6-year cognitive changes across several cognitive variables. As we pointed out at the time, this model fit the data about as well as the model in Figure 8.1 but had radically different implications for how to think about the problem of activity and preserved cognitive function. Which is chicken, and which is egg? After age 60 (the focus of the VLS), does cognitive decline cause reductions in activity levels, or do reductions in activity cause cognitive decline? Perhaps most of the statistical evidence from longitudinal studies of older adults that has been used to support the cognitive enrichment hypothesis could be recast as consistent with the model of Figure 8.2. That is, when people start experiencing cognitive decline, they abandon cognitively demanding activities. The longitudinal studies that are available provide compelling evidence that change in the two constructs are correlated, and that prior level of activity is associated with lower levels of late-life cogni-

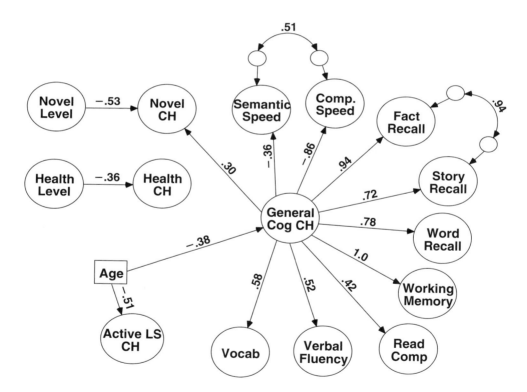

Figure 8.2. Structural equation model depicting relationships among latent changes in contextual variables and general cognitive change. Novel = novel information processing; level = status of variable at Time 1; CH = latent change from Time 1 to Time 3; comp = comprehension; Active LS = active lifestyle; vocab = vocabulary. Reprinted from "Use It or Lose It: Engaged Lifestyle as a Buffer of Cognitive Decline in Aging," by D. F. Hultsch, B. J. Small, C. Hertzog, and R. A. Dixon, 1999, *Psychology and Aging, 14,* p. 259. Copyright 1999 by the American Psychological Association.

tive decline. They do not necessarily establish which variable is leading, which variable is lagging, or what the relative contribution of each variable is in a dynamic reciprocal relationship where each is an influence on the other.

This concern is what led us (Hertzog et al., 1999; Hultsch et al., 1999) to argue that more longitudinal evidence was needed regarding cognitive enrichment effects. Alternative models with very different causal assumptions often fit data equally well, making it difficult to choose the correct model. And the problem is worse than that, actually. Although some longitudinal models (e.g., cross-lagged regression) specify competing lead-lag relationships and/or reciprocal causation (Kessler & Greenberg, 1981), it is not at all clear that the statistical winner in such modeling exercises is the true leading influence. The thorny problem is one of omitted variables. One can never completely rule out the rival explanation that a third variable (e.g., health status, cerebrovascular disease, socioeconomic status) influences both cognitive change and activity change, and that omitting that critical variable produces biased estimates of the relative magnitudes of the lagged relationships. Sliwinski, Hofer, and Hall (2003) provided an excellent demonstration of how unmeasured preclinical Alzheimer's disease could produce individual differences in cognitive change in late life. One obtains "true" causal effects only to the extent that the model is self-contained, that is, all relevant influences on the endogenous variables that correlate with other influence have been measured and modeled (see James, Mulaik, & Brett, 1982, for a clear discussion of this self-containment assumption).

This self-containment assumption is inevitably still an issue for a causal model that has become increasingly popular of late—McArdle's bivariate dual-change score model (BDCSM; McArdle & Hamagami, 2001). It combines a latent growth curve model with latent first-differences and lagged relations among two variables as influences on the growth curves. It has been used to good advantage in a number of recent studies to detect differences in lead-lag relations between two variables. For instance, Lövdén, Ghisletta, and Lindenberger (2005) analyzed data from the Berlin Aging Study and found that social participation had an influence on late-life changes in perceptual speed, whereas perceptual speed did not influence changes in social participation. Likewise, Small and McEvoy (2008) reported BDCSM results from the VLS in which activities had a leading effect on cognitive change, but not vice versa. So far, these models suggest a role for activities in influencing cognitive change, but not vice versa. But the contrarian in me is forced to note that this outcome could be an artifact of omitting critical variables that correlate with the changes in both cognition and activities (e.g., health status, well-being, depressive affect; e.g., Gerstorf, Smith, & Baltes, 2006). Indeed, the classic dual change score model includes only two variables, omitting all others. It, then, is especially dependent on the self-containment assumption. Correlation, no matter how it might be packaged or partitioned in a fancy statistical model, is still not the same as causation.

Such concerns led Salthouse (2006, 2007) to argue strongly that one would only have compelling evidence of mental exercise effects if one ran a randomized intervention design with a control group and engaged in very long-term follow-up to ensure that age was indeed kinder to the more active. There are of course rival explanations for many experimental effects, especially in long-term field studies of the kind suggested here. But most of us are more comfortable with the logic that manipulating a cause should manipulate the effect, and we are willing to ignore the exceptions owing to compromised internal validity or construct validity (Shadish, Cook, & Campbell, 2002).

When Hertzog et al. (1999) commented on possible designs that could generate new, relevant evidence for cognitive enrichment, conducting a long-term randomized control study was not one of our recommendations. From my point of view, such a design is not practically feasible. The kind of long-term follow up Salthouse (2007) envisioned would literally require a wait of between 30 and 50 years for a definitive answer to this important question. As a society, we want and need a provisional answer in the short-term. Besides, if one insisted on an experimental standard of causal proof in all cases, our society would be forced to state that there is no conclusive evidence about a number of well-accepted findings in public health and epidemiology based on correlational evidence, for example, that cigarette smoking causes cancer. Systematic replication, extension, and testing of rival explanations through regression analysis can lead to sound causal inferences from correlational data; it is simply a far more difficult route. The margin of uncertainty and the breadth of untested rival explanations, given the self-containment problem, ensure a long half-life of plausible denial for the contrarian. The major risk, one the contrarian rightly forces us to address, is that we can reify an interpretation by always running one preferred model (in the name of confirmatory analysis) to account for correlational evidence, while ignoring its plausible rivals.

Plausible Neurological Mechanisms for Cognitive Enrichment

Given the foregoing, what has caused me to modify my view on cognitive enrichment effects? Certainly more research is still needed. Nevertheless, there are three major reasons why I believe the available evidence supports the cognitive enrichment hypothesis. First, as just discussed, the preponderance of recent longitudinal evidence on cognitively stimulating activities favors the existence a relationship between intellectually stimulating activities and cognitive change in old age. Although one cannot easily discern the direction of causality or the magnitude of direct effect, this outcome is an important hurdle for the cognitive enrichment hypothesis. The longitudinal data pattern continues to be consistent with the hypothesis.

Second, short-term intervention studies targeting physical exercise in animals and in humans have provided important information about cognitive enrichment effects on both cognition and the neurobiological substrate of the mind: the central nervous system. There is compelling evidence that cognitive performance is substantially improved by physical exercise regimens, even in older populations (e.g., Colcombe & Kramer, 2003; see Hertzog et al., in press, for a review). Importantly, exercise effects are relatively broad-spectrum effects (unlike the specific cognitive effects found in the training literature). Aerobic exercise has tangible benefits for executive functioning and fluid intelligence, and also for many aspects of cognition. Such effects are consistent with the hypothesis that aerobic exercise stimulates circulation in brain regions critical for cognition (e.g., frontal cortex), and also has effects realized through multiple other pathways, such as lowering stress and reducing catabolic effects of stress-related hormones (e.g., cortisol) on the brain (McEwen, 2002). This is the pattern one needs to see to align with the argument that physical activity can be generically associated with preserved cognitive functioning in adulthood.

The animal data show that exercise has effects on brain function and morphology, including creation of new neurons and synaptogenesis (e.g., Cotman, 1995). In fact, the recent literature has supplanted mid-20th-century views of the brain as a relatively static organ with a view of the brain as a highly dynamic structure that is constantly undergoing new cell growth, adaptive connectivity and reconnectivity, and regeneration, even in old age (Kramer, Bherer, Colcombe, Dong, & Greenough, 2004). The benefits of physical exercise for neuronal function in animal populations are likewise broad spectrum effects, affecting many aspects of brain structure and function.

Third, animal studies on enriched social environments continue to show major benefits of these environments on brain structure and function of animals housed in standard cages, and these effects are observed in older animals (e.g., Kempermann, Gast, & Gage, 2002). Given that several studies suggest benefits of social activities for maintenance of cognitive function in old age (e.g., Lövdén et al., 2005; Smits, van Rijsselt, Jonker, & Deeg, 1995; Stine-Morrow, Parisi, Morrow, Greene, & Park, 2007) and given that everyday cognition and memory often occur in social contexts (Hess, 2005), it is also plausible that a socially active lifestyle can have ameliorative effects on cognitive function.

In isolation, none of these streams of research literature provides air-tight evidence for the cognitive enrichment hypothesis. But taken as a whole, the literature is offering evidence of both an association of various kinds of activity with cognition and plausible neurological mechanisms by which such activity could influence brain function. The three types of cognitive enrichment effects I have discussed (specific effects of practicing cognitive skills, knowledge accumulation through intellectual engagement in the world, and broad-spectrum benefits of activity and an engaged lifestyle, especially physical and social activity) have all received substantial empirical support. The case has not been closed, mostly because the problem is an extraordinarily difficult empirical challenge. But I view the available evidence as much more favorable to the cognitive enrichment view than was the case just 10 years ago.

Conclusion

Although the available evidence on cognitive enrichment effects is subject to multiple interpretations, there is sufficient evidence consistent with the hypothesis to ensure that it will continue to receive close scrutiny in the scientific community over the next decade. And meanwhile, the field will ask many new and critical questions concerning cognitive enrichment effects. For example, are more recently born cohorts showing signs of beneficial lifestyle practices to a greater degree than previous generations? Is 60 the new 40 (see chap. 5, this volume)? In addressing these issues, gerontologists will be to a real extent following a trail blazed by K. Warner Schaie and the SLS.

References

Ackerman, P. L. (2000). Domain-specific knowledge as the "dark matter" of adult intelligence: Gf/Gc, personality and interest correlates. *The Journals of Gerontology: Series B. Psychological Sciences and Social Sciences, 55,* P69–P84.

Ackerman, P. L., & Rolfhus, E. L. (1999). The locus of adult intelligence: Knowledge, abilities, and nonability traits. *Psychology and Aging, 14,* 314–330.

Albert, M. S., Jones, K., Savage, C. R., Berkman, L., Seeman, T., Blazer, D., & Rowe, J. W. (1995). Predictors of cognitive change in older persons: MacArthur studies of successful aging. *Psychology and Aging, 10,* 578–589.

Baddeley, A. (1986). *Working memory.* New York: Oxford University Press.

Bahrick, H. P. (1984). Semantic memory content in permastore: Fifty years of memory for Spanish learned in school. *Journal of Experimental Psychology: General, 113,* 1–29.

Ball, K., Berch, D. B., Helmers, K. F., Jobe, J. B., Leveck, M. D., Marsiske, M., et al. (2002). Effects of cognitive training interventions with older adults: A randomized control trial. *JAMA, 288,* 2271–2281.

Baltes, P. B. (1987). Theoretical propositions of life-span developmental psychology: On the dynamics between growth and decline. *Developmental Psychology, 23,* 611–626.

Baltes, P. B., & Baltes, M. M. (1990). Psychological perspectives on successful aging: The model of selective optimization with compensation. In P. B. Baltes & M. M. Baltes (Eds.), *Successful aging: Perspectives from the behavioral sciences* (pp. 1–34). New York: Cambridge University Press.

Baltes, P. B., & Schaie, K. W. (1974). Aging and IQ: The myth of the twilight years. *Psychology Today, 7*(10), 35–40.

Baltes, P. B., & Willis, S. L. (1982). Plasticity and enhancement of intellectual functioning in old age: Penn State's adult development and enrichment project (ADEPT). In F. I. M. Craik & S. E. Trehub (Eds.), *Aging and cognitive processes* (pp. 353–389). New York: Plenum Press.

Basak, C., Boot, W. R., Voss, M. W., & Kramer, A. F. (in press). Can training in a real-time strategy video game attenuate cognitive decline in older adults? *Psychology and Aging.*

Beier, M., & Ackerman, P. L. (2005). Age, ability, and the role of prior knowledge on the acquisition of new domain knowledge: Promising results in a real-world learning environment. *Psychology and Aging, 20,* 341–355.

Botwinick, J. (1977). Intellectual abilities. In J. E. Birren & K. W. Schaie (Eds.), *Handbook of the psychology of aging* (pp. 580–605). New York: Van Nostrand Reinhold.

Bowles, R. P., Grimm, K. J., & McArdle, J. J. (2005). A structural factor analysis of vocabulary knowledge and relations to age. *The Journals of Gerontology: Series B. Psychological Sciences and Social Sciences, 60,* P234–P241.

Cattell, R. B. (1971). *Abilities: Their structure, growth, and action.* Boston: Houghton Mifflin.

Cianciolo, A. T., Grigorenko, E. L., Jarvin, L, Gil, G., Drebot, M. E., & Sternberg, R. J. (2006). Practical intelligence and tacit knowledge: Advances in the measurement of developing expertise. *Learning and Individual Differences, 16,* 235–253.

Colcombe, S., & Kramer, A. F. (2003). Fitness effects on the cognitive function of older adults: A meta-analytic study. *Psychological Science, 14,* 125–130.

Cotman, C. W. (1995). *Synaptic plasticity.* New York: Guilford Press.

Dahlin, E., Stigsdotter-Neely, A., Larsson, A. Bäckman, L., & Nyberg, L. (2008, June 13). Transfer of learning after updating training mediated by the striatum. *Science, 320,* 1510–1512.

Edwards, J. D., Wadley, V. G., Meyers, R. S., Roenker, D. R., Cissell, G. M., & Ball, K. K. (2002). Transfer of a speed of processing intervention to near and far cognitive functions. *Gerontology, 48,* 329–340.

Edwards, J. D., Wadley, V. G., Vance, D. E., Wood, K., Roenker, D. L., & Ball, K. K. (2005). The impact of speed of processing training on cognitive and everyday performance. *Aging & Mental Health, 9,* 262–271.

Ericsson, K. A., & Charness, N. (1994). Expert performance: Its structure and acquisition. *American Psychologist, 49,* 725–747.

Gerstorf, D., Smith, J., & Baltes, P. B. (2006). A systemic-wholistic approach to differential aging: Longitudinal findings from the Berlin Aging Study. *Developmental Psychology, 21,* 645–663.

Gribbin, K., Schaie, K. W., & Parham, I. A. (1980). Complexity of life style and maintenance of intellectual abilities. *Journal of Social Issues 36,* 47–61.

Hertzog, C. (1989). The influence of cognitive slowing on age differences in intelligence. *Developmental Psychology, 25,* 636–651.

Hertzog, C. (2008). Theoretical approaches to the study of cognitive aging: An individual differences perspective. In S. M. Hofer & D. F. Alwin (Eds.), *Handbook of cognitive aging* (pp. 34–49). Thousand Oaks, CA: Sage.

Hertzog, C., Dixon, R. A., Hultsch, D. F., & MacDonald, S. W. S. (2003). Latent change models of adult cognition: Are changes in processing speed and working memory associated with changes in episodic memory? *Psychology and Aging, 18,* 755–769.

Hertzog, C., & Hultsch, D. F. (2000). Metacognition in adulthood and old age. In F. I. M. Craik & T. A. Salthouse (Eds.), *The handbook of aging and cognition* (2nd ed., pp. 417–466). Mahwah, NJ: Erlbaum.

Hertzog, C., Hultsch, D. F., & Dixon, R. A. (1999). On the problem of detecting effects of lifestyle on cognitive change in adulthood: Reply to Pushkar et al. (1999). *Psychology and Aging, 14,* 528–534.

Hertzog, C., Kramer, A. F., Wilson, R. S., & Lindenberger, U. (in press). Enrichment effects on adult cognitive development: Can the functional capacity of older adults be preserved and enhanced? *Psychological Science in the Public Interest.*

Hertzog, C., McGuire, C. L., Horhota, M., & Jopp, D. (2008). *Age differences in theories about memory control: Does believing in "use it or lose it" have implications for self-rated memory control, strategy use, and free recall performance?* Unpublished manuscript.

Hertzog, C., & Nesselroade, J. R. (2003). Assessing psychological change in adulthood: An overview of methodological issues. *Psychology and Aging, 18,* 639–657.

Hertzog, C., & Schaie, K. W. (1986). Stability and change in adult intelligence: 1. Analysis of longitudinal covariance structures. *Psychology and Aging, 1,* 159–171.

Hertzog, C., & Schaie, K. W. (1988). Stability and change in adult intelligence: 2. Simultaneous analysis of longitudinal means and covariance structures. *Psychology and Aging, 3,* 122–130.

Hess, T. M. (2005). Memory and aging in context. *Psychological Bulletin, 131,* 383–406.

Hofer, S. M., Flaherty, B. P., & Hoffman, L. (2006). Cross-sectional analysis of time-dependent data: Mean-induced association in age-heterogeneous samples and an alternative method based on sequential narrow age-cohort samples. *Multivariate Behavioral Research, 41,* 165–187.

Horn, J. L. (1989). Models of intelligence. In R. L. Linn (Ed.), *Intelligence: Measurement, theory, and public policy* (pp. 29–73). Urbana: University of Illinois Press.

Horn, J. L., & Donaldson, G. (1976). On the myth of intellectual decline in adulthood. *American Psychologist, 31,* 701–719.

Hultsch, D. F., Hammer, M., & Small, B. J. (1993). Age differences in cognitive performance in later life: Relationship of self-reported health and activity life style. *The Journals of Gerontology: Series B. Psychological Sciences and Social Sciences, 48,* P1–P11.

Hultsch, D. F., Hertzog, C., Dixon, R. A., & Small, B. J. (1998). *Memory change in the aged.* New York: Cambridge University Press.

Hultsch, D. F., Hertzog, C., Small, B. J., & Dixon, R. A. (1999). Use it or lose it: Engaged lifestyle as a buffer of cognitive decline in aging. *Psychology and Aging, 14,* 245–263.

James, L. R., Mulaik, S. A., & Brett, J. M. (1982). *Causal analysis: Assumptions, models, and data.* Beverly Hills, CA: Sage.

Jennings, J. M., Webster, L. M., Kleykamp, B. A., & Dagenbach, D. (2005). Recollection training and transfer effects in older adults: Successful use of a repetition-lag procedure. *Aging, Neuropsychology, and Cognition, 12,* 278–298.

Jopp, D., & Hertzog, C. (2007). Activities, self-referent memory beliefs, and cognitive performance: Evidence for direct and mediated effects. *Psychology and Aging, 22,* 811–825.

Kempermann, G., Gast, D., & Gage, F. H. (2002). Neuroplasticity in old age: Sustained fivefold induction of hippocampal neurogenesis by long-term environmental enrichment. *Annals of Neurology, 52,* 135–143.

Kessler, R. C., & Greenberg, D. F. (1981). *Linear panel analysis: Models of quantitative change.* New York: Academic Press.

Kliegl, R., & Lindenberger, U. (1993). Modeling intrusion errors and correct recall in episodic memory: Adult age-differences in encoding of list context. *Journal of Experimental Psychology: Learning, Memory, and Cognition, 19,* 617–637.

Kramer, A. F., Bherer, L., Colcombe, S., Dong, W. & Greenough, W. T. (2004). Environmental influences on cognitive and brain plasticity during aging. *The Journals of Gerontology: Series A. Biological Sciences and Medical Sciences, 59,* M940–M957.

Lindenberger, U., von Oertzen, T., Ghisletta, P. & Hertzog, C. (2008). *Cross-sectional age variance extraction: What's change got to do with it?* Unpublished manuscript.

Lövdén, M., Ghisletta, P., & Lindenberger, U. (2005). Social participation attentuates decline in perceptual speed in old and very old age. *Psychology and Aging, 20,* 423–434.

Lustig, C., May, C. P., & Hasher, L. (1999). Working memory span and the role of proactive interference. *Journal of Experimental Psychology: General, 130,* 199–207.

MacKinnon, A., Christensen, H., Hofer, S. M., Korten, A. E., & Jorm, A. F. (2003). Use it and still lose it: The association between activity and cognitive performance established using latent growth techniques in a community sample. *Aging, Neuropsychology, and Cognition, 10,* 215–229.

Masunaga, H., & Horn, J. L. (2000). Characterizing mature human intelligence: Expertise development. *Learning and Individual Differences, 12,* 5–33.

Masunaga, H., & Horn, J. L. (2001). Expertise and age-related changes in components of intelligence. *Psychology and Aging, 16,* 293–311.

McArdle, J. J., & Hamagami, F. (2001). Latent difference score structural models for linear dynamic analyses with incomplete data. In L. M. Collins & A. G. Sayer (Eds.), *New methods for the analysis of change* (pp. 139–175). Washington, DC: American Psychological Association.

McArdle, J. J., & Nesselroade, J. R. (1994). Using multivariate data to structure developmental change. In S. H. Cohen & H. W. Reese (Eds.), *Life-span developmental psychology: Methodological contributions* (pp. 223–267). Mahwah, NJ: Erlbaum.

McClelland, G. H., & Judd, C. M. (1993). Statistical difficulties of detecting interactions and moderator effects. *Psychological Bulletin, 114,* 376–390.

McEwen, B. S. (2002). Sex, stress, and the hippocampus: Allostasis, allostatic load, and the aging process. *Neurobiology of Aging, 23,* 921–939.

McGrew, K. S. (1997). Analysis of the major intelligence batteries according to a proposed comprehensive Gf-Gc framework. In D. P. Flanagan, J. L., Genshaft, & P. L. Harrison (Eds.), *Contemporary intellectual assessment: Theories, tests, and issues* (pp. 151–179). New York: Guilford Press.

Rosen, V. M., & Engle R. W. (1998). Working memory and suppression. *Journal of Memory and Language, 39,* 418–436.

Rybash, J. M., Hoyer, W. J., & Roodin, P. A. (1986). *Adult cognition and aging: Developmental changes in processing, knowing, and thinking.* New York: Pergamon Press.

Salthouse, T. A. (2006). Mental exercise and mental aging: Evaluating the validity of the "use it or lose it" hypothesis. *Perspectives on Psychological Science, 1,* 68–87.

Salthouse, T. A. (2007). Reply to Schooler: Consistent is not conclusive. *Perspectives on Psychological Science, 2,* 30–32.

Salthouse, T. A., Berish, D. E., & Miles, J. D. (2002). The role of cognitive stimulation on the relations between age and cognitive functioning. *Psychology and Aging, 17,* 548–557.

Schaie, K. W. (2005). *Developmental influences on adult intelligence: The Seattle Longitudinal Study.* New York: Oxford University Press.

Schaie K. W., & Willis, S. L. (1986). Can intellectual decline in the elderly be reversed? *Developmental Psychology, 22,* 223–232.

Schaie, K. W., Willis, S. L., Hertzog, C., & Schulenberg, J. E. (1987). Effects of cognitive training on primary metal ability structure. *Psychology and Aging, 2,* 233–242.

Schardt, D. (1997). Exercising the mind: Psychologist K. Warner Schaie interview. *Nutrition Action Health Letter.* Retrieved October 17, 2006, from http://www.cspinet.org/nah/index.htm

Schooler, C. (2007). Use it—and keep it, longer, probably: A reply to Salthouse (2006). *Perspectives on Psychological Science, 2,* 24–29.

Schooler, C., Mulatu, M. S., & Oates, G. (1999). The continuing effects of substantively complex work on the intellectual functioning of older workers. *Psychology and Aging, 14,* 483–506.

Shadish, W., Cook, T. D., & Campbell, D. T. (2002). *Experimental and quasi-experimental designs for generalized causal inference.* Boston: Houghton Mifflin.

Sliwinski, M. J., Hofer, S. M., & Hall, C. (2003). Correlated and coupled cognitive change in older adults with and without preclinical dementia. *Psychology and Aging, 18,* 672–683.

Small, B. J., & McEvoy, C. M. (2008). Does participation in cognitive activities buffer age-related cognitive decline? In S. M. Hofer & D. F. Alwin (Eds.), *Handbook of cognitive aging* (pp. 575–586). Thousand Oaks, CA: Sage.

Smits, C. H. M., van Rijsselt, R. J. T., Jonker, C., & Deeg, D. J. H. (1995). Social participation and cognitive functioning in older adults. *International Journal of Geriatric Psychiatry, 10,* 325–331.

Stine-Morrow, E. A. L. (2007). The Dumbledore hypothesis of cognitive aging. *Current Directions in Psychological Science, 16,* 295–299.

Stine-Morrow, E. A. L., Parisi, J. M., Morrow, D. G., Greene, J., & Park, D. C. (2007). An engagement model of cognitive optimization through adulthood. *The Journals of Gerontology: Series B. Psychological Sciences and Social Sciences, 62,* P62–P69.

Wagner, R. K., & Sternberg, R. J. (1985). Practical intelligence in real-world pursuits: The role of tacit knowledge. *Journal of Personality and Social Psychology, 49,* 436–458.

Willis, S. L., Tennstedt, S. L., Marsiske, M., Ball, K., Elias, J., Koepke, K. M., et al. (2006). Long-term effects of cognitive training on everyday functional outcomes in older adults. *JAMA, 296,* 2805–2814.

Wilson, R. J., & Bennett, D. A. (2003). Cognitive activity and risk of Alzheimer's disease. *Current Directions in Psychological Science, 12,* 87–91.

Wilson, R. J., Barnes, L. L., Krueger, K. R., Hoganson, G., Bienias, J. L., & Bennett, D. A. (2005). Early and late life cognitive activity and cognitive systems in old age. *Journal of the International Neuropsychological Society, 11,* 400–407.

9

Dynamic Emotion–Cognition Interactions in Adult Development: Arousal, Stress, and the Processing of Affect

*Gisela Labouvie-Vief, Daniel Grühn,
and Harold Mouras*

In the past 2 decades, a substantial growth in research on the developmental course of emotions in adulthood and aging took place. The body of research shows that two divergent points of view are currently being debated. On the one hand, some authors argue that aging is related to an increase in emotional well-being that is thought to be the result of general improvements in emotion regulation (e.g., Carstensen, Isaacowitz, & Charles, 1999). On the other hand, some evidence suggests that older adults' ability to process affective information is frequently compromised, especially when impairments of cognitive functions become increasingly evident (e.g., Labouvie-Vief & Marquez, 2004). In this chapter, we suggest a theoretical integration of these two perspectives: dynamic integration theory (DIT). DIT suggests that the relationship between cognition and emotion is inherently dynamic. The integration of emotional schemas relies on the interplay between more stable individual capacities (e.g., cognitive and socioemotional resources) and the dynamic constraints of contextual factors (e.g., emotional or cognitive activation/load). Briefly, DIT proposes that as homeostatic processes of emotion regulation become more vulnerable from middle adulthood to old age, the ability to form well-integrated and complex affect representations is compromised. Nevertheless, certain external and internal constraints on resources (e.g., highly resource-demanding situations, high levels of activation, quality of socioemotional resources) will moderate this impact.

As a consequence of this dynamic interplay, we argue that after a period of general gains in emotion regulation, later life's emotion regulation represents a picture of both gains and losses both within and across individuals. DIT specifies the conditions under which gains or losses are to be expected. In this chapter, we summarize the theory and its implication for aging-oriented research. To do this, we integrate general theoretical principles of cognitive and emotional development with recent findings on the neurobiology of emotion–cognition interactions and illustrate the resulting framework with behavioral and neurobiological findings. Finally, we suggest possible paths for future research and further inquiries.

Principles of Dynamic Integration

DIT integrates two core propositions. The first is derived from a cognitive–developmental view of affect as originally proposed by Piaget (1981) and since then elaborated in a number of more recent theoretical writings (e.g., Case, 1991; Fischer & Bidell, 2006; Harris, 1994; Labouvie-Vief, 2003; Pascual-Leone, 2000). This view states that affective structures, representations, and schemas can be ordered in terms of increasing levels of complexity and integration. As individuals develop more complex representations of emotion-related events, these representations are integrated within schemas that reorganize emotions into patterns of higher complexity, stability, and intentionality. Schemas that are both complex and integrated provide not only complex representations of emotions but highly robust patterns of emotion regulation abilities as well. Nevertheless, the resulting pattern is not static. The second proposition states that, for a given individual, cognition–emotion integration involves a flexible trade-off between emotional activation, the representation and regulation of emotion, and cognitive and socioemotional resources.

Differentiation, Integration, and the Development of Complex Emotions

Following Darwin (1872/1998), emotion theorists view emotions as highly automated response systems whose function is to permit efficient and quick action in emergency situations. These systems appear to organize themselves into distinct primary emotions with differential adaptive response patterns in facial, physiological, hormonal, and behavioral parameters (e.g., Davidson, Scherer, & Goldsmith, 2003; Ekman & Davidson, 1994). Piaget (1981) proposed that these patterns are based on representations that develop and organize themselves similar to other sensorimotor representations. Eventually, they develop into more complex and integrated representations of emotions as well as into more complex and integrated ways of emotion regulation and expression. For example, neonates' emotions are primarily reflex-like responses related to the early brain maturation and regularization of circadian patterns (Sroufe, 1996). These simple and automatic representations involve little active, intentional participation of the neonate's self in his or her inner or outer environment. However, with increasing development, emotions become more consciously directed to relationships with others (i.e., social and moral feelings). In general, with increasing development emotions take on more complexity as indicated by an increasing capacity to manage tension, intentional engagement, understanding of inner states, self–other differentiation, and differentiation and coordination of different emotions.

Complex emotions do not necessarily involve a change in the quality of primary emotions per se but can be embedded in more complex networks of representations, appraisals, and contextually modulated strategies. Some emotions, however, do involve qualitatively new patterns. Shame and other self-conscious emotions, for example, emerge when children become aware of other's evaluations of the self. A more complex emotion is *empathy,* which involves both the capacity to down-regulate automatic emotional resonance (*contagion*) and the awareness of the difference between the states of self and others.

Following Piaget, theories of cognitive–emotional development (Case, 1991; Fischer & Bidell, 2006) describe advances in development as the emergence of "control structures" that provide an integration of different subschemas. From a psychological perspective, these control structures serve to superimpose a stability and coherence on schemas that otherwise would display instability and disorder. More recent neurobiological approaches suggest that such control structures emerge as the early rapid development of automatic, limbic-based emotion schemas become increasingly interconnected with cortical networks that serve to down-regulate emotional activation (Hariri, Bookheimer, & Mazziotta, 2000; Schore, 1994). More generally, activation in specific lateral and dorsal regions of the prefrontal cortex parallels decreased activation in emotional areas such as the amygdala, suggesting an inhibitory influence exerted by the prefrontal cortex.

The concept of complex emotions comprises several important components, such as intentionality, awareness, and self–other differentiation (Labouvie-Vief & Medler, 2002). One aspect, however, that has received the most attention by researchers on aging is the differentiation of affective valence. The ability to organize simultaneously occurring positive and negative information or positive and negative feelings about oneself and other people is an advanced developmental accomplishment that does not fully emerge until adolescence (Fischer & Bidell, 2006; Harter, 1998). To capture the constructs of both integration and complexity, researchers used terms such as *cognitive–affective complexity* (Labouvie-Vief, DeVoe, & Bulka, 1989; Labouvie-Vief & Medler, 2002), *affect complexity* (Ong & Bergeman, 2004; Reich & Zautra, 2002), *emotional awareness* (Lane, 2000; Lane & Schwartz, 1987), and *emotional intelligence* (Mayer & Salovey, 1995). Some authors have suggested that these terms indicate a second criterion of adaptive emotion regulation, in contrast to hedonic and well-being criteria (Helson & Wink, 1987; Labouvie-Vief & Medler, 2002; Ryan & Deci, 2001; Ryff, 1989).

Dynamics of Integration

From a cognitive–developmental, Piagetian perspective, complex cognitive structures have direct significance for the organism. They extend restricted equilibrium-maintaining mechanisms initially provided by simple, automatic schemas through a higher degree of integration and stability across time and context. Such higher order equilibria emerge out of a dynamic interplay between assimilative and accommodative processes. From an emotion perspective, this dynamic parallels the contemporary differentiation between two modes of processing affective information: schematic and conscious processing (Chaiken & Trope, 1999; Clore & Ortony, 2000; LeDoux, 1996; Metcalfe & Mischel, 1999). Schematic processing represents a low-effort, automatic-processing mode in which judgments are framed in a binary fashion: good or bad, right or wrong, and positive or negative. Regulation is oriented at dampening deviations from these binary evaluations. Conscious processing, in contrast, involves an effortful unfolding, elaboration, and coordination of emotional schemas into complex knowledge structures.

Over the course of development from childhood to adulthood, emotional processing shifts from simple and relatively automatic emotion schemas to ones that involve more complex and integrated representations that may require more processing resources. At transition points, this movement from simple to complex representations is characterized by an initial increase in fluctuation, instability, and differentiation before complexity becomes integrated under a structure of higher organization (e.g., de Weerth, van Geert, & Hoijtink, 1999; van Geert, 1994). Piaget seems to assume that these higher order structures are relatively stable and robust. More recent ideas, however, question this assumption. Highly complex and integrated representations are also highly resource-demanding for sufficient processing. Thus, if resources are not sufficiently available, these complex and integrated representations are vulnerable to disintegration and fragmentation. One condition of low available resources is, for example, additional cognitive or emotional load that competes for a limited amount of resources. An example from the sensorimotor domain is postural stability while walking. Postural stability requires processing resources in terms of a continuous coordination and integration of visual, proprioceptive, and vestibular sensory information as well as the coordination of corresponding muscle movements. Although postural stability is based on highly trained representations, young, middle-age, and older adults showed marked declines in walking speed and walking accuracy when they performed simultaneously a mnemonic task (Lindenberger, Marsiske, & Baltes, 2000). Under these resource-demanding conditions such as cognitive or emotional load, integrative complexity is compromised and simple schemas take over. In neurobiological terms, the more automatic, amygdala-based *low road* overrides the more conscious, cortical-based *high road* of processing affective information (LeDoux & Phelps, 2000). Thus, depending on contextual restriction, affective processing can shift from more automatic to more differentiated processing. As a consequence, the burden of processing can be shifted in one or the other direction.

It is important to stress that one mode of processing is not superior to the other. Both modes, the low-road and the high-road processing, are adaptive and effective under different contextual demands. This shift between low-road and high-road processing is itself part of the homeostatic mechanism that maintains equilibrium when environmental demands challenge the organism's system. The how of this shift is addressed by the second proposition of DIT. In principle, an inverse U-shape function is proposed between the level of activation and the degree to which highly integrative and complex processing is possible (Metcalfe & Mischel, 1999; Yerkes & Dodson, 1908). When levels of emotional activation are moderate, complex and well-integrated thinking, planning, and remembering are possible and even facilitated. When levels of emotional activation are low, complex and well-integrated representations are possible, but in the absence of external arousal, processing depends on the internal motivation or activation produced by the effortful processing system. When arousal rises to extremely high levels, however, it tends to disrupt the integration of complex representations. Figure 9.1 depicts the relation between the complexity of emotional representations and the levels of emotional activation from low to high levels. In summary, the shift between low-road and high-road processing helps the organism to maintain equilibrium depending on environmental demands.

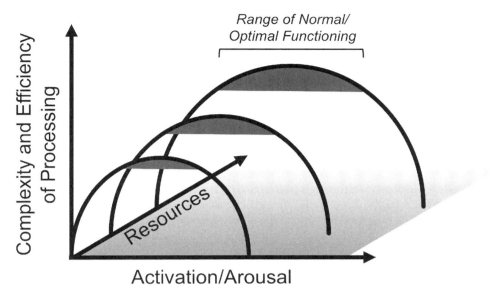

Figure 9.1. Idealized interplay between the processing of affective information, levels of activation, and available resources. In contrast to people with lower resources, people with higher resources (a) process affective information more efficiently, (b) show less degradation of complexity under high-arousing conditions, and (c) show a larger range of normal and optimal functioning.

There is behavioral and neurobiological research supporting the relation between levels of activation and the shift between both modes of processing, the low road and high road. For example, the facilitative effect of moderate levels of emotional activation on cognitive functions has been widely documented (e.g., Eysenck, 1976; Metcalfe & Mischel, 1999). This *emotional facilitation* has been established in behavioral and neuropsychological studies. There is, for example, considerable evidence for the crucial role of arousal in enhancing memory (e.g., Cahill & McGaugh, 1998; McGaugh, 2003): From a neurobiological perspective, increased levels of corticosteroids during arousal affect the functioning of the hippocampus and prefrontal cortex, facilitating encoding of contextual and declarative features (Lupien, Maheu, Tu, Fiocco, & Schramek, 2007; Metcalfe & Jacobs, 1998).

At very low levels of activation, in contrast, cognitive functioning cannot benefit from emotional enhancement. The burden of processing is fully placed on the effortful conscious processing system. A widely known example in the memory literature is the difference between free recall and recognition of stimuli. Whereas recognition is supported by external activation (i.e., making stimuli available), free recall depends solely on internal generation (Craik, 2002). Age differences in memory performance are typically larger for recall than for recognition, suggesting that older adults have difficulties in providing vivid representations in the absence of external activation. Thus, at low and suboptimal levels of activation, age differences are probably more obvious than at optimal levels of activation.

In contrast to moderate levels, very high levels of activation can impair cognitive functioning (e.g., Eysenck, 1976; McEwen & Sapolsky, 1995). Under high-arousing conditions, complex and integrated representations are vulnerable to disruption, disintegration, and fragmentation. As a substitute, nonconscious and automated schemas take over in an effort to maintain the system within tolerable margins.

On a hormonal level, the core mechanism related to the inverted U-shaped function appears to be the interaction between cognitive performance and levels of glucocorticoids (e.g., de Kloet, Oitzl, & Joëls, 1999; Lupien et al., 2007). Glucocorticoids are essential in regulating the organism's homeostasis to stress. The set point of glucocorticoids is, however, related to two types of receptors involved in binding circulating glucocorticoids: the mineralocorticoid receptors (Type I) with a high affinity and the glucocorticoid receptors (Type II) with a low affinity. Basal levels of circulating stress hormones activate only the mineralocorticoid receptors, whereas higher levels involve both receptor types. Superior cognitive performance has been suggested when Type I receptors but not Type II receptors are fully saturated (de Kloet et al., 1999; Lupien et al., 2007). At even higher levels of circulating glucocorticoids, however, memory and cognitive functioning are impaired. If high levels of circulating glucocorticoids are sustained over longer time periods, they can even cause architectural and functional impairments. For example, chronic stress can effect a reorganization of the prefrontal cortex and its functional properties such as a glucocorticoids-dependent blockade of its synaptic plasticity (Jay et al., 2004). Within the amygdala, in contrast, chronic stress reveals somewhat opposite results, for example, a facilitation of synaptic plasticity (Vouimba, Yaniv, Diamond, & Richter-Levin, 2004) and dendritic hypertrophy (Vyas, Mitra, Shankaranarayana Rao, Chattarji, 2002). In summary, the neurobiological evidence suggests that facilitation or degeneration in cognitive functioning vary both with the degree and duration of activation.

In a similar fashion, DIT proposes that the degradation of complex and well-integrated representations resulting from high emotional activation does not automatically result in complete fragmentation but can result in relatively coherent representations and strategies of lowered integration. In such cases, Labouvie-Vief and Marquez (2004) proposed to talk of "graceful" forms of degradation. These forms serve often a compensatory function. One of these forms implies simplified ways to coordinate positive and negative aspects about self and others. In such simplified representations, positive aspects are related to the self, whereas negative affect and information are often projected onto others, resulting in increased black-and-white thinking, stereotyping, and polarization among in-groups and out-groups (e.g., Mikulincer, 1995; Paulhus & Lim, 1994). At the same time, individuals attempt to retreat to safe havens by reducing the range of their action and seeking refuge in close social networks. Erikson (1985) referred to these ways of simplifying psychological complexity as *pseudospeciation,* the exclusion of others from the circle of humanity in which one includes oneself.

The negative sequelae of stress and high levels of activation are particularly likely in individuals who are already vulnerable to high levels of activation, such as those with low or dysfunctional socioemotional resources. These include, for example, persons whose impaired emotion regulation styles already render them vulnerable to overactivation as well as individuals whose lack of proper social support networks compromise their emotion regulation. There is also empirical evidence for the impact of functional or dysfunctional socioemotional resources on hormonal and physiological reactions, especially in terms of buffering the detrimental effects of stress. For example, low social support networks or poor emotion regulation seems to be related to increased stress hormone reactivity (Kiecolt-Glaser, McGuire, Robles, & Glaser, 2002; Laurent & Powers, 2006; Wirtz et al., 2006). Similarly, poor expression of emotions in response to stress is associated with low emotion regulation measured by physiological indices (Brosschot & Thayer, 1998; Fabes & Eisenberg, 1997).

In a sense, trading off differentiation and complexity in favor of optimization makes good sense in situations that pose a threat to the well-being and survival of the self. Such situations stimulate emergency responses in which resources are focused on the self-protective task of restoring equilibrium and securing survival. However, not all individuals try to reduce complexity and take up affect optimization under high-activation or resource-limited conditions. Some individuals may attempt to maintain a differentiated and fairly objective picture of reality. They may try to reduce high levels of activation through intellectual analysis and rumination but not in an integrated manner. This pattern of nonintegrated complexity may be particularly likely in young adults who have high levels of cognitive resources (see Labouvie-Vief & Medler, 2002).

Implications for Aging Research

In summary, DIT postulates an inverted U-shaped function between degree of integration and level of activation. This hypothesis is based on the known interaction between cognitive resources and emotional activation. On a most general level, DIT predicts that resilience to the degrading effects of high levels of activation depends on the availability of cognitive and socioemotional resources. These resources can buffer individuals from high levels of activation. At the same time, the facilitative effect of moderate levels of activation over extremely low ones should be particularly evident for older individuals who are less likely to be able to internally generate sufficient activation for well-integrated performance.

From a general life-span perspective, therefore, the disruption of complex representations is particularly likely in those individuals who are known to possess lower cognitive resources, such as young children or older adults. With respect to aging adults, in particular, there are strong declines in cognitive functioning and prefrontal volume (Raz, 2004; Raz & Rodrique, 2006). One paradoxical effect of age-related declines in cognitive functioning can be a compensatory effect in stronger involvement of the prefrontal cortex. Thus, paradoxically, increases in prefrontal activation in older adults can indicate compensatory effort and less efficient processing (e.g., Mattay et al., 2006; Reuter-Lorenz, 2002).

As we have argued, a disruption of complex emotion processing will result in degradation of complex cognitive–emotional representations, such as more simplified emotion schemas, polarization, and less integration between different representations of the self. These forms of degradation can themselves be quite coherent and efficient, a fact we capture by the term *graceful degradation*. For example, optimization strategies are especially likely to be evident in older individuals whose lowered cognitive resources may prevent the development of complex strategies. In contrast, younger adults should be particularly likely to show a bias toward nonintegrated complexity.

Dynamic Integration in Adulthood: Empirical Findings

The DIT framework is consistent with a large body of research, as already indicated. In addition, for the past few years, it has served as a tool to interpret our own ongoing research as well as initiating new studies. In this section, we provide a selective review of research that supports the theory.

Cross-Sectional and Longitudinal Studies of Affect Complexity and Integration

In several large-scale studies, the senior author and collaborators (Labouvie-Vief, Chiodo, Goguen, Diehl, & Orwoll, 1995; Labouvie-Vief et al., 1989) began to investigate the developmental trajectory of cognitive–emotional complexity across the life span. These studies sampled subjects from the adult life span from 10 years of age to more than 80 years of age. To measure affective complexity, individuals' descriptions of their emotions and their selves were coded. The findings showed a marked increase in affect complexity from adolescence to middle adulthood: Middle-age adults (a) demonstrated more conscious insight into aspects of emotions, (b) revealed a more differentiated view of the self and others, and (c) were more able to integrate positive and negative emotions than adolescents or young adults. However, from middle adulthood to old age, cognitive–emotional complexity declined continuously. These cross-sectional findings about the developmental trajectory of affect complexity have been confirmed in a 6-year longitudinal study (Labouvie-Vief, Diehl, Jain, & Zhang, 2007): Whereas young adults remained fairly stable over 6 years, increasing age was associated with accelerating declines in affect complexity.

The initial results confirmed our expectation that significant growth in affective complexity continues through middle adulthood. However, the results also contained surprises, even disappointments: Not only did growth abate in late middle adulthood, but a significant decline occurred thereafter. These findings highlight the role of middle-age adults as the carriers of complex knowledge integrating mind and emotion. But they also suggest potential problems with emotion regulation in older adulthood. Although as a group older persons reported the highest levels of positive affect, such as joy and interest, they also reported the lowest levels of negative affect, such as sadness and anger. Does this finding indicate increases in resilience among this group? We do not think so, because our notion of declining complexity implies reduced integration of negative affect so that as individuals age, they may find it more difficult to tolerate negative feelings. Thus, we began to suspect that our findings indicate two distinct aspects of emotion regulation: As affect complexity declines, individuals may develop a compensatory tendency to emphasize positive and avoid negative information. We term this strategy *affect optimization*.

In further studies, we therefore developed assessments of these two modes (Labouvie-Vief & Medler, 2002). *High optimizers* were defined as individuals who (a) minimize negative feelings, (b) do not engage in rich exploration of feelings and other nonrational processes (such as intuitions and dreams), (c) tend to ignore unpleasant information, and (d) exhibit low levels of self-doubt. *High differentiators* were defined as individuals who (a) tend to analyze their emotions, (b) exhibit high tolerance of ambiguity, and (c) show low levels of repression. The dimensions of optimization and differentiation were also associated with distinct patterns of person characteristics. High optimizers were characterized by high ratings on self-acceptance, a sense of mastery, and purpose in life. High differentiators, in contrast, scored high on conceptual complexity, personal growth, and empathy. This last finding validates our assumption that understanding another's perspective is a core aspect of affect complexity. Labouvie-Vief and Medler (2002) also reported different cross-sectional age gradients for the two components: Affect optimization increased, whereas affect complexity decreased with age. These divergent developmental trajectories were replicated in longitudinal research by Helson and Soto (2005), as well as in our own data (Labouvie-Vief et al., 2007).

Our results also revealed that the dimensions of optimization and differentiation were empirically uncorrelated. Thus, affect optimization, which involves low levels of negative affect, does not necessarily reflect an integrated mode of affect regulation. Similarly, high complexity does not necessarily reflect integration. Thus, the balance between these two modes may reflect different styles or groups of individuals. We identified four styles (Labouvie-Vief & Medler, 2002): integrated, dysregulated, self-protective, and complex. Following Werner (1957), an *integrated* style is defined by individuals who scored high on using both modes, reflecting differentiation and integration. These individuals displayed the most positive pattern: They reported (a) high levels of positive affect, well-being, and empathy; (b) low negative affect; and (c) a secure relationship style. In contrast, individuals with a *dysregulated* style (low differentiation, low optimization) displayed just the opposite pattern. They showed the most dysfunctional pattern. The remaining two groups, the *self-protective* (low differentiation, high optimization) and *complex* (high differentiation, low optimization) individuals showed a mixed but fairly coherent pattern of adaptation. Compared with the complex, the self-protective scored lower in negative affect but similarly high in positive affect, relationship security, and health. Self-protective individuals placed less emphasis on personal growth but more on environmental mastery than complex individuals. They also scored higher on good impression and conformance but lower on empathy than did complex individuals. This pattern suggests that self-protective individuals tend to dampen negative affect, whereas complex individuals amplify or at least are more willing to experience negative affect. The diverging affective patterns appear to indicate different identity styles, reflecting characteristic variations in how individuals integrate positive and negative affect (Helson & Srivastava, 2001).

According to the principle of dynamic integration, optimization and differentiation strategies are related in a compensatory fashion, especially among individuals with limited resources, such as older adults. This is exactly what our data indicate. When we compared young, middle-age, and old adults, a small number of old adults fell into the complex group, whereas a larger number were classified as self-protective: About 20% of the young and middle-age adults fell into both groups, the complex and self-protective individuals, whereas only 10% of the older adults were classified as complex, but 42% were classified as self-protective. Thus, as individuals grow older and experience declines in cognitive–affective complexity, they tend to rely more strongly on optimization strategies. This pattern was confirmed by our longitudinal data. Over a 6-year interval, declines in differentiation predicted increases in optimization among older adults. On the positive side, however, the number of older adults classified as integrated remained quite stable over the 6-year period. This finding suggests different developmental trajectories for different subgroups of the elderly: One subgroup may be able to enjoy high levels of integration, whereas another subgroup may use more compensatory strategies.

Emotion–Cognition Interactions

To examine whether emotional activation acts differently in young and old adults, we turned to experimental work varying the activation level of stimuli. A first study using an Emotional Stroop task confirmed our interpretation that older adults have difficulties processing high-arousing material (Wurm, Labouvie-Vief, Aycock, Rebucal, & Koch, 2004). In this task, individuals were asked to name the color of emotional words presented in different colors as fast as possible. Words ranged from low- to high-arousing. Findings showed an age by arousal interaction: Young adults did not show differences in response latencies for low- and high-arousing words, whereas older adults showed significant increases in response latencies for high-arousing words compared with low-arousing words. These results indicate that older individuals may have a problem inhibiting high arousal.

Evidence for older adults' difficulties with highly arousing words has also been obtained by Daniel Grühn. To investigate age-related differences in memory for emotionally toned material, Grühn and colleagues conducted two memory experiments. Both studies employed a very similar design to investigate emotional memory. They differed primarily in the type of to-be-remembered material used: One experiment used relatively low-arousing material, namely words (Grühn, Smith, & Baltes, 2005), whereas the other one used high-arousing material, namely emotional pictures (Grühn, Scheibe, & Baltes, 2007), as to-be-remembered material. In both studies, negative material was better remembered than positive and neutral information, suggesting a general emotion-based processing priority for negative information. However, by comparing young and older adults' memory performance for emotional material, age-related differences were clearly evident only for pictorial rather than verbal material: Young adults recognized more negative than positive and neutral pictures, whereas older adults showed almost no difference in recognizing positive, negative, and neutral pictures. One interpretation for the different age pattern between studies might be differences in levels of activation. Pictorial material is generally more emotionally activating than words are. Thus, high arousal may have hindered effective processing.

The interpretation that older adults may have difficulties in remembering high-arousing material is also supported by looking at memorability scores for individual pictures and their associated arousal levels (Grühn & Scheibe, 2008): Whereas young adults showed no specific associations between memorability and arousal levels (partial correlations controlled for valence: $-.04 \leq r \leq .02$), older adults showed a small, but consistent and significant negative relation between memorability and arousal (partial correlations controlled for valence: $-.10 \leq r \leq -.18$). Thus, older adults remembered high-arousing pictures (irrespective of their valence) less well than low-arousing pictures. In context of the proposed inverted U-shaped function, these pictures might be located at the falling, high-arousing part of the function for older adults.

Age Differences in Emotional Reactivity

One domain in which level of activation is crucial is physiological reactivity. Several studies have found reduced responding for subjective and peripheral physiological measures of emotional reactivity in older adults (Labouvie-Vief, Lumley, Jain, & Heinze, 2003; Levenson, Carstensen, Friesen, & Ekman, 1991; Levenson, Carstensen, & Gottman, 1994; Tsai, Levenson, & Carstensen, 2000). In two studies, however, Kunzmann and Grühn (2005) investigated age-related differences in emotional reactivity to sadness-related film clips depicting topics that were specifically relevant for older adults. In one film clip, for example, an older woman realizes that she has Alzheimer's disease. In contrast to previous studies, Kunzmann and Grühn found no differences in physiological reactivity between age groups. Moreover, they found stronger reactions in older adults on subjective, self-report measures of emotional reactivity than in young adults. Compared with previous work that showed less subjective and physiological reactivity, the study reveals that older adults can display strong emotional reactions to age-relevant material. Perhaps one of the reasons for this finding is that the study included highly self-relevant film clips with which individuals strongly identified. Another interpretation might be that these meaningful film clips elicited higher levels of activation than previous film clips did.

Other studies support our interpretation that older adults may be more vulnerable to strong physiological reactions under high levels of activation. For example, Uchino, Holt-Lunstad, Bloor, and Campo (2005) examined cardiovascular reactivity during acute stress in middle-age and older adults. They found, independent from other demographic or health-related factors, an age-related increase in some indicators of cardiovascular reactivity (systolic blood pressure and respiratory sinus arrhythmia) over a 10-month period.

Buffering Effects of Socioemotional Resources

One prediction of DIT is that socioemotional resources should play an important role in protecting individuals from degradation. We examined this hypothesis in a second Emotional Stroop study using attachment styles as correlates of emotion regulation (Jain & Labouvie-Vief, 2008). Young (ages 18–29) and older (ages 60–89) adults were classified into four attachment categories (i.e., secure, dismissing, preoccupied, and fearful; Bartholomew & Horowitz, 1991). Results for both young and older adults revealed longer reading times for the emotion words (i.e., anger-, fear-, and joy-related words) compared with neutral words. For both age groups, results revealed longer color reading latencies for emotion words. However, older adults' reading latencies were significantly higher than young adults' latencies. A triple interaction of age, emotion, and attachment category indicated that color reading latencies were significantly related to attachment style for the older, but not the younger, adults. In addition, older adults' reading latencies varied systematically with attachment style and the specific emotion word. Older adults classified as secure showed a bias toward joy words, whereas older dismissing individuals showed a bias toward fear and anger words. Older preoccupied individuals showed a bias toward fear and joy words, whereas older adults classified as fearful showed a bias toward anger words. The preoccupied and fearful older adults showed also overall longer reaction times than secure and dismissing older adults. It is noteworthy that the specific pattern in older adults conforms to predictions by attachment theory in its accentuation of different emotions. These findings suggest that older adults' processing of affective material is strongly affected by regulation styles. In contrast, the processing of young adults with their high cognitive resources was not affected by regulation styles. This may indicate that older adults' processing, in contrast to that in young adults, is much more vulnerable and depends to a higher degree on socioemotional resources, such as attachment styles.

In the study mentioned earlier about the influence of attachment styles on affective processing in an Emotional Stroop paradigm (Labouvie-Vief et al., 2007), older individuals with a dismissing style appeared to show some protection from emotional activation. According to DIT, however, this protective effect should break down at very high levels of activation. In a recent experiment, Jain and Labouvie-Vief (2008) found empirical support for this prediction. They assessed cardiac reactivity during a face-to-face interaction between older mothers and their middle-age daughters while engaged in three different discussions. These discussions were related to (a) a specific conflict, (b) a happy topic, and (c) a neutral topic. Daughters' heart rates were less elevated by the discussions than mothers' heart rates. However, attachment styles moderated cardiac reactivity for the older mothers but not for the middle-age daughters. In the neutral and happy discussion conditions, secure mothers showed less reactivity than insecure mothers and their daughters. But this protective function of a secure attachment style broke down in the high-arousing conflict condition. In that condition, no differences between secure and insecure mothers were visible. Thus, at high levels of arousal, the protective conditions effective at lower levels of activation break down and the regulation system of the older mothers loses resilience and function.

Another important finding with regard to the protective function of attachment styles was the dissociation between verbal self-reports and physiological measures in individuals with a dismissing attachment style (Jain & Labouvie-Vief, 2008). Dismissing women showed the highest reactivity in heart rates but reported the highest levels of positive well-being (i.e., positive affect, mental health, and physical health). In conjunction with the previous study (Labouvie-Vief et al., 2007), this finding suggests that a dismissing style is only protective against overactivation at rather low levels of activation but breaks down at very high levels of activation, when resources are tied up. Of course, such a pattern is just what one would predict from a defensive pattern of repression. It is noteworthy, too, that this effect held for mothers and daughters alike.

Discussion and Conclusions

In summary, DIT suggests that older adults may have specific problems in dealing with high-arousing situations. Specifically, in contrast to young adults, older adults (a) show difficulties in remembering high-arousing material, (b) show longer response latencies to process high-arousing material, and (c) reveal compromised emotion regulation in high-arousing situations. We suggest that these difficulties reflect a general restriction of homeostatic regulation with advancing age. As a response to this restriction and increased vulnerability to overactivation, many aging individuals appear to develop self-protective, compensatory strategies, that is, a shift from more complex and integrated representations of affect to more simple emotion schemas. The increase in simple emotion schemas fosters polarization such as a more positive view of the self and a more negative view of others. These effects are especially visible under high resource demanding conditions, under which the regulation system of older adults breaks down.

In this chapter, we have primarily dealt with compensatory shifts toward self-protectiveness and optimization. This should be particularly the case under conditions of (a) resource limitations, (b) high levels of activation (i.e., arousal), or (c) low levels of socioemotional resources. Older adults, with their low cognitive resources, are likely to be especially vulnerable to such conditions. However, our data also indicate that a considerable portion of older adults continue to display more positive and integrated patterns of regulation. This suggests that older adults are quite able to show optimal and integrated pattern of emotion regulation under less severe constraints. Such a bifurcation of patterns in older adults is, in fact, in line with our general homeostatic model. Jung (1971), for example, suggested that a decline of cognitive control can initiate a surge of emotional resources that can lead to a more positive reorganization, in which a more mellow, integrated, and wise pattern of adaptation emerges (see also Pascual-Leone, 2000).

References

Bartholomew, K., & Horowitz, L. M. (1991). Attachment styles among young adults: A test of a four-category model. *Journal of Personality and Social Psychology, 61,* 226–244.

Brosschot, J. F., & Thayer, J. F. (1998). Anger inhibition, cardiovascular recovery, and vagal function: A model of the link between hostility and cardiovascular disease. *Annals of Behavioral Medicine, 20,* 326–332.

Cahill, L., & McGaugh, J. L. (1998). Mechanisms of emotional arousal and lasting declarative memory. *Trends in Neuroscience, 21,* 294–299.

Carstensen, L. L., Isaacowitz, D. M., & Charles, S. T. (1999). Taking time seriously: A theory of socioemotional selectivity. *American Psychologist, 54,* 165–181.

Case, R. (1991). *The mind's staircase: Exploring the conceptual underpinnings of children's thought and knowledge*. Hillsdale, NJ: Erlbaum.

Chaiken, S., & Trope, Y. (1999). *Dual-process theories in social psychology*. New York: Guilford Press.

Clore, G. L., & Ortony, A. (2000). Cognition in emotion: Always, sometimes, or never? In R. D. Lane & L. Nadel (Eds.), *Cognitive neuroscience of emotion* (pp. 24–61). New York: Oxford University Press.

Craik, F. I. M. (2002). Human memory and aging. In L. Bäckman & C. von Hofsten (Eds.), *Psychology at the turn of the millennium: Volume 1. Cognitive, biological, and health perspectives* (pp. 261–280). Hove, England: Psychology Press.

Darwin, C. (1998). *The expression of the emotions in man and animals (3rd ed.)*. New York: Oxford University Press. (Original work published 1872)

Davidson, R. J., Scherer, K. R., & Goldsmith, H. H. (2003). *Handbook of affective sciences*. New York: Oxford University Press.

de Kloet, E. R., Oitzl, M. S., & Joëls, M. (1999). Stress and cognition: Are corticosteroids good or bad guys? *Trends in Neurosciences, 22*, 422–426.

de Weerth, C., van Geert, P., & Hoijtink, H. (1999). Intraindividual variability in infant behavior. *Developmental Psychology, 35*, 1102–1112.

Ekman, P., & Davidson, R. J. (1994). *The nature of emotion: Fundamental questions*. Oxford, England: Oxford University Press.

Erikson, E. H. (1985). *The life cycle completed: A review*. New York: Norton.

Eysenck, M. W. (1976). Arousal, learning, and memory. *Psychological Bulletin, 83*, 389–404.

Fabes, R. A., & Eisenberg, N. (1997). Regulatory control in adults' stress-related responses to daily life events. *Journal of Personality and Social Psychology, 73*, 1107–1117.

Fischer, K. W., & Bidell, T. R. (2006). Dynamic development of action and thought. In R. M. Lerner & W. Damon (Eds.), *Handbook of child psychology: Vol. 1. Theoretical models of human development* (6th ed., pp. 313–399). Hoboken, NJ: Wiley.

Grühn, D., & Scheibe, S. (2008). Age-related differences in valence and arousal ratings of pictures from the International Affective Picture System (IAPS): Do ratings become more extreme with age? *Behavior Research Methods, 40*, 1088–1097.

Grühn, D., Scheibe, S., & Baltes, P. B. (2007). Reduced negativity effect in older adults' memory for emotional pictures: The heterogeneity-homogeneity list paradigm. *Psychology and Aging, 22*, 644–649.

Grühn, D., Smith, J., & Baltes, P. B. (2005). No aging bias favoring memory for positive material: Evidence from a heterogeneity-homogeneity list paradigm using emotionally toned words. *Psychology and Aging, 20*, 579–588.

Hariri, A. R., Bookheimer, S. Y., & Mazziotta, J. C. (2000). Modulating emotional responses: Effects of a neocortical network on the limbic system. *Neuroreport, 11*, 43–48.

Harris, P. L. (1994). The child's understanding of emotion: Developmental change and the family environment. *Journal of Child Psychology and Psychiatry, 35*, 3–28.

Harter, S. (1998). The development of self-representations. In W. Damon & N. Eisenberg (Eds.), *Handbook of child psychology: Vol. 3. Social, emotional, and personality development* (5th ed., pp. 553–618). Hoboken, NJ: Wiley.

Helson, R., & Soto, C. J. (2005). Up and down in middle age: Monotonic and nonmonotonic changes in roles, status, and personality. *Journal of Personality and Social Psychology, 89*, 194–204.

Helson, R., & Srivastava, S. (2001). Three paths of adult development: conservers, seekers, and achievers. *Journal of Personality and Social Psychology, 80*, 995–1010.

Helson, R., & Wink, P. (1987). Two conceptions of maturity examined in the findings of a longitudinal study. *Journal of Personality and Social Psychology, 53*, 531–541.

Jain, E., & Labouvie-Vief, G. (2008). *Compensatory effects of emotion avoidance in adult development*. Manuscript submitted for publication.

Jay, T. M., Rocher, C., Hotte, M., Naudon, L., Gurden, H., & Spedding, M. (2004). Plasticity at hippocampal to prefrontal cortex synapses is impaired by loss of dopamine and stress: Importance for psychiatric diseases. *Neurotoxicity Research, 6*, 233–244.

Jung, C. J. (1971). The stages of life. In J. Campbell (Ed.), *The portable Jung* (R. F. C. Hull, Trans., pp. 3–22). New York: Viking Press.

Kiecolt-Glaser, J. K., McGuire, L., Robles, T. F., & Glaser, R. (2002). Emotions, morbidity, and mortality: New perspectives from psychoneuroimmunology. *Annual Review of Psychology 53*, 83–107.

Kunzmann, U., & Grühn, D. (2005). Age differences in emotional reactivity: The sample case of sadness. *Psychology and Aging, 20,* 47–59.

Labouvie-Vief, G. (2003). Dynamic integration: Affect, cognition, and the self in adulthood. *Current Directions in Psychological Science, 12,* 201–206.

Labouvie-Vief, G., Chiodo, L. M., Goguen, L. A., Diehl, M., & Orwoll, L. (1995). Representations of self across the life span. *Psychology and Aging, 10,* 404–415.

Labouvie-Vief, G., DeVoe, M., & Bulka, D. (1989). Speaking about feelings: Conceptions of emotion across the life span. *Psychology and Aging, 4,* 425–437.

Labouvie-Vief, G., Diehl, M., Jain, E., & Zhang, F. (2007). The relationship between changes in affect optimization and complexity: A further examination. *Psychology and Aging, 22,* 738–751.

Labouvie-Vief, G., Lumley, M. A., Jain, E., & Heinze, H. (2003). Age and gender differences in cardiac reactivity and subjective emotion responses to emotional autobiographical memories. *Emotion, 3,* 115–126.

Labouvie-Vief, G., & Marquez, M. G. (2004). Dynamic integration: Affect optimization and differentiation in development. In D. Y. Dai & R. J. Sternberg (Eds.), *Motivation, emotion, and cognition: Integrative perspectives on intellectual functioning and development* (pp. 237–272). Mahwah, NJ: Erlbaum.

Labouvie-Vief, G., & Medler, M. (2002). Affect optimization and affect complexity: Modes and styles of regulation in adulthood. *Psychology and Aging, 17,* 571–587.

Lane, R. D. (2000). Levels of emotional awareness: Neurological, psychological, and social perspectives. In R. Bar-On & J. D. A. Parker (Eds.), *The handbook of emotional intelligence: Theory, development, assessment, and application at home, school, and in the workplace* (pp. 171–191). San Francisco: Jossey-Bass.

Lane, R. D., & Schwartz, G. E. (1987). Levels of emotional awareness: A cognitive–developmental theory and its application to psychopathology. *American Journal of Psychiatry, 144,* 133–143.

Laurent, H. K., & Powers, S. I. (2006). Social-cognitive predictors of hypothalamic-pituitary-adrenal reactivity to interpersonal conflict in emerging adult couples. *Journal of Social and Personal Relationships, 23,* 703–720.

LeDoux, J. E. (1996). *The emotional brain: The mysterious underpinnings of emotional life.* New York: Simon & Schuster.

LeDoux, J. E., & Phelps, E. A. (2000). Emotional networks in the brain. In M. Lewis & J. M. Haviland-Jones (Eds.), *Handbook of emotions* (2nd. ed., pp. 157–172). New York: Guilford Press.

Levenson, R. W., Carstensen, L. L., Friesen, W. V., & Ekman, P. (1991). Emotion, physiology, and expression in old age. *Psychology and Aging, 6,* 28–35.

Levenson, R. W., Carstensen, L. L., & Gottman, J. M. (1994). Influence of age and gender on affect, physiology, and their interrelations: A study of long-term marriages. *Journal of Personality and Social Psychology, 67,* 56–68.

Lindenberger, U., Marsiske, M., & Baltes, P. B. (2000). Memorizing while walking: Increase in dual-task costs from young adulthood to old age. *Psychology and Aging, 15,* 417–436.

Lupien, S. J., Maheu, F., Tu, M., Fiocco, A., & Schramek, T. E. (2007). The effects of stress and stress hormones on human cognition: Implications for the field of brain and cognition. *Brain and Cognition. 65,* 209–237.

Mattay, V. S., Fera, F., Tessitore, A., Hariri, A. R., Berman, K. F., Das, S., et al. (2006). Neurophysiological correlates of age-related changes in working memory capacity. *Neuroscience Letters, 392,* 32–37.

Mayer, J. D., & Salovey, P. (1995). Emotional intelligence and the construction and regulation of feelings. *Applied & Preventive Psychology, 4,* 197–208.

McEwen, B. S., & Sapolsky, R. M. (1995). Stress and cognitive function. *Current Opinion in Neurobiology, 5,* 205–216.

McGaugh, J. L. (2003). *Memory and emotion: The making of lasting memories.* New York: Columbia University Press.

Metcalfe, J., & Jacobs, W. J. (1998). Emotional memory: The effects of stress on "cool" and "hot" memory systems. In D. L. Medin (Ed.), *The psychology of learning and motivation: Advances in research and theory* (Vol. 38, pp. 187–222). San Diego, CA: Academic Press.

Metcalfe, J., & Mischel, W. (1999). A hot/cool-system analysis of delay of gratification: Dynamics of willpower. *Psychological Review, 106,* 3–19.

Mikulincer, M. (1995). Attachment style and the mental representation of the self. *Journal of Personality and Social Psychology, 69,* 1203–1215.

Ong, A. D., & Bergeman, C. S. (2004). The complexity of emotions in later life. *The Journals of Gerontology: Series B. Psychological Sciences and Social Sciences, 59,* P117–P122.

Pascual-Leone, J. (2000). Mental attention, conscious, and the progressive emergence of wisdom. *Journal of Adult Development, 7,* 241–254.

Paulhus, D. L., & Lim, D. T. (1994). Arousal and evaluative extremity in social judgments: A dynamic complexity model. *European Journal of Social Psychology, 24,* 89–99.

Piaget, J. (1981). *Intelligence and affectivity: Their relationship during child development* (T. A. Brown & C. E. Kaegi, Trans.). Oxford, England: Annual Reviews.

Raz, N. (2004). The aging brain observed in vivo: Differential changes and their modifiers. In R. Cabeza, L. Nyberg, & D. C. Park (Eds.), *Cognitive neuroscience of aging: Linking cognitive and cerebral aging* (pp. 17–55). New York: Oxford University Press.

Raz, N., & Rodrigue, K. M. (2006). Differential aging of the brain: Patterns, cognitive correlates and modifiers. *Neuroscience and Biobehavioral Reviews, 30,* 730–748.

Reich, J. W., & Zautra, A. J. (2002). Arousal and the relationship between positive and negative affect: An analysis of the data of Ito, Cacioppo, and Lang (1998). *Motivation and Emotion, 26,* 209–222.

Reuter-Lorenz, P. A. (2002). New visions of the aging mind and brain. *Trends in Cognitive Sciences, 6,* 394–400.

Ryan, R. M., & Deci, E. L. (2001). On happiness and human potentials: A review of research on hedonic and eudaimonic well-being. *Annual Review of Psychology, 52,* 141–166.

Ryff, C. D. (1989). Happiness is everything, or is it? Explorations on the meaning of psychological well-being. *Journal of Personality and Social Psychology, 57,* 1069–1081.

Schore, A. N. (1994). *Affect regulation and the origin of the self: The neurobiology of emotional development.* Hillsdale, NJ: Erlbaum.

Sroufe, L. A. (1996). *Emotional development: The organization of emotional life in the early years.* New York: Cambridge University Press.

Tsai, J. L., Levenson, R. W., & Carstensen, L. L. (2000). Autonomic, subjective, and expressive responses to emotional films in older and younger Chinese Americans and European Americans. *Psychology and Aging, 15,* 684–693.

Uchino, B. N., Holt-Lunstad, J., Bloor, L. E., & Campo, R. A. (2005). Aging and cardiovascular reactivity to stress: Longitudinal evidence for changes in stress reactivity. *Psychology and Aging, 20,* 134–143.

van Geert, P. (1994). *Dynamic systems of development. Change between complexity and chaos.* New York: Harvester Wheatsheaf.

Vouimba, R. M., Yaniv, D., Diamond, D., & Richter-Levin, G. (2004). Effects of inescapable stress on LTP in the amygdala versus the dentate gyrus of freely behaving rats. *European Journal of Neuroscience, 19,* 1887–1894.

Vyas, A., Mitra, R., Shankaranarayana Rao, B. S., & Chattarji, S. (2002). Chronic stress induces contrasting patterns of dendritic remodeling in hippocampal and amygdaloid neurons. *Journal of Neuroscience, 22,* 6810–6818.

Werner, H. (1957). *Comparative psychology of mental development.* Oxford, England: International Universities Press.

Wirtz, P. H., von Kaenel, R., Mohiyeddini, C., Emini, L., Ruesdisueli, K., Groessbauer, S., et al. (2006). Low social support and poor emotional regulation are associated with increased stress hormone reactivity to mental stress in systemic hypertension. *Journal of Clinical Endocrinology and Metabolism, 91,* 3857–3865.

Wurm, L. H., Labouvie-Vief, G., Aycock, J., Rebucal, K. A., & Koch, H. E. (2004). Performance in auditory and visual emotional stroop tasks: A comparison of older and younger adults. *Psychology and Aging, 19,* 523–535.

Yerkes, R., & Dodson, J. (1908). The relation of strength of stimulus to rapidity of habit formation. *Journal of Comparative Neurology and Psychology, 18,* 459–482.

10

The Way We Were: Perceptions of Past Memory Change in Older Adults

David F. Hultsch, Allison A. M. Bielak,
Carolyn B. Crow, and Roger A. Dixon

In the song "The Way We Were," Barbra Streisand sings, "So it's the laughter we will remember whenever we remember the way we were." The implication is that recollection of our personal past is selective and possibly biased toward the positive, adaptive, or self-validating. Indeed, recent research has found a possible emotional "positivity" bias for concurrent remembering (e.g., Blanchard-Fields, 2005). For longer term recollections, psychologists have suggested that recalling the more distant "way we were" is determined substantially by active schema-driven processes that yield a reconstruction of our past rather than by detailed veridical recall of events (Ross, 1989).

This phenomenon is of relevance to gerontologists interested in long-term cognitive changes because of the potentially significant role that beliefs about mental abilities may play in representing and adapting to the aging process. For the purposes of this discussion, we differentiate between two types of beliefs about cognition: (a) *self-referent beliefs,* which consist of individuals' beliefs about efficacy, control, and perceived changes related to their own cognitive functioning (e.g., Bandura, 1977; Berry & West, 1993), and (b) *implicit beliefs,* which reflect largely unconscious and untested beliefs about the nature of cognitive functioning, including putative changes with age (e.g., Greenwald & Banaji, 1995; Sternberg, 1987). The former focuses on explicit assessments and expectations about one's own cognitive functioning, whereas the latter focuses on beliefs about the nature of cognition and its characteristics as they apply to most people.

Ross (1989; Newby-Clark & Ross, 2003; Ross & Newby-Clark, 1998) has suggested that both self-referent beliefs and implicit theories may be central to

David Hultsch is supported by grants from the Canadian Institutes for Health Research and the Natural Sciences and Engineering Research Council of Canada. The Victoria Longitudinal Study is supported by a grant from the National Institute on Aging (R-37-AG008235) to Roger Dixon, who is also supported by the Canada Research Chairs program. Allison Bielak is supported by doctoral scholarships from the Canadian Institutes of Health Research Institute of Aging, the Michael Smith Foundation for Health Research, and the British Columbia Medical Services Foundation. This chapter is based on a master's thesis by Carolyn Crow (Crow, 1998), under the supervision of Roger Dixon. We thank Chris Hertzog for inspiration and ideas on this project.

individuals' constructions of their own personal histories. Specifically, Ross has argued that long-term recall of personal attributes involves two major steps. First, individuals access information about their present status on the attribute in question (e.g., the individual may recollect a number of recent memory failures). Presumably, because of its recency, this information is more salient and more accessible than their status on the attribute or related behaviors at some time in the past. Although this information might be accessed partly through veridical memory for events, it would also probably be significantly influenced by self-referent beliefs regarding the attribute in question (e.g., the individual believes his or her memory is generally poor). Second, in attempting to remember how they once were, individuals may invoke an implicit theory of stability or change on the attribute in question to guide their reconstruction of the past (e.g., memory tends to decline as one gets older). These beliefs may influence both the information retrieved from memory as well as its interpretation. If specific information cannot be recalled, the implicit theory may be used to construct a likely scenario. An implicit theory that contains a strongly held belief of gains or losses over time may lead to constructions of the past that are consistent with these beliefs. For example, individuals may notice a cluster of recent memory failures, endorse the implicit theory of a general decline in memory with aging, and therefore believe that their memory skills must have been better in the past.

In this chapter, we examine some of the issues related to older adults' perceptions of changes in their memory performance. We begin by examining the concepts of self-referent beliefs and implicit theories about memory in later life. We then present previously unpublished data from the Victoria Longitudinal Study (VLS; Dixon & de Frias, 2004) that examine individuals' perceptions of their own memory change over time and the degree to which these perceptions map onto actual changes in performance. We also examine whether individual differences in metacognitive beliefs, affect, or personality appear to moderate individuals' reconstructions of their past abilities. Finally, we discuss how these findings mesh with the conceptual framework outlined in the introduction.

Self-Referent Beliefs About Cognition

Theorists have suggested that it is useful to view self-referent beliefs about cognition as multidimensional and domain specific (Cavanaugh, 1996; Dixon, 2000; Hertzog & Dixon, 2005; Hertzog & Hultsch, 2000). From our perspective, three dimensions focused on the effectiveness, causes, and changes in one's own behavior have been salient in the literature. First, the concept of self-efficacy focuses on the beliefs about the effectiveness of one's own behavior. Briefly, *self-efficacy* may be broadly defined as the belief in one's ability—considering one's motivation, knowledge, cognitive resources, behaviors, and skills—to meet a set of task demands (Bandura, 1977). It may be assessed with reference to a general domain of functioning or a specific task. Second, the issue of the *causes* of behavior is captured in the concept of personal control. Here the focus is on individuals' beliefs about whether outcomes are contingent on their own behaviors as opposed to external influences such as chance or the actions of other individuals or entities (Miller & Lachman, 1999). Beliefs in personal control over cognitive performance can result in adaptive or compensatory actions in everyday life (e.g., Dixon & de Frias, 2007; Hertzog & Dixon, 2005). Finally, the issue of *perceived change* focuses on individuals' beliefs about whether their cognitive functioning has been or will be characterized by gains, stability, or losses over some period of time.

Although these three constructs are related, they are differentiable both conceptually and empirically. At the conceptual level, consider individuals' beliefs related to the task of recalling the names of a dozen people to whom they have just been introduced. Personal self-efficacy beliefs would influence all individuals' assessments of the number of names they could retrieve, as well as their degree of confidence in this assessment. Their sense of personal control would manifest itself in beliefs about the extent to which they could do something that would affect the probability of successfully recalling the names. Finally, their perceptions of change would be reflected in their beliefs about the developmental trajectory of their ability to perform this task. Although these beliefs may coincide, they also may diverge. Thus, older adults may assess their current efficacy to be relatively low, but believe that it could be substantially increased if they applied a compensatory technique (e.g., a mnemonic system, recruiting memory assistance) for remembering names (Dixon, de Frias, & Bäckman, 2001; Hertzog & Dixon, 2005).

Investigators have developed many measures of self-referent beliefs about cognition. Much of the effort has been aimed at developing paper and pencil questionnaires. Although generic measures of constructs such as efficacy and control are available (e.g., Levenson, 1974), it has been argued that examination of the relationship between beliefs and actual behavior requires a domain-specific or task-specific approach (Lachman, 1983; Lachman, Andreoletti, & Pearman, 2006). Since the early 1980s, a number of psychometrically sound multidimensional scales have been developed that are focused on several domains, such as attention (e.g., Tun & Wingfield, 1995), memory (e.g., Dixon, Hultsch, & Hertzog, 1988; Gilewski, Zelinski, & Schaie, 1990; Lachman, Bandura, Weaver, & Elliott, 1995), intelligence (e.g., Lachman, Baltes, Nesselroade, & Willis, 1982), and language (e.g., Ryan, Kwong See, Meneer, & Trovato, 1992). Many of these questionnaires are multidimensional in that they address more than one of the constructs central to self-referent beliefs about cognition described previously. The great bulk of them measure beliefs about memory functioning. More detailed reviews of the conceptual and psychometric characteristics of these measures are available elsewhere (e.g., Cavanaugh, 1996; Dixon, 1989; Gilewski & Zelinski, 1986; Hertzog & Hultsch, 2000).

Given that performance on many cognitive tasks shows a decline with increasing age, it is reasonable to expect that this decline may be reflected in older adults' assessments of their own cognitive performance. Perhaps as a result of the availability of instruments, most studies have been directed toward self-referent beliefs about memory. Although there are inconsistencies across studies, the literature tends to point to both cross-sectional age differences and longitudinal age changes in multiple aspects of metamemory. Many older adults report lower levels of memory efficacy (Gilewski et al., 1990; Hultsch, Hertzog, & Dixon, 1987; Zelinski, Gilewski, & Thompson, 1980), believe their memory has declined more over time (Bielak et al., 2007; Gilewski et al., 1990; Taylor, Miller, & Tinklenberg, 1992), and report less control over their memory functioning (e.g., Bielak et al., 2007; Hultsch et al., 1987; Lachman et al., 1995) than do younger adults (see also Lachman et al., 2006). There are studies that show little or no evidence of age differences in self-referent beliefs about memory (e.g., Crook & Larrabee, 1992), but these findings are in the minority.

Data from longitudinal studies are particularly important because they examine changes in beliefs directly (McDonald-Miszczak, Hertzog, & Hultsch, 1995; Taylor et al., 1992). In an early article from the VLS, McDonald-Miszczak et al. (1995; see also Hertzog & Hultsch, 2000) reported significant changes on several subscales of the Metamemory in Adulthood (MIA; Dixon et al., 1988) instrument for a sample of adults ranging in age from 55 to 86 measured three times over 6 years. Participants reported significant changes in rated memory capacity (lower), perceived stability of memory (more decline), personal control (lower), anxiety about memory (higher), and external strategy use (greater) over the period. It should be noted, however, that the effect sizes for perceived change over the 6 years were relatively modest (range = -0.15 SD to 0.26 SD) and did not vary much across the young-old (ages 55–70) and old-old (ages 71–86) groups. In fact, these effect sizes are somewhat smaller than those observed for longitudinal changes in measures of actual memory performance for word recall (-.30 SD) and fact recall (-.39 SD) obtained over the same interval in the old-old group (Hultsch, Hertzog, Dixon, & Small, 1998).

Longitudinal data also provide important information about individual differences in the amount of change in beliefs. Indicators of self-referent memory beliefs show very high stability over time. McDonald-Miszczak et al. (1995) reported 6-year disattenuated stability coefficients for the subscales of the MIA ranging from .87 to .99. Although there were some individual differences in change in beliefs, roughly 80% to 90% of the true scale variance was associated with stable individual differences. Thus, beliefs about memory functioning and change in memory functioning appear to be relatively stable and enduring characteristics of the individual. It remains to be seen whether such high stability is adaptive, and whether there is a corresponding stability of individual differences in self-referent beliefs regarding the potential efficacy of memory actions (e.g. compensatory efforts; Dixon & de Frias, 2007).

Implicit Theories of Aging and Cognition

Implicit theories have been defined as informal constructions held by individuals about psychological phenomena such as memory or intelligence (Sternberg, 1987). In contrast to *explicit theories,* which are based on systematically collected and analyzed data, implicit theories are the result of earlier experiences that are typically unexamined, or at least not examined systematically (e.g., Chanowitz & Langer, 1981). Implicit theories are often widely shared within a culture or subculture, contributing to stereotypes about characteristic traits or behaviors of members of a certain group and, at least indirectly, influencing memory performance by affected groups (Chasteen, Bhattacharyya, Horhota, Tam, & Hasher, 2005). In addition to dimensions such as gender and race, chronological age represents a fundamental characteristic of persons around which implicit theories are often constructed (Chasteen, Schwarz, & Park, 2002).

Implicit theories about the developmental course of various behaviors and characteristics probably reflect the influence of multiple factors including age stratification and socialization processes that influence opportunities, timing of events, and normative values within a given culture. Given this, it is reasonable to anticipate that implicit theories about change and the causes of change will vary across cultures or even across subcultures within a given society (Morris & Peng, 1994). It is also reasonable to anticipate that implicit theories may have their greatest impact on perceived functioning in the absence of more specific information about a given target person or task. Despite such contextual effects, belief systems about age show substantial consistency within a culture. For example, Heckhausen, Dixon, and Baltes (1989; see also Heckhausen & Schulz, 1995) found that younger, middle-age, and older adults shared a substantial set of beliefs about the degree, desirability, and timing of developmental changes across the adult life span. Of particular interest for the present discussion is the question of adults' beliefs about the trajectory and timing of cognitive changes across adulthood. Overall, there is an expectation that undesirable characteristics will increase with aging, whereas desirable characteristics will decrease (Heckhausen et al., 1989; Kite & Johnson, 1988). Expectations related to cognitive competence appear to be more negative than those associated with personality (Kite & Johnson, 1988). However, even within the cognitive domain there appears to be substantial variation in belief systems across different domains. In particular, relatively early losses are expected in domains such as speed and memory in contrast to gains in areas such as wisdom (Heckhausen et al., 1989).

Although implicit theories about aging and cognition appear to suggest trajectories of both gains and losses, research attention has been focused largely on behaviors that are expected to decline in later life. For reasons noted elsewhere, perhaps the most widely examined domain is memory (Dixon, Rust, Feltmate, & Kwong See, 2007; Zacks, Hasher, & Li, 2000). In general, adults in Western cultures appear to expect that memory functioning will show a loss trajectory with increasing age, with difficulties occurring as early as middle age. Heckhausen et al. (1989) found that participants anticipated that forgetfulness would increase over adulthood with an average age of onset of 55 years. Similarly, Ryan (1992) found that both younger and older adults expected memory failures to increase from young adulthood to middle age, and again from middle age to late life (see also Chasteen et al., 2002; Ryan & Kwong See, 1993). However, the expectation of decline is not uniform. Lineweaver and Hertzog (1998) developed an instrument designed to allow participants to express their beliefs about aging and memory across the entire life span rather than focusing on a few target ages. Multiple items examining the adequacy/effectiveness of memory functioning (efficacy) and the degree to which individuals can influence memory ability and functioning (control) are used. Lineweaver and Hertzog (1998) found, consistent with other studies, that implicit theories about memory and aging in our culture reveal a general expectation of loss. However, they also found substantial diversity across different aspects of memory and evidence that beliefs change as individuals become older and begin to experience actual changes in memory functioning. For example, some specific efficacy beliefs (e.g., memory for faces) are quite similar to global efficacy beliefs, whereas in other specific cases they are somewhat more optimistic (e.g., memory for things that happened long ago) or less optimistic (e.g., names). Lineweaver and Hertzog's analyses also suggest that older respondents may have somewhat more differentiated beliefs, perhaps as a function of experience with the effects of aging on memory in self, friends, and family. In contrast, younger adults' beliefs may be shaped largely by stereotypes about aging.

Cognitive Beliefs and Cognitive Functioning

The literature briefly reviewed previously suggests that adults in Western culture hold moderately multidimensional and multidirectional beliefs about aging and cognition. Although we have differentiated between implicit theories and self-referent beliefs about cognition, these two types of beliefs are likely related. For example, implicit theories of age-related change may influence beliefs related to the self as well as generalized or specific others. In fact, some studies have suggested that there is substantial correspondence between beliefs about others and beliefs about the self. Ryan and Kwong See (1993) asked people to complete ratings of memory ability, intraindividual change, and personal control for both typical adults and themselves at several target ages. They found no significant differences in ratings of self and others for any of the measures. Although self-referent beliefs and generalized beliefs about others within a given domain are significantly related, personal beliefs are not necessarily age-relevant applications of general beliefs to the self. Several studies suggest that this may be the case (Lineweaver & Hertzog, 1998; Ryan et al., 1992). For example, Lineweaver and Hertzog (1998) found that there were substantial correlations between scores of individuals' general beliefs about memory efficacy and control (expectations for most people at a given age) and their personal beliefs about efficacy and control over memory (at the corresponding age). However, the correlations were not so high as to argue that the two beliefs were interchangeable, suggesting there is heuristic value in distinguishing between general and personal beliefs about memory.

Empirical evidence supporting the role of beliefs in peoples' recall of their past standing on personal attributes is available in a number of domains (e.g., McFarland, Ross, & DeCourville, 1989; McFarland, Ross, & Giltrow, 1992). For example, McFarland et al. (1992) reported that implicit theories of age-related gain and loss were important determinants of how older adults recall the characteristics they possessed at an earlier age. For attributes expected to increase with age (e.g., kindness, physical problems), older adults recalled possessing less of the attribute when they were younger than younger adults reported currently. For attributes expected to show decreases with age (memory for names, activity), older adults recalled possessing more of the attribute when they were younger than younger adults did currently.

Cross-sectional results of this sort are limited by the possibility of cohort and selection effects. However, as noted earlier, one VLS longitudinal analysis also offers some support for the role of beliefs in the reconstruction of personal past. McDonald-Miszczak et al. (1995) reported that a sample ranging in age from middle-age to old age and tested three times over 6 years showed significant changes on measures of both perceived memory functioning and actual memory performance. However, they observed only weak relationships between longitudinal changes in memory performance and retrospective perceptions of memory change at the end of the longitudinal period. Although such relationships suggest that adults may monitor or manage changes in their memory ability to some extent (Dixon & de Frias, 2007), other findings were consistent with an implicit theory perspective. Specifically, within-occasion correlations of perceived level of memory efficacy and perceived retrospective change were high and changed together. This result is consistent with the hypothesis that current perceptions of efficacy level drive current perceptions of how memory has changed over time. Further, Bielak et al. (2007) found little evidence that bimonthly changes in memory beliefs were driven by changes in older adults' actual performance, confirming that individuals' perceptions of their memory ability appear to be based on psychologically constructed heuristics rather than on accurate monitoring of memory performance.

In an article that helped inspire the present chapter (see also Crow, 1998), Schaie, Willis, and O'Hanlon (1994) directly examined the accuracy of adults' retrospections about their intellectual functioning using 7-year (two-wave) data from the Seattle Longitudinal Study. They examined actual and self-perceived change in a sample of 837 adults ages 25 to 95 tested on the subscales of the Primary Mental Abilities test in 1977 and again in 1984. At the second testing, participants were asked to rate (from *much better* to *much worse*) how their performance on the concurrent tests compared with their performance 7 years earlier. The percentage of people indicating their performance was worse on the later occasion compared with the earlier occasion was generally higher for older (ages 71–95) than for middle-age (ages 50–70) and younger (ages 29–49) respondents. However, critical for our purposes is the finding that, for virtually all abilities, a majority of respondents, including the older adults, indicated their concurrent performance was either better or the same as their earlier performance. The percentage of participants indicating their more recent performance was worse was substantial (ranging from 17% for Vocabulary to 48% for Spatial Orientation). A typology linking perceived and actual performance was created by grouping participants into those who (a) accurately estimated change in their performance (realists), (b) overestimated positive change (optimists), and (c) overestimated negative change (pessimists). Collapsed across all abilities, approximately 50% of the sample were classified as realists, 30% as optimists, and 20% as pessimists. However, congruence varied across abilities and with age. Of particular interest, older adults were more pessimistic for two of the five abilities tested. Older participants overestimated their decline on inductive reasoning compared with middle-age and younger participants. Similarly, older participants overestimated their decline on verbal meaning compared with younger participants. It was interesting that the younger and middle-age participants overestimated their decline on number compared with the older participants. These results indicate that not all participants evince a belief in cognitive decline. Moreover, although there is evidence that older adults may overestimate decline on some abilities, they also appear to monitor cognitive changes relatively accurately in other cases.

An Empirical Example: New Data
From the Victoria Longitudinal Study

We are pleased to acknowledge that it was the study by Schaie et al. (1994) that motivated us to obtain retrospective estimates of memory performance from our participants in the VLS (Crow, 1998). For this new and previously unpublished study, we focused on memory tasks because, as noted previously, substantial age-related effects are observed for episodic memory and for both self-referent and implicit beliefs about memory (Dixon et al., 2007; Hertzog & Hultsch, 2000). However, although there appears to be a general expectation in our culture that memory declines with age, this belief varies across different types of memory tasks. In terms of actual performance, we used two episodic memory tasks and one semantic memory task. In the VLS and other such projects, episodic memory shows gradual but greater age-related decline than does semantic memory (e.g., Dixon et al., 2007; Hultsch et al., 1998; Zacks et al., 2000). An open question is whether retrospective beliefs would reflect this decline accurately or exhibit a positivity bias about the "way we were." Rather than using rating scales, we chose to ask participants to provide a numeric performance estimate (a postdiction). Ideally, one would have had, for comparative purposes, postdictions for the earlier testing occasions as well. However, the available data enabled us to examine the extent to which participants' concurrent and retrospective postdictions mapped onto their actual memory performance for the various tasks. An implicit theory account would predict increasing divergence between postdicted and actual performance. In addition, to the extent that the individuals' assessments of their current status play a role in the process, estimates of past performance may be moderated by current assessments of memory efficacy or change.

Summary of the Method

The design of the VLS consists of longitudinal sequences in which three main samples of community-dwelling older adults (initially 54–85 years of age) are retested at intervals of 3 years. The general design, participants, measures, and procedures of the VLS have been described extensively elsewhere (see Dixon & de Frias, 2004; Hultsch et al., 1998).

The participants were 164 adults from Sample 1 of the VLS tested in 1995, the fourth occasion of measurement for Sample 1. For purposes of cross-sectional comparison, the participants were divided into two age groups: a young-old group ranging from ages 64 to 75, and an old-old group ranging from ages 75 to 94. Typical of longitudinal samples, the participants are positively selected for education, health, and verbal ability.

Three measures of actual memory performance (word recall, story recall, fact recall) were available for four longitudinal occasions of measurement obtained at intervals of 3 years. Participants completed two versions of each task at each occasion of measurement, and their average performances across the two versions were used as the measures of memory performance in the present analysis. Multiple versions of the tasks were counterbalanced across occasions of measurement to reduce the magnitude of practice effects. The procedures and measures have been presented in detail elsewhere (e.g., Dixon et al., 2004; Hultsch et al., 1998).

The word recall task consisted of immediate free recall of 30 English words (Hultsch, Hertzog, & Dixon, 1990). The word lists consisted of six words from each of five taxonomic categories (e.g., birds, flowers) typed on a single page in unblocked order. Participants were given 2 minutes to study each list and 5 minutes to write their recall. The average number of words recalled correctly across two lists was used as the measure.

The story recall task consisted of immediate gist recall of the contents of narrative stories (Dixon et al., 2004). The stories were approximately 300 words and 160 propositions long and described life events often experienced by middle-age and older adults. Participants were given 3 minutes to read the story and 7 minutes to write their recall. Participants' written recall was scored with reference to the predefined text base of the story, and propositions were scored as correct if the gist of their meaning was expressed. The performance measure used was the average percent recall across two stories.

The fact recall task consisted of 40 questions examining participants' knowledge from several domains, including science, history, sports, geography, and entertainment. No time limits were imposed on the task. The average number of items recalled correctly across two sets of questions was used as the measure.

At the fourth occasion of measurement, participants were asked to make several postdictions of their performance on the three memory tasks. Participants generated these postdictions immediately following the completion of the second version of each memory task that was administered at a given occasion of measurement. Specifically, they were asked to provide an estimate of their just-completed performance as well as their performance on the same task 3, 6, and 9 years previously. Participants did not have access to their just-completed responses on the memory task when making their postdictions.

The scale for participants' numeric estimates of performance varied for the three tasks. In the case of the word recall task, participants were asked to estimate the number of words recalled out of 30. For story recall, they were asked to estimate the number of ideas recalled out of 100. There were actually approximately 160 propositions in the texts. However, because it would have been difficult to convey the concept of a text proposition to participants, we chose to provide an arbitrary figure of 100 ideas as the target for optimal performance. Finally, for fact recall, an estimate of the number of facts remembered out of 40 was elicited.

Several other measures were available to index aspects of memory-related beliefs, affect, and personality, all of which might be assumed to influence assessments of current memory functioning or implicit theories of memory change (e.g., Berry & West, 1993; Bolla, Lindgren, Bonaccorsy, & Bleeker, 1991). These measures were obtained at the fourth occasion of measurement (concurrent with the postdictions).

Memory beliefs were indexed according to three subscales from the MIA (Dixon et al., 1988): (a) The Capacity scale asked participants to rate their memory ability in various everyday situations (e.g., remembering names) and was a good indicator of current memory self-efficacy; (b) the Change scale assessed perceived memory change over varying intervals of time; and (c) the Locus scale measured the degree to which the people believed that their memory could be improved through their own actions. In addition, participants were asked to assess their performance on the three memory tasks relative to that of hypothetical selves or others. The three items used were (a) the average 20-year-old, (b) yourself at age 20, and (c) the best you could do with training. Participants rated each of these items on a 5-point Likert scale ranging from *much better* to *much worse.*

Participants' current affect was assessed by the Bradburn Affect Balance Scale (Bradburn, 1969; for VLS data, see Maitland, Dixon, Hultsch, & Hertzog, 2001). This scale consists of 10 items, including 5 items measuring positive affect and 5 items measuring negative affect. Participants were asked whether they had experienced feelings relevant to each question during the past month. In addition, more stable personality traits were measured using the Neuroticism, Extraversion, Openness, Conscientiousness, and Agreeableness scales of the NEO Personality Inventory (Costa & McCrae, 1985).

Do People Perceive Change in Their Performance Over Time?

As can been seen in Figure 10.1, there was substantial individual variation in perceived change in word recall performance over 9 years. The figures for story and fact belief were similarly diverse. We used random effects models to evaluate the data. Specifically, hierarchical linear modeling was used to statistically examine whether significant change occurred in the participants' beliefs about their performance across the 4 waves. Participants had to have postdiction data on a given task for at least 2 of the 4 waves to be included in a task's analysis. Separate random coefficient models were estimated for each of the three recall tasks. At Level 1, or the within-subjects level, the equation was equivalent to a single regression equation for each individual case, examining individual rates of change across the 4 waves:

$$\text{Level 1: Belief}_{ij} = b_{0j} + b_{1j}(\text{wave}) + e_{ij}$$

At Level 2, or the between-subjects level, the equation evaluated whether stable age group and gender differences were associated with different trajectories of individual change across waves:

$$\text{Level 2: } b_{0j} = \beta_{00} + \beta_1(\text{age group}) + \beta_2(\text{gender}) + \beta_3(\text{Age Group} \times \text{Gender}) + u_{0j}$$

$$b_{1j} = \beta_{10} + \beta_1(\text{age group}) + \beta_2(\text{gender}) + \beta_3(\text{Age Group} \times \text{Gender}) + u_{1j}$$

The random effects for wave slopes were significant for each task, indicating that the interindividual variability observed in Figure 10.1 is associated with reliable differences in perceived change (fact: $z = -8.3, p < .001, \beta = -.78$; word: $z = -3.3, p < .01, \beta = -.49$; story: $z = -4.5, p < .001, \beta = -1.6$). These results indicated that, as wave increased, or the closer the postdiction was to the current occasion, participants' estimates about their ability decreased. In other

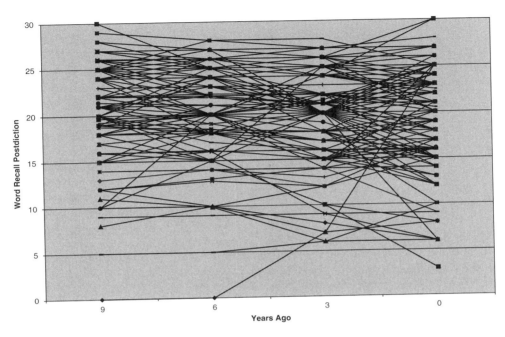

Figure 10.1. Individual trajectories of word recall postdiction scores over 9 years.

words, the estimated level of memory performance was lower at more recent waves (later in life) than at earlier waves. However, there were significant group effects, as men rated their performance on the fact recall task higher ($M = 28.08$, $SD = 7.05$) compared with women ($M = 25.33$, $SD = 7.69$), and young-old adults estimated better performance on the word recall task ($M = 20.56$, $SD = 4.64$) than did old-old adults ($M = 18.78$, $SD = 5.10$). There were no significant interaction effects for any of the tasks.

Does Actual Performance Change Over Time?

A similar series of analyses was conducted on the actual recall performance scores over the four waves. Figure 10.2 illustrates considerable individual variation in word recall performance over time. As with the postdiction evaluations, the individual performance score trajectories for fact and story recall were similarly diverse. Random effects models identical to those described above were used to evaluate individual change in the participants' performance score across the four waves. Again, participants had to have performance data on a given task for least two of the four waves to be included in a task's analysis.

In contrast to the postdiction analyses, random effects for wave slope did not fit the models, indicating the data better fit average group slopes of change in recall performance. However, the results varied more across tasks than in the postdiction analyses. Fixed wave effects were significant for fact ($z = -2.7$, $p < .01$, $\beta = -.37$) and word recall ($z = -4.8$, $p < .001$, $\beta = -.39$), illustrating that as wave increased, recall performance decreased. Interestingly, reflective of the

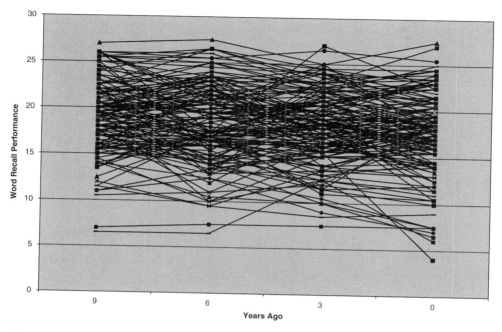

Figure 10.2. Individual trajectories of word recall performance over 9 years.

postdiction estimates, men did in fact perform (overall) better on the fact recall task ($M = 21.84$, $SD = 5.79$) than women ($M = 19.54$, $SD = 5.63$), and young-old adults did recall more words ($M = 19.16$, $SD = 3.60$) than old-old adults ($M = 17.34$, $SD = 4.45$). There were also Wave × Age Group interaction effects for both fact ($z = -2.5$, $p < .05$, $\beta = -.50$) and story ($z = -2.3$, $p < .05$, $\beta = -.90$). Forfact, wave effects were significant only for the old-old adults in that as wave increased, fact recall performance decreased, particularly at the last wave. For story performance, age group differences were significant only for the last two waves, as the young-old adults performed better than the old-old adults.

Do Perceptions Reflect Actual Change?

A series of hierarchical linear models was used to evaluate the effects of wave, age group, and gender on the percent difference between the postdicted score and the actual performance score for each occasion. For word and story recall, random wave effects fit the model best, but could not be fit for fact recall. Figures 10.3 and 10.4 illustrate the correspondence over time between the participants' postdiction estimates of word recall and fact recall, respectively, and the associated recall performance for each. The modeling analyses revealed that for both word and fact recall, the participants' postdiction estimates did not accurately reflect their performance scores regardless of age group or gender. Furthermore, there were no significant wave effects, denoting that the discrepancy between beliefs and actual performance was somewhat stable over time. In contrast, there was a significant wave effect for story recall ($z = -2.95$, $p < .01$,

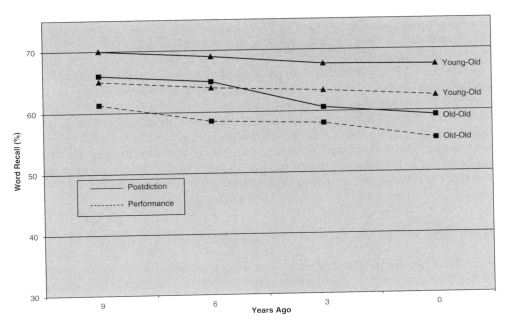

Figure 10.3.   Mean postdiction estimates and word recall performance by age group.

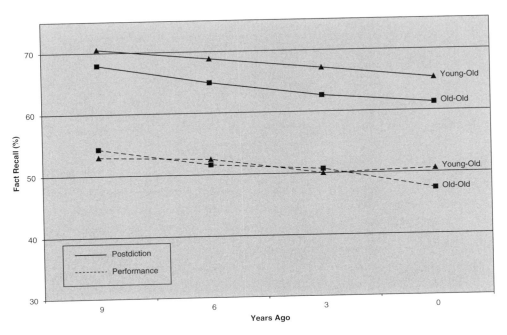

Figure 10.4.   Mean postdiction estimate and fact recall performance by age group.

β = −.013), indicating correspondence between the postdiction and actual score improved over time (see Figure 10.5). Interestingly, there was no group effect for story recall, indicating both age groups appeared to overestimate their abilities by similar amounts.

Figure 10.6 illustrates the correlations between the postdiction and actual performance scores over time. As expected, participants' accuracy in their postdictions increased over time or was more accurate the closer the postdiction was to the current testing period (e.g., estimations about performance 3 years ago were more accurate than estimations about performance 9 years ago). It is interesting that postdiction accuracy was nearly identical for the three recall tasks at the two furthest time points (i.e., 9 years and 6 years ago), and greater accuracy for the word and fact recall tasks only emerged at the closer time points (i.e., 3 years ago and current estimation).

What Determines the Reconstruction of the Past?

A series of hierarchical regressions was used to investigate whether the prediction of past performance by current postdictions were moderated by participants' memory-related beliefs, current affect, or personality. The analyses involved entering each predictor after entry of current postdiction to determine whether the variable significantly predicted 9-year postdiction estimates.

For word recall, MIA Change contributed the most amount of variance after current postdiction ($R^2\Delta = .07$), followed by comparing their current performance to how they would have done at age 20 ($R^2\Delta = .04$), and finally the best they could

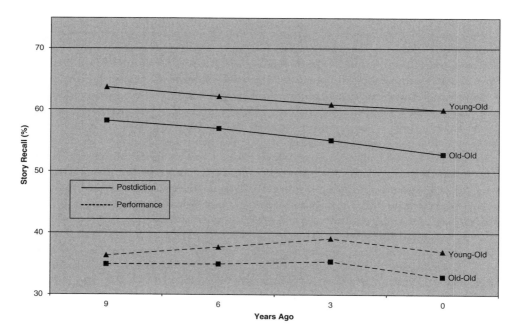

Figure 10.5. Mean postdiction estimate and story recall performance by age group.

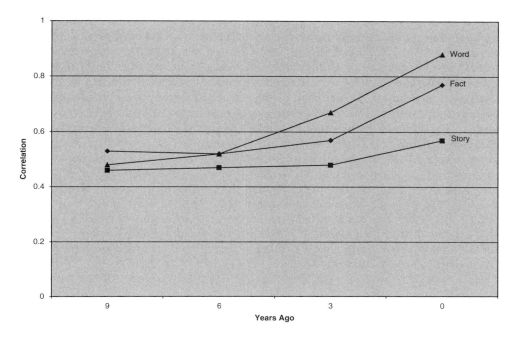

Figure 10.6. Correlations of postdictions and performance at four time points.

have possibly done ($R^2\Delta =. 03$). However, neither of the comparison belief measures predicted any variance over and above that accounted for by MIA Change.

For fact recall, the pattern was quite different, as MIA Change was among other predictors (such as personality) that did not significantly predict 9-year postdiction after taking into account current postdiction. In fact, there were only two significant predictors: individuals' beliefs about how they would have done at age 20 ($R^2\Delta = .02$), and affect balance score ($R^2\Delta = .02$). It is interesting that both variables accounted for unique proportions of variance even after entry of the other. For example, affect accounted for 1.2% of the variance after the yourself-at-20 belief measure, and individuals' belief about their performance at age 20 also accounted for 1.2% of variance after entry of affect.

There were far more significant predictors for 9-year postdiction of story recall, including MIA Change ($R^2\Delta = .014$), MIA Locus of Control ($R^2\Delta = .008$), balanced affect ($R^2\Delta = .014$), comparison with individuals' ability at age 20 ($R^2\Delta = .011$), and comparison with their best possible performance ($R^2\Delta = .006$). A series of further analyses investigated the unique variance of each predictor and found neither MIA Locus of Control nor best-performance beliefs significantly contributed information after MIA Change. Individuals' performances at age 20, however, did ($R^2\Delta = .007$), as did affect ($R^2\Delta = .009$). In fact, both affect and beliefs contributed unique variance. Affect still contributed information after the beliefs measures of both MIA Change and individuals' ability at age 20 were entered into the equation ($R^2\Delta = .008$), but after entry of affect, only MIA Change ($R^2\Delta = .009$), but not individuals' comparison with themselves at age 20, was significant.

We also compared how the relationships between the various belief, affect, and personality measures would change as the postdiction became closer to the current occasion. For word recall, MIA Change remained the only significant predictor of 6-year postdiction, but the effect size was less than half ($R^2\Delta = .03$) that of the 9-year postdiction, and effect size was no longer significant in predicting 3-year postdiction. In contrast, it was affect rather than belief measures that even came close to significantly predicting 6-year fact recall postdiction ($p = .07$), and no variables significantly predicted 3-year postdiction over and above current postdiction. There were numerous significant predictors for 6-year story recall postdiction, including MIA Change ($R^2\Delta = .012$), balanced affect ($R^2\Delta = .008$), and comparison both with individual's age-20 self ($R^2\Delta = .008$) and with their best possible performance ($R^2\Delta = .005$). However, MIA Change beliefs were the only measure to remain significant after the entry of affect ($R^2\Delta = .007$). Furthermore, affect was no longer significant once MIA Change was entered into the equation. Finally, similar to the results for word and fact recall, no measures significantly predicted 3-year story postdiction beyond current postdiction estimates.

Conclusion

Consistent with the results of many other longitudinal studies, the adults in this sample showed decreasing memory performance over time on the word and fact recall tasks. Decreasing performance over the 9-year interval was also observed for the story recall task but only for the old-old adults. A similar pattern was observed when participants reconstructed their performance from the past. Participants' estimates of their performance were lower for recent compared with earlier occasions of measurement, indicating a perception of memory decline over the interval. In the case of the word recall and fact recall tasks, participants' estimates of performance roughly paralleled the amount of actual decline. In contrast, for story recall, the pattern of perceived and actual change diverged (see Figure 10.5). On this task, average performance actually increased across the first three occasions of measurement, followed by a slight decrease from occasions 3 to 4. However, participants estimated that performance declined across the entire 9-year interval. Thus, participants appear to have an overall perception of decline even in the face of increases in actual performance. This pattern is consistent with the idea that individuals may invoke implicit theories of change when reconstructing the past. That this effect is most pronounced for the story task may, in part, reflect the fact that participants had more difficulty calibrating their performance on this task, thus resulting in increased reliance on a reconstruction of the past based on implicit beliefs.

When we consider the discrepancy between participants' estimates of their performance and actual changes, it is clear that older adults are only moderately accurate at evaluating long-term changes in their memory performance. Participants consistently overestimated their performance, although this effect varied substantially across tasks. The discrepancy was least for word recall (3.4%–5.7% depending on the occasion of measurement), higher for fact recall (14.3%–15.6%), and greatest for story recall (20.7%–25.4%). Examination of the correlations between estimated and actual performance (Figure 10.6) shows that participants' accuracy decreased over time. This decrease was most notable for the word and fact recall tasks. Participants provided relatively accurate estimates of performance on these tasks immediately following their completion, but their accuracy decreased substantially as they attempted to reconstruct their performance on the past occasions of measurement. The correlations for the story task showed a flatter profile, but accuracy on this task was rather poor for all occasions of measurement. Indeed, accuracy on all three tasks tended to converge for estimates of performance 9 years in the past with a correlation of approximately .50.

Clearly, other processes must be influencing older adults' reconstruction of the past. In fact, various memory belief and affect measures significantly predicted participants' estimates of their past performance (9-year postdictions) even after entry of their postdiction of current performance. In particular, participants' beliefs about personal memory change (MIA Change scale) and their perceptions of how well they would have completed the same task when they were younger (i.e., 20 years old) emerged almost uniformly as significant predictors across the three tasks. The influence of affect was uniquely significant for both the fact and story 9-year postdiction. It may be the case that affect exerts a greater effect on postdiction perceptions for tasks in which the metric of performance is somewhat ambiguous (e.g., assessing how many propositions one recalled in the story task), and consequently the level of performance is more difficult to estimate. The impact of both the belief and affect factors decreased, however, for the 6- and 3-year postdictions because there were fewer significant predictors for more recent performances. It appears that metacognitive beliefs and affect have a stronger influence in the reconstruction of more distant past performances than they do for more recent performances.

Overall, older adults' reconstructions of their past memory performances are only moderately accurate and may be substantially influenced by overall beliefs about memory decline with aging. However, these memory beliefs appear to have a positivity bias, resulting in consistent overestimations of past performance regardless of age or gender. In fact, it appears that older adults have the same general types of implicit theories regarding memory and aging, one that is quite accurate in perceiving possible change in performance over time (i.e., the discrepancy between beliefs and actual performance was somewhat stable over time). Therefore, implicit memory beliefs may provide reliable guidelines for estimating long-term average memory change, but such general beliefs may not facilitate insight into specific patterns of personal memory changes. Hence, it appears that Barbra was correct: We do distort our personal past in a positive way. At least in terms of our past memory skills, we tend to remember ourselves as being better than we were.

References

Bandura, A. (1977). Self-efficacy: Toward a unifying theory of behavioral change. *Psychological Review, 84,* 191–215.

Berry, J. M., & West, R. L. (1993). Cognitive self-efficacy in relation to personal mastery and goal setting across the life span. *International Journal of Behavioral Development, 16,* 351–379.

Bielak, A. A. M., Hultsch, D. F., Levy-Ajzenkopf, J., MacDonald, S. W. S., Hunter, M. A., & Strauss, E. (2007). Short-term changes in general and memory-specific control beliefs and their relationship to cognition in younger and older adults. *The International Journal of Aging & Human Development, 65,* 53–71.

Blanchard-Fields, F. (2005). Introduction to the special section on emotion-cognition interactions and the aging mind. *Psychology and Aging, 20,* 539–541.

Bolla, K. I., Lindgren, K. N., Bonaccorsy, C., & Bleeker, M. L. (1991). Memory complaints in older adults: Fact or fiction? *Archives of Neurology, 48,* 61–64.

Bradburn, N. M. (1969). *The structure of psychological well-being.* Chicago: Aldine.

Cavanaugh, J. C. (1996). Memory self-efficacy as a moderator of memory change. In F. Blanchard-Fields & T. M. Hess (Eds.), *Perspectives on cognitive change in adulthood* (pp. 488–507). New York: McGraw-Hill.

Chanowitz, B., & Langer, E. (1981). Premature cognitive commitment. *Journal of Personality and Social Psychology, 41,* 1051–1063.

Chasteen, A. L., Bhattacharyya, S., Horhota, M., Tam, R., & Hasher, L. (2005). How feelings of stereotype threat influence older adults' memory performance. *Experimental Aging Research, 31,* 235–260.

Chasteen, A. L., Schwarz, N., & Park, D. C. (2002). The activation of aging stereotypes in younger and older adults. *The Journals of Gerontology: Series B. Psychological Sciences and Social Sciences, 57,* P540–P547.

Costa, P. T., Jr., & McCrae, R. R. (1985). *The NEO Personality Inventory manual.* Odessa, FL: Psychological Assessment Resources.

Crook, T. H., III, & Larrabee, G. J. (1992). Normative data on a self-rating scale for evaluating memory in everyday life. *Archives of Clinical Neuropsychology, 7,* 41–51.

Crow, C. B. (1998). *The way we were: Retrospective evaluations of memory performance in the elderly.* Unpublished master's thesis, University of Victoria, Victoria, British Columbia, Canada.

Dixon, R. A. (1989). Questionnaire research on metamemory and aging: Issues of structure and function. In L. W. Poon, D. C. Rubin, & B. A. Wilson (Eds.), *Everyday cognition in adulthood and old age* (pp. 394–415). New York: Cambridge University Press.

Dixon, R. A. (2000). The concept of metamemory: Cognitive, developmental, and clinical issues. In G. E. Berrios & J. Hodges (Eds.), *Memory complaints and disorders: The neuropsychiatric perspective* (pp. 47–57). Cambridge: Cambridge University Press.

Dixon, R. A., & de Frias, C. M. (2004). The Victoria Longitudinal Study: From characterizing cognitive aging to illustrating changes in memory compensation. *Aging, Neuropsychology, and Cognition, 11,* 346–376.

Dixon, R. A., & de Frias, C. M. (2007). Mild memory deficits differentially affect six-year changes in compensatory strategy use. *Psychology and Aging, 22,* 632–638.

Dixon, R. A., de Frias, C. M., & Bäckman, L. (2001). Characteristics of self-reported memory compensation in late life. *Journal of Clinical and Experimental Neuropsychology, 23,* 650–661.

Dixon, R. A., Hultsch, D. F., & Hertzog, C. (1988). The Metamemory in Adulthood (MIA) questionnaire. *Psychopharmacology Bulletin, 24,* 671–688.

Dixon, R. A., Rust, T. B., Feltmate, S. E., & Kwong See, S. (2007). Memory and aging: Selected research directions and application issues. *Canadian Psychology, 48,* 67–76.

Dixon, R. A., Wahlin, A., Maitland, S. B., Hultsch, D. F., Hertzog, C., & Bäckman, L. (2004). Episodic memory change in late adulthood: Generalizability across samples and performance indices. *Memory & Cognition, 32,* 768–778.

Gilewski, M. J., & Zelinski, E. M. (1986). Questionnaire assessment of memory complaints. In L. W. Poon, T. Crook, K. L. Davis, C. Eisdorfer, B. J. Gurland, A. W. Kaszniak, & L. W. Thompson (Eds.), *Handbook for clinical memory assessment of older adults* (pp. 93–107). Washington, DC: American Psychological Association.

Gilewski, M. J., Zelinski, E. M., & Schaie, K. W. (1990). The Memory Functioning Questionnaire for assessment of memory complaints in adulthood and old age. *Psychology and Aging, 5,* 482–490.

Greenwald, A. G., & Banaji, M. R. (1995). Implicit social cognition: Attitudes, self-esteem, and stereotypes. *Psychological Review, 102,* 4–27.

Heckhausen, J., Dixon, R. A., & Baltes, P. B. (1989). Gains and losses in development throughout adulthood as perceived by different adult age groups. *Developmental Psychology, 25,* 109–121.

Heckhausen, J., & Schulz, R. (1995). A life-span theory of control. *Psychological Review, 102,* 284–304.

Hertzog, C., & Dixon, R. A. (2005). Metacognition in midlife. In S. L. Willis & M. Martin (Eds.), *Middle adulthood: A lifespan perspective* (pp. 355–380). Thousand Oaks, CA: Sage.

Hertzog, C., & Hultsch, D. F. (2000). Metacognition in adulthood. In F. I. M. Craik & T. A. Salthouse (Eds.), *Handbook of aging and cognition* (2nd ed., pp. 417–466). Mahwah, NJ: Erlbaum.

Hultsch, D. F., Hertzog, C., & Dixon, R. A. (1987). Age differences in metamemory: Resolving the inconsistencies. *Canadian Journal of Psychology, 41,* 193–208.

Hultsch, D. F., Hertzog, C., & Dixon, R. A. (1990). Ability correlates of memory performance in adulthood and aging. *Psychology and Aging, 5,* 356–368.

Hultsch, D. F., Hertzog, C., Dixon, R. A., & Small, B. J. (1998). *Memory change in the aged.* New York: Cambridge University Press.

Kite, M. E., & Johnson, B. T. (1988). Attitudes toward older and younger adults: A meta-analysis. *Psychology and Aging, 3,* 233–244.

Lachman, M. E. (1983). Perceptions of intellectual aging: Antecedent or consequence of intellectual functioning? *Developmental Psychology, 19,* 482–498.

Lachman, M. E., Andreoletti, C., & Pearman, A. (2006). Memory control beliefs: How are they related to age, strategy use, and memory improvement? *Social Cognition, 24,* 359–385.

Lachman, M. E., Baltes, P. B., Nesselroade, J. R., & Willis, S. L. (1982). Examination of personality-ability relationships in the elderly: The role of the contextual (interface) assessment mode. *Journal of Research in Personality, 16,* 485–501.

Lachman, M. E., Bandura, M., Weaver, S. L., & Elliott, E. (1995). Assessing memory control beliefs: The Memory Controllability Inventory. *Aging and Cognition, 2,* 67–84.

Levenson, H. (1974). Activism and powerful others: Distinctions within the concept of internal-external locus of control. *Journal of Personality Assessment, 38,* 377–383.

Lineweaver, T. T., & Hertzog, C. (1998). Adults' efficacy and control beliefs regarding memory and aging: Separating general from personal beliefs. *Aging, Neuropsychology, and Cognition, 5,* 264–296.

Maitland, S. B., Dixon, R. A., Hultsch, D. F., & Hertzog, C. (2001). Well-being as a moving target: Measurement equivalence of the Bradburn Affect Balance Scale. *The Journals of Gerontology: Series B. Psychological Sciences and Social Sciences, 56,* P69–77.

McDonald-Miszczak, L., Hertzog, C., & Hultsch, D. F. (1995). Stability and accuracy of metamemory in adulthood and aging: A longitudinal analysis. *Psychology and Aging, 10,* 553–564.

McFarland, C., Ross, M., & DeCourville, N. (1989). Women's theories of menstruation and biases in recall of menstrual symptoms. *Journal of Personality and Social Psychology, 57,* 522–531.

McFarland, C., Ross, M., & Giltrow, M. (1992). Biased recollections in older adults: The role of implicit theories of aging. *Journal of Personality and Social Psychology, 62,* 837–850.

Miller, L. M. S., & Lachman, M. E. (1999). The sense of control and cognitive aging: Toward a model of meditational processes. In T. M. Hess & F. Blanchard-Fields (Eds.), *Social cognition and aging* (pp. 17–41). San Diego, CA: Academic Press.

Morris, M. W., & Peng, K. (1994). Culture and cause: American and Chinese attributions for social and physical events. *Journal of Personality and Social Psychology, 67,* 949–971.

Newby-Clark, I. R. & Ross, M. (2003). Conceiving the past and future. *Personality and Social Psychology Bulletin, 29,* 807–818.

Ross, M. (1989). Relation of implicit theories to the construction of personal histories. *Psychological Review, 96,* 341–357.

Ross, M., & Newby-Clark, I. R. (1998). Construing the past and future. *Social Cognition, 16,* 113–150.

Ryan, E. B. (1992). Beliefs about memory changes across the adult life span. *The Journals of Gerontology: Series B. Psychological Sciences and Social Sciences, 47,* P41–P46.

Ryan, E. B., & Kwong See, S. (1993). Age-based beliefs about memory changes for self and others across adulthood. *The Journals of Gerontology: Series B. Psychological Sciences and Social Sciences, 48,* P199–P201.

Ryan, E. B., Kwong See, S., Meneer, W. B., & Trovato, D. (1992). Age-based perceptions of language performance among younger and older adults. *Communication Research, 19,* 423–443.

Schaie, K. W., Willis, S. L., & O'Hanlon, A. M. (1994). Perceived intellectual performance change over seven years. *The Journals of Gerontology: Series B. Psychological Sciences and Social Sciences, 49,* P108–P118.

Sternberg, R. J. (1987). Implicit theories: An alternative to modeling cognition and its development. In J. Bisanz, C. J. Brainerd, & R. Karl (Eds.), *Formal methods in developmental psychology: Progress in cognitive developmental research.* (pp. 155–192). New York: Springer.

Taylor, J. L., Miller, T. P., & Tinklenberg, J. R. (1992). Correlates of memory decline: A 4-year longitudinal study of older adults with memory complaints. *Psychology and Aging, 7,* 185–193.

Tun, P. A., & Wingfield, A. (1995). Does dividing attention become harder with age? Findings from the Divided Attention Questionnaire. *Aging and Cognition, 2,* 39–66.

Zacks, R. T., Hasher, L., & Li, K. Z. H. (2000). Human memory. In F. I. M. Craik & T. A. Salthouse (Eds.), *The handbook of aging and cognition* (2nd ed., pp. 293–357). Mahwah, NJ: Erlbaum.

Zelinski, E. M., Gilewski, M. J., & Thompson, L. W. (1980). Do laboratory tests relate to self-assessment of memory ability in the young and old? In L. W. Poon, J. L. Fozard, L. S. Cermak, D. Arenberg, & L. W. Thompson (Eds.), *New directions in memory and aging: Proceedings of the George A. Talland Memorial Conference* (pp. 519–544). Hillsdale, NJ: Erlbaum.

Part III

Applying Research Findings

11

The Role of Cognitive Ability in Everyday Functioning: Medication Adherence as an Example

Hayden B. Bosworth and Brian J. Ayotte

Within the past couple of decades, there has been increased interest in everyday cognition, or how older adults address complex cognitive tasks in their everyday lives. This interest has been driven by both methodological and theoretical concerns. Methodologically, researchers who study everyday cognition emphasize external validity as opposed to laboratory-based researchers who emphasize internal validity (Puckett, Reese, & Pollina, 1993). Theoretically, researchers have argued that traditional laboratory-based tests of cognition do not adequately capture older adults' cognitive functioning in everyday life because of the contextual richness of the environment and the frequency in which everyday tasks are faced (Denney & Pearce, 1989; Puckett et al., 1993). Despite this increased focus on everyday cognition, applying basic research to "real world" settings remains one of the biggest challenges identified by cognitive aging researchers (Hershey, Boyd, Coutant, & Turner, 1999). This chapter outlines how basic cognitive functioning underlies performance in applied everyday tasks and illustrates these relationships in the context of medication adherence.

Everyday Cognition

Everyday cognition, also referred to as *practical* or *real-world cognition,* has been defined as the "ability to perform adequately those cognitively complex tasks of daily living considered essential for living on one's own in this society" (Willis, 1996, p. 595). These cognitively complex tasks typically reflect instrumental activities of daily living, which include transportation, food preparation, using

This chapter was coauthored by an employee of the United States government as part of official duty and is considered to be in the public domain. Any views expressed herein do not necessarily represent the views of the United States government, and the author's participation in the work is not meant to serve as an official endorsement.

This chapter was supported by a grant from NHLBI (R01 HL070713) and an Established Investigator award from the American Heart Association to Hayden B. Bosworth. Brian J. Ayotte was supported by a fellowship training grant through the Office of Academic Affairs, Department of Veterans Affairs.

the telephone, managing finances, and taking medications correctly (Allaire & Marsiske, 1999).

There is extensive evidence that performance on traditional tests of cognitive ability tends to decrease with age (Schaie, 1996). However, there are two theoretical approaches to the issue of whether these declines in basic cognitive ability are related to a decline in everyday settings. The first approach emphasizes the knowledge and experience that is gained over one's lifetime (Baltes, 1993). This approach suggests that older adults find ways to adapt to, and compensate for, decreased cognitive functioning in everyday life in a number of ways, including using social partners (Meegan & Berg, 2002), emphasizing automatic processes (Park, 1999), using environmental and contextual cues (Dixon, de Frias, & Bäckman, 2001), and relying on existing knowledge structures (Baltes, 1993). Thus, performance on everyday cognitive tasks does not necessarily have to follow the same pattern of decline as performance on basic laboratory tasks. In fact, if the task is relevant and familiar, then performance may actually increase with age because of the increased experience and domain-specific knowledge. In an early cross-sectional study on everyday cognition, Cornelius and Caspi (1987) found that increasing age was associated with better performance on an everyday problem-solving measure. This study also found that the trajectory of everyday cognition across age groups was more similar to the trajectory of crystallized ability (i.e., increasing through adulthood, then leveling off in older adulthood) than the trajectory of fluid ability (increasing through middle adulthood, then steadily decreasing during older adulthood; Schaie, 1996). *Crystallized abilities* involve the formation of skills and strategies that people have acquired through experience, and *fluid abilities* indicate the ability to deal with novel problems and to perceive and discriminate relations (Bosworth, Schaie, & Willis, 1999).

The second theoretical approach suggests that everyday cognition can be conceptualized as a hierarchy of cognitive abilities (see Willis & Schaie, 1993). This hierarchical perspective implies that (a) encountering everyday problems leads to the activation and application of multiple basic cognitive abilities; (b) the basic cognitive abilities that are activated are dependent upon the type of everyday problem being faced; and (c) in addition to basic cognitive functioning, domain-specific knowledge is often required to solve everyday problems (Willis & Schaie, 1993). This approach predicts that change in everyday cognitive ability should correspond to change in basic cognitive abilities. In a longitudinal study of older adults that supports this approach, Marsiske and Willis (1995) found that a measure of everyday cognition that focused on everyday instrumental tasks decreased with age. In addition, research suggests that performance on measures of inductive reasoning, declarative memory, working memory, and verbal ability are moderately correlated with performance on multiple dimensions of everyday cognitive ability (Allaire & Marsiske, 1999). In addition, Diehl, Willis, and Schaie (1995) found that processing speed, memory, crystallized intelligence, and fluid intelligence were correlated with performance on multiple dimensions of an observable measure of everyday cognition (i.e., food preparation, medication use, and telephone use).

One possible explanation for the inconsistent findings regarding the association between age and everyday cognition may involve the way that everyday cognition is measured. The measures used in studies that find no decline in performance over time have used measures of everyday cognition that include inter-personal, emotional, and *ill-structured* (i.e., requiring open-ended responses, such as listing possible solutions) problems, which may play to the strengths of older adults (Carstensen, Isaacowitz, & Charles, 1999). In addition, some of these measures assess *response fluency* (i.e., the number of possible solutions to a problem; Berg, Meegan, & Klaczynski, 1999) or use a panel of judges to rate the effectiveness of solutions (Crawford & Channon, 2002), thus reflecting creativity of socioemotional awareness (Marsiske & Willis, 1995). Conversely, studies finding age-associated declines in everyday cognitive ability use *well-structured problems* (i.e., the problem has a right or wrong answer) that reflect more formal cognitive processes that actually may reflect competency rather than ability (Allaire & Marsiske, 1999).

Regardless of the theoretical approach, researchers agree that there are important relationships among basic cognitive abilities and everyday cognition. The remainder of this chapter focuses on the cognitive mechanisms underlying a complex everyday task that is very relevant to older adults: adherence to medication.

Cognition and Adherence to Medication

There is clear evidence that with age, many cognitive functions, including speed of information processing, working memory capacity, and long-term memory, decline (Schaie, 1996). Cognitive decline among older adults may be particularly problematic because of older adults' disproportionate use of health care resources and the increased demands of organizing and maintaining their complex medical regimens (Bosworth & Schaie, 1995; Park & Kidder, 1996; Salthouse, 1991).

Prior research has shown that only 50% to 60% of patients are adherent in taking prescribed medications over a 1-year period (Bosworth, 2006; Haynes et al., 2005; Osterberg & Blaschke, 2005; Sabate, 2003) even for medications essential for the treatment of chronic diseases (Avorn et al., 1998). Nonadherence is an important health issue, particularly in chronic disease management (Bosworth, 2006). Medication nonadherence costs an estimated $100 billion annually in the United States, and medications errors and adverse drug reactions account for 10% of hospital administrations (Vermeire, Hearnshaw, Van Royen, & Denekens, 2001).

Cognitive factors are related to all of the components, or stages, of medication adherence, including comprehension, formulating plans, and actually taking medication. For example, nonadherence may be a result of patients' poor understanding of instructions regarding their medications (Ad Hoc Committee on Health Literacy for the Council on Scientific Affairs, 1999; Hoffman & Proulx, 2003). Several recent studies have demonstrated that patients frequently have difficulty reading and understanding medication labels (Davis, Wolf, Bass, Middlebrooks, et al., 2006; Davis, Wolf, Bass, Thompson, et al., 2006; Wolf, Davis, Tilson, Bass, & Parker, 2006). Although patients should receive medication counseling from their health care providers, including physicians and pharmacists, numerous studies have shown that discussions about drugs are often limited (Sleath, Rubin, Campbell, Gwyther, & Clark, 2001;

Tarn et al., 2006) and patients frequently do not remember those conversations (Fletcher, Fletcher, Thomas, & Hamann, 1979; Post & Roter, 1988; Stewart & Liolitsa, 1999), forcing many to rely on drug labels for information. Unfortunately, older adults, compared with younger adults, are more likely to misunderstand instructions on prescription drug labels, leading to an increased number of mistakes (Morrell, Park, & Poon, 1989).

This risk of medication nonadherence and misunderstanding is potentially accentuated for individuals suffering from chronic diseases. Studies have identified associations between certain chronic illnesses, such as hypertension (Swan, Carmelli, & Larue, 1998; Swan et al., 1998) and diabetes (Asimakopoulou, Hampson, & Morrish, 2002; Stewart & Liolitsa, 1999), with subsequent declines in cognitive function. In the case of diabetes, long-standing diabetes results in significant memory deficits, probably due to complications of long-term hyperglycemia and hypertension (Asimakopoulou et al., 2002; Stewart & Liolitsa, 1999). Although these cognitive declines are debilitating in their own right, they are also directly related to health outcomes as many of these age-related declines are necessary for medication adherence (Raz, 2000).

One way to organize components of cognition required for medication adherence is through the construct of medication management capacity. An important aspect of adherence, *medication management capacity* (MMC) has been defined as "the cognitive and functional ability to self-administer a medication regimen as it has been prescribed" (Maddigan, Farris, Keating, Wiens, & Johnson, 2003, p. 33). Measures of MMC typically assess functional skills such as correctly identifying medications, opening containers, selecting the proper dose, and taking the medication at the proper time (MacLaughlin et al., 2005). Low MMC predicts greater emergency department utilization, functional decline, and subsequent residence in assisted-living facilities (Edelberg, Shallenberger, Hausdorff, & Wei, 2000).

Despite the centrality of adherence to successful outcomes, most health care research is focused on improving medical procedures, technologies, and drugs with relatively little concern directed toward the variables that influence whether patients can or will successfully complete medication treatment requirements (Park & Meade, 2007). In this chapter, we discuss factors that contribute to medication adherence at each stage of adherence (i.e., comprehension, planning, and action). In addition, we discuss potential ways to improve each stage, focusing specifically on cognitive and contextual factors. Although this chapter focuses mainly on medication adherence, the topic of adherence is much broader and encompasses a range of medical behaviors, including adherence to lifestyle recommendations (e.g., dietary, weight control, or physical activity) and the use of medical equipment such as a home blood pressure monitor or glucose monitor. In fact, most successful health care outcomes require the recipient of the services to follow a set of instructions, hence requiring the use of various cognitive functions.

Comprehension and Medication Adherence

To take medication successfully or follow medical instructions appropriately, an individual must first be able to comprehend the information, then later remember the instructions or, at least, have written instructions directly available at the time of implementation. However, much of the adherence literature focuses on remembering to take medications, and relatively little addresses the issue of accurate comprehension and remembering of information relevant to medication adherence (Park & Meade, 2007).

To fully comprehend medical information, the patient must understand the words and phrases the physician uses to explain the diagnosis and treatment plan. The patient will often be required to read prescriptions and other materials to successfully follow the recommended treatment plan. However, many of the recommendations and instructions given by physicians are never written, and patients must therefore rely on memory to follow instructions. Even when written information is given, the material often places high demands on working memory, thus limiting retention of key points (Chandler & Sweller, 1991; van den Broek & Kremer, 1998). Patients who are unable to meet the reading and/or the memory demands imposed on them are less likely to follow therapeutic plans and instructions. In addition, sensory impairments may adversely affect comprehension. Older adults often suffer from at least some hearing loss as they age, which negatively affects their ability to retain the temporal order of incoming speech signals as well as the ability to discriminate between speech signals and background noise (Wingfield, Tun, & McCoy, 2005). Many older adults also suffer from impaired visual acuity, which is exacerbated under conditions in which there is low light or the contrast between the letters and background is low. Fortunately, corrective lenses may attenuate age-related differences in visual acuity well into later life (Schieber, 2006).

Morrell et al. (1989) investigated the problem of comprehension by orally presenting young and old adults with a series of fictitious perceptions as they were receiving instructions from a physician. Compared with young adults, older adults showed not only poorer memory for the instructions but also poorer comprehension of the materials. Moreover, when younger and older adults had the instructions available to them in writing and could consult the information when developing a plan for when to take the medications, older adults still consistently made more errors than their younger counterparts.

Between 40% and 80% of information provided by health care providers is forgotten almost immediately (Kessel, 2003). Among older adults, one survey of elderly patients found that only 46% recalled the drugs listed in their medical records (Rost & Roter, 1987), and a second survey indicated that only 58% of older patients were familiar with their dosing instructions immediately after a physician visit (Fletcher et al., 1979). A more recent study involved 172 older individuals recently discharged from the hospital; patients were contacted by telephone and asked about the name, number, dosages, schedule, purpose, and adverse effects of the new medication(s). Of the survey respondents, 86% were aware that they had been prescribed new medications, but fewer could identify the name (64%) or number (74%) of new medications or their dosages (56%), schedule (68%), or purpose (64%). Only 11% could recall being told of any adverse effects, and only 22% could name at least 1 adverse effect. Older patients tended to answer fewer questions correctly ($p = .02$; Maniaci, Heckman, & Dawson, 2008).

In our own work examining comprehension and relationships with age, we created a measure to assess oral comprehension that represents a typical recommendation that a physician may give to a patient with hypertension. Specifically, patients were told, "Your doctor recommends that you stop smoking, start exercising, and take your medication three times a day: once in the morning, in the afternoon, and at bedtime." Patients were then asked to recall the information that was presented, with a score of 10 indicating perfect recall for the components of the statement. Among 636 individuals with hypertension randomly approached for a study on improving blood pressure, we observed that, on average, those less than 65 years of age were able to recall significantly more statements than those 65 years old and older ($d = 0.2$; Bosworth et al., 2007). Thus, numerous studies (e.g., Fletcher et al., 1979; Morrell et al., 1989; Rost & Roter, 1987) have consistently reported that individuals have limited knowledge about their medications, which may have significant public health implications.

Health literacy is the ability to understand and act on health information and is one of the primary determinants of comprehension (McCray, 2005). However, more than 90 million adult Americans—39% of the adults in United States—lack the literacy skills to effectively function in the current health care environment (Institute of Medicine, 2004), and this number has not changed significantly in the past 10 years (U.S. Department of Education, 2005). Low health literacy is found in many different health care settings (Gazmararian, Williams, Peel, & Baker, 2003; Williams et al., 1995) and is most common in older patients, those with lower education levels, immigrants, and racial or ethnic minorities (Wilson, 2003). Prior research has supported the association between literacy and disease knowledge, utilization of preventative services, hospitalization, overall health status, and mortality in older adults (Dewalt, Berkman, Sheridan, Lohr, & Pignone, 2004; Sudore et al., 2006; Wolf, Gazmararian, & Baker, 2005).

A recent multisite study examined primary care patients' abilities to understand and demonstrate instructions found on container labels of common prescription medications. Approximately half (46%) of the patients in the study were unable to read and correctly state one or more of the label instructions on five common prescriptions. Rates of misunderstanding were higher among patients with marginal and low literacy (63%), yet more than one third (38%) of patients with adequate literacy skills misunderstood at least one of the label instructions (Davis, Wolf, Bass, Thompson, et al., 2006). Misunderstanding information at this stage of adherence can have a negative impact on later stages by leading to plans that do not correspond to the instructions and, ultimately, nonadherence to treatment.

Numeracy, or the ability to understand numbers, is especially critical in the health domain, where understanding or not understanding what numbers mean may have life-altering consequences. Researchers have measured it using objective math tests and self-reported perceptions of math ability (Lipkus, Samsa, & Rimer, 2001). Results of the National Adult Literacy Survey indicate that almost half of the general population has difficulty with relatively simple numeric tasks (Kirsch, Jungleblut, Jenkins, & Kolstad, 1993). Having lower numeric skills is associated with lower comprehension and less use of health information. Many patients cannot perform the basic numeric tasks required to function in the current health care environment. For example, 26% of participants in one study were unable to understand information about when an appointment was scheduled (Williams et al., 1995). In summary, numerical competence is needed to understand and weigh the risks and benefits of treatment, to decipher survival and mortality curves, and to navigate medical insurance forms and informed consent documents (Nelson, Reyna, Fagerlin, Lipkus, & Peters, 2008).

Understanding risk–benefit information is another important dimension of health literacy, and a hierarchy of skills is needed to comprehend and use this information. First, patients must be able to acquire accurate and timely information from reading tables, charts, or text, or from listening to speech. Then patients often must make calculations and inferences. For example, given survival rates for chemotherapy versus hormone therapy, a patient with cancer must calculate the difference between therapies and infer the meaning of that difference. Next, patients must remember information either for a short period (if the decision is made quickly) or after an extended delay (if the decision is made after an extended period of time), and memory ability differs across patient populations. Finally, patients must be able to weigh factors to match their needs and values to arrive at a health decision. Unfortunately, people appear to have problems even with relatively simple interpretations of risk magnitudes. In fact, one study suggests that 16% of highly educated people incorrectly answered straightforward questions about risk magnitudes (e.g., "Which represents the larger risk: 1%, 5%, or 10%?"; Bastian et al. 2001). If these errors occur in highly educated people, then it is important to ensure proper understanding of risks and benefits in patients who may have lower cognitive ability because of disease, low education levels, or the aging process.

In summary, patients are required to read medical information and comprehend what to do and when to do it. Patients may be required to perform numeric tasks, including calculating the number of tablets for a single dose of medicine. They are expected to monitor themselves for both beneficial and adverse effects, know what to do if they miss a dose of medication, and master whether, when, and how to obtain refills of their medication (Gazmararian et al., 2003). Chronic illnesses in the elderly population often require following an intensive and complex medical regime (e.g., medications, daily monitoring, routine physician visits, tests) such that the adverse consequences of low health literacy in this population may be particularly pronounced and require serious consideration (Parker & Gazmararian, 2003).

Planning and Integrating a Medication Regimen

After being prescribed medications, patients must be able to successfully integrate the medication regimen into their daily lives. There are five primary elements associated with this integration: (a) reading the instructions; (b) correctly interpreting the instructions; (c) opening the bottle; (d) cutting pills, if required; and (e) planning the dosage and timing of the medication (Isaac & Tamblyn, 1993). Thus, to ensure planning and integration of one's medication regimen, a number of cognitive resources are brought to bear, many of which are described next.

Executive functioning (Fuster, 1997; West, 1996) is required for medication adherence. Executive functioning involves higher order management of cognition, including planning, problem solving, working memory, and anticipation of possible consequences of a particular course of action (Stuss, 1992).

Insel, Morrow, Brewer, and Figueredo (2006) found that an index of executive function ability was strongly correlated with medication adherence over time. Unfortunately, this study did not specifically address how executive function ability was related to actual planning and the integration of a medication regimen with the daily lives of older adults.

Additional cognitive processes such as retrospective memory, working memory, and inhibition are also related to planning. For example, memory is important in this stage of adherence because after developing a plan to take medications, patients must actually remember the plan (Kliegel, McDaniel, & Einstein, 2000). In a comprehensive laboratory study investigating the association between cognitive abilities and planning in a prospective memory task, Kliegel et al. (2000) sought to elucidate how age and specific cognitive domains were related to plan elaboration, recall, and initiation in older and younger adults. With regard to plan elaboration, younger adults tended to develop much more elaborate plans than older adults. However, there were no age differences in how well the plans were actually remembered. Thus, making less elaborate plans may have been adaptive for older adults. Unfortunately, less elaborate plans were related to poorer performance on the task. In other words, older adults made plans that they could remember, but the plans were not necessarily adequate to ensure adherence. With regard to plan initiation, both working memory and inhibition ability were positively related to the likelihood that the plans developed by participants would be initiated, as well as the performance on the actual task. These findings suggest that planning plays an integral role in real-world prospective memory tasks, such as adherence. However, additional work is needed to identify the cognitive components related to planning and integration in a real-world setting.

In addition to executive processes and working memory, medication planning and integration may depend on the encoding and storage of information about the medicine (e.g., why the medicine is important, why the person needs to take it) and instructions as to when and how (e.g., with food) the medicine is to be taken. For example, Rice and Okun (1994) found that older adults remembered more information when it was consistent with prior beliefs or experience compared with when information was contrary to prior beliefs or experience. In addition, encoding entirely new information was easier than trying to correct or change preexisting knowledge. These findings are consistent with the concept of cognitive schemas, or cognitive frameworks. Information that is consistent with a person's schema is remembered better than information that is inconsistent with the schema. This has direct effects on the integration of a medication regimen into a person's daily life. If a person has been unknowingly taking medications incorrectly for a period of time, it would be much more difficult for him or her to remember corrected information regarding instructions. Likewise, if a patient's medication schedule is changed or if the instructions are not congruent with the patient's beliefs or schema, integrating the medication schedule into his or her daily life might prove difficult.

Inductive reasoning involves the recognition of patterns and the generalization of available information (Heit, 2000). The ability to recognize patterns and generalize instructions may be useful for planning medication usage, particularly if a person is taking multiple medications. If a person is planning his or her medication schedule, being able to recognize that the dosage is in the same relative place on the label would make it easier to actually create a schedule. Inductive reasoning is strongly associated with scores on everyday problem-solving measures, which often include a medication component (Allaire & Marsiske, 1999; Diehl et al., 2005). For example, the revised Observed Tasks of Daily Living measure (Diehl et al., 2005) includes items assessing a person's ability to understand medicine-related information. In a large clinical trial, Willis et al. (2006) found that training participants on reasoning tasks was associated with better self-reported instrumental activities of daily living (e.g., managing health, financial responsibilities) 5 years later. Additional research needs to be conducted to determine how inductive reasoning specifically is related to medication adherence.

Automatic processes, or cognitive processes that occur with minimal awareness or conscious effort (Bargh & Fergusen, 2000), may also be involved in integrating medication into one's schedule. Imagining a detailed plan to engage in a certain behavior, or creating what have been termed *implementation intentions,* makes it much more likely that the behavior will be automatically triggered by appropriate retrieval contexts—thus increasing the likelihood that a person will actually perform the planned behavior in the future (Gollwitzer, 1999). It is interesting to note that Brandstätter, Lengfelder, and Gollwitzer (2001) found that creating and mentally rehearsing plans to engage in a relatively simple laboratory task increased the likelihood of enacting the plans regardless of cognitive load. This finding has implications for people with decreased cognitive capacity due to illness or the aging process and suggests that implementation intentions may improve adherence, even in patients with some type of cognitive impairment. Additional research is needed to further establish the efficacy of creating implementation intentions for increasing (or maintaining) levels of adherence.

In summary, planning and integrating a medication regimen into a patient's daily life involves a number of complex cognitive processes. Not only is comprehension of the information required, but patients also must be able to recall relevant information, keep this information readily available when developing their plan, and recognize patterns in their medication in order to develop an effective medication schedule. The next step is to actually implement the plan.

Action: Implementing the Plan

Once information is comprehended and a plan is formulated, the act of remembering to perform a medical instruction is often called *prospective memory,* which refers to remembering to perform a planned action. Prospective memory requires not only that people remember the particular action that is to be performed but also that they remember to perform that action when it is appropriate to do so (McDaniel, Einstein, Stout, & Morgan, 2003).

Einstein and McDaniel (1990) made a distinction between event-based prospective memory and time-based prospective memory. In an *event-based prospective memory* task, the occurrence of an environmental event signals the appropriateness of performing the intended action. For example, an individual may form the intention to take one's blood pressure medicine when one has his or her cereal in the morning. At breakfast the next morning, the cereal can act as an environmental cue or signal for triggering one's memory to take the medication. To the extent that these cues stimulate remembering of the intention, they reduce the self-initiated retrieval processing required for prospective memory. For *time-based prospective memory* tasks, it is appropriate to execute the action at a certain time or after a certain period of time has elapsed. For example, it may be appropriate to measure one's blood glucose level at a certain time of day. In terms of medication taking, the medication-taking regimen may require remembering after specified periods of elapsed time—say after every 8 hours if one is on a three-times-a-day regimen. For time-based tasks, there is no obvious and specific external cue that might help stimulate prospective remembering. Instead, retrieval of the prospective memory intention likely requires a high degree of self-initiated processing. As might be expected based on the amount of self-initiated processing that is required, research suggests that there are larger age differences on time-based prospective memory compared with event-based prospective memory (Einstein, McDaniel, Richardson, Guynn, & Cunfer, 1995; Park, Hertzog, Kidder, Morrell, & Mayhorn, 1997).

Working memory is also relevant in actually taking medication. Remembering to take a medication at the proper time is irrelevant if a person cannot keep the intention to take medicines active in working memory while doing others things, such as going to the room where the medication is kept, checking the time, pouring a glass of water, and getting medicines. In one study examining how delay in performing an intended action was related to the likelihood of that action actually being performed, McDaniel et al. (2003) found that even a brief delay of 5 seconds resulted in poorer performance in older adults. One possible explanation for this loss of memory is that older adults are less able to inhibit internal and external distractions (Hasher & Zacks, 1988). In practice, this means that older adults who are busy, thinking about other things, or are in an environment that has a lot of distractions may forget to take their medications even if they had the intention to do so.

Adherence also requires patients to remember whether they actually took their medication. In other words, patients must monitor the output of a prospective memory task, an ability that becomes more difficult when the action is repetitive (e.g., taking medication) and as people get older (Einstein, McDaniel, Smith, & Shaw, 1998). For instance, patients may confuse the thought of taking a medication with the memory of actually taking the medicine (Johnson & Raye, 1981). This is referred to as *internal-source monitoring* (Einstein et al., 1998). Likewise, patients may confuse a recent memory of taking their medications for a more distal memory of the same action, which is reflective of a problem of temporal memory (Einstein et al., 1998). Both of these memory errors can result in errors of repetition or omission.

In general, adhering to a medication regime is dependent on accurate comprehension of information as well as successfully developing a plan and integrating the medication regime into daily life. In addition, prospective memory ability, working memory, and output monitoring are all associated with actually taking medication. Despite knowledge about the cognitive correlates of adherence, rates of actual adherence remain low. However, a number of promising approaches might increase adherence.

Approaches for Improving Medication Adherence

Despite knowledge about the cognitive correlates of adherence, rates of actual adherence remain low. However, a number of promising approaches might increase adherence.

Presentation of Information

Efforts to improve the presentation of prescription medication are needed to ensure proper understanding and interpretation of instructions (see Exhibit 11.1 for a summary of recommendations to improve medication adherence). A growing body of research, for example, has found that patients frequently misinterpret prescription drug labels. Challenges in reading and understanding labels may represent one cause for the high rates of medication errors and poor adherence. The extent to which deficits in labeling contribute to poor adherence or unsafe use of medications is unknown, but it is worth striving for improvements in those domains.

Exhibit 11.1.   Health Literacy Interventions

Fundamental techniques
- Simplified materials
- Simplified language
- Lower reading level
- More attractive format/layout
- Lower concept density
- Context provided first
- Use of pictograms or graphic devices
- Culturally sensitive

Technology-based communication techniques
- Audiotapes
- Videotape
- CD-ROM
- Interactive multimedia programs
- Computerized decision aids
- Telephone-delivered interventions (education, counseling, and reminders)

Personal communication and education
- Classes on health education sessions
- Health care provider communication techniques
- Interactive communication strategies

Tailored approaches
- Viewpoints and experiences of the intended population to determine the optimal context, channels, and content
- Computer-based algorithms that take patient characteristics into account (language, age, gender, ethnicity, reading ability, health literacy levels, and specific goals/needs)

People tend to comprehend more and make better-informed decisions when the presentation format makes the most important information easier to evaluate and when less cognitive effort is required (Peters, Dieckmann, Dixon, Hibbard, & Mertz, 2007). For example, Shrank, Avorn, Rolon, and Shekelle (2007) summarized in their systematic review that when optimizing content, patients prefer information about the indication for the medication, expected benefits, duration of therapy, and a thorough list of potential adverse effects, in addition to typical information identifying the drug's name, directions for use, and warnings. When optimizing label formats, lists, headers, and white space enhance readability, and content should be organized to follow the schema that patients use to understand medication information. The print should be the largest size possible of fonts that are easiest to read, and language should be simple, precise, and devoid of formal medical terminology.

Unfortunately, the medication labels and patient information leaflets that patients rely on for pertinent drug information are often difficult for them to understand. Font size influences readability and comprehension in both consumer medication information (e.g., leaflets created by the private sector) and container labels. The small print size that appears on many product labels necessitates a visual acuity of at least 20/50, making it hard for many individuals, especially older individuals, to read (Holt, Hollon, Hughes, & Coyle, 1990). In one randomized controlled trial, 101 older adults and 109 young adults were presented with 12 otherwise identical over-the-counter drug bottles with varied container labels along three dimensions, one of which was font size (7-point vs. 10-point; Wogalter & Vigilante, 2003). Whereas younger participants performed equally well in the small and large font size label groups, elderly patients had significantly reduced recall and understanding after reading the small-font labels. Regardless of performance, both young and elderly participants preferred the larger font labels.

A recent review suggests that pictures can be especially helpful to patients with low literacy skills (Houts, Doak, Doak, & Loscalzo, 2006). Specifically, research suggests that pictures can help people with low literacy skills understand relationships, provided that they understand the elements being related. The authors also concluded that spoken information can, with the help of pictures, be recalled to a high degree by people with low literacy skills, enabling them to make optimum use of information spoken by medical staff (Houts et al., 2006). The success of pictorial aids depends on their use of culturally appropriate, simple, realistic pictures that convey a clear, singular meaning (Katz, Kripalani, & Weiss, 2006).

Morrow, Leirer, and Altieri (1995) found that older adults' comprehension and subsequent memory of medical information are improved when the information is presented in a list format (rather than a paragraph format). Repeating medical information also helps older adults better remember it (Morrow, Leirer, Carver, Tanke, & McNally, 1999). Recall can be aided by presenting instructions in a clear and simple manner, using concrete and specific advice, repeating and stressing the importance of the critical components of the advice, checking understanding, and providing feedback (Sanson-Fisher, Campbell, Redman, & Hennrikus, 1989).

Training

One approach to improving medication adherence has been to train the component processes thought to underlie medication adherence, such as speed of processing, reasoning, and memory (Park & Meade, 2007). However, Ball et al. (2002) demonstrated that training on component processes did not necessarily transfer to activities of daily living (e.g., medication adherence). As such, this avenue may not be the most promising for interventions aimed at improving adherence.

A potential strategy for improving adherence may rely on automatic cognitive processes that require little cognitive effort and remain intact with age (Jacoby, 1991, 1999; Park, 2000). For example, the act of imagining a detailed plan to perform a specific action actually increases the probability that one will implement the plan (Gollwitzer, 1999). Forming implementation intentions entails the explicit imagining and then rehearsal of how one will initiate a desired behavior when he or she encounters appropriate cues in the environment. Later, when the individual encounters these specific cues, they automatically cue the person to perform the imagined behavior. Forming implementation intentions appears to be an effective strategy for improving older adults' prospective memory (remembering to perform future actions) because the strategy relies on age-invariant automatic processes rather than explicit recollection of information from memory (Chasteen, Park, & Schwarz, 2001).

Environmental Aids

One commonly available and frequently used intervention to assist medication adherence is medication organizers or medication containers that are sold over the counter. Whereas these devices may be beneficial for some, they require good comprehension of the medication regimen if the organizers are to be loaded correctly. Park, Morrell, Frieske, and Kincaid (1992) investigated how over-the-counter pillboxes and medication charts affected adherence to medication in a sample of younger and older adults. Results of this study indicated that older adults who were given the pillbox and the chart were significantly more adherent than those who got none or one of the external aids. It should be noted, however, that the evidence on the efficacy of using pillboxes is inconsistent, with some studies finding that using this type of aid does not increase adherence compared with a control group (e.g., Littenberg, MacLean, & Hurowitz, 2006). Potential explanation for the inconsistent findings using pillboxes may be attributed to individuals' initial knowledge and ability to periodically load their pillboxes correctly.

Maintenance of Behavioral Change

Because problem solving occurs within a person's short-term memory (Newell, Shaw, & Simon, 1956), when memory capacity is exceeded, patients resort to heuristics or rules of thumb that result in less than optimal decision making (Kahneman, Slovic, & Tversky, 1982). Thus, even if patients succeed in solving problems and making initial behavioral changes, it may be unlikely that these new behavioral changes are maintained (Committee on Communication for Behavior Change, 2002; Wing & Phelan, 2005). Low levels of behavioral maintenance may be difficult because maintaining information needed for good decision making in one's short-term memory is burdensome. Consequently, as behaviors are integrated into a person's daily routine (e.g., taking a pill before bedtime), the person may pay less attention to the task and relapse to former behavior patterns (Langer & Imber, 1979; Sharps & Martin, 2002).

Summary of Interventions

Presentation of information, training, and environmental aids can all positively influence medication adherence. Unfortunately, many of the studies examining the efficacy of interventions aimed to increase adherence have not included long-term follow-ups or have not examined adherence rates postintervention (McDonald, Garg, & Haynes, 2002). Thus, it is not clear whether these strategies have extended benefits for medication adherence. Regardless, the literature does seem to suggest that relatively simple and easily implemented cognitive interventions can increase adherence in at least the short term. Further work is needed to examine barriers and facilitators of long-term medication adherence. In addition to observational studies to determine factors related to long-term adherence, interventions that occur in real-world settings under typical conditions are needed to increase generalizability and subsequent implementation.

Case Study

In this section, we describe a typical individual interacting with the medical environment and subsequent issues related to medication adherence. Mr. Jones is an 85-year-old man with a high school education; he lives alone and has a score of 44 out of a possible 66 on the Rapid Estimate of Adult Literacy in Medicine (REALM; Parker, Baker, Williams, & Nurss, 1995), indicating low literacy. Mr. Jones smokes a half-pack of cigarettes per day, has glaucoma and difficulty seeing, and is being treated for diabetes, hyperlipidemia, and hypertension.

Before his next primary care visit, Mr. Jones was asked to bring in all the medications he was currently using and was queried by his health care provider as to how he took each medication. He reported taking one tablet of atenolol (treatment for hypertension) per day. However, the label instructions were for him to take two tablets per day. When asked if he was having any problems taking his medications, Mr. Jones replied that he was unsure why he was taking one tablet, could not recall what the doctor told him at his last visit, and could not recall the purpose of the medication. He acknowledged that he was confused about when he should take his medications. After clarifying these for Mr. Jones, the health care provider asked him to repeat the information back to her. To facilitate adherence, the patient was mailed a medication calendar that he could take to his next appointment and have the physician fill in the correct medications and dosages.

At his next primary care visit 6 weeks later, Mr. Jones brought his daughter along so that she could also be aware of his medication schedule. During the visit, a nurse asked him what medications he was currently taking and whether he was having any problems with taking his medication. She gave him a written reminder describing when each of his medications should be taken. He told the nurse that he wears a watch that beeps every 12 hours to remind him to take his medication daily.

In general, patients tend to overestimate their medication adherence (Dunbar-Jacob, Dwyer, & Dunning, 1991), and unless a patient is not responding to therapy, it may be extremely difficult to identify a medication adherence problem. Asking patients about their medication use is often the most practical means of ascertainment, but it is prone to inaccuracy. A key validated question is "Have you missed any pills in the past week?"; any indication of having missed one or more pills signals a problem with low adherence (Haynes, McDonald, & Garg, 2002). Compared to pill counts as the reference standard, asking nonresponders about their medication adherence using this single question will detect 55% of those with less than complete adherence, with a specificity of 87% (Stephenson, Rowe, Haynes, Macharia, & Leon, 1993). Other practical measures to assess adherence include watching for those who do not respond to increments in treatment intensity and patients who fail to attend appointments. Finally, simply asking patients to describe their medication regimen, for example, when they take their medication and what it is for, can often be very informative.

Summary of Cognition and Medication Adherence

The relationship between cognitive function and medication adherence has not been consistent. Cognitive impairment has been associated with twice the risk of nonadherence use in the elderly population (Salas et al., 2001). Insel et al., (2006) observed, consistent with prefrontal cortex theory, that executive function and working memory were related to medication adherence. However, retrospective memory did not predict medication adherence. One possible reason for these inconsistent findings is that cognitive abilities are differentially related to each of the three components of adherence discussed in this chapter (e.g., comprehension, planning and integration, action). For example, retrospective memory should, by default, be related to output monitoring (remembering if a medication was taken or not). However, the relationship between retrospective memory and self-reported adherence might not be apparent because if a person made an internal-source monitoring error, he or she might actually believe that the medication was taken. Given the complexity and multidimensional nature of medication adherence, a better understanding of how cognitive abilities are related to the components of adherence will likely clarify these inconsistencies. Improving medication adherence will become ever more important as the cost of medications continues to increase, advances in medication treatment for various diseases continues, and the use of these medications increases as the population ages. Effective interventions aimed at increasing medication adherence should consider multiple cognitive components required for effective medication adherence in order to maximize the likelihood that patients experience the benefits of their medication regimes.

Conclusion

The previous discussion focuses mostly on medication use, a major focus of examination of everyday cognition within an applied setting. One can theorize that this is because older adults consume more medications than any other group and the potential public health implications of medication nonadherence are significant. To fully understand health care instructions such as medication, exercise, diet, and rehabilitation guidelines, patients must pay attention to the health professional, encode or learn the treatment plan so that it can be recalled accurately from long-term memory at a later time, and integrate this new regimen into their daily activities.

As discussed previously, recalling health information is a complex task that requires processing and memory (Morrow, Leirer, Altieri, & Tanke, 1991). For instance, health information in the health care setting is often presented verbally, which requires patients to listen and encode the information without the benefit of having written material to refer back to at a later time (Johnson & Sandford, 2005). Consider the recommendations a provider may provide to an individual with osteoarthritis, a prevalent disease among older adults. Patients have to remember a number of important pieces of information, including information regarding diet, exercise, and in some cases, medication use that involves dosage, timing, possible interactions, and whether the medication should be taken with food (Morrow, Leirer, & Sheikh, 1988). The extent to which this information fits into cognitive schemas can influence how well patients recall the information at a later time (Rice & Okun, 1994).

It is important to also acknowledge that information management in patient decision making is often a significant problem, particularly among older adults who have increased prevalence of chronic diseases. Individuals with chronic diseases are expected to engage in varying degrees of self-management. Self-management consists of the following components: Engaging in activities that promote physical and psychological health; interacting with health care providers and adhering to treatment recommendations; monitoring health status and making associated care decisions; and managing the impact of the illness on physical, psychological, and social functioning (Barlow et al., 2002; Bayliss et al., 2007). The role that comprehension, planning and integration, and action play in the health care system is significant, yet our understanding of the role that cognition plays in everyday health care requires further work.

References

Ad Hoc Committee on Health Literacy for the Council on Scientific Affairs, American Medical Association (1999). Health literacy: Report of the Council on Scientific Affairs. *JAMA, 281,* 552–557.

Allaire, J. C., & Marsiske, M. (1999). Everyday cognition: Age and intellectual ability correlates. *Psychology and Aging, 14,* 627–644.

Asimakopoulou, K. G., Hampson, S. E., & Morrish, N. J. (2002). Neuropsychological functioning in older people with type 2 diabetes: The effect of controlling for confounding factors. *Diabetes Medicine, 19,* 311–316.

Avorn, J., Monette, J., Lacour, A., Bohn, R. L., Monane, M., Mogun, H., et al. (1998). Persistence of use of lipid-lowering medications: A cross-national study. *JAMA, 279,* 1458–1462.

Ball K., Berch D. B., Helmers K. F., Jobe, J. B., Leveck, M. D., Marsiske, M., et al. (2002). Effects of cognitive training interventions with older adults: A randomized controlled trial. *JAMA, 288,* 2271–2281.

Baltes, P. B. (1993). The aging mind: Potentials and limits. *Gerontologist, 33,* 580–594.

Bargh, J. A., & Ferguson, M. J. (2000). Beyond behaviorism: On the automaticity of higher mental processes. *Psychological Bulletin, 126,* 925–945.

Barlow, J., Wright, C., Sheasby, J., Turner, A., Hainsworth, J., Tattersall, R. L., et al. (2002). Self-management approaches for people with chronic conditions: A review. *Patient Education and Counseling, 48,* 177–187.

Bastian, L. A., Lipkus, I. M., Kuchibhatla, M. N., Weng, H. H., Halabi, S., Ryan, P. D., et al. (2001). Women's interest in chemoprevention for breast cancer. *Archives of Internal Medicine, 161,* 1639–1644.

Bayliss, E. A., Bosworth, H. B., Noel, P. H., Wolff, J. L., Damush, T. M., & McIver, L. (2007). Supporting self-management for patients with complex medical needs: Recommendations of a working group. *Chronic Illness, 3,* 167–175.

Berg, C. A., Meegan, S. P., & Klaczynski, P. (1999). Age and experiential differences in strategy generation and information requests for solving everyday problems. *International Journal of Behavioral Development, 23,* 615–639.

Bosworth, H. B. (2006). Medication adherence. In H. B. Bosworth & M. Weinberger (Eds.), *Patient treatment adherence: Concepts, interventions, and measurement* (pp. 147–194). Mahwah, NJ: Erlbaum.

Bosworth, H. B., Olsen, M. K., Dudley, T., Orr, M., Neary, A., Harrelson, M., et al. (2007). The Take Control of Your Blood Pressure (TCYB) study: Study design and methodology. *Contemporary Clinical Trials, 28,* 33–47.

Bosworth, H. B., & Schaie, K. W. (1995). Medication knowledge and health status in the Seattle Longitudinal Study. *Gerontologist, 35,* 24.

Bosworth, H. B., Schaie, K. W., & Willis, S. L. (1999). Time to death in the Seattle Longitudinal Study: Cognitive, cognitive style, and sociodemographic risk factors. *The Journals of Gerontology: Series B. Psychological Sciences and Social Sciences, 54,* P273–P282.

Brandstätter, V., Lengfelder, A., & Gollwitzer, P. M. (2001). Implementation intentions and efficient action initiation. *Journal of Personality and Social Psychology, 81,* 946–960.

Carstensen, L. L., Isaacowitz, D. M., & Charles, S. T. (1999). Taking time seriously: A theory of socioemotional selectivity. *American Psychologist, 54,* 165–181.

Chandler, P., & Sweller, J. (1991). Cognitive load theory and the format of instruction. *Cognition and Instruction, 8,* 293–332.

Chasteen, A. L., Park, D. C., & Schwarz, N. (2001). Implementation intentions and facilitation of prospective memory. *Psychological Science, 12,* 457–461.

Committee on Communication for Behavior Change in the 21st Century, Institute of Medicine (2002). *Speaking of health: Assessing health communication strategies for diverse populations.* Washington, DC: National Academies Press.

Cornelius, S. W., & Caspi, A. (1987). Everyday problem solving in adulthood and aging. *Psychology and Aging, 2,* 144–153.

Crawford, S., & Channon, S. (2002). Dissociation between performance on abstract tests of executive function and problem solving in real-life-type situations in normal aging. *Aging and Mental Health, 6,* 12–21.

Davis, T., Wolf, M. S., Bass, P. F., Middlebrooks, M., Kennen, E., Baker, D. W., et al. (2006). Low literacy impairs comprehension of prescription drug warning labels. *Journal of General Internal Medicine, 21,* 847–851.

Davis, T., Wolf, M. S., Bass, P. F., Thompson, J. A., Tilson, H. H., Neuberger, M., & Parker, R. M. (2006). Literacy and misunderstanding prescription drug labels. *Annals of Internal Medicine, 145,* 887–894.

Denney, J. A., & Pearce, K. A. (1989). A developmental study of practical problem solving in adults. *Psychology and Aging, 4,* 438–442.

Dewalt, D. A., Berkman, N. D., Sheridan, S., Lohr, K. N., & Pignone, M. P. (2004). Literacy and health outcomes: A systematic review of the literature. *Journal of General Internal Medicine, 19,* 1228–1239.

Diehl, M., Marsiske, M., Horgas, A. L., Rosenberg, A., Saczynski, J. S., & Willis, S. L. (2005). The revised observed tasks of daily living: A performance-based assessment of everyday problem solving in older adults. *Journal of Applied Gerontology, 24,* 211.

Diehl, M., Willis, S. L., & Schaie, K. W. (1995). Everyday problem solving in older adults: Observational assessment and cognitive correlates. *Psychology and Aging, 30,* 478–491.

Dixon, R. A., de Frias, C. M., & Bäckman, L. (2001). Characteristics of self-reported memory compensation in older adults. *Journal of Clinical and Experimental Neuropsychology, 23,* 650–661.

Dunbar-Jacob, J., Dwyer, K., & Dunning, E. J. (1991). Compliance with antihypertensive regimen: A review of the research in the 1980s. *Annals of Behavioral Medicine, 13,* 31–39.

Edelberg, H. K., Shallenberger, E., Hausdorff, J. M., & Wei, J. Y. (2000). One-year follow-up of medication management capacity in highly functioning older adults. *The Journals of Gerontology: Series A. Biological Sciences and Medical Sciences, 55,* M550–553.

Einstein, G. O., & McDaniel, M. A. (1990). Normal aging and prospective memory. *Journal of Experimental Psychology: Learning, Memory, and Cognition, 16,* 717–726.

Einstein, G. O., McDaniel, M. A., Richardson, S. L., Guynn, M. J., & Cunfer, A. R. (1995). Aging and prospective memory: Examining the influences of self-initiated retrieval processes. *Journal of Experimental Psychology: Learning, Memory, and Cognition, 21,* 996–1007.

Einstein, G. O., McDaniel, M. A., Smith, R. E., & Shaw, P. (1998). Habitual prospective memory and aging: Remembering intentions and forgetting actions. *Psychological Science, 9,* 284–289.

Fletcher, S., Fletcher, R. H., Thomas, D. C., & Hamann, C. (1979). Patients' understanding of prescribed drugs. *Journal of Community Health, 4,* 183–189.

Fuster, J. M. (1997). *The prefrontal cortex anatomy, physiology, and neuropsychology of the frontal lobe* (3rd ed.). Philadelphia: Lippincott-Raven.

Gazmararian, J. A., Williams, M. V., Peel, J., & Baker, D. W. (2003). Health literacy and knowledge of chronic disease. *Patient Education and Counseling, 51,* 267–275.

Gollwitzer, P. M. (1999). Implementation intentions: Strong effects of simple plans. *American Psychologist, 54,* 493–503.

Hasher, L., & Zacks, R. T. (1988). Working memory, comprehension, and aging: A review and a new view. *The Psychology of Learning and Motivation, 22,* 193–225.

Haynes, R. B., McDonald, H. P., & Garg, A. X. (2002). Helping patients follow prescribed treatment: Clinical applications. *JAMA, 288,* 2880–2883.

Haynes, R. B., Yao, X., Degani, A., Kripalani, S., Garg, A., & McDonald, H. P. (2005, October 19). Interventions to enhance medication adherence. *Cochrane Database of Systematic Reviews, 4.* Available from http://www.cochrane.org

Heit, E. (2000). Properties of inductive reasoning. *Psychonomic Bulletin & Review, 7,* 569–592.

Hershey, D. A., Boyd, M. L., Coutant, K. M., & Turner, K. (1999). Cognitive aging psychology: Significant advances, challenges, and training issues. *Educational Gerontology, 25,* 349–364.

Hoffman, J., & Proulx, S. M. (2003). Medication errors caused by confusion of drug names. *Drug Safety, 26,* 445–454.

Holt, G. A., Hollon, J. D., Hughes, S. E., & Coyle, R. (1990). OTC labels: Can consumers read and understand them? *American Pharmacy, NS30,* 51–54.

Houts, P. S., Doak, C. C., Doak, L. G., & Loscalzo, M. J. (2006). The role of pictures in improving health communication: A review of research on attention, comprehension, recall, and adherence. *Patient Education and Counseling, 61,* 173–190.

Insel, K., Morrow, D., Brewer, B., & Figueredo, A. (2006). Executive function, working memory, and medication adherence among older adults. *The Journals of Gerontology: Series B. Psychological Sciences and Social Sciences, 61,* P102–P107.

Institute of Medicine. (2004). *Health literacy: A prescription to end confusion.* Washington, DC: National Academies Press.

Isaac, L. M., & Tamblyn, R. M. (1993). Compliance and cognitive function: A methodological approach to measuring unintentional errors in medication compliance in the elderly. *The Gerontologist, 33,* 772–781.

Jacoby, L. L. (1991). A process dissociation framework: Separating automatic from intentional uses of memory. *Journal of Memory and Language, 30,* 513–541.

Jacoby, L. L. (1999). Ironic effects of repetition: Measuring age-related differences in memory. *Journal of Experimental Psychology: Learning, Memory, and Cognition, 25,* 3–22.

Johnson, A., & Sandford, J. (2005). Written and verbal information versus verbal information only for patients being discharged from acute hospital settings to home: Systematic review. *Health Education Research, 20,* 423–429.

Johnson, M. K., & Raye, C. L. (1981). Reality monitoring. *Psychological Review, 88,* 67–85.

Kahneman, D., Slovic, P., & Tversky, A. (1982). *Judgment under uncertainty: Heuristics and biases*. New York: Cambridge University Press.

Katz, M. G., Kripalani, S., & Weiss, B. D. (2006). Use of pictorial aids in medication instructions: A review of the literature. *American Journal of Health Systems Pharmacy, 63*, 2391–2397.

Kessel, R. P. C. (2003). Patients' memory for medical information. *Journal of the Royal Society of Medicine, 96*, 219–222.

Kirsch, I., Jungeblut, A., Jenkins, L., & Kolstad, A. (1993). *Adult literacy in America: A first look at the results of the national adult literacy survey*. Washington, DC: National Center for Education Statistics.

Kliegel, M., McDaniel, M. A., & Einstein, G. O. (2000). Plan formation, retention, and execution in prospective memory: A new approach and age-related effects. *Memory & Cognition, 28*, 1041–1049.

Langer, E. J., & Imber, L. G. (1979). When practice makes imperfect: Debilitating effects of overlearning. *Journal of Personality and Social Psychology, 37*, 2014–2024.

Lipkus, I. M., Samsa, G., & Rimer, B. K. (2001). General performance on a numeracy scale among highly educated samples. *Medical Decision Making, 21*, 37–44.

Littenberg, B., MacLean, C. D., & Hurowitz, L. (2006). The use of adherence aids by adults with diabetes: A cross-sectional survey. *BMC Family Practice, 7*, 1.

MacLaughlin, E. J., Raehl, C. L., Treadway, A. K., Sterling, T. L., Zoller, D. P., & Bond, C. A. (2005). Assessing medication adherence in the elderly: Which tools to use in clinical practice? *Drugs and Aging, 22*, 231–255.

Maddigan, S. L., Farris, K. B., Keating, N., Wiens, C. A., & Johnson, J. A. (2003). Predictors of older adults' capacity for medication management in a self-medication program: A retrospective chart review. *Journal of Aging and Health, 15*, 332–352.

Maniaci, M. J., Heckman, M. G., & Dawson, N. L. (2008). Functional health literacy and understanding of medications at discharge. *Mayo Clinic Proceedings, 83*(5), 554–558.

Marsiske, M., & Willis, S. L. (1995). Dimensionality of everyday problem solving in older adults. *Psychology and Aging, 10*, 269–283.

McCray, A. T. (2005). Promoting health literacy. *Journal of the American Medical Informatics Association, 12*, 152–163.

McDaniel, M. A., Einstein, G. O., Stout, A. C., & Morgan, Z. (2003). Aging and maintaining intentions over delays: Do it or lose it. *Psychology and Aging, 18*, 823–835.

McDonald, H. P., Garg, A. X., & Haynes, R. B. (2002). Interventions to enhance patient adherence to medication prescriptions. *Journal of the American Medical Association, 288*, 2868–2879.

Meegan, S. P., & Berg, C. A. (2002). Contexts, functions, forms, and processes of collaborative everyday problem solving in older adulthood. *International Journal of Behavioral Development, 26*, 6–15.

Morrell, R. W., Park, D. C., & Poon, L. W. (1989). Quality of instructions on prescription drug labels: Effects on memory and comprehension in young and old adults. *The Gerontologist, 29*, 345–354.

Morrow, D. G., Leirer, V. O., & Altieri, P. (1995). List formats improve medication instructions for older adults. *Educational Gerontology, 21*, 151–166.

Morrow, D. G., Leirer, V. O., Altieri, P., & Tanke, E. D. (1991). Elders' schema for taking medication: Implications for instruction design. *Journal of Gerontology, 46*, 378–385.

Morrow, D. G., Leirer, V. O., Carver, L. M., Tanke, E. D., & McNally, A. D. (1999). Repetition improves older and younger adult memory for automated appointment messages. *Human Factors, 41*, 194–204.

Morrow, D. G., Leirer, V. O., & Sheikh, J. (1988). Adherence and medication instructions: Review and recommendations. *Journal of the American Geriatrics Society, 36*, 1147–1160.

Nelson, W., Reyna, V. F., Fagerlin, A., Lipkus, I., & Peters, E. (2008). Clinical implications of numeracy: Theory and practice. *Annals of Behavioral Medicine, 35*, 261–274.

Newell, A., Shaw, C., & Simon, H. A. (1956). Elements of a theory of human problem solving. *Psychological Review, 55*, 151–166.

Osterberg, L., & Blaschke, T. (2005). Adherence to medication. *New England Journal of Medicine, 353*, 487–497.

Park, D. C. (1999). Aging and the controlled and automatic processing of medical information and medical intentions. In D. C. Park, K. Shifrin, & R. W. Morrell (Eds.), *Processing of medical information in aging patients* (pp. 3–22). Mahwah, NJ: Erlbaum.

Park, D. C. (2000). Medication adherence: Is and why is older wiser? *Journal of the American Geriatrics Society, 48,* 458–459.

Park, D. C., Hertzog, C., Kidder, D. P., Morrell, R. W., & Mayhorn, C. B. (1997). Effect of age on event-based and time-based prospective memory. *Psychology and Aging, 12,* 314–327.

Park, D. C., & Kidder, D. P. (1996). Prospective memory and medication adherence. In G. E. M. Brandimonte & M. A. McDaniel (Eds.), *Prospective memory theory and application* (pp. 369–390). Hillsdale, NJ: Erlbaum.

Park, D. C., & Meade, M. L. (2007). A broad view of medical adherence: The importance of cognitive, social, and contextual factors. In D. C. Park & L. L. Liu (Eds.), *Medical adherence and aging: Social and cognitive perspectives* (pp. 3–20). Washington, DC: American Psychological Association.

Park, D. C., Morrell, R. W., Frieske, D., & Kincaid, D. (1992). Medication adherence behaviors in older adults: Effects of external cognitive supports. *Psychology and Aging, 7,* 252–256.

Parker, R. M., Baker, D. W., Williams, M. V., & Nurss, J. R. (1995). The test of functional health literacy in adults. *Journal of General Internal Medicine, 10,* 537–541.

Parker, R. M., & Gazmararian, J. A. (2003). Health literacy: *Essential for health communication. Journal of Health Communication, 8*(Suppl. 1), 116–118.

Peters, E., Dieckmann, N., Dixon, A., Hibbard, J. H., & Mertz, C. K. (2007). Less is more in presenting quality information to consumers. *Medical Care Research and Review, 64,* 169–190.

Post, K., & Roter, D. (1988). Predictors of recall of medication regimens and recommendations for lifestyle change in elderly patients. *Gerontologist, 27,* 510–515.

Puckett, J. M., Reese, H. W., & Pollina, L. K. (1993). An integration of life-span research in everyday cognition: Four issues. In J. M. Puckett & H. W. Reese (Eds.), *Mechanisms of everyday cognition* (pp. 3–19). Hillsdale, NJ: Erlbaum.

Raz, N. B. (2000). Aging of the brain and its impact on cognitive performance: Integration of structural and functional findings. In F. I. M. Craik & T. A. Salthouse (Eds.), *The handbook of aging and cognition* (pp. 1–90). Mahwah, NJ: Erlbaum.

Rice, G. E., & Okun, M. A. (1994). Older readers' processing of medical information that contradicts their beliefs. *The Journals of Gerontology: Series B. Psychological Sciences and Social Sciences, 49,* P119–P128.

Rost, K. R., & Roter, D. (1987). Predictors of recall of medication regimens and recommendations for lifestyle change in elderly patients. *Gerontologist, 27,* 510–515.

Sabate, E. (2003). *Adherence to long-term therapies: Evidence for action.* Geneva, Switzerland: World Health Organization.

Salas, M., In't Veld, B. A., van der Linden, P. D., Hofman, A., Breteler, M., & Stricker, B. H. (2001). Impaired cognitive function and compliance with antihypertensive drugs in elderly: The Rotterdam study. *Clinical Pharmacology and Therapeutics, 70,* 561–566.

Salthouse, T. (1991). *Theoretical perspectives in cognitive aging.* Hillsdale, NJ: Erlbaum.

Sanson-Fisher, R. W., Campbell, E. M., Redman, S., & Hennrikus, D. J. (1989). Patient-provider interactions and patient outcomes. *Diabetes Education, 15,* 134–138.

Schaie, K. W. (1996). *Adult intellectual development: The Seattle Longitudinal Study.* New York: Cambridge University Press.

Schieber, F. (2006). Vision and aging. In J. E. Birren & K. W. Schaie (Eds.), *Handbook of the psychology of aging* (pp. 129–162). San Diego, CA: Elsevier.

Sharps, M. J., & Martin, S. S. (2002). "Mindless" decision making as a failure of contextual reasoning. *Journal of Psychology, 136,* 272–282.

Shrank, W., Avorn, J., Rolon, C., & Shekelle, P. (2007). Effect of content and format of prescription drug labels on readability, understanding, and medication use: A systematic review. *Annals of Pharmacotherapy, 41,* 783–801.

Sleath, B., Rubin, R. H., Campbell, W., Gwyther, L., & Clark, T. (2001). Physician-patient communication about over-the-counter medications. *Social Science & Medicine, 53,* 357–369.

Stephenson, B. J., Rowe, B. H., Haynes, R. B., Macharia, W. M., & Leon, G. (1993). Is this patient taking the treatment as prescribed? *JAMA, 269,* 2779–2781.

Stewart, R., & Liolitsa, D. (1999). Type 2 diabetes mellitus, cognitive impairment and dementia. *Diabetes Medicine, 16,* 93–112.

Stuss, D. T. (1992). Biological and psychological development of executive functions. *Brain and Cognition, 20,* 8–23.

Sudore, R. L., Mehta, K. M., Simonsick, E. M., Harris, T. B., Newman, A. B., Satterfield, S., et al. (2006). Limited literacy in older people and disparities in health and healthcare access. *Journal of the American Geriatrics Society, 54,* 770–776.

Swan, G. E., Carmelli, D., & Larue, A. (1998). Systolic blood pressure tracking over 25 to 30 years and cognitive performance in older adults. *Stroke, 29,* 2334–2340.

Swan, G. E., DeCarli, C., Miller, B. L., Reed, T., Wolf, P. A., Jack, L. M., et al. (1998). Association of midlife blood pressure to late-life cognitive decline and brain morphology. *Neurology, 51,* 986–993.

Tarn, D., Heritage, J., Paterniti, D. A., Hays, R. D., Kravitz, R. L., & Wenger, N. S. (2006). Physician communication when prescribing new medications. *American Journal of Managed Care, 12,* 657–664.

U.S., Department of Education. (2005). *National assessment of adult literacy: A first look at the literacy of America's adults in the 21st century.* Washington, DC: National Center for Education Statistics.

van den Broek, P., & Kremer, K. (1998). The mind in action: What it means to comprehend during reading. In B. M. Taylor, M. F. Graves, & P. van den Broek. (Eds.), *Reading for meaning: Fostering comprehension in the middle grades* (pp. 1–31). New York: Teacher's College Press.

Vermeire, E., Hearnshaw, H., Van Royen, P., & Denekens, J. (2001). Patient adherence to treatment: Three decades of research: A comprehensive review. *Journal of Clinical Pharmacy and Therapeutics, 26,* 331–342.

West, R. L. (1996). An application of prefrontal cortex function theory to cognitive aging. *Psychological Bulletin, 120,* 272–292.

Williams, M., Parker, R. M., Baker, D. W., Parikh, K., Pitkin, W. C., Coates, W. C. et al. (1995). Inadequate functional health literacy among patients at two public hospitals. *Journal of the American Medical Association, 274,* 1677–1682.

Willis, S. L. (1996). Everyday cognitive competence in elderly persons: Conceptual issues and empirical findings. *The Gerontologist, 36,* 595–601.

Willis, S. L., & Schaie, K. W. (1993). Everyday cognition: Taxonomic and methodological considerations. In J. M. Puckett & H. W. Reese (Eds.), *Mechanisms of everyday cognition* (pp. 33–54). Hillsdale, NJ: Erlbaum.

Willis, S. L., Tennstedt, S. L., Marsiske, M., Ball, K., Elias, J., Koepke, K. M., et al. (2006). Long-term effects of cognitive training on everyday functional outcomes in older adults. *JAMA, 296,* 2805–2814.

Wilson, J. F. (2003). The crucial link between literacy and health. *Annals of Internal Medicine, 139,* 875–878.

Wing, R. R., & Phelan, S. (2005). Long-term weight loss maintenance. *American Journal of Clinical Nutrition, 82*(Suppl.), 222S–225S.

Wingfield, A., Tun, P. A., & McCoy, S. L. (2005). Hearing loss in older adulthood. *Current Directions in Psychological Science, 14,* 144–148.

Wogalter, M. S., & Vigilante, W. J., Jr. (2003). Effects of label format on knowledge acquisition and perceived readability by younger and older adults. *Ergonomics, 46,* 327–344.

Wolf, M. S., Davis, T. C., Tilson, H. H., Bass, P. F., & Parker, R. M. (2006). Misunderstanding of prescription drug warning labels among patients with low literacy. *American Journal of Health-System Pharmacy, 63,* 1048–1055.

Wolf, M. S., Gazmararian, J. A., & Baker, D. W. (2005). Health literacy and functional health status among older adults. *Archives of Internal Medicine, 165,* 1946–1952.

Index

About the Editors

Hayden B. Bosworth, PhD, is a gerontologist and health services researcher. He is the associate director of the Center for Health Services Research in Primary Care at the Durham VA Medical Center in North Carolina. At Duke University Medical Center, he is a research professor in the Department of Medicine, Division of General Internal Medicine; a research professor in the Department of Psychiatry and Behavioral Sciences; and a research professor in the School of Nursing. He is also an adjunct professor of health policy and administration in the School of Public Health at the University of North Carolina at Chapel Hill. He received his master's and doctoral degrees from the Pennsylvania State University in 1994 and 1996, respectively, under the mentorship of K. Warner Schaie.

Dr. Bosworth's research focus has been on developing interventions to improve health behaviors and treatment adherence to improve patient outcomes among those with chronic diseases. He has published over 145 peer-reviewed articles that have examined the effects of patient characteristics and social environment on chronic diseases such as coronary heart disease, stroke, and hypertension. Funding for his work has been provided by various sources, including the National Institutes of Health, the U.S. Department of Veterans Affairs, the American Heart Association, the Robert Wood Johnson Foundation, and the Kate B. Reynolds Foundation. He is the recipient of various awards, including the Gerontological Society of America's Margaret M. Baltes Early Career Award in Behavioral and Social Gerontology in recognition of outstanding early career contributions in behavioral and social gerontology. Dr. Bosworth is a fellow of the Gerontological Society of America and of the American Psychological Association's Divisions 20 (Adult Development and Aging) and 38 (Health Psychology).

Christopher Hertzog, PhD, is a professor of psychology at the Georgia Institute of Technology. He received his doctoral degree in 1979 from the University of Southern California, where he worked with K. Warner Schaie on the Seattle Longitudinal Study. After a 2-year postdoctoral fellowship at the University of Washington, under the supervision of Earl Hunt, he was an assistant professor of human development at the Pennsylvania State University until 1985, when he moved to Georgia Tech. Dr. Hertzog's research interests focus on individual differences in adult cognitive development. He has conducted longitudinal research on adult developmental change using multivariate statistical models and has participated in studies grounded in experimental cognitive psychology as a basis for understanding effects of aging on memory, skill acquisition, and intelligence. His recent work has focused in large part on adults' metacognition and strategic self-regulation in cognitive tasks. Dr. Hertzog is a fellow of the American Psychological Association (APA) and past-president of APA's Division 20 (Adult Development and Aging).